SCHOOL HEALTH EDUCATION

School Health Education

DR. S.L. GOEL
Vice-President, Executive Council,
Indian Institute of Public Administration, New Delhi
Editor, The Indian Journal of Public Administration, New Delhi
Professor of Public Administration (Retd.)
Panjab University, Chandigarh
Emeritus Fellow, University Grants Commission
Director, State Bank of India (Local Board), Chandigarh
Director, National Horticulture Board, Ministry of Horticulture,
Government of India, New Delhi
Formerly Member UGC, Member Distance Education Council
and Member All India Board of Management, AICTE

DEEP & DEEP PUBLICATIONS PVT. LTD.
F-159, Rajouri Garden, New Delhi-110027

SCHOOL HEALTH EDUCATION

ISBN 978-81-8450-053-0

Typeset by S.S. COMPOSERS,
3190, Mohindra Park, Shakur Basti, Delhi-110034.

Printed in India at MAYUR ENTERPRISES,
WZ Plot No. 3, Gujjar Market, Tihar Village, New Delhi-110018.

Published by DEEP & DEEP PUBLICATIONS PVT. LTD.,
F-159, Rajouri Garden, New Delhi-110027.
Phones: 25435369, 25440916
E-mail: ddpbooks@yahoo.co.in • ddpubs@gmail.com
Showroom:
2/13, Ansari Road, Daryaganj, New Delhi-110002 • Telefax: 23245122

Contents

Preface

Happiness, Happiness, Happiness
It may be of any bend
Happiness of being Healthy
Is the real Happiness

The education as is obtained today is not all aimed at character building with the result that we find even highly educated men who have so much of power and service machinery at their command fail miserably when tackling problems in the right way, in the human way, in the interests of our nation. Highly talented individuals are there in every field, second to none, but devoid of patriotic spirit and personal integrity, the impact they produce is minimal. Today, we are urgently in need of men and women of character, integrity and dedication and of tremendous capacities happily blending dignity of man with dignity of labour.

Concentration of mind, its purity and charity alone can bring out the amazing qualities and capacities that lie hidden in the human mind. Lack of these has created a student community who are debilitated, inhuman, selfish and indifferent to human values. Swami Vivekananda stresses the value of Shraddha, faith, as one of the most potent factors capable of elevating human life. He wanted this "Life-saving, great, ennobling, grand doctrine "to be taught to our children from their very birth. Where the different streams of consciousness in man, namely, concentration of mind, purity of life, faith in oneself, strength of body and fearlessness of mind are combined together in a single personality, the force of that character becomes invincible. Men of such stature alone can rebuild a shattered society. It is such men that our educational system should create to safely carry over our country to the 21st Century.

To build a truly great character is the most glorious of human achievements. Such a man-making education, in which India has all the technical know-how, handed down from time immemorial, should form the basis of our national efforts in the field. In most exquisite words have our ancient Masters sung the glory of such a true education.

Asato maa sadgamya.
Tamaso maa jyotir gamaya,

Mrutyor maa amrutam gamaya,
Om Shanti, Shanti, Shanti.

Lead Me From the Unreal to the Real,
Lead Me From Darkness to Light,
Lead Me From Death to Immortality,
Om Peace, Peace, Peace.[1]

As stated in a WHO Publication, "Primary School Physical Environment and Health", 1999, "By the year 2000 there will be over 1400 million children between the ages of 5 and 14 years, approximately 87% of whom will be living in developing countries. Children in this age group are 14 times more likely to die between their fifth and fifteenth birthdays than their age-mates in the industrialized market-economy countries.

It is widely recognized that schools can play an important role in promoting society's health. Much effort has been invested over recent years in health education techniques for schools in low-income communities, including child-to-child methods, curriculum development, and the production of locally appropriate education materials. However, the impact of the actual fabric and management of school premises on child health has been relatively neglected. Many schools fail to provide healthy environments for their pupils. Poorly designed and maintained schools can be a source of disease and ill-health. Sick children also make poor learners.

Characteristic Problems

While there is no such thing as a typical school in a developing country, certain characteristics will be familiar to many observers. These include:

- overcrowded classrooms, designed for 25 children but catering for 50 children, under one overworked teacher;
- little or no furniture, with what there is in poor repair;
- darkness due to too few windows or windows that must be kept covered with shutters to keep out the sun or wind, and no electricity;
- dilapidation due to lack of maintenance, with disintegrating floors, broken doors and windows, and holes in the roof;
- no water supply, or an intermittent or inadequate supply;
- toilets which no longer work and grounds littered with facial material;
- toilets which may work but which are padlocked since there is no water for flushing or because the children are not trusted to use them properly;

1. Dr. M. Lakshmi Kumari, President, V.K. Yogas, Kanyakumari, pp. iii-iv.

- schools where everything that can be stolen has been taken;
- underpaid, undertrained teachers who often have to travel long distances to work;
- lack of accommodation for staff;
- an absence of blackboards, school books, writing materials for the children, and didactic materials for the teachers; and
- girls kept away either permanently or every month, during their periods, because decent and private sanitation facilities for them are lacking.

It is tempting to suggest that all these problems are the products of poverty and that the answer is simply more money. Many developing countries can boast showpiece examples of good, clean, well-equipped schools—schools with in-house health services, pristine washrooms, well-tended grounds, and well-trained teachers working in classrooms equipped with computers, televisions and videos. For the lucky few these model schools are undoubtedly delivering a high quality of education in an environment conducive to physical and mental health. Where both money and focused attention is available, such things are possible. And there is no doubt that education does merit a larger share of the world's resources. But the evidence suggests that, aside from these showpiece examples, simply throwing more money at the problem does not necessarily result in sustainable solutions. Many examples exist where well-intentioned governments and donors have made significant investments in new and improved schools but with disappointing results.

WHO documents suggests that:

Good Design is not Enough

Exhaustive guidelines on classroom design are not enough to improve school environments. In fact, model designs often assume an unrealistic availability of resources. More importantly, a healthy school is dependent on good management, commitment and maintenance.

Standard Designs Assume Standard Conditions

Designs for model schools are only useful if applied intelligently and with care. If standard designs are used in circumstances for which they were not intended, the result can be counter-productive.

Schools are more than Classrooms

While much attention has been given to classroom design, many of the elements which influence child health lie outside the classroom. There is a need to think about the total school environment and the way in which schools are run. In particular, the involvement and needs of the local community should be considered.

The Greatest Need is to Improve Existing Schools

Before large amounts of resources are devoted to building new schools, better use should be made of existing schools. This can be achieved through better management and larger financial allocations for maintenance and repairs. It is also important to ensure that pupils and staff with disabilities are able to use facilities at existing schools.

School is a place where children from primary to secondary classes get education and learn values, norms, standards essentials for socialization and development of personality. That is why Kothari Commission in 1966 remarked that the destiny of a nation is shaped in her class-rooms. Thus, it becomes imperative for Government at Union, State and Local levels to provide congenial environment in schools for children so that they grow as enlightened citizens. The development of the country depends on how we are nurturing our children in schools. The children being in their formative years can be moulded in desired direction. To achieve, the schools must provide a stimulating environment wherein children can develop their physical, intellectual and spiritual potentialities. Since we are concentrating on health of school children, it is therefore, essential to teach children all essential attributes and lifestyles, which can help them in achieving physical, mental, social and spiritual health. The first important parameter for this is the need of good environment in the school.

Before 1976, education was the exclusive responsibility of the States. The Constitutional Amendment of 1976, which included education in the Concurrent List, was a far-reaching step. The substantive, financial and administrative implications required a new sharing of responsibility between the Union Government and the States. While the role and responsibility of the State in regard to education remain unchanged, the Union Government accepts a larger responsibility to reinforce the national and integrative character of education, to maintain quality and standards including those of the teaching profession at all levels, to study and monitor the educational requirements of the county.[2]

The National Policy on Education, 1986, as modified in 1992, has highlighted the need for a simultaneous focus on improving access, retention and quality. The Revised Programme of Action, 1992, provided for the launching of a National Mission for the achievement of the goal of UEE. This mission was to have the central objective of mobilizing all resources, human, financial and institutional, necessary for achieving the goal of UEE. The Sarva Shiksha Abhiyan (SSA) is an effort to operationalize this policy commitment by promoting decentralized planning with full involvement of Panchayati Raj Institutions. Though a large number of schemes are currently contributing towards improvement in the outreach of the

2. India 2004, Ministry of Information and Broadcasting, GOI, p. 193.

elementary education system and its quality, it is felt that by adopting a holistic and convergent approach at the district level, it may be possible to facilitate this process.

The SSA has evolved from the recommendations of the State Education Minister's Conference held in October 1998, to pursue Universal Elementary Education in a mission mode. A National Committee of State Education Ministers under the Chairmanship of Minister of Human Resource Development was set-up on the recommendation of the conference to work out the approach to the mission mode. The Committee submitted its report in October, 1999. The draft framework for a holistic and convergent approach to UEE in the mission mode was circulated to the states for their comments. The Scheme of SSA was revised incorporating the suggestions made by the states and then discussed in an Education Secretaries' Conference in November 1999.[3]

The Parliament has passed the Constitutional 86th Amendment Act, 2002 to make elementary education a Fundamental Right for children in the age-group of 6-14 years. It is proposed to bring in a follow-up legislation with detailed mechanism to implement this act.[4]

The programme covers the entire country and addresses the needs of 192 million children in 11 lakh habitations. 8.5 lakh existing primary and upper primary schools and 33 lakh existing teachers would be covered under the scheme. The programme seeks to open new schools in habitations, which do not have schooling facilities and strengthen existing school infrastructure through provision of additional class rooms, toilets, drinking water, maintenance grant and school improvement grant. Existing schools with inadequate teacher strength would be provided additional teacher under the programme. Extensive training and provision of academic support structure would build the capacity of existing teachers. The SSA has a special focus on girls and children of weaker sections. A number of initiatives, including free textbooks, target these children under the programme have been launched. The SSA also seeks to provide computer education even in rural areas to bridge the digital divide. The approach is community-owned and village education plans prepared in consultation with Panchayati Raj Institutions will form the basis of district elementary education plans. The Sarva Shiksha Abhiyan covers the entire country with a special focus on educational needs to girls, Scheduled Castes and Scheduled Tribes and other children in difficult circumstances.[5]

In line with the commitment of augmenting resources for education, the allocation for education has, over the years, increased significantly. Plan outlay on education has increased from Rs. 151 crore in the First Five-Year Plan to Rs. 43,825 crore in the Tenth Five Year Plan (2002-07). The

3. Annual Report, Ministry of HRD, Department of Education, 2001-02, p. 55.
4. India 2004, Ministry of Information and Broadcasting, GOI, p. 195.
5. *Ibid.*, pp. 195-97.

expenditure on Education as a percentage of GDP also rose from 0.64 per cent in 1951-52 to 3.98 percent in 2002-03 (BE).[6]

The above statistics reveal that the Governments at the Union and State levels are serious to promote school education. However, in practice, the situation is far from satisfactory. The school environment, facilities and teachers' sincerity are lacking. Most of the schools lack basic amenities like toilets and drinking water.

Let us illustrate with some examples:

Government Primary School at Jindra village (Punjab) is crying for attention. It has only one teacher for 81 students of five classes.

The only teacher was on leave and an intermediate girl who had been appointed as temporary teacher was managing the students. Some of the bright students were teaching their classmates.

The school doesn't have a boundary wall, toilet and proper drinking water arrangements. The students were being taught in the open as there is no power connection in the schools. Classrooms are in a shambles and one of the rooms was servicing as a store-*cum*-kitchen.

Government Primary School at Chak Jindra village (Punjab) has now turned into a gurdwara. A village resident, Hari Singh, said the school had a single teacher and it functioned for five six years. It closed down owing to poor quality of education and lack of facilities. The villagers then decided to make it a gurdwara. Most of the schools have the same story.[7]

Health Education is an important discipline, which must be taught, in schools, Ministry of Health and Family Welfare and Department of Education, Ministry of HRD made efforts to promote health education through Central Health Education Bureau. However, this idea remained only on paper and was not translated into practice.

Today, we are spending public and private money on health facilities. Our health problems to a large extents, are the cause of our wrong habits and poor knowledge of health services. Therefore, there is a need of practical health education in schools, which would have its chain effect on families and nation.

The present book, "School Health Education" is an attempt to remind the Union and State Governments to provide facilities in schools to promote health education. Health Education at a young age would be of great benefit to the country through its healthy citizens.

Healthy Children—Healthy Families—Healthy Nation.

G.K. Vishwakarma, former Director-General of Health Services rightly mentioned:

Health Education as a means to improve the quality of life by helping people to acquire health by their own efforts within available resources has been accepted by all. For this reason it has been duly emphasized in both

---

6. *Ibid.,* pp. 193-95.
7. Perneet Singh, in his article in *The Tribune* News Services, Tuesday, September 14, 2004.

the National Health Policy and National Education Policy. In developing countries, school-age children form a sizable portion of the total population of these countries. As such, inclusion of Health Education as part of core curriculum from Class I to X in the National Curriculum for Primary and Secondary Education by the National Council of Educational Research and Training (NCERT) is a significant step. The importance of health education to help children remain healthy by adopting healthy lifestyles so that they may be able to reap the full benefit of all the inputs made in the field of education for their alround development as a physically healthy, socially useful, economically productive and personally satisfied citizens of the country has been clearly established by including, health education in the National Curriculum Framework by the NCERT.

At this juncture, it is imperative that teachers are properly oriented to plan, implement and evaluate an objective-based health education curriculum for different levels of school education. The present module is an attempt to help teachers, principals, education supervisors and administrators along with personnel from other sectors to understand the school-age child and his/her health needs and problems, understand the nature and scope of health education for this group of population and to have an insight into their own role for working towards health promotion of school-age children. These children may be those, who are enrolled in schools or have dropped out from schools for various reasons, or did not have an opportunity even to enter a school and are either helping their parents in their family vocations or are employed as child labour. This material also highlights that health is not the sole responsibility either of health personnel or education personnel or personnel from Departments of Women and Child Development, Information and Broadcasting or parents, etc., but is a joint responsibility of all those concerned with national development and prosperity in general and child welfare in particular.

Health Education should equip individuals How to Think rather than tell them what thoughts to have, To Understand Themselves in terms of their own needs, and To Value without establishing a set of values for them, the role of the educator in this process is not of a teacher but that of a resource person who helps people (i) to develop a desire to be healthy, (ii) to identify health hazards around them including superstitions, misconceptions, myths, fads, and wrong beliefs, (iii) to set their own goals considering their capabilities and available resources and constraints, and (iv) to achieve these goals with their own efforts seeking help from concerned professionals. To summarize, health education should encourage these people to (a) WANT to be healthy, (b) KNOW how to stay healthy, (c) DO what they can individually and collectively to maintain their own health, health of their family members and of those around them in the community, (d) SEEK help when needed from available community resources, and (e) CONTRIBUTE to improved preventive and promotive self-care, behaviour in family and community.

Parents and school teachers need to be oriented by Primary Health Care professionals to impress upon them the importance of regular health appraisal of school-age children, immunizations suitable for their age, and importance of healthy habits. This will enable them to create a desire and appreciation of good health among these children to accept and utilize available services. There is also a need to orient both parents and teachers about common signs and symptoms of deviations from normal health and monitor growth of these children. This will help them to refer or take the child suspected of any deviation to the first level of formal health system. At this point a Cumulative Health Card may be issued in respect of each referred child. However, in case of minor ailments, the teachers may be provided orientation to treat minor ailments on the spot. In case of out of school children either parents may be trained to treat minor ailments using home remedies or primary health workers may provide the same during home visits. These workers should also visit schools regularly to examine all school students periodically and send reports to first level health officers referring children needing specialist examination. The medical officer may prepare his programme of school visits according to these priorities.

In case of chronic diseases the first health professional would refer the child to specialist. The follow-up of treatment would rest with teachers and parents in respective cases. This would also include referral and follow-up in case of psychological problems.

Both parents and teachers need to be impressed upon that the only way to motivate young children to practise healthy habits is to follow the same in school and home themselves. Thus, both parents and teachers in consultation with primary health care professionals may decide about A Code of Health Practices to be followed by all in home and school for prevention of common health problems prevalent among children and community and for health promotion. Necessary basic minimum facilities for practicing this code be jointly arranged as discussed earlier. Flash Cards, stickers with brief catchy key health messages for (i) Prevention of prevailing disease and disabilities, (ii) limiting the existing diseases, and (iii) health promotion, preferably with pictorial messages be prepared and given to schools or flashed on T.V. Safe, sanitary and wholesome physical environment should be provided in home and school where children can participate in normal activities in home and school with a minimum of interface, disturbance and frustration.

To develop a meaningful programme of health education either for school children or for out of school children it has to fit into a well thoughtout framework for curriculum development or programme planning. The broad steps include:

(i) Understanding of current points of view of Health Education and Primary Health Care.

(ii) Awareness of health hazards or health problems at individual, family, school and community level.

(iii) Establishing the BASELINE in terms of knowledge, attitudes and practices; and determining NEED which indicates the gap between programme objectives (what ought to be) and the baseline (what is).
(Need = what ought to be—what is)

(iv) Formulation of measurable behaviour objectives in context with available resources and constraints, and directed towards the Goal of Health For All.

(v) Deciding contents highlighting KEY HEALTH MESSAGES depending upon local and national health programmes in a language understandable by local people.

(vi) Identification of learning opportunities that will best enable school-age children to attain specific objectives related to development of desirable health practices, understandings/concepts, and attitudes.

(vii) Preparing a Plan of Work, deciding appropriate approaches suitable for school students and out of school children, considering their availability, and responsibilities of professionals for programme implementation.

(viii) Implementation of Programme.

(ix) Deciding indicators for concurrent and terminal evaluation of programme objectives and to evaluate the accomplishment of these objectives.

(x) Review and modification of steps.

Programme for Healthful School Living and Healthful Living in Home and Community be drawn jointly by teachers, parents, students (school-age) and professionals in accordance with the steps laid down in the framework. This is likely to lead them to understand what health is, how to protect it, and what to do when it goes wrong with an understanding of the limits of self-healing so that they know when to contact the first level of the formal health system.

It is hoped that this book would be beneficial to experts in health and education in schools. "School Health Education" is an attempt to lay the foundation of the country through the health, vitality, character and general education of the students. It is hoped that the book would be beneficial to policy-makers, planners, implementor of elementary and secondary education. School faculty would be benefited most as once they start taking interest in children's health, they would be doing an excellent work, as health is wealth.

Healthy Child—Healthy Nation

Chandigarh S.L. GOEL

CHAPTER I

SCHOOL HEALTH EDUCATION: NATURE, SCOPE AND SIGNIFICANCE

> Healthy living can help the nation avoid much of its disease burden resulting in a huge cost saving as well as curbing of the suffering of millions of individuals. This is particularly pertinent now with the rising incidence of lifestyle related diseases (such as cancer and cardio-vascular diseases), accidents and traumas, drug addiction and smoking, etc. There should also be compulsory health education in schools and a behavioural change campaign.
>
> —*Voluntary Health Association of India, New Delhi*

School Health Education: Nature, Scope and Significance

To quote Mahatma Gandhi: "If we are to reach real peace in this world and if we are to carry on a real war against war, we shall have to begin with children; and if they will grow up in their natural innocence we won't have to struggle, we won't have to pass fruitless ideal resolutions but we shall go from love to love and peace to peace."

INTRODUCTION

Children's Health and Development

Information and motivation have all the more punch when they are directed towards the younger elements. They are most effective during the early school years.

The role of the school itself in modern life goes far beyond mere academic instruction; it has an important, indeed essential, social task of forming the child's personality. This is much more than teaching children to read, write and do sums, or preparing candidates for examinations or competitions. The school has to contribute towards forming a sound personality, and in particular towards ensuring total physical and mental health for children, so that they can face the difficult world of adults with the maximum chance of success.

To do this, the teaching staff should receive during their years of training a fair knowledge of the biological, psychological and social factors, which leave their imprint on the child's growth and development.

If the first years of a child's life lay down the foundations of its future personality, it is during the school years that the structure begins to take shape. This is when physical growth and psychic development

CHART 1.1

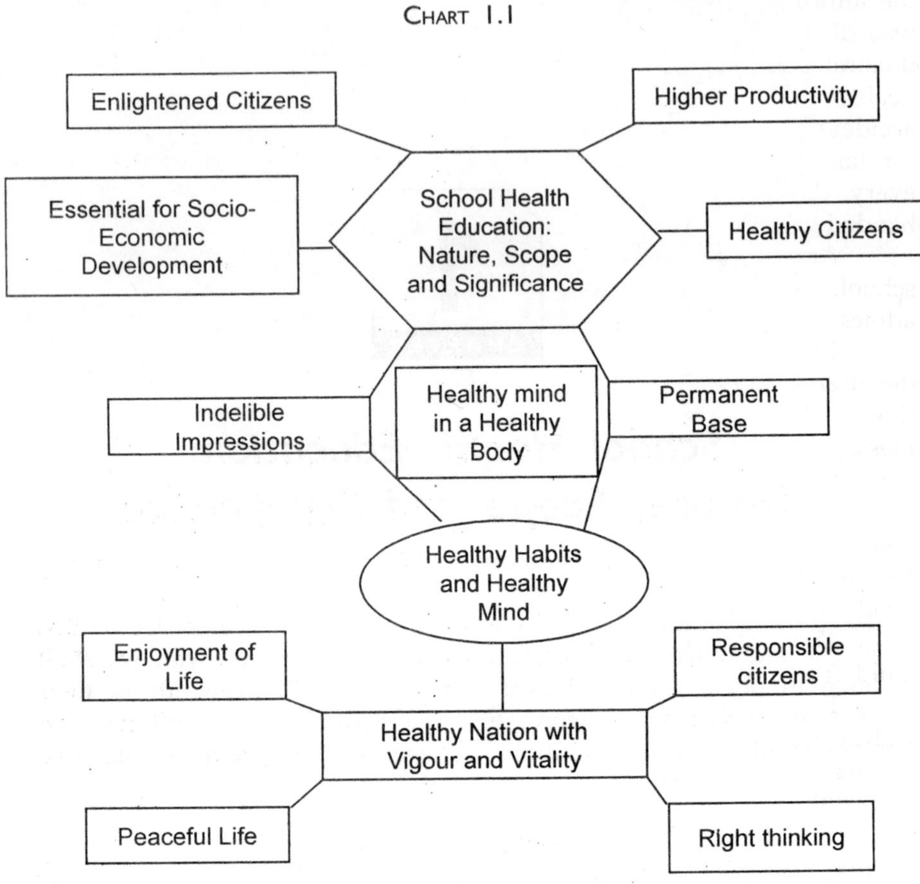

require constant and careful attention, and when close collaboration between parents, teachers and health personnel assumes particular importance. All these people are working with the same human materials. Their techniques may differ but all of them have the same cares and the same goal: to help the children in their charge to grow up in the best possible way.

An experiment undertaken recently in the West African state of Benin explored how to make schoolchildren themselves responsible for their own health and that of their community. The first stage was to hold a number of information sessions in Porto Novo for teachers of both sexes, doctors and nurses, who got down to analyzing the problems posed by the health of school-age children and set in train a practical programme of health education in the schools.

The second stage required a working group composed of primary school inspectors, school doctors, nurses and collaborators from the Paris-based International Children's Centre to draw up a manual of schoolchildren's health, on the basis of recommendations made during the information sessions. The manual was intended for teaching staff and was distributed to all the country's schools. Using practical examples, it illustrates six main issues: the school's role in promoting and protecting health, the growth and development of the child, diet and nutrition, accident prevention and basic first-aid, the environment, and preparation for family life. School "pharmacies" or medical kits, comprising simple every day medicines that cannot possibly do any harm, have been handed out to teachers in some of the rural schools.[1]

Another important source of health information should be the school, yet health is all too often excluded from the training of the adolescent, both in classes and in the overall school environment.[2]

Child development is integral to over all socio-economic development of a nation. "Children's health—tomorrow's wealth", the theme affords and occasion to convey to a world-wide audience the message that children are a priceless resource, and that any nation which neglects them would do so at its peril. World Health Day, 1984 thus highlighted the basic truth that we must all safeguard the healthy minds and bodies of the world's children, not only as a key factor in attaining health for all by the year 2000, but also as a major part of each nation's health in the twenty-first century.[3]

There is an old saying, attributed to Jesuit teachers: "Give me the child for seven years and I will give you the man for life."

Regarding the welfare of the children—Mahatma Gandhi said very rightly that Prayer of the Nation is child's smile and fortune. Pt. Jawaharlal Nehru said: "Nation marches on the tiny feet of the children". IYC slogan of India was Happy Child is Nation's Pride.

Children's health is linked to many inter-sectoral factors, e.g. health, environmental and nutritional needs, social and psychological need, educational needs and special attention of girl child:

Improving Health through Schools

If we consider what is taken to create health, the school emerges as an ideal setting for action. The Ottawa Charter for Health Promotion (1986), a product of the First International Conference on Health Promotion in Industrialized Countries, states that health is created by people in the settings in which they live. It also suggests that health is created by caring for oneself and others, by being able to make decisions and have control over one's life circumstances, and by ensuring that society creates conditions that allow the attainment of health by all its members. (Box 1.1)

Schools can help young people to acquire basic skills needed to create heatlh. Such skills, sometimes called life skills, include decision-making, problem-solving, critical thinking, communication, self-assessment and coping strategies. When people have such skills they are more likely to adopt a healthy lifestyle.

If we consider how best to invest in health, school health

Box 1.1

Life Skills Improve Lifestyles

In Mexico, a study of a sex education programme, based on life skills, Planeando tu vida, which is taught in over 200 schools, showed that adolescents, especially boys, who took part in the programme before they became sexually active were much more likely to use contraceptives in later relationships than those who had not.

In the USA, a study of a life-skills-based health education curriculum Teenage Health Teaching Modules (THTM), involving 5000 students, showed a reduction in self-reported drug use, alcohol consumption and cigarette smoking among students who were educated with the modules.

programmes emerge as very good investments. Last year, the World Bank and WHO compared the cost-effectiveness of various public health programmes. They concluded that among the most cost-effective investments in health are programmes to: expand immunization and micronutrient supplementation; increase knowledge about family planning, nutrition and health care; reduce consumption of tobacco, alcohol and other drugs; and prevent AIDS and sexually-transmitted diseases. Clearly, school health programmes play a major role in addressing these issues, and investments in such programmes are perhaps the "very best of the best".

Schools that provide services to reduce certain health problems, participate in community health projects and encourage people to adopt healthy behaviour clearly benefits large number of people. (Box 1.2)

Box 1.2

School Health Projects Benefit the Community

A very successful programme to reduce intestinal worms was initiated in the Republic of Korea in the mid-1960s. The programme was directed mainly to student groups through schools, was expanded to whole communities, and included mass chemotherapy, health education and environmental sanitation.

It resulted in:

- The prevalence of intestinal worms among schoolchildren decreasing from over 80% in the 1960s to 0.2% in 1992.
- Their prevalence in the general population of the country decreasing from 84% in 1971 to 3.8% in 1992.

Indeed, schooling alone has been shown to be a powerful way to influence health, worldwide. Its impact is most apparent in the benefits to maternal and child health when girls receive schooling.[4] (Box 1.3)

Box 1.3

Education Improves Health!

- Surveys in 25 developing countries show that, all else being equal, 1 to 3 years and schooling among mothers reduced child mortality by about 15% and by much more when mothers had more education. The Peru for example, seven or more years of schooling reduced the mortality risks by nearly 75%.
- Data from 13 African countries for 1975-85 show that a 10% increase in female literacy rates was accompanied by a 10% reduction in child mortality.

UNIVERSALIZATION OF ELEMENTARY EDUCATION

Universalization of Elementary Education (UEE) has been accepted as a national goal. In pursuance of the Constitutional Directive and the need for provision of elementary education as a crucial input for nation-building, the National Policy on Education 1986, as revised in 1992, staged that free and compulsory education of satisfactory quality should be provided to all children up to the age of 14 years, before the commencement of the 21st Century. The Department of Elementary Education and Literacy have state that though considerable progress has been made towards achieving the targets, more rigorous and sustained efforts are required to achieve UEE by the end of Ninth Five Year Plan.

The Department has further submitted that concerted efforts towards UEE have resulted in mani-fold increase in institutions, teachers and students. Access to schools is no longer a major problem. At the primary stage 94 per cent of the country's rural population now has schools within a distance of one kilometer. At the upper primary stage, 84 per cent of the rural population has schools within a distance of three kilometers.

The Table 1.1 on next page indicates the growth of recognized educational institutions since 1994-95.

Some of the initiatives taken by the Department of Elementary Education and literacy towards achieving Universalization of Elementary Education and promoting women's education are discussed.[5]

Children are our future and our most precious resources. The quality of tomorrow's world and perhaps even its survival will be determined by the well being, safety and the physical and intellectual development of children today. To predict the future of a nation, it has been remarked, one need not consult the stars; it can more easily and

TABLE 1.1

Years	Primary	Upper Primary	High/ Hr. Sec./ Inter/ Pre.-Jr. Colleges
1994-95*	581305	163605	92252
1995-96*	590421	171216	98134
1996-97*	598354	176772	102183
1997-98*	610763	185506	107100
1998-99*	626737	190166	112438

* Provisonal.
Source: Sixth Report, Lok Sabha, December 2001, New Delhi.

plainly be read in the faces of its children. Children are the mirror of a nation. Abraham Lincoln nicely explained the role of the child when he said,

> "A child is a person who is going to carry on what you have started. He is going to sit where you are sitting, and when you are gone attend to those things which you think are important. You may adopt all the policies you please, but how they are carried out depends on him. He will assume control of your cities, states, and nations. He is going to move in and take over your Churches, Schools, Universities and Corporations. All your books are going to be judged, praised or condemned by him. The fate of humanity is in his hands."

The UN General Assembly in the Resolution comprising the Second Development Decade has stated:

> "Today youth, everywhere is in ferment. The 1970's must mark a step forward in securing the well-being and happiness not only of the present generation but also of the generations to come."[6]

One of the specific objectives of the Second Development Decade is that "the well-being of children shall be fostered."[7] Dr. P.C. Chunder, former Minister of Education and Social Welfare, Government of India in his Foreword to the National Plan of Action for International Year of the Child", 1979 has rightly said that,

> "A Nation's children are its supremely important asset and the nation's future lies in their proper development. . . . An investment in children is indeed an investment in the Nation's future. A

healthy and educated child of today is the active and intelligent citizen of tomorrow."[8]

To quote C. Subramaniam, the former Finance Minister in the Government of India:

"Giving high priority to children's welfare means singling out a target group which is intermingled with the rest of the population right down to the level of individual families. Therefore, it requires building up an organizing and an administrative set-up that goes all the way from international agencies to each village and town of less-developed countries."[9]

Effective national policies and plans regarding children can make a decisive contribution to all other long-term development activities and particularly to the success of the programmes aimed at raising the quality of life of lower income groups and at building national capacities and self-reliance.

Health-related habits formed during childhood can play a crucial role in determining whether an adult will be destined to enjoy a long and healthy life.

The ultimate objective of procreation is to have children who will become healthy, happy adults and will continue so during a long life. More and more are we realizing, and finding, that the foundation for such a desirable state is laid in the earliest stages of a child's growth and development. Much attention needs to be paid to this vital fact. We are getting better at reducing our infant mortality rates. This is admirable. But we need to ask the question: If an infant now escapes becoming an infant mortality statistic, what is the outcome for that infant? Is he or she intact? Will he or she arrive at adulthood complete and healthy?

How early are these vital years? The wise Chinese celebrate their children's first birthdays when they are born. This tradition is based on the far-sighted realization that a very important period of growth and development has been occurring in the 40 weeks growing before birth. In modern biomedical terms, then, many of the secrets and foundations of later health are hidden and to be found in the prenatal period. Growth and development start at conception; and while birth is of the greatest importance to the family involved, it is not, comparatively speaking, of such great biomedical importance. Perhaps for certain purposes we should talk of the Vital Weeks.[10]

The first years are crucial in laying the foundation of good health and improving the quality of life.

There is need to understand that while the task of safeguarding the health of today's children is urgent, it cannot be accomplished through conventional means. What is required is a radical new approach emphasizing the just distribution of health resources; mobilization of national and international resources; imaginative use of traditional medicine and its practitioners; research and development of appropriate health technologies relevant to local needs; and close cooperation among the nations of the world.[11]

Education and health are the two most important sectors of national development, and proper coordination between these sectors is of paramount importance. The delivery system of both these sectors need to work hand-in-hand to achieve the cherished goals of self-reliance[12].

It is imperative that our young children should acquire knowledge, skills and attitudes which will shape their health and have positive impact on their lifestyle and thereby play a vital role in improving the health status of their community and nation at large.

Emphasizing the importance of the School Programme, the National Health Policy has recommended that "Organized school health services integrally linked with the general preventive and curative services would require to be established within a time limited programme".

The policy further states, "The recommended efforts on various fronts would bear marginal results unless nation-wide health education programme backed by appropriate communication strategy are launched to provide health information in easily understandable form to motivate the development of attitude for healthy living. The public health education programmes should be supplemented by health, nutrition and population education programme in all educational institutions at various levels. Simultaneously efforts would require to be made to promote universal education especially adult and family education without which the various efforts to organized preventive and promotive health activities, family planning and improved maternal and child health cannot bear fruit".

The National Policy on Education (1986) has emphasized the need for the overall development of the young child. It states, "Recognizing the holistic nature of child development, viz., nutrition, health and social, mental, physical, moral and emotional development. Early Childhood Care and Education (ECCE) will receive high priority and be suitably integrated with the Integrated Child Development Services Programme, wherever possible". The policy further states, "A full integration of child care and pre-primary education will be brought about, both as a feeder and a strengthening factor for primary education and for human resource development in general. In continuation of this stage, the School Health Programme will be strengthened.

The section on vocational education in the Education Policy also stresses on the development of appropriate categories of health worker. It states, "Health planning and health service management should optimally interlock with the education and training of appropriate categories of health manpower through health-related vocational courses. Health education at the primary and middle levels will ensure the commitment of the individual to family and community health, and lead to health-related vocational courses at the +2 stage of higher secondary education."

It is heartening to note that the national intention in both the policies are complementary and need to be judiciously integrated in the programmes of actions to attain the major goals.[13]

HEALTH EDUCATION SERVICES IN SCHOOLS

The Central Council of Health also recognized the importance of adequate health services for student community in the county. It, therefore, adopted the resolution at their Third Meeting held in 1955.

> "The Central Council of Health viewing with concern the lack of adequate student health services throughout the country and recognizing the urgent need of adequate health services for this most important group in the community, recommends that all State Governments should take immediate steps to establish a student health service under their health departments so as to give the entire student population proper medical care including nutrition and physical education".

The Estimates Committee of the Parliament in 1958-59 (Forty-fourth Report), gave the following recommendation on school health education:

> "The committee are of the view that a comprehensive programme for improving the standard of health of school children is necessary and should be based on surveys already conducted or to be undertaken. In this connection the Committee were informed that the Ministry propose to appoint an expert committee presided over by a leading public man interested in the subject to examine the lines on which health survey of school children should be conducted and also to suggest ways and means for the promotion of nutrition among the school children. The Committee felt that the proposal has a substantial value because if the health of the school children deteriorates, the future of the country will be at stake. It further suggested to consider the feasibility of harnessing medical profession through the local medial association for the purpose."[14]

V.T. Tatochenko in his article: "Education for Health" stresses that while general education has contributed immensely to the health improvement of the people, the importance of special health education efforts aimed at parents, children and adolescents has always been recognized in most health service systems.

Traditionally, health education aims at fostering hygienic habits, promoting adequate nutrition, and creating environmental conditions conducive to a healthy physical and mental growth and development.

Much importance is attached in prevention of disease, recognition of the first signs of illness and elementary treatment procedures. At school, children are introduced to the basic knowledge of anatomy, physiology and hygiene, which constitute the core of school health education programmes.

In the USSR, hundreds of thousands of primary health care workers—district pediatricians and public health nurses, school physicians and nurses, and feld-shers and midwives in rural areas—carry out both individual and group health education. A part of their duty hours is routinely devoted to health education activities. The process starts with the education of the mother before childbirth, continues throughout childhood and adolescence, and enters a new cycle with the preparation of young people at school for parenthood and family life[15].

Government of India (1961) Report of the schools education committee made the following recommendations for Health Education in Schools:

RECOMMENDATIONS (HEALTH EDUCATION)[16]

1. Health education should be included as part of general education in the primary, middle and secondary schools. The basic education system, as expounded by Mahatma Gandhi, contains the essential ingredients of a school health education programme.
2. Steps should be taken to keep the school environment in a sanitary condition. The school administration should provide the right environment to promote health, prevent disease and furnish opportunities to children to practise good health habits.
3. School authorities should employ teachers who are in sound health and should take steps to see that conditions under which they are working are conducive to healthy living.
4. The health personnel should assist the teacher in carrying out his health education responsibilities. They should also help parents to provide facilities for the children to practise at home the health habits learnt at schools.
5. The State Administration should play a vital role in the effective implementation of the school health education programme and in setting up standard in the State in accordance with the national policies.
6. The State Administration should take immediate steps to publish text books on health education and to have health lessons included in other appropriate text-books. Books and teaching aids should be kept up-to-date with scientific health information and adopted to the development level of pupils for whom they are intended.

7. The Central Health Education Bureau (CHEB) and the National Institute of Audio Visual Education, in cooperation with appropriate advisors in various fields of education should develop "type" instructional material and teaching aids for use in school health education programme. These materials should serve as guides for the States to develop their own aids and material.
8. In primary grades, the emphasis should be placed on practicing healthful living. The teaching should be practical and related to pupil's past experience, his home conditions and his present needs.
9. The learning experiences in middle classes should be "life centred" rather than "book-centred". In schools where there are special subject teachers, the health content of the curriculum may be correlated with the specific subjects taught. Where the class teacher is responsible for all teaching in the class, he should be responsible for health teaching as well.
10. The health curriculum for secondary schools should be carefully planned so as to avoid unnecessary duplications and serious omissions, with appropriate health topics being incorporated within the respective special subjects. Wherever facilities exit, health should be included in the list of optional subjects offered.
11. The draft syllabi on health education for the children of the age groups 6-11, 11-14 and 14-17 be prepared by the Committee on Health and Nutrition Education, constituted by the Ministry of Education should be adopted for health teaching in schools with slight modifications to suit local needs.
12. The School Health Education (SHE) section in the Central Health Education Bureau and the Students' Health Education Unit in SHEBs should be developed to provide leadership in different aspects of School Health Education.

V. Tatochenko feels that health education in schools should not be merely taught but make the children aware of its use in day-to-day life.

The transfer of knowledge cannot be considered the final gals of health education; the child has to learn how to use this knowledge and how to make the best choice in a given situation.[17]

Rapid changes in lifestyles, and the evolution of views on health and disease call for new departures in health education. A quick glance at health education material of even one generation ago will show how fast it tends to get out of date. Medical facts, it has been estimated, get outdated within a decade or so. Effective health education therefore requires a continuous stream of knowledge, development of the people's ability to absorb it, and decisions taken on the basis of a constantly changing body of information.

There is another, and perhaps more important reason for new health education efforts to be made. The WHO definition of health stresses that health is not only the absence of disease or infirmity but a state of complete physical, mental and social well-being. Such a concept of well-being should include not only the individual's ability to function normally under optimal or near-optimal conditions, but also to stand up to increased loads, strains and stresses by summoning up resources that usually lie dormant.

RAISING THE QUALITY OF LIFE

If the contents of "traditional" health education are analyzed from this stand-point, it would be clear that a substantial part of it is aimed at prevention of diseases and creation of optimal environmental conditions for the child's growth and development, while a comparatively minor role is given to health promotion that would prepare an individual to function properly under the stressful conditions of life today. This is not to say that "traditional" health education has not value—which it certainly has—but there is need to underline the importance of health education aimed at health promotion and at raising the quality of life, and not limited merely to prevention of disease or health protection.

One of the best examples of such an approach is to engage children in physical training and sports, which lead to harmonious growth and increased capacity for physical work. In the USSR, a set of indicators, differentiated by age-groups, has been developed, to serve both as a target of physical training of school children and as a measure of physical activity performance by individual children. Research is needed to formulate precise indicators for physical training of pre-school children, as well as of children with various infirmities who need physical exercise as much, if not more, than healthy children.

However, the aim of physical education goes even beyond this: it should help to create in adolescents an internalized need for physical activity, an ability to maintain a balance between physical and mental work, which is the best way to combat hypodynamia—diminished power—a quickly spreading modern "disease".

It is well known that even children in equally good health do not react the same way to various stress factors. For example, some may catch cold even after a short exposure to cold weather, while the majority of children remain unaffected. "Tempering" or toughening-up of the children to gradually increase their resistance to cold is one of the most important elements of healthy development, particularly in cold climates. Introduction of tempering (for example, through shower baths of decreasing temperature) in many pre-school institutions in the USSR brought down respiratory morbidity to one-half or one-third. These measures cannot, however, be effective if parents are not made to stop over clothing the children and keeping them in a hot-house atmosphere. Hence the need for systematic educational efforts in childhood and adolescence to motivate future parents.[18]

PROGRAMME INTERVENTIONS IN CHILD HEALTH

The poor environmental factors are also reflected in the causes of the death of children in the developing world. If we examine the Table 1.2, we discern that the main causes of death of children in the developing world are diarrhoeal diseases and respiratory infections followed by communicable and preventable diseases such as whooping cough and measles.

From the above statements about the health problems of children in the developing world, it is evident that no specific health measures and no single set of actions can remedy these problems. The real "Iceberg" of which excessive infant mortality is but one visible tip consists of poverty, hunger, malnutrition, ignorance and many other socio-economic ills. In order to control this total "iceberg", we must take care of the broad socio-economic development programmes directed at the root of these ills.

TABLE 1.2

Leading Causes of Child Deaths

	Developed Country	*Developing Country*
Infants	Births injuries	Enteritic, Diarrhoeal disease
	Congenital anomalies	Influenza, Pheaumonia
	Influenza, Pheaumonia	Bronchitis, etc.
	Enteritis, diarrhoeal diseases	Whooping cough
1-4 years	Accidents	Enteritic, Diarrhoeal disease
	Congenital anomalies	Influenza, Pheaumonia
	Malignant neoplasms	Bronchitis, etc.
		Measles
5-9 years	Accidents	Enteritic, Diarrhoeal disease
	Malignant neoplasms	Influenza, Pheaumonia
	Congenital anomalies	Accidents
	Heart diseases	Measles
10-14 years	Accidents	Influenza, Pheaumonia
	Malignant neoplasms	Accidents
	Congenital anomalies	Enteritic, Diarrhoeal disease
	Heart diseases	Measles

Source: Summarized from WHO Technical Report Series No. 600.

ISSUES OF HEALTH EDUCATION IN SCHOOLS

In a document, "Health Education for School-Age Children: A Framework" brought out by Central Health Education Bureau poses certain issues which need solution to formulate realistic school health education policy.

Issues

1. What is the most effective way to integrate health education in the total school programme? Should it be:
   - An independent subject to be taught by a subject teacher?
   - Integrated with other subjects?
   - A part of management of physical, mental, emotional and social environment in school?
   - A part of school health services?
   - Pervasive to total school programme?
2. How much time should be allotted to health education transaction out of the time allocated to "Health and Physical Education" at different levels in the National Curriculum for Primary and Secondary Education and National Curriculum for Higher Secondary Education.
3. How can more effective links be established among schools, families and other agencies of communities, including the mass-media, to minimize conflicts in value systems and maximize positive health learning?
4. How can long-sought, but rarely found effective coordination of effort between the health and education sectors be achieved at national, state, district and local levels in areas such as:
   - curriculum planning/revision/transaction;
   - preparation of instructional materials;
   - preparation of educational personnel through pre-service and in-service education;
   - improvement of school environment;
   - health appraisal, referral and follow-up of students;
   - enlisting community participation and participation of students in community-based health programmes; and
   - monitoring and evaluation.
5. To what extent can already overburdened teachers teaching other subject be reasonably expected to shoulder—additional responsibilities of health education transaction; observing and screening students for defects and deviations from normal health and maintaining health records?
6. How can teachers, lacking expertise and training in transaction and evaluation of health education as per minimum learning outcomes for each level of school

education, be prepared to deal with the subject competently and confidently?
7. What should be the strategy of preparing health education faculty for teacher education institutions, health education planners and administrators for national, state and district level health education and educational institutions?
8. What strategy will be most effective for health education transaction for out-of-school children?
9. What will be most effective mechanism to monitor health education transaction and environmental facilities in school for healthful living?

All these issues need to be tackled for the successful implementation of the health education policy. Efforts have been made to address to these questions in this document.[19]

The same document suggests the objective, content areas and course material at different levels:

Long-Range Objective

Schools need to organize and provide learning experiences to their students with a view to achieving the following long-range objectives:

- Develop a desire to be healthy;
- Become aware of meaning and concept of health;
- Be familiar with the factors and conditions that promote or adversely effect health;
- Acquire relevant health knowledge; develop positive attitude and practices to stay healthy;
- Do what he/she can individually and collectively to promote—(i) his/her own health: (ii) health of his/her family members, and (iii) health of others in the community; and
- Promote improved preventive and promotive self-care health behaviour in families and in the community.

Content Areas

Health education content at various school levels may be organized under the following illustrative broad areas:

(i) Personal health including rest, sleep, exercise, posture, etc;
(ii) Environmental/community health;
(iii) Nutritional health;
(iv) Mental health;
(v) Growth and development;
(vi) Prevention and control of disease and disorders;
(vii) Safety, first-aid, home nursing;
(viii) Family life and reproductive health;

(ix) Contemporary health problems: smoking and chewing of tobacco, drug-abuse, alcoholism and special problems of the community;
(x) Consumer education; and
(xi) Health Education Planning and Implementation.

Health Education Transaction

Health education in school should not be considered as the sole responsibility of a single teacher. Development of healthy lifestyles through healthful living in a school is to be shared by all teachers. They themselves have to present an example of desirable behaviour they intend to develop among their students. Similarly, day-to-day observation of signs of deviation from normal health, screening students under their charge for height, weight, vision and hearing, maintaining health record of students, referring them to health personnel through their parents and following instructions regarding making any adjustment should be the responsibility of all the teachers.

Health education concepts have been integrated in subjects like environmental studies, language, social sciences, biology, physical education and population education. It should be taught consciously by the teachers teaching these subjects, keeping in mind the objectives for each level of school education. Besides, health education will be taught by physical education teachers as a separate subject. The time allocated for health education transaction as per objectives laid down for each level of school education viz: Primary, upper-primary, secondary and higher secondary will be 50% of the time allocated to Health and Physical Education as recommended in the "National Curriculum for Primary and Secondary Education" and "National Curriculum for Higher Secondary Education" developed by NCERT.

Minimum learning outcomes need to be developed under each content area according to priorities to be accorded to practices, attitudes and knowledge at each of level.

Primary Education Level (Classes I-V)

The emphasis at this stage will be on development of health practices through conscious planning and supervision. The teacher will present an example of health behaviour he/she wishes to develop among students. An illustrative list of health practices may be developed as minimum learning outcomes. Students may be observed for these practices. The HEALTH CODE consisting of selected practices to be developed according to priority may be prepared. The health problems of students revealed by a medical examination may also be used in evolving the health code. The "Health Code" to be followed by all in the school may be displayed listing the practices and showing pictures thereof for younger children who cannot read. After these practices become habits, other practices may be included in the "Health Code" and revised code may be prepared and displayed. The process may continue till almost all practices become habits. Emphasis should be on development of proper skill involved in these practices. Habits and practices exhibited by the teacher provide an educational opportunity for his/her students to initiate his/her behaviour. Activities such as demonstrations, drawing/ collection of pictures, skits, dramas, role-play, responsibility for checking health practice(s) of others on a particular day, proper use and improvement of environmental facilities in school may be planned.

Parental cooperation in this effort will be of immense value in achieving the goal of health. Older students may be given the responsibility of developing health practices among their younger brothers and sisters by presenting an example of these practices to them.

The healthy practices based on correct skills and supported by scientific knowledge appropriate to the age of these students will lead to development of right attitudes/influencing preferences and feelings of these students about healthy lifestyles.

Teachers have to keep an eye on the common signs and symptoms of deviation from normal health among students under their charge and periodically screen them for height, weight, vision and hearing. Observations about deviations from normal health have to be communicated or referred to the school health services personnel through parents or in case of absence of such a scheme to the parents who may make their own arrangements to take their children to qualified physicals. In addition, teachers may plan the school day in such a manner so as to ensure a mentally and emotionally healthy environment for his/her students besides meeting their needs for rest, play and recreation.

Upper Primary Level (Classes VI-VIII)

The guidance and supervision of the health practices initiated during the primary school level will continue. However, opportunities will be required to be provided to discuss cause and effect relationship of health practices with prevention and control of disease. The emphasis in selecting such opportunities will have to be laid on learning by students rather than teaching to them. Interaction with the health personnel for collecting information and relevant materials providing additional information on topics listed in the syllabus and textbooks may be facilitated wherever and whenever possible. Efforts should be made in selecting a method of instruction which may provide maximum participation from pupils.

At this stage, the first priority should be given to development of right attitudes among students, like—

- acceptance of personal responsibility for health promotion;
- application of health knowledge and understanding to solve health problems;

- confidence in scientific health principles/practices;
- awareness that prevention is preferable to treatment or cure:
- conviction that any deviation from normal health status requires immediate medical attention and care;
- reliance on scientific medicine;
- rejection of superstitions and quackery;
- respect for the health of others;
- willingness to suffer inconvenience for the protection of health of others; and
- ideal of attaining vigorous high level of health.

An effort should be made to ensure that the learning opportunities provided to transact health instruction lead to the evidence of above attitudes.

Secondary School Level (Classes IX-X)

By this time, the consensus effort on the part of teachers to develop practices into habits may have resulted into a healthy lifestyle. But the efforts to develop right attitudes would continue to establish a strong foundation for a healthy way of life. There would be more emphasis on academic learning about the nature and concept of health and disease, health problems, factors and conditions responsible for health and disease, and resources available to meet the challenge to protect, preserve and promote the individual and community health through self-care health behaviour. The activities will be participatory in nature.

Assignments of exploratory nature may be given in the form of individual and/or group projects, opportunities may be provided to document observations and conclusion, present the results, answer questions and provide clarifications. Students may be involved in planning, preparing and using such methods as symposium forum, panel discussions, role-play, putting up exhibitions using multi-media to present their findings.

Higher Secondary Level (Classes XI-XII)

Health instruction at this stage will become more academic in nature. Besides classroom instruction opportunities for greater student community interaction will be planned and provided. Student participation will be ensured from the planning stage through organization and implementation to evaluation stages. Besides, emphasis on self-learning through library reading and observation of community projects and programmes by health care providers, both official and non-official, opportunities may be provided for students to interact with technical personnel either by interviewing them, cooperating with them in their projects or by inviting them to present their experiences through symposia, panel discussions, etc., where they can elicit information they need.

The opportunities may be directed to develop Five Basic Communication Skills—

I. Talk with Health Care Provider(s);
II. Listen and Learn;
III. Ask questions;
IV. Decide what to do, with the help from the health care provider; and
V. Do-follow through.

Students may be involved in taking up health education projects in the community either through activities under 'Work Experience' or though National Service Scheme (NSS) to help people solve their health problems through self-care (community participation).

Transaction for Health Education in Non-Formal Education

The objectives and content of health education will be same as for various stages of formal education viz. (a) primary level (6-11 years), Upper primary level (11-14 years), Secondary level, (14-16 years), Higher Secondary level (16-18 years). The implementation strategies may be formulated according to the organizational structure of the non-formal centres, community resources and facilities for inter-sectoral coordination.

Evaluation

Evaluation is a process of assessing the effectiveness of any effort in terms of results. It can be planned as a concurrent or on-going activity as well as a terminal activity, which indicates pupil's progress towards educational objectives. It reveals the strength and weakness of a programme and provides information for use in reviewing specific objectives, developing new learning strategies and improving methods and material.

Evaluation implies establishment of a baseline before an activity is planned and implemented as well as to set-up an indicator for future comparisons. In case of evaluation of school health programme for improving health status students, it may includes:

I. Appraisal of facilities (including technical professional preparation of personnel) for health promotion of students:
   - healthful school environment;
   - school health services;
   - health instructions; and
   - coordination between Health, Education and other sectors and between School, Home and Community Services.

II. Appraisal of transaction of School Health Programme including:

- maintenance and improvement of school environment for health promotion;
- utilization of results of health appraisal for health education and for developing self-care behaviour;
- transaction of curriculum to achieve desired change in knowledge, attitudes and practices of students; and
- utilization of coordination mechanism for optimizing resource utilization and minimizing value conflict between school and home.

The assessment can be done by using such tools as: Observation, interviews, checklists, project reports, records and tests.

In evaluating knowledge, attitudes and practices at various school levels, viz., primary, upper primary, secondary and higher secondary, the weightage to be given to 'allocation of time' in health education programme, and to 'allocation of percentage of marks for developing and evaluating knowledge (K), Attitudes (A), and Practices (P) may be in the following order of priority:

		1 2 3
(a)	Primary level (Classes I-V)	P A K
(b)	Upper primary level (Classes VI-VIII)	A P K
(c)	Secondary level (Classes; IX-X)	K A P
(d)	Higher Secondary level (Classes XI-XII)	

The proper transaction of health instruction in schools presupposes adequate pre-service and in-service preparation of teachers in health education content appropriate to each school level (minimum learning outcomes), formulation of measurable (behavioural) objectives, selection and use of appropriate educational methods, establishment of base-line, curriculum planning and evaluation techniques.[20]

ESSENTIALS

I. Need of Effective Co-ordination between Health and Education Sectors this has been Beautifully shown in Chart 1.2

Since health affects and is affected by education, therefore, there is a need of effective co-ordinates between the two.

Effective coordination of school health services and school health education can be achieved if policy planning and decision-making bodies at national, state, district and local levels have adequate representation from education and health sectors. At the national level, a coordination committee needs to be established. Such a measure will ensure liaison between all programme officers from MHRD and MHFW, and help in formulation, implementation, review and modification of school health education and school health service programmes. The coordination at the national level between NCERT and CHEB and at the state level between SCERT and SHEB need to be strengthened and streamlined.

On the coordination bodies from the national level to local levels, there should be representation from coordinating bodies at the lower level. This would ensure a steady flow of information from top to bottom level and also from the bottom level up to the top level for facilitating monitoring of programmes.[21]

CHART 1.2

Management of Monitoring and Evaluation

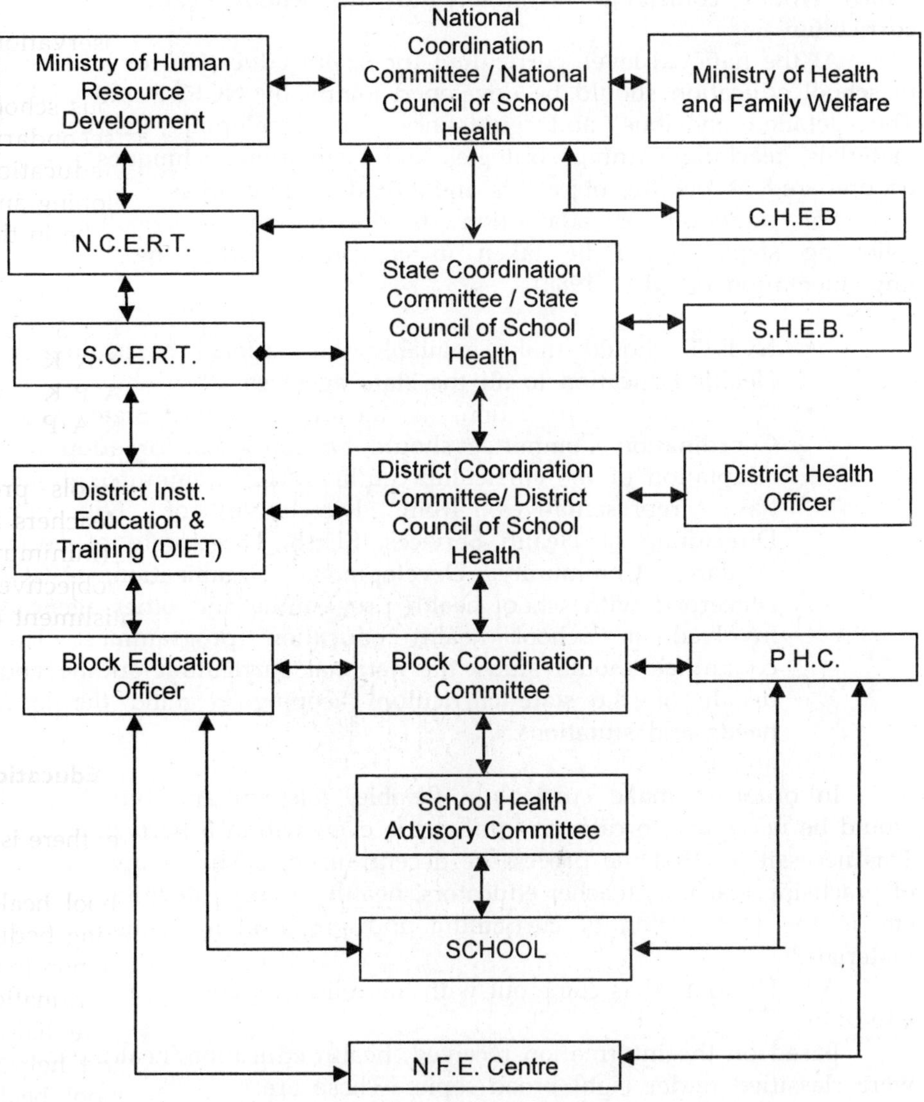

Source: CHEB: Health Education for School Age Children.

2. Designing Curriculum: The Same Report Suggests that: Formulation and Adoption/Adaptation of the National Curriculum Framework

Although curriculum planning is primarily the responsibility of education departments planning for school health education should be a joint responsibility of education and health personnel. The health personnel should ensure the accuracy of content and health needs of the learner. Personnel with responsibility for school health services and healthful school environment should ensure those essential components, which would contribute favourably to the school health education curriculum.

At the national level, curriculum for health education for all stages of school education should be developed jointly by NCERT and CHEB. The detailed syllabus and guidelines for developing instructional materials, teaching-learning strategies and evaluation techniques should be prepared as per the objectives and broad content areas.

For adoption or adaptation of the national curriculum, the following steps should be taken in consonance with the POA for implementation of NPE (1986).

- NCERT should make available the national curriculum in Health Education to all the state agencies.
- As a follow-up action, a meeting of the State Level Coordination Committee should be convened for adoption/ adaptation of the curriculum outline. This Committee should have representatives from Directorate of Education, Directorate of Health Services, SHEB, Directorate of Social Welfare, Community Development Organization, NGOs concerned with school health programme and other agencies involved in school health education programmes. This committee should study the national curriculum outline and decide on the state curriculum keeping in mind the local needs and situations.

In order to make curriculum flexible, relevant and functional it would be necessary to cater to local needs even within a particular state. This necessitates that the process be decentralized, ensuring involvement of practising teachers, teacher educators, health workers, doctors, parents, etc. in the formulation of curriculum and preparation of instructional materials.[22]

A.B. Hiramani has come out with the following core areas in health education.

Based on the information received, health education/health aspects were classified under eight broad topics. These are:

I. Personal Hygiene;

II. Water and Environmental Sanitation;
III. Food, Nutrition and Health;
IV. Food Sanitation Practices;
V. Communicable and Non-Communicable Diseases;
VI. Human Biology;
VII. Safety and First-aid; and
VIII. Health/Medical Care.

Although these broad categories apparently seem to be exclusive, the topics or components included in the curricula under each of the broad subjects are not exclusive. There is un-avoidingly an overlapping.

I. Personal Hygiene

1. Significance;
2. Cleanliness;
3. Care of all parts of the body;
4. Dangers of spitting indiscriminately;
5. Health habits and care of the body;
6. Eyes, teeth, ear defects in general; and
7. Hygiene rules for keeping good health.

II. Water and Environmental Sanitation

1. Relationship between water and environmental sanitation and health;
2. Cleanliness of house, school and surroundings;
3. Disposal of garbage and refusal;
4. Need of urinamental sanitation;
5. Environmental pollution, nature, sources and prevention, and harms caused by environmental pollution;
6. Need of pure and safe water for health;
7. Water pollution, nature, source of prevention;
8. Diseases caused due to polluted water and hazards of contaminated water;
9. Importance of clean body; and
10. Well-ventilated and sanitary houses.

III. Food, Nutrition and Health

1. Need of energy foods for human body;
2. Food-sources of energy for body/need of food;
3. Types of food;
4. Nutrients and their functions and sources;
5. Balanced diet;
6. Importance of raw food;

7. Foodstuff and their functions;
8. Malnutrition;
9. Protein deficiency/deficiency diseases—causes and remedy;
10. Necessity of different types of food for human body according to age;
11. Type of work, conditions and climate;
12. Food and health; and
13. Food and nutrition (for energy, body-building and protection).

IV. *Food and Sanitation Practices*

1. Food habits and hygienic practices in family;
2. Proper storage of cooked food;
3. Food preservation;
4. Hygiene of food items and hygienic way of cooking;
5. Methods of cooking and health; and
6. Effects of adulteration.

V. *Communicable Diseases and Non-Communicable Diseases*

1. General knowledge of communicable diseases;
2. Nature, causes and epidemiology;
3. Ways of transmission of communicable diseases;
4. Prevention/Measures for controlling communicable diseases;
5. Need of vaccination;
6. Non-communicable diseases-their symptoms, causes, prevention and cure.

VI. *Human Physiology*

1. Different types of bones and their functions;
2. Muscles and their functionings;
3. Different types of systems and their functions—nervous system, respiratory system, excretory system, digestive system, circulatory system and reproductive system;
4. Human body—organs of body and their functions;
5. Hormones and Enzymes and its importance for human body;
6. Human scultry system; and
7. Sense organs.

VII. *Safety and First-Aid*

1. Principles of first-aid;
2. Health and Safety measures;
3. Accident and first-aid;
4. Type of bandages and their applications;

5. Fractures, wounds, shocks and their treatment;
6. Common poison and their treatment;
7. Artificial respiration;
8. Treatment of burn and bleeding;
9. Safety habits in home and school;
10. Principles of home safety;
11. Safe drinking water;
12. Man-made disaster; and
13. Natural disaster.

VIII. Health/Medical Care

1. Medical care for sick/care of the patient;
2. Help to the sick persons;
3. Health care;
4. Drug addiction and health;
5. Home nursing;
6. Infant mortality—cause and prevention;
7. Child care;
8. Preparing preventive habits;
9. Correct postures; and
10. Meaning and importance of good health.[23]

As a whole, the Renuka Committee recommended induction of health education at two levels: in the teacher training programme; and second, in the curricula of various stages of education. Firstly, the teacher training is of vital importance; unless the teacher is trained in contents and methods of health education he will not impart effectively health education to the pupil. The curriculum recommended by the Committee was so comprehensive to achieve better standard of health of school going children. The broad subject areas of recommended curriculum is given in Table 1.3

Interdisciplinary Approach: Health in the School Curriculum

What is the relationship between these subjects like mathematics geography, science, history, biology and the promotion of health care? The common point between them is that all these subjects are taught in most schools throughout the five continents, and they therefore represent the basis of the educational process for millions of school-children all over the world. A simple adaptation of the approach to these subjects and of their contents so as to involve health issues will be an important step towards reaching a goal which is desirable for doctors, educators and health authorities everywhere: the stimulation of a degree of concern in children, from an early age, for the maintenance of their health and the prevention of diseases.

Teachers of different subjects can find many ways to introduce the

TABLE 1.3

Broad Topics of Health Recommended by the Renuka Committee in the Syllabus for Different Age Groups (different stages of education)

Age groups/Class of Study	*Broad topics*
6-11	(i) Personal Hygiene; (ii) Environmental Hygiene (Healthful School living); (iii) Control of Diseases; (iv) Food and Nutrition; (v) Health conditions in town or village; (vi) Growth; (vii) Rest, sleep, exercise, posture; (viii) Caring for animals; (ix) Safety and First-aid; (x) Health Organizations; and (xi) Family life education including sex education;
11-14 (Classes VI-IX)	(i) Personal Health; (ii) Environmental Hygiene (Healthful living); (iii) Control of communicable Diseases; (iv) Food and Nutrition; (v) Health Conditions in village, town or country; (vi) Growth; (vii) Rest, Sleep, Exercise, Posture, Leisure Activities; (viii) Caring for Animals; (ix) Safety and First-Aid Home Nursing; (x) Health Organizations; (xi) Family Life Education including Sex Education; (xii) Mental Health; and (xiii) Pioneers in Health;
14-17 years (Classes X-XII)	(i) Personal Health; (ii) Environmental Hygiene; (iii) Control of Communicable Disease; (iv) Food and Nutrition; (v) Health conditions in village, town or country; (vi) Growth; (vii) Rest, sleep, exercise, posture; (viii) Caring for Animals; (ix) Safety, First-Aid and Home Nursing; (x) Health Organizations; (xi) Family Life Education including Sex Education; (xii) Care of Eyes, Ears, Nose, Teeth; (xiii) Mental Health; and (xiv) Pioneers in Health.[24]

principles and concepts of health care and health maintenance among students. We have already seen that integrating other relevant topics (such as environmental issues) within the context of formal teaching has proved successful wherever it has been tried, and there are clear indications that it is perfectly possible in regard to health care topics.

The urgent need to adopt this interdisciplinary approach at the earliest possible age—especially in developing nations—is underlined by the fact that most of the health problems present in those countries result from a lack of public awareness about their origins, how they are transmitted and how they can be prevented. Lack of information is the chief culprit for encouraging the continuing transmission of certain diseases, such as schistosomiasis, typhoid fever and cholera, which could be largely avoided if we could bring about simple changes in the behaviour of children. The educational process is one way of stimulating such changes of attitudes, and teachers of all subjects can collaborate in this process by making minor adaptations in their classroom approach.

During the teaching of mathematics, for instance, teachers can use examples related to the number of insect species, which transmit diseases such as malaria or Changas disease. Such example will help to stimulate the students' ability to do simple sums or more complex calculations (the object of the lessons), but will also enable them to identify the vectors of disease and at the same time will increase their concern about the presence of certain insects in their homes.

In geography lessons, teachers have an opportunity to relate geographical areas to the incidence of certain diseases. The study of rivers or lakes (even for the young children in the first years of school) offers a chance to talk about water-snails and the part they play in transmitting schistosomiasis (bilharziasis). In affected areas, the lessons can warn students to avoid bathing in certain places. In the context of subject like science (in the early years) or biology, it is clearly easier to stimulate in students a sense of concern about their own health and that of others.

It this kind of approach to the teaching of curriculum subjects is to develop its full potential in teaching health awareness, a great deal of commitment is necessary from teachers themselves. Many countries have already introduced health issues into the teaching system in the form of specific subjects created for the purpose, but restrictions imposed by the timetable and other factors impede the success of such a strategy. If, in a world-wide effort to stimulate a sense of health care among young people, every teacher could assume a little of the responsibility for passing on to their students some basic knowledge about aspects of hygiene and health maintenance, the final result would be amazing. Health and education are closely linked subjects. To integrate them in this way would be a most effective way of preventing the spread of another very serious "disease" which affects all too many people: the lack of information![25]

Youth represents a tremendous potential for society. Provided it is channeled in the right direction, the enthusiasm, initiative and idealism of young people can help others, including the elderly, the handicapped, the poor, and in so doing can create a happier and more balanced society.

Young people's participation in community activities—particularly in primary health care—is a key precondition for health for all.[26]

3. Preparation of Manpower

For effective implementation of school health education, the functionaries at all levels need to be strengthened and provided with professional support in school health education at national, state, district and local levels. There is also a need for preparing trained resource persons for providing expertise to the Teacher Training Institutions (TTIs).

Preparation of Resource Persons

The present post-Graduate Diploma Course in Health Education is inadequate to meet this demand. It may be desirable to start a separate Diploma Course in School Health Education. Alternatively, the existing Diploma Course should have a modular course in School Health Education. This, in the long-run, will be necessary to supply trained manpower to such organizations and agencies as NCERT, CHEB, SIEs,/ SCERTs, SHEBs, DIETs, TTIs, district health set-up under CMO, etc.

Preparation of Teachers

Proper transaction of health education would depend on the effective teacher preparation. The training should equip teachers with innovative practices related to teaching-learning strategies and evaluation procedures. Teacher preparation in health education should be addressed to both practicing teachers and pupil teachers.

For In-service Teachers

Special orientation courses in health education should be organized for all levels of school education. The training programme for these teachers may be organized as a part of the programme of in-service training of teachers, under POA of NPE (1986) in States/UTs.

The Experts from the teacher training wings of State Health Education Bureau (SHEB) or the personnel from Directorate of Health Services should be utilized for this purpose. Other resource persons for such training programmes should be drawn from other state and district level health agencies such as CMO's office, Department of Social and Preventive Medicine of medical colleges. The NCERTs, DIETs, and TTIs should seek assistance from these agencies.

At the primary stage, all teachers should be given training in health education. At the upper primary and secondary stages those teachers responsible for giving instruction in health education should be trained.

In case, there are specialized teachers for Physical Education with degree in Physical Education, they may be entrusted with teaching this subject area. A teacher with B.A. or B.Sc. Home Science may also teach health education. These teachers will need special orientation courses. However, in most cases where these categories of teachers are not available, a three-month special training course should be devised for those teachers who will be teaching health education.

To prepare future teachers of health education the Pre-service teacher education programme should be revised and revamped. The Teacher Training Institutes and Colleges of Education should be strengthened to provide professional support and expertise in health education. The orientation programme in health education should be organized for teacher educators of these institutions. The syllabus for teacher training programme should be revised to include these components. The concepts and methodology tried out under Project NHEES should be incorporated in the teacher education curriculum of TTIs. Activities related to school health programme should form an integral part of the internship programme of pupil teachers.

The scheme of orientation and training for school health education should be closely linked with the overall net-working of technical support structure of teacher training envisaged for implementation of NPE 1986.[27]

4. Providing Proper Environment in which Students can Learn for Themselves

Young people need to be healthy in order to attend regularly and take full advantage of the opportunities provided by schools. School-based efforts that improve health in turn help to improve the learning potential and school performances of young people. (Box 1.4)

Not all schools—whether in developing or developed countries—

Box 1.4

Health Improves Learning Potential

- Poor diet impairs learning and development. Studies show that the academic performance and mental ability of pupils with good nutritional status were significantly higher than those of pupils with poor nutritional status, even when family income, school quality, teacher ability or mental ability were taken into account.
- Whipworm infestations adversely affect school performance. In Jamaica, the removal of whipworms among school-age children led to a significant improvement in short-term and memory. After nine weeks, treated children showed no significant difference from uninfested children.
- Iron deficiency influences a child's ability to benefit from classroom instruction. Studies show that when iron-deficient anaemic children first enroll in school, they are at a disadvantage in terms of their aptitudes. This disadvantage disappears when their iron levels become sufficient through supplements to the diet.

American countries concluded that facilities entailing serious health risks are more common than positive examples of clean school environments. Such situation obviously must be changed.

"Health for All" and "Education for All" are expressions of the United Nations' commitment to health and education. Because these goals are inseparably lined, they must be achieved concurrently. This will require strong alliances between health and education agencies, including WHO and UNESCO, national ministries and non-governmental agencies.

Strategies that can assist agencies to work together were discussed at the Third International Conference on Health Promotion held in Sundsvall, Sweden in 1991. While concerted actions are essential, the impetus for action resides with individuals. Young people, as well as adults, can play a significant role in creating support for school health by raising and acting on such questions as:

- Does our school promote health?
- Is our school a healthy place to live, work and visit?
- Does our school help students, school personnel and families to address their health needs?
- What can I do both individually and with others to bring about needed change?

To turn the world's schools into "Health-promoting schools", we will need to work together. Indeed, it will require the mobilization of people and resources at local, national and international levels to work in a concerted effort to bring about change. WHO, in collaboration with the US Centers for Diseases Control and Prevention and other organizations, is preparing to initiate such an effort. They hope to unite the organizational capacities of agencies at all levels into a powerful force for health in a global school health initiative.[28]

Notes and References

1. WHO: Etienne Berthet, A new role for teachers, *World Health,* May 1979, pp. 24-25.
2. WHO: Matine Allain-Regnault, Communication both ways, *World Health,* January-February 1985, p. 22.
3. Dr. H. Mahler, Children's Health Tomorrow's Wealth, in *World Health,* January-February, 1984, p. 3.
4. WHO: Jack Jones, Ilona Kickbusch and Desmond O' Byrne, *World Health,* March-April 1995, p. 10.
5. Sixth Report, Ministry of Human Resource Development, Department of Elementary Education and Literacy, Department of Secondary Education and Higher Education, Lok Sabha Secretariat, New Delhi, December 2001/ Agrahayana, 1923 (Saka), pp. 11-12.
6. UN General Assembly, Second Development Decade, Report of the Second Committee (Part 1) A/8/24.

7. Second Development Decade Resolution 2626 (XXV), para 18.
8. Govt. of India: Ministry of Education and Social Welfare, Department of Social Welfare: National Plan of Action for International Year of the Child (1979), New Delhi, September 1978.
9. Subramaniam, C., "A World Charter for Children," *The Hindu*, 28 September 1978.
10. Frank Falkner, "The Vital years", World Health Organization, February-March 1979, p. 8
11. Dr. H. Mahler, World Health Organization, February-March 1979, pp. 2-3.
12. P.L. Malhotra, Health Education for School-Age Children, (Forward), CHEB and NCERT, 1988.
13. CHEB and NCERT: Health Education for School-Age Children, A framework, New Delhi, 1988, pp. 1-2.
14. Quoted in the Report of the School Health Committee, Part-I, 1961, p. 10.
15. WHO: V. Tatochenko, "Education for health", *World Health*, February-March 1979, p. 24.
16. Government of India (1961): Report of the School Health Committee, New Delhi.
17. V. Tatochenko, "Education for health" February-March 1979, p. 24.
18. *Ibid.*, pp. 24-25.
19. Health Education for School-Age Children, December 28, 1987 to January 2, 1988-New Delhi, *op. cit.*, pp 3-5.
20. *op. cit.*, pp. 7-14.
21. Health Education for School-Age Children: A Framework, (December 28, 1987 to January 2, 1988, New Delhi), pp. 16-17.
22. CHEB: Health Education for School-Age Children, December 28, 1987 to January 2, 1988, New Delhi, pp. 17-18.
23. A.B. Hiramani, Health Education—An Indian Perspective, Delhi, B.R. Publishing Corporation, 1996, pp. 155-58.
24. *Ibid.*, pp. 151-53.
25. WHO: Walter Leal Filho, Health on the Curriculum, *World Health*, November 1988, p. 18.
26. WHO: Healthy Youth: Our Best Resources, *World Health*, January-February 1985, p. 17.
27. Health Education for School-age Children (December 28, 1987 to January 2, 1988, New Delhi), pp. 19-20.
28. WHO: Improving Health through Schools, *World Health*, March-April 1995, pp. 10-11.

7. Second Development Decade ... [illegible]
8. Govt. of India, Ministry of ... [illegible] Welfare, Department of Social Welfare: National Plan of Action for International Year of the Child [illegible], New Delhi, [illegible].
9. [illegible] World Charter for Children [illegible], 1978.
10. Frank Falkner ... [illegible] World Health Organization, [illegible].
11. Dr. H. Mahler, World Health Organization ... [illegible] March 1979, pp. [illegible].
12. [illegible] Health Education for [illegible] and [illegible].
13. CHEB and NCERT, Health Education for School-age Children [illegible], New Delhi, [illegible].
14. Quoted in the Report of the School Health Committee [illegible], pp. [illegible]
WHO [illegible]
15. [illegible]
16. [illegible]
17. [illegible]
18. [illegible]
19. Health Education [illegible]
20. [illegible]
21. [illegible]
22. [illegible]

CHAPTER 2

GOALS, OBJECTIVES AND CONTENT AREAS OF HEALTH EDUCATION

> To enhance and promote health education of school children in every possible manner; to enable them to adopt measures to remain healthy; and develop in them self-reliance, social responsibility and better quality of life, not only as children of today but also as adults of tomorrow.
>
> —*Author*

Goals, Objectives and Content Areas of Health Education

The integrated family unit is essential—all the experts in the field of child health, welfare and education agree—if today's children are to grow up healthfully and happily.[1]

There is an old saying attributed to Jesuit teachers: "Give me the child for easy years, I give you the man for life." How far is this true for health? Can we really expect the effects of childhood education to last for a lifetime?

Many highly placed observers are optimistic. For example, the former U.S. Secretary for Health, Joseph Califano, said in 1977 that "effective health education early in life can help prevent the major diseases in adulthood". But not everyone agrees. Margaret Witton, a community leader in North London, commented a few years ago—on hearing that her health authority employed seven health educators in local schools—"It's an appalling waste of money . . . when the essential services are desperately short." A hard look at the available evidence suggests that there is some justification for both points of view.

Regrettably, in the industrialized countries, health education often turns out to be little more than a fig leaf, funded by governments, which are dependent on tax revenues from cigarettes and alcohol. The only surprise, in this situation, is that school health education has no effect at all.

Finally, we need to begin from "where the children are at." We need to know their priorities—and often, more important—their parents' priorities. Detailed planning has to be locally based, always commencing with surveys of existing knowledge and practice. We cannot expect to make lasting progress except by involving the community from the beginning. Otherwise, any gains made will disappear as soon as central support is withdrawn. Inevitably, progress will vary from topic to topic and country to country. But where it is possible to unite local opinion leaders and the community generally in a sustained movement for health promotion, we can indeed expect schools to make major contributions towards achieving a lifetime of good health.[2]

GENERAL OBJECTIVES

- To make the child aware of the concept of health and factors influencing health.
- To help the child develop awareness of health problems and to seek help from the teachers, parents and members of peer group and community leaders in solving them.
- To help the child develop healthy habits relating to personal and environmental cleanliness, exercise, rest sleep, posture and food.
- To help the child to make wise decisions in respect of applying principles and practices of common health with special reference to his physical well-being.
- To help the child develop an understanding of safety measures and to develop the skills of providing first-aid and home nursing.
- To make the child realize the importance of immunization against communicable diseases as an important measure of achieving positive health.
- To help the child develop appropriate human relationship in order to promote mental and social health.
- To help the child develop abilities of transferring health knowledge and health promoting activities in the community.

PRIMARY STAGE

Cognitive Domain

- To know and understand the external parts of the human body and their functions.
- To understand that adequate nutritious food is necessary for the growth of the body and maintenance of health.
- To understand the importance of cleanliness and sanitation of his surroundings.
- To understand the importance of taking care of different parts of the body.
- To recognize the common diseases prevalent in the locality and understand their preventive and control measures including immunization.

CHART 2.1

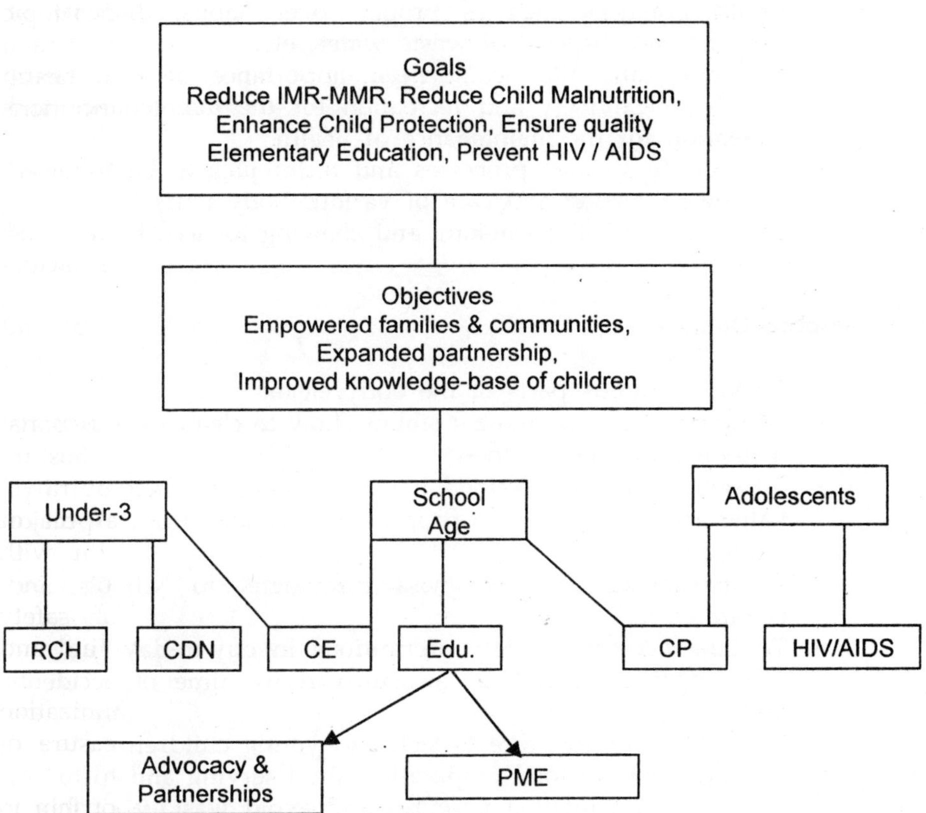

Notes: RCH = Reproductive and Child Health;
CDN = Child development and Nutrition;
CE = Child's Environment—Sanitation, Hygiene and Water Supply;
Edu = Elementary Education;
CP = Child Protection; and
PME = Planning, Monitoring and Evaluation

Source: Master Plan of Operations, 2003-07, GOI in Cooperation with the United Nations Children's Fund (UNICEF).

- To establish relationship between nutritional intake in daily diet and nutritional disorders and deficiency diseases.
- To recognize the need and importance of personal cleanliness for healthful living.
- To develop elementary knowledge about first-aid and care of the sick at home.
- To learn the concept of safe water and develop the method or techniques of keeping the water safe.

- To develop an understanding of personal and community health practices such as proper toilet habits, disposal of garbage and disposal of waste water, etc.
- To understand the health needs-importance of rest, sleep, exercise, cleanliness and recreation for the maintenance and recreation for the maintenance of health.
- To identify various processes and techniques to be followed for the protection and care of various body parts.
- To understand that smoking and chewing tobacco is injurious to health.

Psychomotor Domain

- To keep various parts of the body clean.
- To demonstrate to younger sibling, how to clean various parts of their body and clothes.
- To select and identify food items according to their nutritive value and to eat food in proper combinations from all major food groups.
- To participate in cleanliness campaigns in schools and community.
- To take necessary safety precautions in day-to-day life and take appropriate first-aid measures at the time of accidents and emergency.
- To provide proper care to sick and young children.
- To participate in food preparation, food serving and to follow proper food sanitation practices and avoid wastage of food.
- To demonstrate simple techniques of making water safe for drinking.

Affective Domain

- To take interest in finding out how different external parts of the body function.
- To take interest in selecting and develop taste in eating food from different food groups and finding out what kinds of food are available in the locality.
- To appreciate the need of avoiding wastage of food at all levels.
- To appreciate the importance of physical, mental and social well-being.
- To acquire a taste for the good and beautiful things in the environment and develop interest in finding out how the environment can be kept clean and beautiful.
- To appreciate the importance of consuming safe water.
- To appreciate the role of home, school, community and other agencies in promoting healthy living.

- To appreciate the importance of first-aid and care of the sick.
- To appreciate the harmful effects of smoking and chewing tobacco.

Content Areas

Based on the above objectives the learning opportunities in health education will be made available in the following content areas:

- External parts of human body-structure and functions;
- Care of external body parts;
- Personal cleanliness;
- Personal health practices;
- Food-types, values, sources;
- Food consumption, desirable practices, avoiding wastage and spillage, etc.;
- Environmental cleanliness and sanitation;
- Communicable diseases, causes, transmission, prevention and control;
- Accidents, first-aid and care of the sick; and
- Harmful effects of smoking or chewing tobacco, consuming alcohol, etc.

Upper Primary Stage

Cognitive Domain

- To explain and discuss various organ systems and functions of body including the process of reproduction
- To understand the concept of nutrients, their value in daily diet and to select appropriate food items in order to prepare balanced diet.
- To explain the causes of deficiency diseases and establish their relationship with deficiency.
- To learn about various techniques and procedures of food preservation and storages and rules of food sanitation.
- To discriminate and distinguish between safe and unsafe water and learn the ways of purifying water.
- To explain the process of how communicable diseases spread and the measures taken for their prevention.
- To discuss the growth and development characteristics and find out contrast in growth patterns between boys and girls.
- To identify personal and community health practices conducive for healthy environment in the home, community and village.
- To recognize ill-effects of tobacco, drugs and narcotics on health.

Psychomotor Domain

- To develop skills of taking care of eyes, ear, teeth, and genital part of body.
- To demonstrate safety and first-aid measures during accidents and emergencies.
- To provide essential care to the sick at home.
- To participate in environmental sanitation in home, school and locality.
- To demonstrate procedures and techniques of purifying water for drinking.
- To observe socially accepted norms of behaviour in day-to-day life.

Affective Domain

- To imbibe regular health habits of keeping body parts clean.
- To develop positive attitudes towards observance of health rules in schools and the community.
- To develop the habit of consulting health personnel in the state of sickness and not to take to self-medication.
- To develop regular habits of washing hands before taking food, not wasting food and cleaning eating place before and after food.
- To inculcate regular habits of taking food at regular time and in adequate quantity.

Content Areas

To translate the objectives of this stage into contents, the learning opportunities can be woven around the following major areas:

- Internal organizations of the human body and the functioning of different systems with special reference to reproduction.
- Nutrients, food groups, balanced diet—its concept, deficiency diseases and disorders, food preservation and food sanitation.
- Concept of safe water, precautions necessary for keeping water safe.
- What is disease—how it travels and spreads, difference between communicable and non-communicable diseases—their causes, symptoms and preventive measures.
- Desirable personal and community health practices for the prevention of communicable diseases.
- Meaning of growth and development characteristics of growth in boys and girls—physical, mental, social, and environmental, facilities conducive for growth/stages of growth and development.

- General principles and procedures of first-aid, safety and home nursing.
- Harmful effects of tobacco, drugs and narcotics on health.

Secondary Stage

Cognitive Domain

- To identify the nutrients and other constituents of different types of food items and understand their functions for promotion of health.
- To decide the quantity and amount of different types of food consumed to make the daily diet balanced.
- To understand the concepts of malnutrition and under-nutrition and their relationship with different deficiency diseases prevalent in the family and the community and the measures to prevent and control them.
- To identify the signs, symptoms, mode of transmission of different communicable diseases at the community level and their prevention and control through immunization and other measures.
- To establish relationship between the health status of an individual and community and the personal and community health practices.
- To identify community health problems and establish their relationship with population growth, issues and problems.
- To identify socio-cultural values and beliefs prevalent in society and establish their relationships with health practices.
- To discuss social engineering aspects which are directly or indirectly related to the promotion and protection of health, i.e. child survival measures, status of women education and employment of women; age at marriage; birth spacing; equality of sexes; and effective safe-motherhood, etc.
- To explain the basic quality of responsible parenthood and its implications to the quality of life, as well as on the health of the people in the family and society.

Psychomotor Domain

- To enlist the major pollution problems in the neighbourhood and community and participate in their prevention and control.
- To provide first-aid to injured in the family, school and community.
- To list the harmful effects of alcohol and narcotics, tobacco and betel chewing on health.

- To recognize the adulterated food items sold in the local market and report to the health authorities for necessary action.
- To select locally available food items in order to make the daily diet balanced and nutritious.
- To participate in the health campaigns organized at the school and community level.
- To participate effectively by helping people at the time of epidemics and natural calamities such as floods, storms, droughts, etc.
- To help in organizing immunization camps in the village to educate people in respect of observing desirable health practices in the community.
- To help local agencies of maintaining healthful environment in the community.
- To motivate people to adopt small family norm as a way of life.

Affective Domain

- To develop positive attitude towards the observance of health rules in their life.
- To realize the importance of timely immunization for child survival.
- To accept small family norm as an essential component for improvement of quality of life.
- To adopt voluntary participation in community cleanliness and sanitation programme as an integral part of duties.
- To follow desirable health practices and nutritional habits in day-to-day life.
- To extend cooperation and support in health-related intervention programmes in order to make these a part and parcel of the lifestyles of the people.

Content Areas

- Concept of health and factors influencing health.
- Personal and community health practices and their bearing on the health status of the individual, community and society.
- Communicable, non-communicable and deficiency diseases their causes and prevention.
- Child survival measures—immunization, growth monitoring, breast-feeding, food supplements, ORS, birth spacing and female education.
- Principles of safe motherhood-age of marriage, health risks with frequent pregnancy and other risk factors.

- Elements of responsible parenthood, importance of observance of small family norm for better quality of life, equality of sexes.
- Socio-cultural beliefs and values conducive to health promotion.
- Harmful effects of tobacco, narcotics, betel-chewing and alcohol.[3]

ASPECTS OF CHILD HEALTH

Comprehensive, child health services including preventive, promotive and curative services are being provided to those who seek care in secondary and tertiary health care institutions. At primary health care level, the spectrum of services available is narrower, focus is mainly on essential newborn care, essential child care including ARI and ORT programmes, immunization, Vit. A and anemia prophylaxis programmes, Effective utilization of available services for prevention and detection of under nutrition in under five population is the aim of ICDS programme during the ninth plan period. Efforts are being focused on improving quality of screening of children for early detection of health and nutrition problems and improving the referral services so that person requiring care in secondary and tertiary level institutions receive them without delay.

Once the general policy has been determined, the problem is as to how can we devise programmes, which ensure that this policy is implemented. Let us now discuss the various ingredients, which can help in the effective formulation of the plan for fulfilling the health needs of children.

I. Change the Outlook of Planners

Planners and administrators should be enlightened to look upon the provision of health services for children as an investment in human resources, rather than a social welfare activity. The planners must be persuaded that a higher priority to the development of services for the young child would be beneficial to the modernization of the country. Secondly, the planners should not bother too much about the economic development in the narrow sense of increasing the GNP, but should talk in humanistic terms. There should be good communication between the health planners and the general planners. Thirdly, while planning, we should allocate more resources to the development of children. When funds are cut for the children who need help the most, we mortgage the present to the future. Fourthly, the planners should understand that the benefits of child welfare programmes are being enjoyed by the urban children, who are already getting their needs fulfilled. The imbalance needs to be corrected and in future more resources may be invested for the development of the unprivileged children living in rural areas, urban slums and tribal areas.

2. Establish Objectives/Goals and Targets

On the basis of the gravity of the problem inferred from the statistical analysis, the objectives/goals and targets may be set-up for each area—national, regional and local; and activity health, nutrition, environment. On the basis of the present information, we may accomplish the goals of:

(a) Reduction in maternal, pre-natal, infant and childhood mortality;
(b) Reducing the child morbidity ensuring minimum maternal and child health services through proper cooperation with other development activities;
(c) Promotion of health through the provision of safe drinking water, primary health care, and nutritional services;
(d) Effective involvement of the community in delivering all these services;
(e) Ensuring proper knowledge and utilization of family welfare services; and
(f) Promotion of wider community education or health and nutrition.

3. Adopt Basic Services Approach

The UN General Assembly in its Resolution 2.26 (XXV) has advocated the basic services approach for development. The main emphasis in this approach is on the involvement and active participation of the people of the communities; the use of responsible volunteers or part-time workers in providing services essential to the well-being of children; and the re-orientation of national structure to direct and support this approach, using more para-professional workers. Through such methodology, the whole population can have access to services and not only better-off people in better-off areas. This approach would improve the conditions of family and community life. Improved mid-wifely, minimal preventive health measures, improved water supply and sanitation, cleanliness in the home, basic mother and child health care, knowledge on the part of the parents of family planning, better nutrition, campaigns for immunization and distribution of Vitamin A to prevent blindness. All this can be carried out by basic village workers to help the small child grow to his full potential.[4]

Such services rapidly improve living conditions, they are labour-intensive, they demonstrate what community responsibility and self-reliance can achieve.

4. Adopt Family as a Unit

Healthy families make healthy people. The family can provide the most effective and socially appropriate milieu in which the physical and emotional development of children can be ensured. Family is a planning unit of health care, a front line in the sequence of education, prevention, diagnosis, treatment and rehabilitation of its members. According to Ihsan Dogramaci, Executive Director of the International Pediatric Association in Paris:

He further adds that "This integrated family unit becomes the keystone of the healthy community in which it lives. And within such a family, this child emerges as a psychologically well-developed human being who is happy with herself or himself, with parents, relatives and the surrounding society. Form such children and such families will one day evolve a world, which leaves aggression behind and builds a future of peace. Let us all have the courage to face this challenge and do all in our power to ensure that what is known in theory is applied in reality for the benefit of all children."[5]

N.N. Mashalaba, Director of Maternal and Child Health Programme in the Ministry of Health of Botswana has rightly mentioned that, "Promoting better health for mothers and children and through them better health for the whole family, is the vital nucleus of action towards better health for all."[6]

The family, in addition to being a social unit, is also a health unit. Family health is something greater than the sum of the health of the family members who live in the same household: illness of a child affects the entire family—the parents, grandparents, siblings and others who may be living within the same group. And concern for the child begins from the moment of conception—or even before, since with proper family planning, the spacing between children and their dates of arrival should be arranged and predictable.

The family is a most important factor in the life of the child, whose health from fetal growth on through the pre-school years probably determines its growth and development to adulthood, its behaviour, and its ability to be an adequate parent to the next generation.

Who is to be responsible for the guidance, the preventive measures, the education in health and sanitation matters, and the health and sanitation matters, and the health care of the child and its family? In the first place, families themselves are responsible, but health and other community workers have an important role to play.[7]

5. Expand and Re-orient Health Care Services

The population covered by a PHC should be reduced to 25,000. One of the doctors at the PHC should have orientation in maternal and child health, and a community health-nursing supervisor should be added to the staff. The sub-health centres should be made responsible for a population of 2,500 instead of 5,000 for better delivery of health services. Under 5-clinics or baby welfare clinics may be set-up in these centres. Newborn observation units should complement obstetric units at all levels.

Delivery of basic health services at the village level should involve the members of the village community.

Training needs of all categories of health workers should be identified, and the relevant programme developed. The need to shift the emphasis in medical education from the narrow confines of hospital work to a broader social level should be given high priority. Training should be village-based. Neera Kuckreja Sohoni in an article, "Organizational Structure to Meet Children's Needs" concludes that:

> "It must be conducted that any effort to recognize existing structures so as to have greater functional efficiency can only be attempted with great care and caution, and after careful study of all the procedural and programmatic ramifications. Equally, what needs to be acknowledged as hard core reality is that existing structures are deficient and in need of organizational overhaul. Unless this is undertaken, child welfare objectives and pursuits will remain at best platitudes and, at worst, a mockery."[8]

6. Meet the Challenge of Nutritional Deficiency

Nutritional deficiency has increased among lower income groups. There has been a rise in per capita income; however, the position of these groups has not changed, because the prices of basic commodities, especially food, have risen steeply. Nutrition education to improve utilization, storage and consumption of locally available nutritive foods, should be launched all over the country. This should be done through projects like kitchen gardens, poultry and dairy units and fisheries. The community may be taught the right method of cooking and eating through demonstration projects. Para-professional must carry out intensive nutritional monitoring of children.

In the words of Dr. Halfdan Mahler, WHO's Director-General, "Poor malnourished parents produce malnourished children who in turn will become poor and malnourished parents". This vicious spiral must be broken by improving child health and nutrition levels. This is a challenge to the government of the world and to the international community during the International Year of the Child and in the years to come. The well-being of the majority of the world's population is at stake.[9]

Thus, education for health in modern society should be carried out not only by health professionals, but by parents, teachers and also by other social figures. A multidisciplinary approach becomes indispensable as soon as the problem is seen in a wide perspective beyond its "medical" and "prevention and cure" aspects. The medical profession will no doubt continue to play an important role, particularly health professionals who come in close contact with people. But new tasks call for an increasing use of non-medical perons, such as parent and teachers, with medical workers serving them as resource persons, consultants and, in many respect, educators.[10]

7. Plan for Safe Environment

Potable water supply and its proper drainage must be provided. Sanitary latrines must be popularized.

Health-related habits formed during childhood can play a crucial role in determining whether an adult will be destined to enjoy a long and healthy life. There is increasing evidence that many prevalent and disabling adult diseases are related to environmental and community factors. Exposure to pollutants and health-related habits formed during childhood can play a crucial role in determining whether an adult is healthy or is to suffer from cardiovascular or lung diseases, or cancer. The most appropriate motto to characterize those vital years of childhood is surely, "Sapines Qui Prospicit". . . he is wise who looks ahead.[11]

8. Plan for Health Education

Health Education must be provided to school children and the community. In schools, health, hygiene, nutrition environmental sanitation should be introduced. Yogic exercises may be made compulsory in schools. Games should be popularized.

The transfer of knowledge cannot be considered the final goal of health education; the child has to learn how to use this knowledge and how to make the best choice in a given situation. Rapid changes in lifestyles, and the evolution of views of health and disease call for new departures in health education. A quick glance at health education material of even one generation ago will show how fast it tends to get out of date. Medical facts, it has been estimated, get outdated within a decade or so. Effective health education therefore requires a continuous steam of knowledge, development of the people's ability to absorb it, and decisions taken on the basis of a constantly changing body of information.

9. Plan for Educational, Psychological and Social Needs of the Child

Educational efforts should be geared to stimulate the child's intellect and creativity. According to Professor Piaget:

> The principal goal of education is to create men who are capable of doing new things, not simply of repeating what other generations have done—men who are creative, inventive and discoverers. The second goal of education is to form minds, which can be critical, can verify, and not accept everything they are offered. The great danger today is of slogans, collective opinions, ready-made trends of thoughts. We have to be able to resist individually, to criticize, to distinguish between what is proven and what is not. So we need pupils who are active, who learn early to find out by themselves, partly by their own spontaneous activity and partly through material we set-up for them; who learn early to tell what is verifiable and what is simply the first idea to come to them.[12]

All children should be covered by educational efforts. The education system should cater according to the needs of the children living in a particular area. Instead of a single entry point in schools, a multi-point entry should be introduced, and the sequential system should be removed, so that children can enter schools and complete their courses at their own pace, according to their age and ability. The search for talented students should start from the primary classes. The idea of neighbourhood school suggested by the Education Commission should be implemented.

Quality of primary school education should be improved by development of teachers through in-service training, and publication of attractive children's literature in regional languages.

10. Safeguard Children from Labour

India has all along followed a proactive policy in the matter of tackling the problem of child labour, and always stood for constitutional, statutory and developmental measures that are required to eliminate child labour. India has ratified six ILO conventions relating to child labour and three of them as early as in the first quarter of the twentieth century. Legislative provisions have been made in various laws to protect children from exploitation at work and to improve their working conditions. In addition, a comprehensive law, namely, the Child Labour (Prohibition and Regulation Act), 1986 prohibits employment of children in certain hazardous occupations and processes and regulates their employment in some other areas.

The National Policy on Child Labour was formulated in 1987 which apart from requiring enforcement of legal provisions to protect the interests of children, envisages focusing of general development programmes for the benefit of child labour and project-based plan of action in areas of high concentration of child labour.

Leisure and the chance to play are not luxuries for children, but essentials for normal health growth. Long hours of work have a stultifying effect on youngsters and may often cripple them emotionally. Children, our most precious resources, are literally the key to the future of our planet. Every effort should be made to provide the young of our species with the time to grow, to play and to learn during that period which we call childhood, to provide them from the beginning with the potential for leading better adults. The value we accord to life is affirmed in our treatment of our children.

Francis Blanchard, Director-General of the International Labour Office issued a declaration endorsing the aims of IYC. The declaration calls for action based on the following principles:

(a) a child is not a 'small adult' but a person entitled to self-fulfilment through learning and play so that his adult life is not jeopardized by his having had to work at an early age;

(b) government should, in cooperation with all the national organizations concerned, take all necessary social and legislative action for the progressive elimination of child labour; and

(c) pending the elimination of child labour, it must be regulated and humanized.

These children are employed for various reasons. *The Tribune* editorial has rightly mentioned that:

> "The International Labour Organization suggestion to ban child labour is obviously meaningless for this part of the World. The harshness that greets him at work can only be mitigated by accepting the fact that child labour cannot be wished away."

At the present moment, preventive legislation may be enacted to safeguard the health, safety and welfare of working children below 18 years of age. Such a legislation should cover working hours, rest periods, wages, leave, prevention of health and safety hazards and prevention of cruelty and exploitation of children in employment or apprenticeship training. Sufficient social security measures may be made for the children.

> "Until better laws are framed and public sympathy is evoked, employment bureaus should be opened at the District level for children below 14. The employment Bureaus can at least create public opinion against employers who exploit children."[13]

Much of the legislation regarding child labour throughout the world is sound, and is certainly a necessary first step. The only trouble is that, given present circumstances, it is difficult to enforce in some of the poorer countries. It is all very well and good to pass laws insisting that children cannot work and must be in school, but in many areas there are simply not enough schools.

It is clear that child labour will never be fully eliminated until the conditions on which it thrives are eradicated. Child labour is the product of poverty and uneven development. Until development is seen, not in terms of higher gross national products but as a balanced growth leading to generalized adult employment and fairer income distribution patterns, it is likely to stay with us.

11. Emphasis on Prevention through Vaccination and its Integration with General Development

Health is wealth that can be preserved. Immunization protects children against infectious diseases such as measles, tetanus, diphtheria, whooping cough, polio limelights, and tuberculosis. Personal hygiene prevents many diseases, particularly diarrhoea. Breast feeding, followed by correct weaning and well-balanced nutrition, protects against malnutrition and strengthens resistance to infection. Day care activities, where play and exercise stimulate both body and mind, contribute to the harmonious development of the child.

Through vaccination and its integration with General Development, immunization provides a means of helping to break the vicious cycle of high infant and childhood mortality rates. By permitting more of a family's children to survive, it reduces the number of births desired by a family which, in turn, acts in strong synergy with family planning activities, and makes the further expansion of immunization services one of the best bargains available for primary health care and national development.

From a wider development perspective, immunization must go hand in hand with not only improvements in health services, water supply and sanitation, nutrition, family planning and education, but also economic development, which in the industrialized countries, virtually eliminated infectious diseases in recent history. Visionary initiatives like the CVI can have an enormous impact on human development within this larger picture.

It is the most opportune time to start planning effectively to meet the diverse needs of the children. Since the development of the children is the responsibility of many sectors and agencies at all levels, there is a need of coordinate planned efforts. The superiority of the integrated planning approach lies in that the various actions affecting the conditions and development of children are analyzed and decided upon simultaneously and in relation to each other. "The interplay of inter-sectoral and intra-sectoral integration of services for children has assumed greater importance from plan to plan; it seems well accepted that inter-sectoral linkages cannot be disregarded in the formulation of policies and programmes for children and in carrying out the needed services for them in the most effective manner. Inter-sectoral linkages have to be established not only at the national and state levels, but also the field levels in order to obtain the best results."[14]

The problem of coordination must be worked out in detail to avoid conflicts and delay. Past efforts to attain such inter-developmental coordination have not been very successful at the field level. It would be necessary to review the present organization and provide additional support if the goods and services are to be delivered to the needy children. Effective Planning for the health needs of the children require dynamic and integrated approach, which is capable of assessing the various backward and forward linkage effects that any programme of children development is found to have. Fanny Edeleman, Secretary of the Women's International Democratic Federation (WIDF) stressed while speaking in a seminar on "Child in Asia" held (from 30 January to 2 February 1978) in India that:

"the problem of child development should be tackled by coordinating technical resources and know-how instead of taking isolated and adhoc action on individual issues and problems"

In this venture, a broad participation is crucial. Directorates of Health of Union, State and Union Territories, medical and Nursing Colleges, autonomous institutions, universities, Social Welfare and Education Departments, and voluntary organizations must pool their expertise to make a rational plan for the all-round development of children. The foreign resources, wherever needed, may be tapped through the UNICEF and utilized judiciously.

Children welfare is to be planned and organized on a comprehensive basis by taking all aspects of the child's personality into account.

SPECIAL PROGRAMME FOR THE GIRL CHILD

SAARC declared 1990 "The Year of the Girl Child" and 1991-2000 as the "Decade of the Girl Child". During this period programmes are proposed to:

- Increase public awareness of the value of the girl child;
- Reach girls with basic services for their survival and development;
- Ensure their participation in programmes of child development, health, nutrition and education;
- Increase the age of marriage; and
- Create a positive environment to allow girls to develop into productive and confident young women.

A National Plan of action for the Girl Child for 1991-2000 A.D. has been drawn up by the Government. The Plan recognizes the rights of the girl child to equal opportunity, to be free from hunger, illiteracy, ignorance and exploitation.

Towards ensuring survival of the girl child, the objectives are to:

- Prevent cases of female foeticide and infanticide and ban the practice of amniocentesis for sex determination;
- End gender disparity in infant mortality rate;
- Eliminate gender disparities in feeding practices, expand nutritional interventions to reduce severe malnourishment by half and provide supplementary nutrition to adolescent girls in need;
- Reduce deaths due to diarrohea by 50% among girl children under 5 years and ensure immunization against all forms of serious illnesses; and

- Provide safe drinking water and ensure access to fodder and drinking water nearer home.

Protection of the girl child is to be ensured through the following:

- Relief for those girls who are economically and socially deprived and belong to special groups;
- Intervention to sensitize various agencies on the need to protect the girl child and adolescent girls from exploitation, assault and physical abuse;
- Education and sensitization of male members of the family to the special needs of the girl child;
- Equal treatment, dignity and respect for girl children in the family and community as well as providing support and help in their day-to-day work so that they get time to avail of the opportunities for self-development;
- Rehabilitation services to reduce the growing instances of exploitation of girl-children and adolescent girls; and
- Protection of girl-children and adolescent girls from prevalent social evils such as dowry, child marriage, prostitution, rape, incest, molestation, etc. through appropriate legislation and proper enforcement.[15]

NEW DEVELOPMENT: HEALTH PROMOTING SCHOOLS

Regional office for South-East Asia, World Health Organization, New Delhi has brought out a document based in the Health Jamboree for Secondary School students of South-East Asia Region: Report of an inter-country meeting Feydhoo Finolhu Island, Maldives, 13-15 September 2001, (SEA/HE/187) which deals with Health promoting schools. To quote:

Schools are strategic settings for providing students with educational qualifications and to improve their opportunities for employment Fostering good health is equally important to help student lead socially and economically productive lives in the future.

As part of the Healthy Settings Approach, the concept of Health Promoting Schools is now being promoted and implemented in the South-East Asia Region. The approach adopts policies that support efforts to empower students for healthy living and carry the health messages beyond their class rooms to their families and local communities. Health-promoting schools build a safe and a healthy psychosocial environment by promoting the involvement of parents and community. The role of students in promoting these environments as well as take actions to promote health is as essential as the role of headmasters, principals, teachers and school management.

Every child has a right to good health. Students can be effective advocates to promote the concept of health-promoting schools itself. Students can advocate for health promoting schools not only among themselves but also to policy-makers. Participants to the Regional Consultations on Comprehensive School Healthy Education in Colombo, 1995 and Health Promoting Schools in Bangkok, 1997 strongly recommended the active involvement of school children and youth in school health programmes.

Students can voice their rights at both national and international fora, which could help shape national policies towards the health of the young. The Regional Meeting of the Students of South-East Asia Member Countries could provide an essential platform for the youth of the Region to discuss the health challenges they face now and can face in the future. They can also offer strategic decisions for dealing with adolescent health problems, and suggestions to government to implement health-promoting schools.

Students of secondary schools are in the adolescent phase—an intermediary phase between childhood and adulthood—a phase in which their bodies are subjected to a spurt of hormonal changes. Many do not understand these changes and are bewildered, not only at how their bodies are changing, but also as to how their emotions seem to be running wild on uncharted tracks.

Many do not have recourse to discuss their worries, fears and dilemmas, while at the same time, they are required to cope with changing parental, societal and peer norms, resulting, very often in emotional and behavioural near-crisis.

A health Jamboree for secondary school students was held in Feydhoo Finolhu Island, Maldives, from 13 to 15 September 2001.

The Jamboree aimed at providing a conducive forum for these students to discuss and understand their problems, exchange ideas, and attempt to work out strategies to cope with their own changing world against the backdrop of their different cultural and societal expectations.

Objectives

The following were the objectives of the Jamboree:

(1) To explore the holistic concept of health;
(2) To share observations, experiences on prevalent health problems which they might have experienced as adolescents, as well as other public health problems in the communities;
(3) To discuss existing school health programmes in their respective countries and explore ways of involving themselves in the same;
(4) To develop strategies for better health at various levels; and
(5) To understand the importance of diet and exercise in ensuring and promoting health and incorporating the same in their daily lives.

Mr. Ahmed Abdullah, Minister of Health then addressed the gathering:

Welcoming all the participants, he gave a background in how the health jamboree came to be conceived. He noted that school children all over the world have gatherings for sports, cadet camps, jamborees, class picnic, science exhibitions, but had never got together to focus on health issues.

He felt that children are very important and strong change agents and that health promotion activities in schools would benefit everybody. Children in the adolescent phase faced a lot of challenges to their physical, mental and social health and so the idea of holding a Jamboree focusing on adolescent heath, with adolescent school girls and boys from different countries was born.

He was very happy at the response to the Jamboree. He urged the students to make full use of the Jamboree to open up their minds to self-awareness, the health problems they face and the harmful lifestyles that they could be lured into. The Jamboree was an opportunity for them to learn healthy lifestyles and to interact with students from other cultures. He hoped they would learn a lot in the three days and take back lessons, which they could share with their families, colleagues and communities.

RECOMMENDATIONS

- There should not be too great a lapse of time between the planning and the implementation phases as some loss of continuity can occur.
- The teachers/officials should be oriented to their roles and responsibilities, so that they can be better involved.
- Guidelines for presentation of school health programmes should be outlined at the time of sending the invitations, so that this session stays more focused and gives the necessary information.
- The Jamboree could be extended to a period of five days, as the programme was very tight and many resource persons felt rushed and could not do justice to analyzing the processes involved.
- Linkages between the topics need to be established.
- More time could be given to sports, physical exercises and other leisure activities.
- Though the food was very good, the needs of vegetarians could be better addressed.
- There is a need for training of resource persons.

We could encourage such projects in schools so that they are not only benefited themselves but help others in the family based on the health education knowledge gained.

CRITICAL APPRAISAL

Inspite of repeated assertions through National Education Policy, 1986 and National Health Policy that school health education should be given priority through teaching and actions of the health education in schools. Many committees on school health education have been formed but the ground reality in that majority of schools especially the village schools lack the concept of school health education. There was earlier a practice to get the students examined medically by Doctors out of medical fund collected from students. This was a mere formality as it was eyewash and in the real sense of the term, there was no medical examination. Health school education is defunct and there is a need to take strong policy decision to introduce health education. Let us discuss the facts and suggestions based on personal visits to schools and discussion with students, teachers and parents.

(1) Lack of infrastructure—For school health education, we need a good infrastructure with weighing machine, library, charts, which are non-existent.

(2) No time to study and practice health education—Now-a-days students become too busy to prepare their future careers that they find no time or interest for health education. Students and teacher both consider it a wastage of time and money.

(3) Dearth of qualified teachers to teach health education—Since health education in schools is included in most of the subjects, but there are few teachers who can integrate health education in school curriculum. They themselves are as ignorant as students.

(4) Families do not care about health education—Students coming from families, where no interest is shown in health education, do not evince any interest in health education. It is a vicious circle that is health education can either start from the family or the school; the result would be beneficial to both.

(5) Enamoured by modern lifestyles—Students do not want to follow any health education principles with exercises, balanced diet, clean habits, good values. They consider these, as the sign of backwardness. Students even come to school in cars, buses, and cycles from nearly. They find no time for physical work. Hence the environment and values for health education are lacking.

SUGGESTIONS

(1) Education and Health Departments need to take School Health Education seriously—The State and Union Government Departments of health and education must make a thorough

preparation for implementation of school health education seriously, e.g.

(i) There must be orientation programme of teachers to make them effective teachers in school health education. It would rather be more appropriate if health education is included as a compulsory subject in B.Ed., JBT courses.

(ii) Government must provide infrastructure facilities, which can sustain the interest of teachers and students in health education.

(iii) Government must make a provision to make use of experts in health in Government Health Centres to lecture in schools on topics of school health education.

(iv) Rates of medical fund for students may be increased or government may allot grants for school health education.

(2) Redesigning the syllabus to provide scope for school health education—Students in schools are already too burdened that they hardly find any time for activities like health education. Rather, the need is that top priorities may be given to health education, value education rather than other subjects, Yoga Education which means physical, mental and spiritual development of children for total personality development. There is a need to redesign the school syllabus.

(3) Communities must also attend to health education to make schools conscious of health education as schools are a part of communities—New policies for health education then, must include first of all clear, unequivocal mandates for community involvement in health planning, and development of health education. People have the right and the duty to participate individually and collectively in the planning and implementation of their health care.

(4) Shortage of Health teaching and learning materials—One of the greatest handicaps under which training programmes are being undertaken is the grave shortage of relevant teaching and learning materials for use by teachers. Central Education Bureau should help in making these materials available.

CONCLUSION

There is a need for school health education. It should be taken seriously. Half-hearted attempts result in wastage of resources with no benefit. We should start from the scratch, as at present health education in schools is non-existent.

Need of School Health Education

School is a fit place where students are in learning mood. They form habits during this period. If the teachers harness the potential of students, they can be agile and active citizens and asset to the community and country. Health is wealth. Healthy children can take the country to greater height. Let us discuss the important benefits. That can result for good school health education:

1. Good Style of Life

School life is such when students adopt the style of life, i.e. whether of hard work or sluggishness. The teachers should encourage positive thinking among students.

Swami Vivekanand says that: stand up, be bold, be strong. Take the whole responsibility on your shoulders and know that you are the creator of your own destiny. All the strength and succour you want is within you. Therefore, make your own future.
Aldous Huxley observed that: there is one corner of the Universe you can be certain of improving and that is your own self.

Systematically, therefore, we must train and discipline the mind for right thinking and correct diligent activity. Right thinking is a habit that can be cultivated. Substitution of positive thoughts and flooding the mind with creative ideas are methods by which we can flush out the floor of the mind, littered as it is now with the filth of incomplete thoughts and decaying ideas. Having recognized a thought as negative or wrong, do not waste time in upholstering it to look neat and attractive, but reject it immediately and totally—the owner of right thinking expels all false thoughts and induces healthy conceptions, adding to the effectual dynamism in the seeker.

Behind every achievement that we see in this world today, is the unseen hand of the human will. The material comforts, scientific achievements are all the products crystallized out of the human will and determination. The human will-power has conquered nature, and made her slave for the welfare of mankind, and in the process, has even created things, which were not even available in the world before. Behind all the technological progress are the determined efforts of hundreds of dedicated men and women, who faced all the challenges to make their dreams come true.

The human body and mind act as an antenna which transmits thought waves, propagates and interacts with other human beings and influences them accordingly. So one good thought spreads globally and influences others to become good and do good and similarly the *vice versa*. In the same way the human body and mind act as receiving antenna and receives all thought waves of others and are being influenced by them. So one is not fully responsible for his activity, as he is governed and influenced by so many such radiations but human brain with its intellect structural arrangements can plan, act and lead a harmonious life on understanding the nature of these radiations.

Love is the elixir of life. It has been found to have power even to cure physical and mental disorders. One who has hatred in his mind not only loses his mind, but also undermines his health and life. On the other hand, love, sympathy, and friendship not only contribute towards building one's peace of mind, but also create a balanced outlook. A man who develops these qualities will acquire serenity, joy and peace in spite of all external circumstances.

2. *Balanced Diet*

Students may be taught about balanced diet, i.e. adequate amount of all ingredients essential for body. Today, many diseases are the product of junk food.

3. *Healthy Living*

Teachers must teach the students about healthy living which depends upon exercise, food and thinking, etc.

Ideas for Action . . . in the School

Children are our future, and will benefit most from learning about health. As a school teacher, you have an essential role in the struggle for health, here are some suggestions for activities that could easily be organized in the school.

1. Prepare a flannel graph or poster with the main types of food and ask the children to group them according to those that provide proteins, fats and so on. Make the point that may foods fit into more than one category.
2. Ask individual children to list the health-supporting foods they ate the day before.
3. Conduct a class survey to find the most popular health-supporting foods. Allow each child two votes. Display the results and discuss them.
   Note: It is important to help the children put their knowledge into practice. What the children have learned will remain "school knowledge" unless you are able to help them to transfer it to their lives in some relevant and practical ways. If at all possible, involve the parents in the activities.
4. Organize a class or school festival. Ask the children to help plan a festival, which must include a feat or a meal. The festival could be in memory of the founder of the school, or could mark a sprots or academic achievement or other similar event. Tell them to choose special foods to suit the occasion and to decide whether these are well balanced. Help the children to devise a ceremony to give the occasion special atmosphere. Invite parents and community leaders.
5. Plan a meal for the family. If it is possible to communicate

with the parents, ask whether the children might plan and prepare a main meal for the whole family. The children might work best in small groups with your supervision and guidance.

6. Prepare a school lunch box. Some children might bring lunch boxes with them and small groups could help to plan different menus for several days.
7. Plan school meals. Meals are offered in some schools and, if the supervision of such meals could be persuaded to cooperate, the children could take turns to help plan and prepare different meals each day for a week.

These suggested school activities are extracted from Food, Environment and Health: A Guide for Primary School Teachers by Trefor Williams, Alysson Moon and Margaret Williams, World Health Organization, Geneva, 1990.[16]

Notes and References

1. WHO, *World Health*, Feb-March 1979, p. 20.
2. WHO: Donald Reid, Learning good health, *World Health*, Jan.-Feb., 1984, pp. 5 and 7.
3. Health Education for School-Age Children, December 28, 1987 to January 2, 1988, New Delhi, pp. 31-39.
4. UNICEF, A Strategy for Basic Services, p. 14.
5. *Ibid.*, p. 33.
6. *Ibid.*, p. 31.
7. Ihsan Dogramaci, "The keystone of the community", World Health Organization, Feb.-March 1979, p. 20.
8. Neera Kuckreja Sohoni, "Organization Structure to Meet Children's Need" in *The Indian Journal of Public Administration*, Vol. XXV, No. (July-Sept. 1979), p. 50.
9. Ihsan Dogramaci, "The keystone of the community", World Health Organization, Feb.-March 1979, p. 19.
10. V. Tatochenko, "Education for health", World Health Organization, Feb.-March 1979, p. 26-27.
11. Frank Falkner, "The Vital years", *World Health*, March 1979, p. 11.
12. Professor Piaget: Report of the Jean Piaget Conferences at Cornell University and the University of California: Conference on Cognitive Studies and Curriculum Development, Cornell University and the University of California, 1964; Piaget Rediscovered; Richard E. Ripple and Verne N. Rocakcastel, eds., p. 5.
13. *The Tribune*, Chandigarh, 29 August 1979.
14. UNICEF, Study of the Young Child: Indian Case Study, NIPECD, 1976, p. 93.
15. S.L. Goel, "Health Care System and Management", New Delhi, Deep & Deep, 2001, Vol. 2, pp. 272-73
16. WHO: Tumsifu N. Maletnlema, "Politics and nutrition in Africa", July-August 1991, p. 16.

CHAPTER 3

SCHOOL ENVIRONMENT

A school environment, which is carefully planned and well maintained helps to promote the health of the students and staff, and decreases the possibility of infection and injury. It provides the atmosphere for more effective teaching and learning, and serves as an example to the community of good environmental hygiene. Studying in clean and pleasant surroundings enhances the quality of life, and participation in keeping the school clean and beautiful develops in both students and staff a sense of pride and ownership.

What is a healthful school environment? There are many requirements that are necessary to make the school a healthful place for children. While the ideal cannot always be achieved, every school should endeavour to reach certain minimum standards of health and safety.[1]

—Ministry of Health and Family Welfare, GOI, New Delhi

CHAPTER 5

SCHOOL ENVIRONMENT

School Environment

In order to remain healthy, besides living in a healthful environment, it is very important to develop clean personal habits. These habits should be developed in young children as early as possible, both at home and at school. In this way these habits will become a normal part of each person's daily life. The primary school years are thus the ideal time for educating the child about health and for forming important lifelong habits.[1]

While teaching children to develop healthy habits, it is essential that you yourself serve as a model for the children by practicing good health habits. In talking about personal hygiene you must be careful not to hurt any child's feelings. Always try to relate the need for personal cleanliness with the desire to be healthy.[2]

—*MOHFW*

School is the most important place where character and attitudes are being formed of children. The first necessary step in this direction is the school environment. Schools today are located in dirty places and the teachers and government are not bothered about school environment.

Schools are most neglected in our country, as Government is not attending to school environment causing an unhealthy environment. Children even do not like to go to schools and feel happy in holidays. What is the reason? The schools lack basic sanitation, drinking water facilities and proper environment. There is a need of improvement of school environment, which would have chain effects on family and the community. It is time to provide good environment.

We cannot continue dosing
What we have always done
Tomorrow cannot be just more of yesterday

We need flexibility and Pragmatism
As much as innovation
But the Stress must invariably be on Action

The teachers spend the productive time of the day in working for the school children to earn their livelihood. However, most teachers consider official work as a drudgery to be avoided and postponed on one pretext or the other and this makes their life dull, insensitive and non-creative. In contrast, if the teachers take pleasure in discharging their duties, they can remain active, healthy and efficient. Life would thus remain always joyful. Employment provides extra opportunity to meet and share views with colleagues as well as with the students. The quality of job content and the situational context are equally important for gaining job satisfaction. While much has been written about the working in schools, enough attention has not been paid to the ambience/ environmental factors which are so critical for ensuring the desired outputs.

It is commonly seen and felt that the teachers do not seem to be bothered about the place they are working, its surroundings and the general atmosphere. A visit to most organizations would reveal the following: (see Chart 3.1)

Chart 3.1

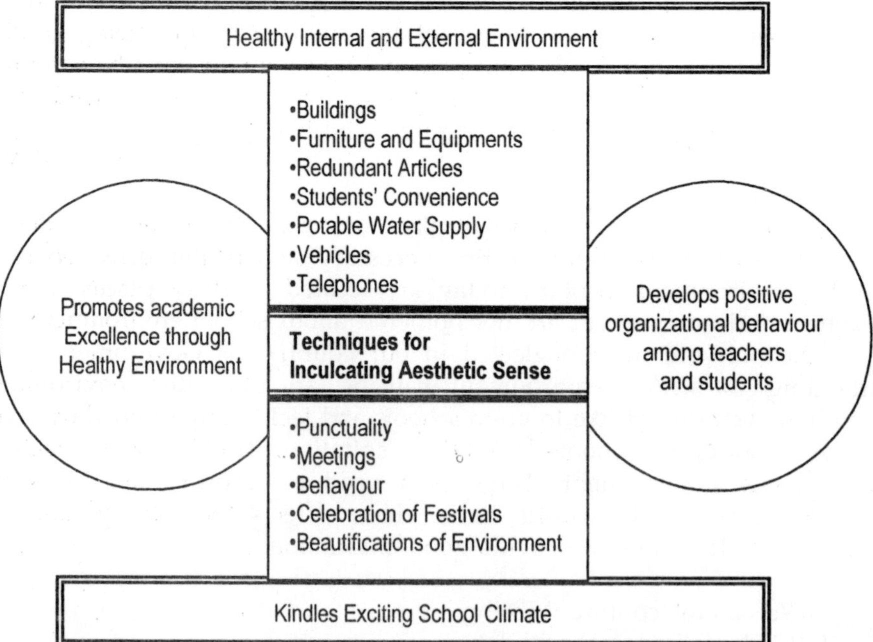

(i) The outlay of the school is dull, shabby and disorderly. Various pieces of furniture do not match, and are so positioned that it appears to be lying scattered and uncared for.

(ii) The bathrooms are and where these exist are stinking, making it unbearable and unusable. Besides, drinking water of good quality is not available, which leads to many diseases.

(iii) Disorderly parking of vehicles outside the school premises causes inconvenience to visitors and the whole place looks like an unorganized market area.

(iv) The teachers come to the school at their own time, disregarding all norms of punctuality, depicting an attitude of apathy and indifference.

(v) Building maintenance is poor and it appears that teachers have no concern with the surroundings. Most of the walls and floors have been spoilt by spitting, throwing refuse, painting and pasting posters/slogans, etc.

(vi) We find many useless articles, equipments, papers, etc. scattered all over, causing repulsion for any visitor and students. There is no display of aesthetic sense in decorating the building and its exteriors with plants, flowers, etc.

(vii) Most of the teachers are always busy in one meeting or the other, leaving very little time for substantive work or even interaction with the students.

(viii) We find that most teachers start quarreling with the students on one pretext or the other, assuming themselves to be the owners of the school rather than being public servants/facilitators.

(ix) We often find teachers talking on a telephone for long, thus wasting office time and reducing efficiency.

(x) The senior teachers draw more and more peons and clerical staff to their personal establishments in keeping with their 'status' and 'prestige'. This deprives the school of its productive hands leading to decrease in overall efficiency.

(xi) There are no occasions for intellectual discussions, lectures, symposia, etc. wherein the teachers can open up and suggest ways of improving the school outlook, work culture and academic practices.

(xii) Holidays are observed on important days without having even adequate knowledge about them and the necessity felt for celebrating them.

The question is how to manage all these inputs? How to make the quality services available? Although above issues are considered to be peripheral and incidental yet these are actually the pre-requisites for building an efficient school. For example, a good school layout helps in the following: These are considered to be unimportant but otherwise, these are the pre-requisite on which to build efficient schools.

1. Proper utilization of school space.
2. Effective work flow.
3. Seedy communication.
4. Better use of school equipments.
5. Proper supervision.
6. Necessary comfort and reduced fatigue.
7. High morale of the teachers.
8. Improved overall efficiency of the school.

The old maxim "As is the teacher so is the school" may be basically sound; but it overlooks the fact that children learn from their environment and that the condition of a building, as well as the qualifications of teachers who make up the staff, leaves its imprint upon the habits and tastes of pupils. Classrooms that are ill kept, improperly lighted, poorly ventilated, durty painted, and disorderly arranged create pupil reactions that are not conducive to efficient learning. A principal, therefore, cannot afford to overlook his responsibility to supervise the housekeeping duties of teachers, custodian, and pupils. To do this efficiently he needs to possess some practical knowledge pertaining to toilet room facilities, floors and cleaning materials, chalkboard surfaces, illumination, sanitation, playground surfaces, hearing and ventilating, and several other phases of plant management.[3]

Let us discuss the various aspects of school environment:

A. BUILDING MANAGEMENT

Buildings should be well maintained to keep the minds of students and teachers happy as well as to create good image in the minds of the visitors. Most of the school buildings especially in the fields are in dilapidated conditions. PWD, an organization created at the union and state levels to maintain and upkeep these buildings has failed to discharge its duties because of corrupt practices as well as shortage of staff and finances. What can be done to maintain buildings?

(i) Each building should be placed under the control of a caretaker, and the responsibility of maintaining that building should be with a single person. The care-taker must examine the building at regular intervals and not all the problems being faced, so that timely repairs can be executed to save sudden collapse.
(ii) A committee should be constituted and empowered to effect the required changes.
(iii) White washing and painting of walls and doors respectively

should be done as and when required instead of fixed intervals. Maintenance contracts would be awarded accordingly.

(iv) Safety of the buildings should be regularly examined and those found unfit for occupation should either be demolished or reclaimed in order to prevent danger to the life and property.

(v) Adequate lighting and fan arrangements may be made as per the need of each room/seating patterns rather than sticking to uniform standards of space.

(vi) Leakages in buildings may be checked in time so as to avoid permanent damages.

(vii) Modifications/alterations may be made only under the advice of architects having innovative ideas for efficient and effective use of space.

An intelligent and well-informed custodian can be of great assistance in keeping the building in good order. But this employee because of his limited training qualifications cannot appreciate the full educational significance of housekeeping activities. The principal has to be in a position to appraise the condition of the building at all times. To do this he has to know what's right and what's wrong about the building and the way it is being operated and maintained.[4]

B. MANAGEMENT OF FURNITURE AND EQUIPMENT

Furniture is essential to provide comforts and working atmosphere to teachers and students. Furniture costs money and hence must be used carefully and maintained properly. We can take the following steps to make the furniture serve our purpose:

(i) Proper assessment of the needs of all rooms/teachers/students may be done before ordering new equipment. It has been seen that because of lack of coordination furniture at one place is lying surplus while at another place it is in demand causing artificial scarcity. Sometimes the stores are full of old furniture which can be made of good quality with minor repairs and polishing while the orders are placed for buying fresh furniture.

(ii) Peons employed for the upkeep of furniture need be trained in the upkeep of furniture through regular dusting, spraying to avoid rusting, and keeping them in good conditions.

(iii) Furniture should be neatly arranged to provide aesthetic outlook and presentable.

(iv) Every year/every single article of furniture should be physically counted and examined for repairs polish or condemnation, etc.

(v) Furniture, which is unserviceable and beyond repairs, needs to be condemned rather than piling them up in stores and wasting precious spaces.
(vi) The staff should be convinced about the importance of cleaning, inspecting and keeping equipment in good order; of reporting defects immediately; and or returning equipment to its correct place after use.
(vii) There is no easy way to convince the teachers/students of the need to clean equipment and to keep it in good condition. The best way is for the Headmaster to set a good example by ensuring that equipments are cared for and in a good condition (dirty or damp equipment deteriorates more rapidly than when it is kept clean and dry).
(viii) An inspection checklist and inspection schedule should be drawn up and duties decentralized among responsible teachers and students irrespective of their administrative charges. These officials should help in detecting discrepancies and taking remedial action.

Thus, good management can take care of the management of equipments by:

- Instructing and motivating staff to feel responsible for the equipment they use;
- Ordering supplies when needed;
- Storing them safely; and
- Controlling their use.

The salient advantages of such a system would be:

(a) Reduction in idle time and continuous availability of equipment.
(b) Increased life of the equipment.
(c) Continued service.
(d) Less operational costs.
(e) Satisfactory quality of services.
(f) Safety of operation.

C. MANAGEMENT OF REDUNDANT ARTICLES

Schools are full of redundant articles and no one takes pains to write them off. These articles on one hand present an ugly look and on the other hand block the space, especially in big schools, where the value of space is quite prohibitive. Thus articles/papers/equipments which have become useless need to be discarded as early as possible. How can we go about it? We suggest a few measures as follows:

(i) There should be stocktaking in every section, once a quarter to identify of what is relevant and what is not. This exercise would help in disposing of unwanted articles.
(ii) The auctioning of discarded items should be decentralized to schools. The depreciated value rather than book value should be the criteria for evaluating the auction bids.
(iii) Removal of redundant articles should thus be a continuous process.
(iv) There may be many articles like fans, tube lights, heaters, boilers, etc. which have become outdated or inefficient. These need to be discarded on regular intervals and substituted by efficient models.

D. MAINTENANCE OF STUDENTS' CONVENIENCES

Bathrooms and toilets in school premises are the most essential infrastructural component for teachers and students especially women and girls as well as visitors. Most of the schools in villages do not have public conveniences. They should be kept clean, as cleanliness is next to godliness. Many of the diseases are the product of insanitary conditions prevailing in many schools besides causing physical discomfort and inconvenience to the users. We suggest here the following action to keep them clean:

(i) Sweepers engaged for cleaning bath rooms may be given training by pinpointing the importance of cleanliness in the upkeep of bath rooms.
(ii) Necessary materials like phenyl, cleansing agents, etc. may be supplied regularly.
(iii) Some persons may be appointed to supervise the upkeep of bathrooms regularly and maintaining a record of the action taken.
(iv) Bathrooms may be constructed away from sitting places so that the stink does not adversely affect the working of employees.
(v) Employees and visitors may be requested to keep the bathrooms clean.
(vi) Sufficient water arrangements may be made.
(vii) Privatization of cleanliness of bathrooms can be tried.

From the standpoint of health as well as the esthetic needs of children, the matter of sanitation deserves first consideration. Lack of care and improper care are the chief causes of bad sanitary conditions in schools. It is not uncommon to find unsanitary conditions in school toilet rooms. The latter should be free of all strong odours, including those, which are produced by the use of chemical deodorants and disinfectants. A pupil should not be subjected to unpleasant smells or sights when he goes to a toilet room. Proper construction, ventilation, sunlight, and frequent cleaning are the only means of correcting bad toilet room conditions and insuring proper asthetic and health standards.

The principal himself should know and, if necessary, should advise the central office of the fact that all fixtures, floors, and walls in toilet rooms should be constructed of material that has a smooth, non-absorbing finish. Tile floors and walls are vastly superior to concrete for toilet rooms since the latter material is permeable and is more difficult to keep clean. If the central administration cannot supply a new tile floor at once. An intermediate step may be substituted. A concrete floor can be improved by painting it with floor enamel. Moreover, penetrating seals are temporarily effective when applied to terrazzo and concrete.

Another factor in improving sanitary conditions in toilet rooms relates to the supplies furnished by the custodian for cleaning. Suitable brushes (several of which are now on the market) for washing toilet bowls and other plumbing fixtures when furnished by the custodian will encourage regular cleaning. The custodian's task in keeping toilet rooms sanitary should be made as pleasant as the nature of the assignment will permit. Given the right equipment, the job becomes less objectionable than otherwise.

Cleanliness is a trait, which schools generally profess to include among their curricular aims. Unfortunately, school systems often fail to provide the environmental conditions, which encourage children to practice cleanliness consistently in their everyday habits. Many toilet rooms have washbowls but no towels for drying hands. This leaves children with the alternatives of omitting washing their hands altogether, drying them with toilet paper, or using their handkerchiefs. The latter practice leads children to do a superficial job of washing and at best results in the child's returning to the classroom with a soiled handkerchief in his pocket.

Administrators sometimes argue that it is impractical to provide children with paper towels because they are so destructive and wasteful. They sometimes tear them up, throw them on the floor, or litter up the corridors with them. This makes extra work for the custodian. While there can be no denying that this situation obtains in some schools, it does not follow that all hand-wiping facilities. Rather it suggests some improvement in supervision and in the general morale of the school.

Schools have experimented with at least three types of hand drying arrangements: cloth towels, air dryers, and paper towels. Cloth towels are not practical in large schools; the cloth roller towel is insanitary and the individual cloth towels are expensive both from the standpoint of laundering and original cost. Air dryers tend to slow up traffic somewhat where large number of children are involved. They are, however, reasonably economical to operate once they are installed and they have the advantage of being completely sanitary.

Paper towels are unquestionably the most popular form of hand drying provision. They are available in rolls and in individual cabinets. Until some better provision is discovered principals are justified in recommending good quality-paper towels for use in toilet rooms. They should be placed in a container and not left on windowsills. Needless to say, the containers should be filled regularly.[5]

E. SUPPLY OF POTABLE WATER

Water is the basic requirement of every human being. Most of the students and teachers get health problems and infections because of poor quality of water. They cannot afford bottled water available at a high cost. The organization should attend to management of supply of good water for all students and visitors. The following can be done in this direction:

(i) Water storage should be done in clean tanks. Besides tanks should be washed on Saturdays/Sundays when schools are closed. Besides insecticides like potassiumpermagnate may be used once a month to keep the water infection free. Tanks, which have become too dirty should be discarded.

(ii) Students, Teachers and visitors should be requested not to waste the precious resource, i.e. water. Taps may not be kept open.

(iii) Plastic jugs and glasses used for taking water in the rooms are mostly dirty. They need be regularly cleaned and well maintained.

(iv) Contract for mineral water at cheap rates may be tried if feasible.

(v) Water testing may be got done through laboratories once in six months to assess its quality.

We may educate the students on the following points:

F. SAFE DISPOSAL OF REFUSE

Refuse may consist of paper, polythene bags, fruit skins and seeds, leftover food, leaves, twigs, etc. If refuse is left lying around, it is not only unsightly and creates a bad odour, but the heap of refuse also serves as a breeding place for rats, flies and other vermin. Flies carry disease germs on their bodies, wings and legs. When the flies settle on food, the germs get into the food. When the food is eaten, the germs enter the body and cause diseases like diarrohea, dysentery, typhoid fever or cholera. When flies sit on the face or eyelids of a child who has sore eyes or trachoma, they pick up the germs and carry them to the face or eyes of healthy children who also get the disease. Rats harbour diseases like plague and typhus. The fleas, which live on the rats suck up the disease germs from the rats' blood and carry them to human beings who then get the disease.

Banana skins, orange peel and jamun seeds left lying about on the ground are a hazard as someone can slip on them and fall.

You should ensure safe disposal of refuse as follows:

(i) See that there is a proper place for collecting rubbish. Place litter baskets all over the school compound and see that each classroom has a wastepaper basket. If there is a school meal programme, see that there is a covered dustbin in the kitchen.
(ii) See that the litter wastepaper baskets and garbage cans are emptied daily when school gets over.
(iii) In a corner of the compound get a pit dug in which the rubbish can be dumped and composted or burned. The compost from this heap is excellent manure for the kitchen garden. Ask the Health Guide or the Health Worker Male from the Sub-centre to help in the construction of the compost pit.

Points for Health Education

1. Teach children not to throw paper, banana skins, etc. on the ground, but to use the litter basket provided. In this way they can:
   - help to keep their school clean and beautiful;
   - prevent breeding of rats, flies and other vermin which cause diseases; and
   - prevent accidents from people slipping on fruit peel and seeds.
2. Get children to help in preparing the compost pit and using the compost as manure for the kitchen garden.

F. PUNCTUALITY

Punctuality, which was cherished by all, has become a casualty causing great problems. It is good for better time management.

(i) Head of School should show seriousness about this issue by calling for all teachers and students to be punctual as a preventive and educational measure.
(ii) Induction training may be given to all teachers and students to be punctual as preventive and educational measure.
(iii) Late arrivals should lead to deduction of half-day casual leave

and 3 consecutive defaults invite censure and advise entry in SRs and CRs.

(iv) Punching of cards to mark attendance can be introduced.

(v) Habitually non-punctual teachers may be served warning/censures/stoppage of increment and even suspension including termination.

(vi) Extra-benefits in the form of deputation for training, other assignments, etc. may be refused to those who are not punctual.

(vii) Strict monitoring may be done to prohibit late coming.

The Administration Reforms Commission (ARC) has rightly stated that, "the healthy functioning of the administration depends not only on the competence of its personnel, but also on the maintenance of a high standard of personal conduct and the observance of discipline. It is, therefore, essential that there should be a clearly enumerated code to correct official behaviour and a provision for the punishment of those who deviate therefore. There would, of course, also be provision for punishing slackness and inefficiency."

Punctuality enforcement is not a difficult task provided the culture of non-punctuality is discouraged. Teachers are being paid for devoting time as time is money. How can we pay them if they are not producing? The Indian Administration is suffering a lot on this count. Government of India and State Government must give top priority to this issue as we find that because of non-punctuality of doctors, teachers, administrative staff, people suffer a great agony in waiting for them. The government and school management must be harsh and no leniency should be exhibited to persons who are not punctual. This is the first and foremost requirement of any school success and prestige.

G. SCHOOL SAFETY AGAINST FIRE

We find that large number of schools in the country are not safe. There have been frequent incidents of fire in schools e.g. Mandi Dabwali in Haryana and recently the death of 100 children in a South Indian State School (Tamil Nadu). This has taken the shape of epidemic. We must train the teachers and students as to how to cope with such emergency situation. The Government must ensure that all the schools, whatever their status should possess facilities to protect the teachers and students against hazards like fire, floods, earthquake, etc.

As many as 90 children were burnt alive when fire engulfed Lord Krishna High Secondary School at Kumbakonam in Tamil Nadu. The fire and the death of so many children for no fault of theirs sent shock waves throughout the country.

The Tribune dated 24.7.2004 carried out a survey of schools in some districts of Punjab, which presents a pathetic outlook. We must take action and not forget the recent fire incident in a school waiting till another fire engulfs children. Just to quote the survey:

Ludhiana has a number of government, private and aided schools, which are being run from dingy rooms and old multistoried buildings located in narrow streets of the old city with a single exit door. Although their location in the congested and crowded markets makes them fire prone, no efforts have been done by the school authorities to instal fire-fighting system. A survey of these schools conducted by *The Tribune* team revealed that regardless of the recent tragedy and the directions given out to them by the board officers, the school authorities refused to install proper fire extinguishers on the campus. Those who have installed the system have not got them refilled for years together.

Many multistoried schools in Purana Bazar, Trunk Bazar, Katehra, Bandiya Da Mohalla, Gur Mandi, Mochpura, Katra Nauhria Mal, Hazuri Road, Islam Ganj, Dera Bhajan Garh, Kidwali Kangar, Abdullapur Basti, Salim Tabri, Haibowal and Dugri, which are situated in narrow lanes, flout all fire safety norms. While there are no arrangements to douse fire, the exit and entry points are guarded by sliding grill gates, leaving space for only one child to enter or leave.

In many schools, like in Arya Girls Senior Secondary School, Purana Bazar, a small exit point, guarded by grills, opens into a narrow (about 10-feet) street. The school, which houses 900 students any day, is virtual tinderbox. The three-storey building with a single staircase in each block and rooms hoping each other make the students once vulnerable in the case of fire. Moreover, a fire engine cannot enter the school since the entrance is through a winding narrow lane.

The most dangerous situation in terms of fire threat was posed by private schools located in narrow lanes of the city. Hundreds of such schools exist in the urban areas of the district. Thousands of students study in such schools that have been built in gross violation of the designs approved for schools. Let aside fire fighting equipment even the fire tenders cannot approach such schools in case of an emergency. Three Kendriya Vidyalaya schools being run by the Army at Pathankot are, however, a fortunate exception. The army has maintained proper fire fighting equipment in all the schools being run by it. The equipment was also tested in a time bound manner by the fire fighting experts of the army.

In Amritsar, thirty-six schools of Amritsar have been declared unsafe while 22 elementary schools are in a bad condition. Most of the schools in the walled city are located in the narrow lanes that make it almost impossible for fire tenders to reach the spot in the case of a fire. Almost all are without a proper fire-fighting equipment. Many schools need urgent repairs of staircases. A large number of schools in the walled city located in the narrow lanes and congested bazaars have little or no arrangements for any exigency. In a locality called Shatiriyan Wala Bazaar where five schools have one entry and exit point.

Fire safety is something most of the schools in Patiala are not even aware of. Surprisingly even a few schools, which are frequented by the upper crust do not follow fire safety norms. Schools in the inner city are highly unsafe as they are situated in two to three-storeyed buildings in narrow lanes with only a single door, which serves as both an entrance and exit.

A random survey revealed that many of the schools in the city had not incorporated any fire safety measure in their premises. What to talk of fire extinguishers; most of the schools do not even have any sand baskets or emergency fire exits. None have an emergency fire plan to evacuate children in an orderly manner in case of a fire.

A few schools, which are frequented by wards of the so-called upper crust and charge high fee are also not following the requisite safety measures. One such case is the British Coed School in the city. The school, which is situated in an old building with narrow staircases and small classrooms, does not have any fire extinguisher on its premises. The school has more than 600 children on its rolls, most of them in the junior classes.

In the inner city, a tragedy is waiting to happen at many of the premises with no precaution being taken against fire. At the National School's nursery and middle wing in Dharampura Bazaar one saw children of the primary wing huddled in rooms, which open into one another without any corridor. There is only one entrance to the primary wing from where children would have to be evacuated in case of an emergency. School Principal Avtar Singh when questioned said he did not feel any need to install any extinguisher, as the fire brigade's service was very good. He also said that earlier he had bought a fire extinguisher but he did not get the gas replenished after one year as it entailed an expenditure of Rs. 1,000.

District Education Officer (Secondary) Pritpal Kaur said she could get fire extinguishers installed in government schools only if the government released a special grant for the purpose.

H. BEHAVIOUR MANAGEMENT

Most of the problems today are the result of rude behaviour of majority of teachers towards students and citizens. Their behaviour has alienated the people from the functioning of school. Inspite of 73rd and 74th amendment, people still have not been given their due place and recognition in public governance. How to go about it. We may suggest the following remedies:

(i) Training may be imparted in the art and science of communication.

(ii) Teachers using filthy language should be dealt with strictly by imposition of fines or recording the demeanour in the confidential reports.

(iii) A column about behaviour should be incorporated in ACR.

(iv) Teachers should be encouraged to be polite, nice and courteous. Superiors should set a personal example by observing same standards while dealing with their bosses as well as subordinates or members of public.

(v) Supervision should be done strictly and if required dialogues of citizens and teachers depicting different situations—very negative, negative-positive, very positive, be recorded for training purposes. To quote Aristotle, "Anyone can become angry—that is easy. But to be angry with the right person, to the right degree, at the right time, for the right purpose and the right way is not easy."

(vi) A new concept called "Equilibrium Thinking" has been tried out with police trainees both with veterans having thirty years experience and freshly recruited officer trainees. Several of the trainees reported remarkable breakthroughs in managing anger and other emotions. Equilibrium is produced when positive values or vices are balanced. The positive values need to be affirmed or reinforced and the negative values need to be denied, weakness and uprooted.

Current success literature talks only of the power of positive thinking but mere positive thinking does not generate sufficient power to overcome the challenge of ingrained negative attitudes, habits forces and values. Mere positive thinking does not produce an equilibrium that comes from a habit of self-realization. The method is quite simple. Continuously hold the words Beat it in one's mind. In order to overcome anger, continually issue the following commands to self:

1. Be calm	Beat anger
2. Be gentle	Beat stress
3. Be peaceful	Beat tension
4. Be patient	Beat impatience
5. Be poised	Beat imbalance
6. Be tactful	Beat tactlessness
7. Be cheerful	Beat depression

It takes only about 10 seconds to run the series of commands through one's mind. So even if one repeats the exercise ten times a day it will take only 100 seconds.

The repetitive reinforcement on a daily and continuous basis will help in internalizing values and overcoming flows and weaknesses. Equilibrium thinking lends itself to the all round development of the human personality and character.[6] There is the need for making the administration sensitive to the citizens' needs. To quote him:

	Do's	*Don'ts*
1.	Make haste, slowly.	Don'ts merely make haste.
2.	List areas of interface.	Don't be unrealistic.
3.	Phase out areas for introduction of small steps.	Don't take on more than you can commit.
4.	Involve customer and staff in formulating and implementing it.	Don't involve only senior officers in the formulation and implementation.
5.	Prepare a Master Plan for formulation and implementation over five years and budget for it.	Don't rush into an overall package for the whole Ministry/ Department/Organization.
6.	Win consumer confidence with small, highly visible measures.	Don't promise more than you can deliver.
7.	Remember, citizens' charter process, constantly evolving.	Don't look upon it as a one-time exercise, with a final outcome.
8.	Inform the customer of the proposed commitments.	Don't inform the customer unless you are sure of delivering the service.
9.	Use simple language.	Don't use difficult language or jargon.
10.	Train your staff.	Don't leave yourself out.
11.	Delegate power.	Don't centralize.
12.	Set-up system for feedback and independent scrutiny.	Don't continue blindly without regular, periodic reassessment of performance.

We are now on the threshold of the twenty-first century. In the new millennium, above all, the schools would need to re-invent itself to become students-citizen-centric.

I. CELEBRATION OF FESTIVALS AND IMPORTANT EVENTS

In order to promote patriotism, national integration and enlightened citizenship, it is essential that the ministry/department/ subordinate offices/schools should celebrate festivals and important events for small duration wherein, the following activities can be undertaken.

1. A brief lecture about the purpose of festival/event.
2. Cultural programme.
3. Discussions.
4. Simple tea and snacks.

Such acts would promote the bond of friendship among the teachers in the schools and help in building a good team. This would also take care of regionalism, caste and narrow loyalties.

J. BEAUTIFICATION OF ENVIRONMENT

Internal and external physical environment should be soothing and stimulating to generate enthusiasm, activity and high spirits. Visits to most of the schools reveal that school in this aspect pays no attention.

Essential for Beautification

(i) Plants in pots may be kept at various locations. These may be changed according to the season. The weeds should also be regularly removed through contract arrangements.

(ii) Proper spraying may also be done to ensure infection free atmosphere. Some sprays with fragrance may also be used. Spread of rodents, flies, mosquitoes should be checked.

(iii) Proper play cards may be displayed for the guidance of visitors.

(iv) Dustbins and waste paper baskets may be provided to avoid littering and proper disposal of waste material.

(v) Preparation of Tea/Coffee or any other article may be banned in the individual rooms. Tea/Coffee, etc. can be had only in the canteen. Canteen should be equipped with proper exhaust fans to avoid pungent smells.

(vi) Good ideas may be written on the board specially provided for the purpose at the entrance of the building to infuse good thoughts.

(vii) If there is space surrounding the office/ministry/department, it should be well maintained. There should be regular removing of the congress grass and weeds and planting of flowering plants depending upon the season.

The dynamics of school management can thus be summarized in a graphical form as on next page: (See Chart 3.2).

The task before the schools today is to manage the appropriate inputs in such a way that the schools strives towards excellence.

We can thus conclude that the dynamism in the schools cannot be declared by fiat, nor can it be generated artificially imposing systems, procedures, and job demands. The enthusiasm and the aesthetic sense of teachers and students expressed about their jobs, about each other and about schools is a priceless corollary of effective management. Without it, the whole management effort can easily become a kind of drudgery, never moving beyond a mechanical process with little sense of personal

CHART 3.2

Dynamics of Managing School Aesthetic

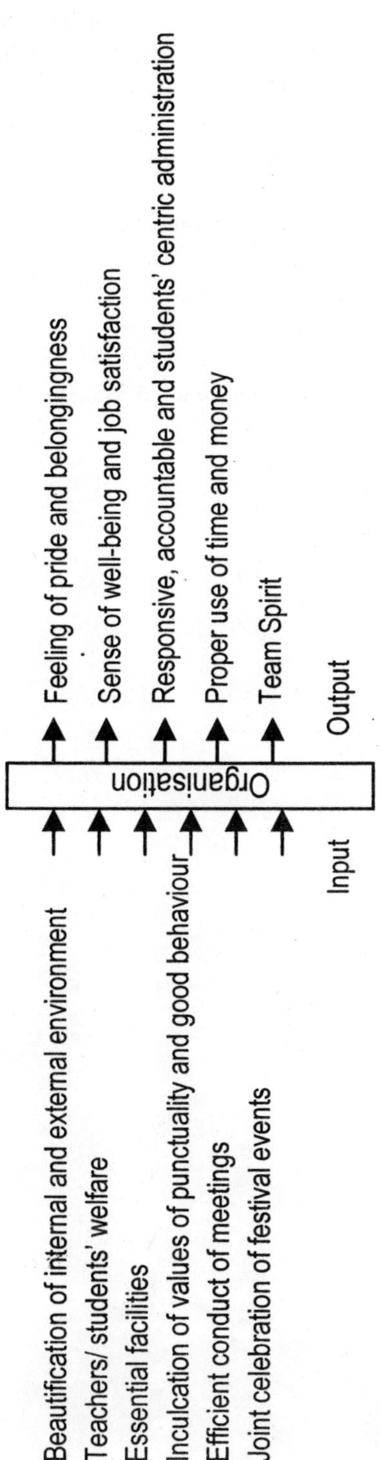

involvement. The teachers and students have a great potential which need be optimized through the development of their attitudes and philosophy through aesthetic development.

Notes and References

1. School Health, Primary School Teachers, M/o Health and Family Welfare, GOI, New Delhi, p. 5.
2. *Ibid.*, p. 17.
3. *Ibid.*, p. 174.
4. *Ibid.*
5. *Ibid.*, pp. 175-76.
6. Partap, Philip, Managing Anger, Aggression and Stress, in *Management in Government*, Jan.-March 2000, pp. 45-48.

CHAPTER 4

PERSONAL HYGIENE: SCHOOL HEALTH EDUCATION

> The physical dimension of health is probably the easiest to understand. The state of physical health implies the notion of "perfect functioning" of the body. It conceptualizes health biologically as a state in which every cell and every organ is functioning at optimum capacity and in perfect harmony with the rest of the body. However, the term "optimum" is not definable.
>
> —*K. Park*

Personal Hygiene: School Health Education

The signs of physical health in an individual are: "a good complexion, a clean skin, bright eyes, lustrous hair with a body well clothed with firm flesh, not too fat, a sweet breath, a good appetite, sound sleep, regular activity of bowels and bladder and smooth, easy, coordinated bodily movements. All the organs of the body are of unexceptional size and function normally; all the special senses are intact; the resting pulse rate, blood pressure and exercise tolerance are all within the range of "normally" for the individual's age and sex. In the young and growing individual there is a steady gain in weight and in the future this weight remains more or less constant at a point about 5 lbs (203 kg) more or less than the individual's weight at the age of 25 years (12). This state of normality has fairly wide limits. These limits are set by observation of a large number of "normal" people, who are free from evident disease.[1]

—*K. Park*

The word 'hygiene' is derived from the Greek word 'Hygeia' the goddess of health who was supposed to look after the health of the people. It has been rightly said that cleanliness is next to Godliness. The first aim of Health Education is to keep oneself clean, which is within one's own capacity but generally neglected.

Personal hygiene involves the essential steps that we must take to ensure that we can protect ourselves from infection and disease. It is in fact much more than mere warding-off illness. It involves care and actions, which enable us to lead a healthy, active and fulfilling physical, mental and social life at the maximum of our efficiency and potential.

CHART 4.1

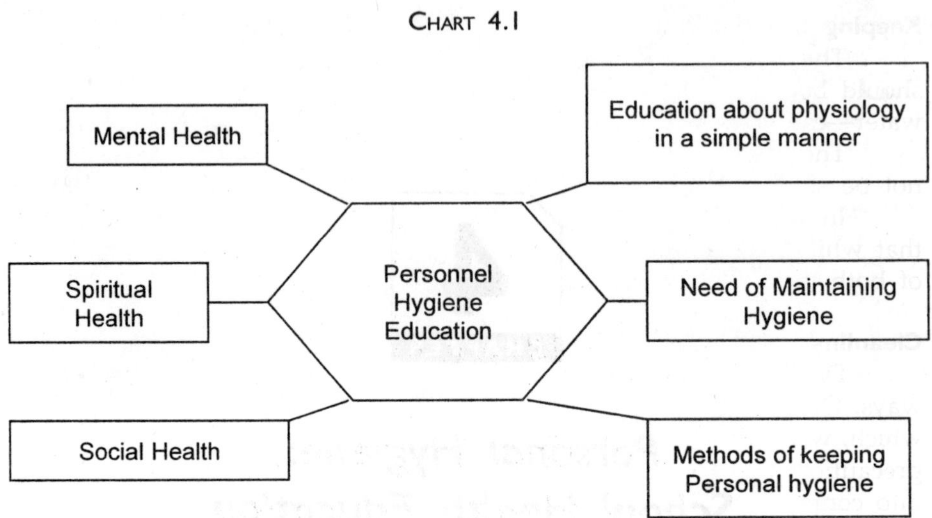

Hygiene deals both with the individual and community. What the individual has to do to preserve and to improve the health of his body and mind comes under the purview of personal hygiene, and what the organized community needs to do to maintain, protect and improve the health of the people as a whole comes under the purview of public health. Personal hygiene promotes Community Health. That aspect of public health, which is concerned with keeping, the external surroundings clean and healthy is termed sanitation.

Environmental sanitation is concerned with all those things in a man's surroundings that affect his body and mind's development, his health and his life. It is concerned with safe drinking water, pollution-free air and surroundings, proper sewage disposal, sanitary conditions and food supply, regulations for house and building.

In order to remain healthy, besides living in a healthful environment, it is very important to develop clean personal habits. These habits should be developed in young children as early as possible, both at home and at school. In this way these habits will become a normal part of each person's daily life. The primary school years are thus the ideal time for educating the child about health and for forming important lifelong habits.

While teaching children to develop healthy habits, it is essential that you yourself serve as a model for the children by practicing good health habits. In talking about personal hygiene you must be careful not to hurt any child's feelings. Always try to relate the need for personal cleanliness with the desire to be healthy.[2]

Let us discuss the essentials of personal hygiene: Personal hygiene if followed from childhood can save us from lot of health hazards. Let us discuss about cleanliness of some essential parts of the body.

Keeping the Physical Body Clean

The best way to clean the body is to clean it with water. We should be having a bath or else wipe our body with a cloth dipped in water—called a sponge bath.

The body should be dried with a fluffy towel. Bath towels should not be shared to avoid infection.

In India, we take bath in the morning as we worship God after that while in some countries, bath is taken before sleeping. The purpose of both is to keep the body clean.

Cleanliness of Hands, Feet and Nails

Disease germs can enter the body only in a limited number of ways. One of these is through the skin. The skin is a protective covering which, when broken, can admit harmful bacteria or viruses easily. Simple precautions are very effective in minimizing this. Hands and feet come into contact with the agents of contamination more than any other parts of the body. Therefore, they should be washed whenever they have been exposed to dirt before preparing or handling food or drinks, before eating, and after using the lavatory. This is the first principle taught in homes by parents and teachers. Similarly, foot must be protected through proper footwear, which can avoid direct contamination from ear.

Nails are extensions of the epidermis, or outer layer of the skin. Nails should be kept short so that nothing accumulates under them. One should make a special effort to clean under nails while washing hands. A nail that is polished right down to the base prevents its live tissues from 'breathing', which is not conducive for a healthy nail. Nail polish should therefore not be used all the time.

Cleaning Mouth and Teeth

The condition of the various parts of your mouth, i.e., the tongue, teeth and gums must be good. Halitosis or offensive mouth odour is indicative of poor oral hygiene. The foul smell is primarily a result of cell decay, and the odours are characteristic of the growth of some micro-organisms. Halitosis can also result from infected or diseased gums, decaying teeth, or oral tumours.

For good oral sanitation one should brush one's teeth every morning and before going to sleep at night. Mouth and teeth are the entering point of food and therefore that must be kept clean to avoid any infection.

Care of Hair

Hair originates in tiny sacs or follicles deep in the dermis layer of skin tissue. Hair follicles are closely connected to the sebaceous glands, which secrete oil to the scalp and give hair its natural sheen. Baldness is basically related to sex, age and heredity, but bacterial or fungal infections, allergic reactions to particular medicines, radiation, or continual friction may also cause baldness.

Care of Eyes and Ears

The eye performs two major functions—it transforms light energy into vision, and it focuses. The outer layers of the eye, and the fluids in them are a protection for the delicate parts inside. Tears provide the moisture for lubricating the movement of the eyeballs, and also act as disinfectants for the eyes.

Eyes, specially of school age children, should be examined periodically to detect and treat defects if any.

Ears give us the sense of hearing and the sense of balance. Two special types of sense receptors within the tunnels and chambers of the ear make this possible. The major parts of the ear consist of the auditory canal, middle ear, and the inner ear.

Any infection of the ear and any discharge from it should be promptly attended to. Earache is one of the most common complaints of childhood.

Refuse may consist of paper, polythene bags, fruit skins and seeds, leftover food, leaves, twigs, etc. If refuse is left lying around, it is not only unsightly and creates a bad odour, but the heap of refuse also serves as a breeding place for rats, flies and other vermin. Files carry disease germs on their bodies, wings and legs. When the flies settle on food, the germs get into the food. When the food is eaten, the germs enter the body and cause diseases like diarrohea, dysentery, typhoid fever or cholera. When flies sit on the face or eyelids of a child who has sore eyes or trachoma, they pick up the germs and carry them to the face or eyes of healthy children who also get the disease. Rats harbour diseases like plague and typhus. The fleas, which live on the rats suck up the disease germs from the rats' blood and carry them to human beings who then get the disease.

Banana skins, orange peel and jamun seeds left lying about on the ground are a hazard as someone can slip on them and fall.

You should ensure safe disposal of refuse as follows:

(i) See that there is a proper place for collecting rubbish. Place litter baskets all over the school compound and see that each classroom has a wastepaper basket. If there is a school meal programme, see that there is a covered dustbin in the kitchen.

(ii) See that the litter wastepaper baskets and garbage cans are emptied daily when school get over.

(iii) In a corner of the compound get a pit dug in which the rubbish can be dumped and composted or burned. The compost from this heap is excellent manure for the kitchen garden. Ask the Health Guide or the Health Worker Male from the Subs centre to help in the construction of the compost pit.

Points for Health Education

1. Teach children not to throw paper, banana skins, etc. on the ground, but to use the litter basket provided. In this way they can:
   - help to keep their school clean and beautiful;
   - prevent breeding of rats, flies and other vermin which cause diseases; and
   - prevent accidents from people slipping on fruit peel and seeds.
2. Get children to help in preparing the compost pit and using the compost as manure for the kitchen garden.

Care of External Genitals

Cleanliness of the sexual organs is even more important than that of the other parts of the body partly because of their proximity to the anus and the urethra where bacterial contamination can be high. Every time one uses the toilet, this part of the body must be cleaned well with water. In the case of uncircumcised male organ it is important to retract the foreskin in the bath and wash the secretions that collect underneath. If this is not done the collection of secretions will get affected by bacteria and cause irritation. In the case of females the vulva should be washed well every time a toilet is used. During menstruation it is more important to have regular and frequent baths. While washing yourself after fecal discharge care should be taken not to infect the vulva with the fecal matter. Thorough washing is essential.

Rest and Sleep

Adequate amount of rest and sleep are vital for good health and good appearance. They also influence mental alertness, physical performance as well as human relationships. It is believed that during sleep the body replaces tissue cells and eliminates waste products created by fatigue, at a faster rate than when awake. During sleep the blood pressure is lower and the heart muscle contractions are slower, this gives rest to the heart and blood system. Lack of sleep increases fatigue and also susceptibility to a number of ailments, including the common cold.

A good seven-to-eight hours sleep refreshes us to face the challenges of the day. Alcohol, sleeping pills and tranquilizers are never the right answer to fatigue.

Exercise, Fatigue and Posture

Physical upkeep can be achieved with little or no exercise equipment. All that is required is a little timing each day and a great deal of determination and patience. Regular exercise causes the hear-beat to grow stronger and steadier, and breathing to become deeper. As the flow of blood through the tissues is improved, waste products of the cells are removed more effectively; the body uses energy more efficiently in both physical and mental task; coordination is improved.[3]

Points for Health Education

Teach children the following:

(i) Go to bed early and rise early.
(ii) Sleep in a clean, quiet, well-ventilated room.
(iii) Use a light covering in summer and a blanket or quilt in winter.
(iv) If necessary use a mosquito net or apply a mosquito repellant on the body before sleeping.
(v) Do not sleep in a closed room in which there is a charcoal fire or sigree burning.
(vi) Sleep in a separate bed.
(vii) Wear clean loose garments to sleep in.
(viii) In the morning air the bedding and roll it up nearly or make up the bed.
(ix) Put the bedding in the sun from time to time.
(x) Change and wash the bed linen frequently.
(xi) Take regular exercise.
(xii) Take active part in physical training and outdoor games in your school.
(xiii) Always keep you back straight when you sit, stand or walk. A boy or girl who has a good posture looks much more attractive than one who stoops or walks with a slouch.
(xiv) Good posture helps the different parts of your body to function normally.

This helps to keep your healthy.

Leisure and Recreation

Besides studying, working, playing games, taking exercise, taking meals, keeping ourselves and our surroundings clean, resting and sleeping, most of us still have some spare time left in which we can do what we like best.

There are a variety of hobbies and interests, which we can develop, and which can give us enjoyment and provide recreation for our minds and bodies. For some of us these hobbies involve physical activity such as walking, cycling, swimming, gymnastics, or playing cricket, kabbadi or other sports; others may be interest in less active pursuits like carpentry, model-making, sewing, cooking, gardening, or indoor games like chess or carom; still others prefer to spend their spare time in listening to or making music, painting, pottery, stamp, collecting, reading or writing.

There are any number of ways in which we can spend our spare time that can help to keep us healthy and happy, and can add delight to our waking hours.[4]

Mental Health

Mental Health is more important than physical health.

More recently, mental health has been defined as "a state of balance between the individual and the surrounding world, a state of harmony between oneself and others, a coexistence between the realities of the self and that of other people and that of the environment.[5]

There is a need to promote self-confidence and positive thinking, which can lead to mental strength and equanimity.

During recent years there has been increasing recognition of the influence of schools on children's psychosocial development, and of the potential of the educational system as a means of fostering mental health. At first sight it may not be obvious why schools should have an important place in preventive programmes; after all, schools do not cause mental disorder, so why should improved schooling aid in the prevention of psychiatric problems? Yet schools are important in prevention, because a vulnerability to mental disturbances is much affected by people's life circumstances. For children, schooling occupies a high proportion of their waking hours during much of their growing years.

Research has shown that schooling is most effective when it has the support of parents and makes good use of parents' skills. Most parents want their children to do well at school, but many feel alienated by the professional competence of teachers and discouraged by their own educational limitations. This need not happen if schools take the time and trouble to involve parents in ways that enhance, rather than detract, from parental responsibilities. This has been most strikingly shown in work with nursery schools but it is equally evident with older age groups. Thus, one study showed the marked benefits of getting parents (even those who were semi-literate) to listen to their children reading. Later, too, the role of the family will have an important bearing on children's commitment to learning, and on educational advancement when compulsory education comes to an end.

Finally, there is a very substantial association between child psychiatric disorders and learning difficulties. For that reason, steps that are effective in aiding the learning of children with special educational difficulties are likely to have psychiatric benefits. But this must be done in a way that increases the children's sense of self-esteem and enables them to cope successfully in ordinary society. This is probably best accomplished by improving the standard of schools generally rather than by creating separate institutions for children with special needs.

Schools cannot be expected to compensate for the ills in the rest of society. Nevertheless they can be a force for the good, with benefits that are especially marked for the disadvantaged. The overall psychological impact of the school is relatively modest compared with that of the family. But in terms of prevention, schools have a major advantage in that they can affect many children, while at the same time society has the power to ensure that the schools do indeed provide good environments in which to live and to learn. That is no small advantage, but its potential for preventing mental ill-health has not yet been fully realized.[6]

Dr. M.L. Lakshmi Kumari, President, V.K. Yogas, Kanyakumari, says that:

The aim of all education, undoubtedly, is the attainment of human excellence and perfection, not just in any field of knowledge or activity but life in totality. Education should be the means to fashion excellent characters out of the very ordinary human raw material. This means culturing of the qualities of head and heart in a way congenial to the growth and development of oneself and others around him. In practical life, it has to be translated as qualities of truthfulness, righteous living, purity in personal life, self-confidence, integration of body, mind and intellect, love and compassion towards all living beings and surrender to Almighty. These are steps leading to the unfoldment of perfection already in man. Such a truly educated and cultured man alone can meet the challenges, internal and external, in a positive way, converting them into opportunities, helping in his ultimate evolution. Pursued further, one's entire thought behaviour and life itself would come to express the spiritual oneness of the creation and this would be the manifestation also of the divinity inherent in man. A truly educated man, like a true scientist, satisfied with nothing but the one truth has to be necessarily spiritual as well.

Swami Vivekananda stressed on man-making, character-building education. To quote him, "Education is not the amount of information that is put into your brain and runs riot there undigested all your life. We must have life-building, man-making, character-making assimilation of ideals. We want education by which character is formed, strength of mind is increased, the intellect is expanded, by which one can stand on one's feet. What we want is Western science coupled with Vedanta, Brahmacharya as the guiding motto and also Shraddha and faith in one's own life". Education is the panacea for all the ills affecting us individually, socially and nationally.

The education as is obtained today is not at all aimed at character building with the result that we find even highly educated men who have so much of power and service machinery at their command fail miserably when tackling problems in the right way, in the human way, in the interests of our nation. Highly talented individuals are there in every field, second to none, but devoid of patriotic fervour and personal integrity, the impact they produce is minimal. Today, we are urgently in need of men and women of character, integrity and dedication and of tremendous capacities happily blending dignity of man with dignity of labour.

Connection of mind, its purity and chastity alone can bring out the amazing qualities and capacities that lie hidden in the human mind. Lack of these has created a student community who are debilitated, inhuman, selfish and indifferent to human values. Swami Vivekananda stresses the value of Shraddha, faith, as one of the most potent factors capable of elevating human life. He wanted this "Life-saving, great, ennobling, grand doctrine" to be taught to our children from their very birth. Where the different streams of consciousness in man, namely, concentration of mind, purity of life, faith in oneself, strength of body and fearlessness of mind are combined together in a single personality, the force of that character becomes invincible. Men of such stature alone can rebuild a shattered society. It is such men that our educational system should create to safely carry over our country to the 21st century.

To build a truly great character is the most glorious of human achievements. Such a man-making education, in which India has all the technical know-how, handed down from time immemorial, should form the basis of our national efforts in the field. In most exquisite words have our ancient Masters sung the glory of such a true education.

Asato maa sadgamaya.
Tamaso maa jyotir gamaya,
Mrutyor maa amrutam gamaya,
Om Shanti, Shanti, Shanti.

Lead Me From the Unreal to the Real,
Lead Me From Darkness to Light,
Lead Me From Death to Immortality,
Om Peace, Peace, Peace.

Human mind today is completely out of control, flowing in all directions. It is like a river in spate. Our primary attempt should be to prevent the flow spreading in all directions by controlling, harnessing and regulating it. This is achieved by reinforcing the banks. In the river of thoughts, the intellect represents the banks, which decide the direction of flow. Hence, the intellect has to be chastened and chiseled with the help of the scriptures.

In order to live and to bring out the maximum happiness from ourselves, to work out the best for ourselves, everyone of us must have a goal in life, a mission, an inspiring ideal; looking up to that ideal and hitching our eyes to it, we must work on in the world outside. Thereby, the work becomes chastened; the work itself become its own reward for the individual and a great joy wells up in his mind, not in terms of what he gets on the first of the month, but what he gives to the society as best as he can, from the place where he is.

Social Health

Social well-being implies harmony and integration within the individual, between each individual and other members of society and between individuals and the world in which they live. It has been defined as the "quantity and quality of an individual's interpersonal ties and the extent of involvement with the community."

The social dimension of health includes the levels of social skills one possesses, social functioning and the ability to see oneself as a member of a larger society. In general, social health takes into account that every individual is part of a family and of wider community and focuses on social and economic conditions and well-being of the "whole person" in the context of his social network. Social health is rooted in "positive material environment" (focusing on financial and residential matters), and "positive human environment" which is concerned with the social network of the individual.[7]

The life of harmony can be lived by rising above our limited egocentric view of things and happenings, and expanding our mind to accommodate a constant awareness of the totality of the world, the entirety of mankind and the vastness and wholeness of the universal problems. When this total and consummate perception is developed and maintained, man's individual problems sink into insignificance and absurdity.

Our life of harmony with the ampler scheme of the cosmos brings to our heart an inward peace and poise. When poise is maintained within us, problems and challenges vanish like mist before the rising sun.[8]

Spiritual Health

The core of the human personality is the Consciousness, which is the "Life Centre" around which all the activities of the body, mind and the intellect revolve. It remains ever changeless and immovable like an axle in the wheel, but causes all changes and movements to occur. When man succeeds in identifying with this changeless, immovable conscious principle within him, he is no longer victimized by the changing phenomena of perceptions, emotions and thoughts, but becomes the Supreme Lord of them all. The intellectual pursuits, emotional attachments and physical cravings of such a man naturally wither and fall away like petals of a flower when the fruit emerges.

Religion teaches us this art of focusing our attention on the spiritual core which is our Real Nature, and when we understand the infinite dimension of our being, we develop, in our experience of the Supreme Bliss, a total dispassion for anything that the material world can offer.[9]

CONCLUSION

Personal hygiene is the most important as the practice of it can protect a person from health complications at a later stage. However, most of the people neglect personal hygiene on one pretext or the other. They forget the proverb, "A Stitch in time saves nine". The quality of life becomes very low. Therefore, the following Health Education measures must be applied to make the individuals families, community conscious of personal hygiene.

(1) The mothers must be given health education either by Government Health System or NGO's or other measures so that they make their children conscious of personal hygiene. Family should also practice personal hygiene wherein children would automatically observe the required personal hygienic measures.
(2) Teachers in Pre-Nursery and Nursery Schools should give more emphasis on education to the tiny tots in personal hygiene rather than teaching them other subjects. The teachers can teach personal hygiene though play way methods, songs, etc. The purpose that the education of personal hygiene must leave an indelible impressions on the minds of the tiny tots so that these become reflex actions for them in their life.
(3) When children attains maturity, they can be educated in the reasons behind observing principles of personal hygiene. This type of health education would be enduring and permanent for them in life.
(4) There can be Sunday Schools for children where children can be given health education on personal hygiene.
(5) Health System of the country should not be merely for patient treatment but more important function need be performed by health system, i.e. providing health education.

When personal hygiene becomes well established through all the agencies, the rush for medical care would be limited thus saving huge resources being spent on hospitals and super-specialty Hospitals. Most of the problems arise out of individuals not following the principles of personal hygiene. The policy-makers, planners and health administrators must give top priority to provide health education to people on top priority.

Teachers' Involvement

Active involvement of teachers is very important as they are the pivot of the whole programme. Their involvement will be sought in the following areas:

(i) Intensive health education of the students using child-to-child approach for developing self-health care.
(ii) Inculcation of healthy habits with a view to developing healthy lifestyles.
(iii) Observation of students to identify deviation from normal health and diseases.
(iv) Screening of vision and hearing, along with taking of height and weight of students.
(v) Maintain health card for each student and discuss health problems of pupils with the Medical Officer, parents and health workers, link mothers and youth leaders.

(vi) Identify health education opportunities in the school.
   1. At the morning prayer.
   2. In the class room and relate with health contents given in the text books.
   3. Organize enjoyable out-of-class activities like health poems, songs, skits, plays.
   4. Include health activities in cultural programmes during special events such as annual days, national days, etc.
   5. Supervise personal hygiene practices during lunch, after using toilet facilities and after games.
   6. Organize school health days or weeks.

(vii) The above activities may be organized with the involvement of National Service Scheme Volunteers, wherever available; otherwise, involve health workers, the community people or youth leaders and link mothers.

(viii) Encourage students of Classes V and IV to check the personal hygiene of students of Classes III, II and I at the time of prayer, at lunchtime, during recess and at home. By doing so, the older children will become conscious of their own healthy habits; it will also generate a sense of leadership.

(ix) Each child of Classes V and IV adopt two children of lower classes, i.e. III, II and I and teach them health messages. They will also observe their practices.

(x) Coordination with Primary Health Centre for medical examination, treatment, the referral and follow-up.

(xi) Follow up the regularity of treatment prescribed and ensure visit to Primary Health Centre.

(xii) Liaison with parents, link mothers and community for mobilizing their resources for improving environmental conditions of the schools.

(xiii) Form parent-teacher associations and seek their active involvement.

(xiv) Ensure community participation in the promotion of school health programmes by dividing the community into manageable units and allot these units to every child.

   It is observed that about 10% of the population of any community consists of primary school-age children. On an average, there will be 100 primary school students in a village with 1000 population. A population of 1000 will have on an average 200 households. So one primary school student will have to look after two households, i.e. one his own and another that of the neighbour.

   Children should be used as health communication for two households. They may disseminate health information to the members of the allotted households, observe the health habits of siblings in the home, and those of friends in the neighbourhood.

(xv) Minimal records are suggested to be maintained at the schools to avoid unnecessary burden on the teachers. A quarterly report on the activities will have to be sent to the Block Medical Officer with a copy to the Central Monitoring Cell and State Coordinator.

(xvi) Provide necessary assistance to the health team for organizing specialists' camps. These camps will be set-up in the school buildings/Primary Health Centre/Community Centre depending on the convenience, availability and easy accessibility to a large number of students or a group of villages.

(xvii) Help National Service Scheme volunteers and youth leaders of Nehru Youva Kendra to organize village health camps by providing necessary assistance. These are:
- Physical facilities for the camps including accommodation.
- Establishing contacts with village leaders.
- Planning need-based activities like mass meetings, film shows, group-discussion, immunization campaigns, nutrition demonstration, Oral Rehydration Solution demonstration, filling up its improvement of environmental conditions, etc.

(xviii) Enhancing the nutrition status of children by seeking support for programmes of better nutrition of students, providing correct and adequate nutrition knowledge and encouraging school/home nutrition gardens.

(xix) Organizing health/environmental sanitation camps and campaigns with community participation.

In order to keep the interest of the teachers sustained or to generate strong motivation, following incentives need to be provided:

1. Health check-up for teacher at the time of training and treatment in case there is need.
2. Award of certificates at the end of the training course.
3. Award of running trophies of the best school within the district Gradation of schools on the basis of their performance may be made with the following criteria:
   - Improvement in environmental conditions.
   - Improvement in Health Status of children.
   - Improvement in personal hygiene of students.
   - Development of nutrition garden.
   - Involvement of parent community in school health programme.
   - Application of Child-to-Child and Youth-to-Child approaches.
   - Formation of school health committee.

- Collaboration with NSS volunteers, youth leaders and health workers.

4. Award of merit certificate/incentive to the best health education teacher based on individual performance.
5. Training of teachers regarding their role in school health services programme will be provided by coordinating the resources like the Advisors of ICDS programme, Regional Health and F.W. Training Centres, State Council for Educational Research and Training (SCERT), Training Orientation/Research Coordinators (TORCs) of National Services Scheme and Programme Officers of National Services Scheme, State Institutes of Education and Resources available with other special programmes.
6. A minimum of five days' training for teachers along with National Services Scheme volunteers of colleges/schools, where available, and for only teachers wherever National Services Scheme is not available, has been considered necessary. Teachers must be apprised regarding portions of health cards to be filled up by them, their referral slips and the proforma for health education information to be maintained in separate notebooks.
7. The training programme will be coordinated by the State Project Coordinators of State Health Programme.
8. The roles and responsibilities of health and educational personnel have been drawn up exhaustively, It would be desirable to involve local functionaries during the training programme to finalize these by raising the following questions:
   (i) How may of these activities are they already performing?
   (ii) How many more can they conveniently accept?
   (A copy of finally agreed roles and responsibilities of each functionary may be forwarded to the nodal officer.)
9. A sum of Rs. 100 will be provided to the teachers as honorarium of the five-day training.
10. These teachers will be considered to be on duty for the period of training and will draw their TA from the source of their salary as per the State/UT rules. This issue may be settled at the District Coordination Committee meetings.[10]

Notes and References

1. K. Park: Preventive and Social Medicine, M/s Banarsidas Bhanot, 1167, Prem Nagar, Jabalpur, 1997, pp. 12-13.
2. School Health, Primary School Teachers, M/o Health and Family Welfare, GOI, New Delhi, p. 17.
3. Environmental Sanitation and Safety-2, IGNOU, Public Health and Hygiene, pp. 47-54

4. School Health, Primary School Teachers, M/o Health and Family Welfare, GOI, New Delhi, p. 28.
5. K. Park: Preventive and Social Medicine, M/s Banarsidas Bhanot, 1167, Prem Nagar, Jabalpur, 1997, p. 13.
6. WHO: Michael Rutter, The Role of Schools, *World Health*, August-September 1985, pp. 28-29.
7. K. Park, Preventive and Social Medicine, M/s Banarsidas Bhanot, 1167, Prem Nagar, Jabalpur, 1997, p. 13.
8. Swami Chinmayananda, Kindle Life, Central Chinmaya Mission Trust, Mumbai, pp. 40-41.
9. *Ibid.*, pp. 58-59.
10. Intensive Health Education, M/o Health and Family Welfare, Kotla Road, New Delhi, pp. 8-10.

CHAPTER 5

TRAINING OF SCHOOL TEACHERS IN SCHOOL HEALTH EDUCATION

Many of the things we need can wait.
The child cannot.
Right now is the time,
his bones are being formed,
his blood is being made,
and his senses are being developed.
To him we cannot answer 'Tomorrow'.
His name is 'Today'.

—*Gabriela Mistral*

Training of School Teachers in School Health Education

"The vital years," observed that "Health-related habits formed during childhood can play a crucial role in determining whether an adult will be destined to enjoy a long and healthy life."

—*Frank Falkner*

The first step, therefore, is to encourage teachers to accept the promotion of health as an integral part of education. Even in countries where preventive medicine is a desperate necessity, an excessive regard for the academic approach may still linger, to the detriment of health promotion. Information about the value of latrines may have a lower priority than understanding atomic structures, for example, especially if examination results and jobs are dependent on it.

The second obstacle to success with school health education lies in the possible conflict of values between school and community. For example, it is obviously useless to preach the advantages of a balanced diet to teenagers, if their parents offer them fried food at every meal. Nor is a theoretical knowledge of the value of animal proteins much use of children whose staple diet is cassava.

If health education is to be fully effective, we must consider the context in which it is taught. We therefore need to identify the factors, which predispose, enable, or reinforce good health. Thus, if our goal is to reduce unintended teenage pregnancy, it is not sufficient to provide knowledge, or improve instruction. We must also ensure that acceptable sources of supply for contraceptives are available before commencing any educational programme; this has been successfully achieved in Minnesota, USA, and the island of Gotland in Sweden. Similarly, reminders to local tobacconists not to sell cigarettes to under-age children (in countries where this is illegal) should accompany the introduction of school anti-smoking programmes.

In the end, we really need to turn the whole question upside-down. Instead of asking how we can make health education effective, we need to start with a clearly defined health problem and identify all of the factors, which can contribute to its solution. Within this framework, we can then assign a particular role to health education, but we cannot expect it to be fully effective except in conjunction with a variety of other measures.

For example, improving children's dental health may require the following: controls over the consumption of sugar—perhaps affecting the sale of sweets in school shops; large-scale fluoridation of water; provision of an adequate supply of toothbrushes; education for parents; and all of these should be combined with an effective school programme. Education for children cannot be expected to achieve much by itself. Health education then, is not to be seen as an end itself. Instead, it is simply one of several approaches towards the promotion of health by preventive methods.

Community influences themselves are important when we consider the disappointingly short-term effects of some school programmes. Every teacher knows that new ideas are rapidly forgotten if they are not reinforced, that is, by referring to the same topic again, perhaps from a different perspective on each occasion. This explains the failure of "health weeks". Schools need to plan health education as part of a spiral curriculum, returning to each major topic every two or three years.

But by far the strongest source of effective "reminders" lies in the community. Provided parents are actively involved in the programme, much of the reinforcement can be supplied by them. But if parents, governments and industry are all pulling in the opposite direction to schools (as often occurs with nutrition), school health messages will be as effective as a whisper in a thunderstorm.

As Lawrence Green pointed out in the April-May 1983 issues of *World Health*, health education, or rather health promotion, cannot successfully be imposed from above. Similarly, major advances in health promotion cannot occur without wholehearted community support. Innumerable health schemes for schools have failed to survive the departure of outside development teams—whether the school is in the African bush or in the urban jungles of Europe and North America. The wholesale adoption of Western approaches to sex education in parts of Nigeria proved totally inappropriate to the solution of teenagers' problems in a developing nation. So while suggestions and support from the centre will always be helpful, detailed planning and implementation must be carried out at local level.

If so, as Green points out, the first step towards effective health promotion is to arouse community awareness. In the United Kingdom, schools can now obtain standardized questionnaires developed by John

Balding at the University of Exeter to measure and compare student, teacher and parent opinions on priority topics for health education. They can also obtain questionnaires on student-reported health behaviour, and compare their results (anonymously) with other schools. This simple idea has led to major changes in teaching practice, initiated and carried out entirely by the local teaching staff without any need for further intervention by outsiders.

Similarly, Peter Homel and colleagues in Australia have found marked changes in health behaviour relating to smoking, drinking and probably also physical fitness, in a project jointly supported by the New South Wales Health and Education Authorities. This involved, essentially, asking the teachers in a particular community to plan and organize their own ideal approach to health education, and then providing them with the resources to do so. This "bottom-up" style of curriculum development is in marked contrast to the traditional "top-down" style, for which so many failures have been recorded.

If we want to change lifestyles, we cannot realistically expect to achieve this through education alone. We must instead identify every possible obstacle to health, and try to tackle as many as we can simultaneously. Education will then usually be found to have a crucial role in every form of health promotion.

For example, if the key to better health lies in a change in the law, the first step many be to educate the law-makers. This may, in some respects, be simpler to achieve (at least conceptually) in developing countries. In many cases, their need for improved health at minimum cost is too obvious to require debate. In the context of specific projects designed to tackle major local problems (for instance, the Pikine Project, *World Health*, August 1983), health education can play a major role.

The past decade has seen major advances in both the quality and quantity of school education. However, until recently, evaluation suggested that it had little effect on lifestyles. In general, the message seemed literally to "go in one ear and out the other."

As E.L. Thompson pointed out in 1978, when reviewing school programmes in the English-speaking countries directed against smoking: "Most methods have shown little success."

This may have been the result of over-reliance on traditional teaching methods, with too much emphasis on "talk and chalk"—that is, long lectures delivered with the help of a blackboard. Since then, radical changes have occurred, at least in some schools. Such pioneers as Richard Evans in Texas, Trefor Williams in Britain and Leif Aaro in Norway have developed new approaches based on social learning theory.

Modern health education programmes now rely on "doing" as an aid to learning, with emphasis on role play, individual learning from assignments, and well-produced visual aids. Much more attention is given to fitting the activity to the personality of the learner. As a result, we can now "chalk up" an impressive list of successes for school health education. We know that, at least in some schools, good health education can produce cleaner teeth, higher rates of rubella (German measles) immunization, and fewer smokers.

Favourable reports have also been received from some countries concerning the influence of schools on alcohol consumption and teenage fertility. We cannot be certain how far into adulthood these benefits will last but there are some grounds for optimism, at least in relation to smoking.

Nevertheless, substantial negative areas still remain. For example, school programmes rarely appear to have any impact on eating habits, especially the type of "junk food" diet favoured by Western teenagers. More seriously, many of the favourable results already mentioned are often relatively short lasting. A study made in the United Kingdom showed that impressive improvements in tooth brushing techniques may last for as little as six months after lessons have been given.

So we are left in some doubt—why is school health education effective for some topics but not for others? And why are its effects sometimes so shortlasting? To find out, we need to look more closely at the relationship between health education and health.

The first difficulty with school health education is that teachers do not always see a necessary connection between health education and health. The aims of many school programmes are often "to provide information," or "to improve decision-making skills." Changes in health-related behaviour are not necessarily seen as an expected, or even as a desirable, outcome. As one teacher put it: "Well, I tell them about smoking, but it's up to them after that, isn't it?" If a school programme is not intended to influence health, we should not be too surprised if it doesn't.[1]

The ultimate objective of procreation is to have children who will become healthy, happy adults and will continue so during a long life. More and more are we realizing, and finding, that the foundation for such a desirable state is laid in the earliest stages of a child's growth and development. Much attention needs to be paid to this vital fact. We are getting better at reducing our infant mortality rates. This is admirable. But we need to ask the question: If an infant now escapes becoming an infant mortality statistic, what is the outcome for that infant? Will he or she arrive at adulthood complete, and healthy?

How early are these vital years? The wise Chinese celebrate their children's first birthdays when they are born. This tradition is based on the far-sighted realization that a very important period of growth and development has been occurring in the 40 weeks a growing before births. In modern biomedical terms, then, many of the secrets and foundations of later health are hidden—and to be found—in the prenatal period. Growth and development start at conception; and while birth is of the greatest importance to the family involved, it is not, comparatively speaking, of such great biomedical importance. Perhaps for certain purposes we should talk of the Vital Weeks.[2]

Environmental Factors

There is increasing evidence that many prevalent and disabling adult diseases are related to environmental and community factors. Exposure to pollutants and health-related habits formed during childhood can play a crucial role in determining whether an adult is healthy or is to suffer from cardiovascular or lung diseases, or cancer.

Science can provide the know-how for keeping our atmosphere clean and it can provide the evidence for the harmful effects of smoking. But we have to decide whether we will inaugurate the improvements, cost what they may. The alternative is to pay the bill of adult disability and ill-health, and thus face even greater costs.

The most appropriate motto to characterize those vital years of childhood is surely "Sapiens Qui Prospicit"—he is wise who looks ahead.[3]

There is need to understand that while the task of safeguarding the health of today's children is urgent, it cannot be accomplished through conventional means. What is required is a radical new approach emphasizing the just distribution of health resources; mobilization of national and international resources; imaginative use of traditional medicine and its practitioners; research and development of appropriate health technologies relevant to local needs; and close cooperation among the nations of the world.[4]

The tragic fact is that the great majority of children in the Third World fall into this category of those requiring "special care" because of their socio-economic disadvantages. The parameters of suffering and the problems of children in the Third World are silent and insidious: death by degrees; the surface drama of disease often only crowns and concludes, but largely obscures, the gradual disintegration produced by protein-energy malnutrition, common infectious diseases and social deprivation. This slow "social" dying is too often met with indifference by the majority of those rich in power and wealth. We cannot claim any satisfactory solution in any of the areas of food, human settlement, health, education or human rights until we have, as a primary obligation, confronted the critical vulnerability of children and secured their future.[5]

There are many successful experiences in recent years, which have shown how major improvements in the health of millions of children can be accomplished in a very short period of time. We must look together to gain inspiration from these experiences in order to meet the challenge we face. This brings us back to trusting in people, and giving value to the love of children—as our richest resources for today's—and tomorrow's—human development. This is basic to what we mean by the slogan: a healthy child, a sure future.[6]

Children of school-going age from a very high proportion of India's population, both in rural and in urban areas. It is, therefore, important that the physical and mental health of this segment of the population should be the concern of all those responsible for ensuring the health of the people. Healthful habits as regards personal hygiene, clean surroundings, nutritious diet, exercise, rest and recreation, if formed at an early stage, will remain with a person throughout life and will help to develop healthy citizens in the full and positive sense of the term—viz. persons who are in a state of complete physical, mental and social well-being.

Teachers is schools besides teaching can play an important role:

The American Commission on Teacher Education rightly observes, "The quality of a nation depends upon the quality of its citizens. The quality of its citizens depends not exclusively, but in critical measures upon the quality of their education, the quality of their education depends more than upon any single factor, upon the quality of their teachers.

The Ministry of Education document "Challenge of Education: A Policy Perspective" (1985) has mentioned, "Teacher performance is the most crucial input in the field of education. Whatever policies may be laid down, in the ultimate analysis these have to be interpreted and implemented by teachers as much through their personal example as through teaching-learning process.[7]

Teachers are not supposed merely to make their students literate but ensure an all round development of personality. Health is a very important component of his personality; therefore, teachers must be trained in the art and science of health education.

School health programmes have the following broad goals:

1. To prepare the younger generation to adopt measures to remain healthy so as to help them to make the best use of educational facilities, to utilize leisure in a productive and constructive manner, to enjoy recreation, and to develop concern for others.
2. To help the younger generation to become healthy and useful citizens who will be able to perform their role effectively for the welfare of themselves, their families, the community at large and the country as a whole.

To achieve these goals the school health programme comprises the following components:

1. Regular medical check-up of school children enabling early detection of defects and disease and prompt referral for treatment.
2. Protection of all school-going children against preventable diseases by immunization according to the National Immunization Schedule.
3. Health and population education programmes in schools.

4. Ensuring a healthful school environment, e.g. as regards safe drinking water, sanitation, accident prevention and food hygiene.
5. Nutrition education and providing, wherever possible, nutritional supplements or mid-day meals to school children.[8]

Among the aims of health education stressed by the Athens conference was improvement of the children's or adolescents' ability to mobilize their own resources for their health care and to make effective decisions on the basis of the information acquired. This means that mere transfer of knowledge cannot be considered the final goal of health education: the child should learn to use this knowledge, and to make the best choice in a given situation.

One of the most important elements in health education is active participation in it of children and adolescents. This was strikingly demonstrated in a project undertaken in one country to decrease the number of traffic accidents among school-children. The children themselves were invited to study the traffic pattern in their area, and to calculate transport densities. Pedestrian's movements, and so on. The result was that even during the observation, collation of data and its discussion, there was a considerable decrease in accidents. The participation of children in health education activities can range from playing the role of "sanitarians", and keeping a watch on personal hygiene of children, to the planning of physical training loads by young sportsmen and group discussions of psycho-social aspects of their health.

The above ideas and others discussed in Athens represent a "positive" approach to health. It is not a completely new approach. Its main elements have long been known. But it is only now that it has moved high on the agenda, now that health for all—and not for the chosen few—has become a universal slogan proclaimed through the Declaration of Alma-Ata. Disease, misery and hunger are still widely prevalent in today's world, and call for concerted measures against them. But is also time to start work to promote the health of those who will live and work in the 21st century: the children of today.[9]

The above-mentioned needs of children can be met only if teachers provide the children education about healthy life at home as well as in school. That is why teachers are held in high esteem and is considered national builder.

RESPONSIBILITIES OF SCHOOL TEACHERS IN THE SCHOOL HEALTH PROGRAMME

I. Provision of Health Instruction of School Children and Promotion of Healthful Practices among them

1. Serve as a health counsesllor for the school children.

Chart 5.1

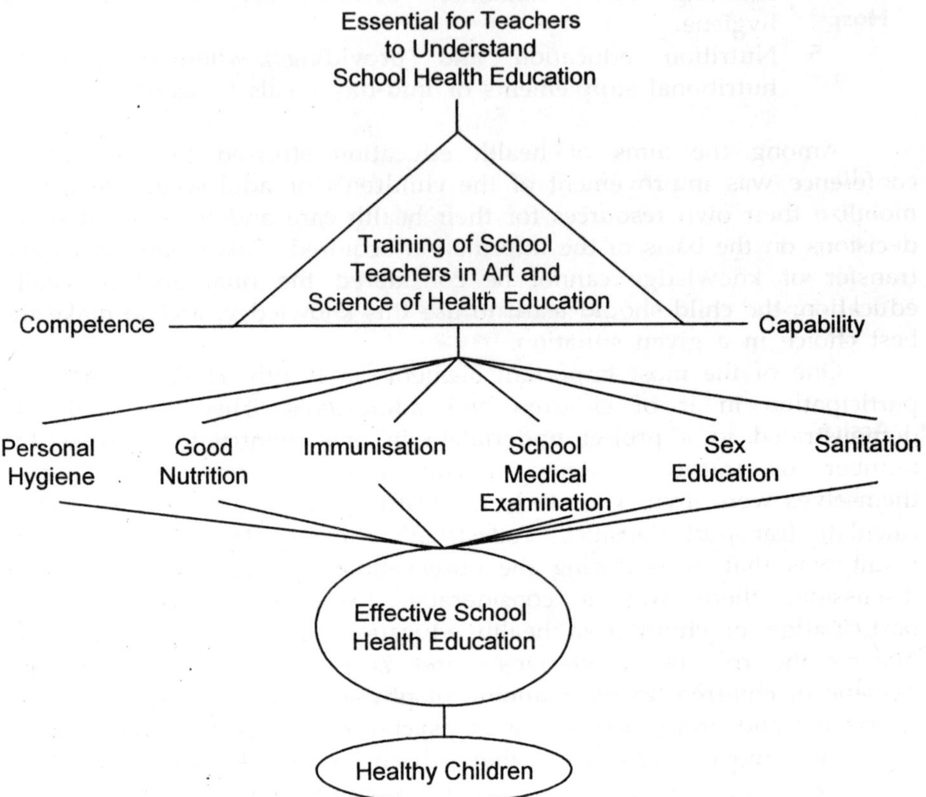

2. Identify the activities and situations that may jeopardize the health or safety of the school children and take the necessary steps to correct or improve the situation.
3. Observe the health practices of school children as regards personal hygiene, habits and posture, and encourage them to develop good health practices.
4. Encourage the students to help in maintaining a clean and safe school environment.
5. Supervise food sanitation practices when food is prepared, procured, stored or served in the school and encourage children to develop healthful food habits.
6. Plan for health educational activities in the school based on the specific health needs, interests and practices of the students.
7. Involve the students in organizing health campaigns and health projects in the school and in the community.
8. Plan with parents to develop a common health practice code to be followed both at school and in the home.

II. Detection of Deviations from Normal Health, Provision of First-aid in Accidents, and Referral of Children to the Medial Officer, PHC/ Hospital

9. Observe students for defects and deviations from normal health and refer them for examination and treatment to the PHC.
10. Observe students for signs and symptoms of communicable diseases, arrange for their leave from school and inform the Health Worker/Health Assistant/MO PHC of the nearest Sub-centre/PHC.
11. Give simple treatment for minor ailments.
12. Provide first-aid in the case of accidents and arrange for transfer of those in need of special care to the PHC/hospital.

III. Assistance in Health Check-up and Immunization of School Children

13. Prepare the list of new entrants for health check-up and for immunization.
14. Prepare the students for medical examination and immunization and inform the parents about the programme.
15. Take the height, weight, and chest measurement of the children.
16. Encourage the parents to ensure that any defects detected in their children are corrected and that their children are given regular and complete treatment for any disease detected in them.
17. Coordinate with parents for referral and follow-up of cases in whom defects or deviations from health are detected.
18. Arrange parent-teacher meetings at regular intervals to discuss educational and health problems of children and measures to be taken to solve these problems.
19. Assist in the rehabilitation of students who have recovered from illness or defects.

IV. Maintenance of Health Records of School Children

20. Complete the relevant portions of the individual Student's Health Record.
21. Make entries about the treatment for minor ailments provided to them in the school.
22. When a student is referred to the PHC/hospital, fill in the referral on the Student's Health Record card, which should be returned to you after treatment.

Let us discuss the role of teachers under the following points:

1. Personal Hygiene

Personal hygiene is the most important. Positive habits developed in early years of life remain for the whole life.

Teach children the following:

(i) Go to bed early and rise early.
(ii) Sleep in a lean, quite, well-ventilated room.
(iii) Use a light covering in summer and a blanket or quilt in winter.
(iv) If necessary use a mosquito net or apply a mosquito repellant on the body before sleeping.
(v) Do not sleep in a closed room in which there is a charcoal fire or sigree burning.
(vi) Sleep in a separate bed.
(vii) Wear clean loose garments to sleep in.
(viii) Walk in the morning air, roll up the bedding neatly or make up the bed.
(ix) Put the bedding in the sun from time to time.
(x) Change and wash the bed linen frequently.
(xi) Take regular exercise.
(xii) Take active part in physical training and outdoor games in your school.
(xiii) Always keep your back straight when you sit, stand or walk. A boy or girl who has a good posture looks much more attractive than one who stoops or walks with a slouch.
(xiv) Good posture helps the different parts of your body to function normally. This helps to keep you healthy.[10]

2. Good Nutrition Education

Poor nutritional status of children reflects poor development potential and prospect. Nutrition plays an important role in national development. People with malnutrition contribute little to national progress and become a big burden. Malnourished children who grow into adulthood have poor stamina, poor mental and psychomotor competencies. Chronic malnutrition in the early years of life causes not only stunt in growth of children but leaves permanent mental and physical scars which hinder the process of brain development to its optimum, affect their intelligence and make them unable to attain their full intellectual potential. So, it is very imperative to assess the nutritional status of school-going children who are the future citizens of the country. Teply (1979) has stated that over 15 million children die each year in developing countries and in over half of these deaths; malnutrition is either a direct or an associated cause (pp. 3-5). India is one of the children and where more than 1/3 of all children born alive die from malnutrition and disease before they reach the age of five and those who survive, a major segment suffers from several nutritional maladies. Orissa being one of the poorest states of India requires top priority in the assessment of nutritional status of school-going children.

Health is wealth. A healthy person has sound mind. "Health is a dynamic balance between individual, the group and the environment. Health reflects harmonious development of the person on all levels; biological, psychological and social. It depends on the way in which each individual adjusts to a constantly changing environment" (Ghorai, 1987, p. 212).

There are evidences indicating severe malnutrition experienced in the initial phase of life of a growing child-affecting not only expression of a genetic potential for physical growth and development but also context, the school children need special care and attention from nutritional point of view. Adequate, good and balanced nutrition is one of the most influential factors for the development of physical fitness, good health status and sound mind. There are numerous studies in the past in developing countries indicating the close relationship between malnutrition and subsequent impaired intellectual development and school performance (Winick, 1970, p. 1413; Latham and Cobos, 1971, p. 1307; Hertzig *et. al.*, 1972, p. 814; El-Wakeil *et. al.*, 1980a; Karla *et. al.*, 1980, p. 109 and Zaki *et. al.*, 1985).[11]

Donn (1983) said that, according to M.S. Rose, an outstanding nutritionist, "Nutrition deals with the scientific laws governing the requirements of human being for maintenance, growth, activities, reproduction and lactation", he also said that, according to another well known nutritionist E.N. Todhunter, "Nutrition deals with all that makes a man a healthy, functioning creative human being through a well chosen diet." (p. 4)

Robinson (1966, p. 206) has defined nutrition as "The science of foods, the nutrients and other substances therein; their action, interaction and balance in relationship to health and diseases; the processes by which the organism ingests, digests, absorbs, transports utilizes, nutrients and disposes of their end products. In addition, nutrition must be concerned with social, economic, cultural, and psychological implication of food and eating."[12]

Growth is the increase in the size and weight of the body and of its various parts, while development is the progress in the functioning of the body and its various parts.

From the time of birth until about the age of 17 to 18 years, a child is constantly growing and developing, both physically as well as mentally. The rate of growth varies at different ages. In the infant and very young child growth is rapid. By about 5 to 6 years the rate of growth slows down until the child reaches 9 or 10 years. At this age, there is again a spurt in growth, which continues through adolescence—the transition period between childhood and adulthood. Usually by about 17 to 18 years, the adolescent reaches his or her full height and does not grow any taller.

The rate of growth is also different between boys and girls. In the first 5 or 6 years of life, boys and girls of the same age are about the same height. After this age, boys tend to be slightly taller than girls. Between 10 and 13 years, girls grow much faster than boys and are usually taller and heavier than boys of the same age. By 14 to 15 years, however, boys catch up with the girls and overshoot them, so that by 17 or 18 years, boys are usually taller and heavier than girls.

From birth to maturity, a child develops its physical, mental and social abilities. The infant goes through the stages of holding up its head, turning on its tummy, grasping things, sitting, crawling, standing and walking. The child learns to hop, jump and run, and to use his hands to build with bricks, mould clay or use a needle and thread. So also, the child's mental capacity, understanding, judgment and power of reasoning increase, as he grows older. He develops from an individualistic, self-centre little creature, whose main needs are food and sleep, into a social being who loves and wishes to be loved by his family and friends, who is able to adjust to those around him, to control his feelings, and to fit himself for taking his place as a member of the world in which he lives.

The different body organs grow and reach full development at different rates. For instance, the eyes and brain stop growing in size by the age of ten; the permanent teeth usually appear by the age of 14, except for the third molars or 'wisdom teeth' which erupt between 18 and 25 years; the genital organs grow very little until the age of puberty and rapidly thereafter until adulthood is reached.

It is important to remember, however, that there are wide variations among individuals in growth and development. In the same age group, some children will be tall, others short, and some will be fatter than others; some will be stronger, or can run faster, or are more skilled in games which require good muscular coordination; others may be more quick to understand, to remember facts, to solve mathematical problems; and some children will be more talented than others in singing, dancing, or painting.

Individual growth and development depend on a number of factors. Most important among these are hereditary tendencies, nutrition, and the occurrence of illness or injury. At present we cannot do much to change our genes, which are responsible for our hereditary tendencies. However, we can take steps to avoid certain illnesses and injuries by taking the necessary immunizations and safety measures. So also, by taking the right kind of food in the right quantities, we can:

- ensure normal growth; and
- avoid disease caused by deficiency of certain food factors.[13]

Breast milk is the perfect food for babies. It is nature's way of ensuring a sound healthy start to life, and it meets all the nutritional needs of the baby, safely and adequately. There is no better food.

It is unique because it also provides the baby with defences that protect against many of the illness in early infancy. Breast-feed babies are less likely to suffer from gastro-intestinal infections, respiratory infections, and other common diseases which are among the major causes of infant death.

The close contact of baby and mother while breast-feeding provides the warm, secure environment needed for the health and well-being of the baby, and for a happy relationship between mother and child.

Aside from these health advantages, breast milk also has other values. It requires no preparation and is always available at the right temperature. It avoids complicated sterilization of bottles, and saves the mother both time and money.[14]

In the words of Dr. Halfdan Mahler, WHO's Director-General, "poor malnourished parents produce malnourished children who in turn will become poor and malnourished parents". This vicious spiral must be broken by improving child health and nutrition levels. This is a challenge to the governments of the world and to the international community during the International Year of the Child and in the years majority of the world's population is at stake.[15]

Nutritious Diet

Good nutrition means that the body is getting the food, which is, required. Malnutrition occurs when a person does not get the proper kind of food in the amounts that are needed for keeping healthy.

A nutritious and balanced diet consists of foods, which contain sufficient amounts of each of the following food substances or nutrients:

(i) Proteins

These help in repairing worn-out body cells, in the formation of blood, and in developing antibodies, which help the body to resist disease. They are present in milk and milk products, eggs, meat, fish, dals, pulses and nuts.

(ii) Carbohydrates and Fats

These provide the body with energy and fuel to carry out its various activities. Without enough energy there cannot be good growth, because when the daily diet is deficient in carbohydrates and fats, the body will use up proteins for supplying energy instead of for repair of body tissues and growth. Fats are also needed for the proper utilization of vitamin D by the body. Carbohydrates are present in cereals, e.g. rice or wheat, sugar, gur (jaggery), potato, banana and chikku, while fats are present in oil, ghee and butter.

(iii) Vitamins

These are protective substances, which are found in small quantities in several kinds of foods. There are different kinds of vitamins.

Some are needed for good vision and healthy eyes (Vitamin A); others for blood formation, for keeping the skin healthy, and for proper development of the nervous system (Vitamin B); some are required for increasing resistance to infection and for early healing of wounds (Vitamin C); while others are needed for strong teeth and bones (Vitamin D). Since the body cannot itself produce vitamins, it is very important that they are supplied through the food we eat. Foods which are rich in vitamins are as follows:

Vitamin A

Vitamin A or retinal is essential for maintenance of normal external epithelium mucous membranes of mouth, eyes, respiratory tract and genitourinary tracts and it promotes normal body growth, particularly of bones and teeth, prevents night blindness and maintains normal vision. Vitamin A deficiency, which is very common in the world, occurs amongst the children. Its deficiency produces night blindness, blindness, Xerophthalmia, horny, dry and scaly skin, damaged mucous membranes leading to easy invasion of infection, diseased gums and deformed teeth and stunted growth. But when taken in excess produces some toxic effects.

Green leafy vegetables such as palak, methi or drumstick leaves; yellow fruits and vegetables like mango, papaya, carrot and pumpkin, eggs, liver, meat and curds.

Vitamin B

The family of B complex vitamin consists of eight vitamins. Although the function of all the Vitamin B complex family has similar in activity in the body still some of them have got specific function.

Thiamine (B-1) is essentially required for metabolism of carbohydrate, fat and protein and to release energy for growth, activity, body maintenance and repair of body tissues. It also maintains normal muscle tones especially on the digestive system and in the heart. It has got important role in producing a healthy nervous system and mental function. Deficiency of Vitamin B-1 (Thiamine) produces low appetite, constipation, irritability, fatigue, beriberi, nervous disturbances, cardiovascular disorders, oedema and muscle cramps.

Vitamin B_2 (Riboflavin) necessary for growth and reproduction and plays an important role in metabolism of carbohydrates, fats, lipids and proteins to release energy in the cells, hence this vitamin is essential for healthy body tissues, especially skin, eyes and CNS. It is more needed during pregnancy and lactation. Excess of this vitamin is encreched in urine and very limited quantity is retained in the muscle tissues, so regular supply of this vitamin in the diet is essential. When its deficiency occurs, especially in vegetarian persons it produces stunted growth, affects skin on the face, particularly around mouth and lips.

Niacin (Nicotine acid) plays an essential role in cellular metabolism of carbohydrate and is found in circulating blood, heart, brain, muscles, kidney and liver. The deficiency of niacin (nicotinic acid) produces pellagra with reddish skin rash, a sore mouth and tongue and intestinal disorders, dermatitis, mental disorder. Normally amino acid tryptophan is converted into niacin in the human body (60 mg. Tryptophan = 1 mg. of niacin).

Vitamin B-6 (Pyrodoxine) also plays an important role in metabolism of amino acids, fats and carbohydrates. The body can synthesize non-essential amino acids with the help of this vitamin and also it is needed to convert tryptophan to niacin. Its deficiency produces anaemia, muscular and nervous disorders.

Pantothanic acid acts as a component of coenzyme involved in the metabolism of carbohydrates, fats and amino acids. The deficiency of this vitamin causes Gopalan's syndrome wherein the person complaints of burning pain over soles of feet.

Biotin plays an important role in the metabolism of carbohydrate, fatty acids and amino acids. Its deficiency occurs when a person consumes large quantity of raw eggs daily since protein in egg while inactivates biotin.

Folic acid (Folacin) is required for normal growth and reproduction and to prevent one type of anaemia and is involved in celluar metabolism, particularly certain amino acids.

Vitamin B-12 is an important component of enzymes involved in metabolism of fat, carbohydrate and protein and is essential to prevent pernicious anaemia. It is necessary in less quantity for the growth of infants and children but in more quantities during pregnancy and lactation. Its deficiency causes pernicious anaemia with symptoms like sore tongue, weakness, loss of weight, anaemia, sensory and mental disorders.

Parboiled rice, hand pounded rice and unmilled rice whole wheat (atta) or dalia, millet (bajra); groundnuts, pulses and beams; milk and milk products, eggs, meat, liver and fish.

Vitamin C

Vitamin C (Ascorbic acid) prevents scurvy and is required in metabolism of amino acids and in the formation of folic acid. It helps absorption of iron from the intestine, maintains healthy blood vessels and helps in formation of tooth and bone. Its deficiency causes scurvy characterized by swollen painful joints, delayed would healing, spongy gums, loose teeth and haemorrhages, particularly near the bones, joints or under the skin.

Citrus fruit such as sour lime and orange, guava, amla and tomato; green leafy vegetable, cabbage, coriander.

Vitamin D

Vitamin D regulates the metabolism of calcium and phosphorous and helps in their absorption from the intestine, and promotes proper mineralization of bones and teeth. Its excess intake can produce toxic effects. Its deficiency can cause rickets in growing bones which become weak and fragile, malformed skeleton, bow legs, knock knees, enlarged bones about the joints and narrow distorted chests.

Exposure to sunlight is the cheapest way to get this vitamin; fish liver oils have a high content of vitamin D; butter, ghee, eggs and groundnut oil.

Vitamin E

Vitamin E otherwise known as tocopherol is essentially required in the body to protect Vitamin A, Vitamin C and unsaturated fatty acids from oxidation and to protect the cell structure. Deficiency of Vitamin E in diet may result in sterility, macrocytic anaemia, abnormal termination of pregnancy, muscular dystrophy, diabetes, coronary heart disease and skin disorders.

Vitamin K

Vitamin K by forming prothrombin in the liver helps in the coagulation of blood. This vitamin is known to be synthesized in the intestines out of the available nutrients by bacteria. Deficiency of Vitamin K produces defective blood coagulation and internal haemorrhages.[16]

(iv) Minerals

These are also protective substances, which are needed by the body for the formation of blood (iron), the development of strong teeth and bones (calcium and phosphorus), for blood clotting (calcium), and for normal growth and development (iodine).

There are many minerals known to have essential role to play in the formation of healthy human body. These minerals are present in human body in different quantity, some are in more quantity known to be macro-minerals and some are present in small quantity known as micro-minerals.

Macro-minerals

Calcium and phosphorous play a major role in the formation of bones, hence essential for growth of human body. Calcium is required for clotting of the blood and normal functioning of nerve tissues and is necessary for muscle construction.

Phosphorus is usually an accompaniment of calcium and both of them are required and stored in the body in equal proportion. Phosphorus increases the rigidity of bones and teeth. It plays an important role in cell metabolism and metabolism of carbohydrate, fat and protein. It is involved in normal growth and development of teeth and bone and in maintaining normal blood levels, metabolism of normal nerve tissues, muscle energy metabolism and is involved in many enzyme systems.

Magnesium is required in the body catalyses chemical reactions, particularly of enzyme system. It also regulates body temperature and is involved in constructions of nerves and muscles and synthesis of proteins. Deficiency of magnesium minerals causes dysfunction of neuromuscular system with tremor and convulsion and sometimes behavioural disturbances.

Potassium being an important component of lean body tissue is very essential for human body. It also influences the ability to the muscles to contract and to affect response of nervous tissues. Its deficiency causes muscular weakness, nervousness, mental confusion and cardiac irregularities. Its deficiency occurs usually whenever there is muscle breakdown due to starvation, protein deficiency or injury or inadequate consumption, prolonged diarrhoea, abnormal kidney function due to rental disease or diabetic complications.

Sodium is an essential macro-mineral required for normal functioning of the body. It is the principle element in the extra cellular fluid. It maintains acid base balance in the body fluids. Its deficiency occurs rarely in healthy individuals. When its deficiency occurs in the body acid-base balance in the body fluid is deranged and the person becomes dehydrated.

Chlorides are required for formation of hydrochloric acid of the gastric juice, which is essential for proper absorption of Vitamin B-12 and iron. It also maintains acid-base balance in fluids throughout the body.

Sulphur is present in all body tissues and is required essentially as a component of B-Complex Vitamin as Thaimine and Biotin and certain Amino acids like cystine, methionine and cystene. It maintains rigidity of nails, skin and hair in the body.

Micro-Minerals

Chromium is necessary to maintain normal glucose metabolism. Its deficiency is normally found in old age, pregnancy and PEM.

Cobalt is component of Vitamin B-12′ hence it is necessary in metabolism of Vitamin B-12 in the body.

Copper is very essential to prevent anaemia and for normal development of the bones, healthy CNS and formation of connective tissues. With copper deficiency in human brain there is cerebeller ataxia and tremor (Evered *et. al.*). In children with deficiency of copper genetically there is retinal dystrophy (Danks, 1980, pp. 209-25).

Fluorine as a component of human body present in bones and teeth. It prevents dental caries, so it is essential for growing children for development of teeth and bones.

Iodine is very essential in the metabolism of thyroid hormones and its deficiency causes simple or endemic goiter.

Iron being a constituent of haemoglobin, myoglobin, and number of enzymes plays an important role in transporting oxygen from the lungs. Iron is also a component of enzymes that are involved in cellular metabolism of glucose and fatty acids. Synthesis of haemoglobin of blood requires iron in the presence of copper and adequate amount of protein. In its deficiency anaemia results manifesting signs of pallor of skin and tissues, weakness, fatigue, tiredness, headache and softness of breath, lack of concentration and loss of memory. Hence, iron plays an important role in the growth, maintenance and repair of the tissues of the body.

Manganese is essentially required for normal tendon and bone structure, reproduction and normal function of the CNS and plays a role in enzyme system in the body. Manganese deficiency in young animals results in defective otolith development in the untricle and saccule (Shradar, *et. al.*, 1967, pp. 443-60). There is ataxia, alongwith dysequilibrium, head retraction and tremor (Everson *et. al.*, 1959, pp. 49-57; Hurley *et. al.*, 1958, pp. 309-20).

Molybdenum is essentially required in the enzyme action of Xanthin oxidase and adlerhyde exidase.

Selenium is considered to be an essential micro-mineral due to the fact that it appears to be related to Vitamin E in its function and acts as an antioxidant to preserve the cellular membrane.

Pups born of nickel deficient rats are reported to be less active than controls (Pollitt *et. al.*, eds., 1982, p. 16).

Zinc deficiency in rats leads to impaired learning ability. In human being there is a defective taste acuity and poor appetite due to its deficiency (Hambidge, 1974, pp. 171-82). As observed in Iranian and Egyptian males, this deficiency causes retraction in growth and hypogonadism with delayed or absent sexual maturation (Pollitt *et. al.*, eds., 1982, p. 16).[17]

Foods, which are rich in minerals, are as follows:

Iron

Green leafy vegetables, pudina, radish, kerela, bajra and ragi, gur, meat, liver and eggs.

Calcium

Milk, cheese, dried fish, ragi, green leafy vegetables.

Iodine

Fish, spinach, brinjal, garlic, ginger, vegetables grown near the sea, seaweed.

In order to remain healthy, each person should eat at least one food from each of the five food groups every day. These five food groups are as follows:

Group A

Foods such as rice, wheat, maize, ragi, jowar, bajra, potato, yam, sugar, gur.

Group B

Foods such as milk, panir, curds, buttermilk, groundnut, dal, gram, beans, eggs, meat, fish.

Group D

Vegetables such as carrot, pumpkin, leaves of spinach (palak), mustard (sarson ka sag), cabbage, drumstick, radish, fenugreek (methi), amaranth (chaulai), peas, bhindi, brinjal, cauliflower, tomato, capsicum, karela.

Group E

Foods such as oil, ghee, butter.[18]

Vitamin A Deficiency

Lack of vitamin A in the diet causes changes in the eye, which can result in partial or total blindness. This is a severe health problem in our country, especially among children between 1 to 5 years of age. The deficiency often occurs in malnourished children during or immediately following an illness such as measles, pneumonia, whooping cough, diarrhoea or malaria.[19]

Healthy Dietary Habits

Another important goal of health education is to foster healthy dietary habits in parents and in children. In many countries health education helped to combat malnutrition by spreading awareness about local foods and their proper use. It must now be applied to another aspect of malnutrition: overfeeding and obesity, a major public health problem in some countries. The answer is proper nutrition education, which should be individualized to take into account constitutional and behavioural factors, such as level of physical activity and heredity.

Parents should also be educated in the correct handling and feeding of children. Permissiveness at the table may lead to overeating, and forced feeding to loss of appetite. New approaches to parent education in this respect are badly needed since over-feeding—as well as over protection in general—has deep instinctive roots.[20]

Tuberculosis

TB is caused due to a bacterial infection that most commonly affects the lungs. In childhood it causes symptoms such as fever, irritability, poor appetite, weight loss, fatigue, etc. If felt untreated, it can cause death. Immunization is with BCG vaccine, which should be administered at birth or soon after.

Polio

Polio is an acute viral infection caused by polio virus, which mainly affects children under five. The initial symptoms include fever, fatigue, headaches, vomiting, constipation, (or less commonly, diarrhoea), stiffness in the neck, and pain in the limbs. In a few children, the disease causes paralysis, which is almost permanent, and in the more severe cases, polio can lead to death by asphyxiation. Though there is no cure, it can be easily prevented by a simple oral vaccine.

3. SCHOOL MEDICAL EXAMINATION

The school medical examination is a convenient time for instruction about the dangers of communicable diseases and the efficacy of vaccines; the traffic accident that happens nearby can illustrate a lesson on road safety; the athletics contest or football match which excites the local community will serve as a model to demonstrate good health and the value of physical education to community development.

The school medical examination is a very important occasion in the health activities of the school. It serves as an opportunity for the following:

(i) Each child is given a thorough health check-up by the Medical Officer. Any defects or deformities are detected, advice and treatment are given, and if necessary the child is referred for further investigations and treatment.

(ii) The teacher brings to the notice of the doctor and health staff any observations, which he/she has made about the child's health. The teacher is able to check whether his/her observations were correct.

(iii) The school medical examination can also serve as an opportunity for continuing education of the teacher by the doctor or health staff as regards procedures for detecting defects or deviations from normal in children.

There are many preparations to be carried out before this event. If these are carried out systematically, the school medical examination can proceed in an orderly and efficient way, with no loss of time and with no fear or anxiety among the students.

The following are some of the things teachers should do to prepare for the school medical examination.

1. Fix the date(s) of the school medical check-up well in advance according to the convenience of the Medical Officer and health staff as well as of the school. As far as possible the school medical examination should take place at about the same time each year. If many students are to be examined the medical check-up may continue for more than one day in consultation with the MO PHC.

One Week Prior to the Medical Examination and Immunization Programme

2. Inform the parents or guardians of the date on which their children are to be examined. This can be done personally or by sending a message with the children. You can also take the help of the local Health Guide for this purpose. Request the parent/guardian to ensure that the child attends school on that day.
3. Go through the Student's Health Records and see that the entries are complete. If any information is missing, try to obtain it, if necessary by meeting the parent or guardian. Fill in your observations on each student.
4. Meet with the Health Worker and find out what will be required by the health staff on the day of the medical examination.
5. Inform the Health Worker about the number of children in each class who are to be examined. Also inform the Health Worker of the number of children in each class who are to be given diphtheria and tetanus (DT), tetanus toxoid (TT), and typhoid vaccination, so that the worker can arrange for the supply of vaccines and for the preparation of the necessary equipment.
6. Prepare the children for the medical examination and immunization programme. Tell them what will be done during the examination and reassure them that there is nothing to be afraid of. Tell them that they will be given vaccinations to protect them from certain diseases. Tell them they can help the doctor and his team to carry out the programme if they cooperate by doing what they are asked to do. Teach them to greet the doctor and the health team when they go in for examination and to thank them when the examination is over.

On the Day before the Medical Examination

7. Select and arrange the room where the medical examination and immunization programme is to be carried out and get it swept, swabbed and dusted.
8. Arrange one end of the room for the doctor and health staff. This part of the room should be well-ventilated and well-lit. Arrange if possible two tables, one for the doctor and one for the other health staff, and three or four chairs. Screen off this part of the room by a curtain or sheet hung across the room.
9. Carry out the following screening tests on the children class-wise on the day prior to the medical examination and enter the results in their health cards—

(i) Measurement of height;
(ii. Measurement of weight;
(iii. Chest measurements: during inspiration
during expiration

On the day of the Examination and Immunization Programme

10. Ensure that the room where the medical examination and immunization are to be carried out is in order.[21]

Maintenance of Health Records

As a part of teacher's responsibilities regarding the school health programme, teachers will be required to maintain a health card of each child in their school. In maintaining the Student's Health Record, teacher should keep the following points in mind:

(i) Keep all the health cards up to date.
(ii) Ensure that the entries are accurate. Incorrect entries are misleading and are worse than no entries at all.
(iii) Make the entries neat and legible.
(iv) Store the Student's Health Records in order, i.e., class-wise, either according to the students' roll numbers, or according to the students' surnames in alphabetical order. In this way, any student's record can be easily and quickly found when it is wanted.
(v) Keep the Student's Health Records in a safe place. If the student moves to another school, his/her record should be transferred with the leaving certificate to that school. When the student finishes his/her school education, the health record should be handed over to the student's parent or guardian.
(vi) After teachers have finished making entries in the Student's Health Record, always return it to its proper place to avoid its being misplaced.
(vii) Always treat records as confidential. Do not leave them lying about for any inquisitive person to pick up and read. Do not allow any unauthorized person to have access to them.[22]

4. SANITATION

The outreach of the School Sanitation is going to increase in the future. Schools have been recognized as a tremendous resource that can be harnessed. The education system, with its strength of over 7 lakh primary and upper primary schools, over 30 lakh teachers and more than 100 million students, offers a readymade infrastructure that can be mobilized to influence children, parents, and the community. Moreover, the schools can function as demonstration centers and the teachers as social animators for promoting hygiene practices and generating a demand for sanitation facilities among the communities.

The Rajiv Gandhi National Drinking Water Mission, in the Guidelines of the Restructured Centrally Sponsored Rural Sanitation Programme, has changed policy to include coverage of rural schools with sanitation facilities. It envisages an improved quality of life in rural areas through coverage of sanitation in rural schools. It adopts the strategy of introducing rural school sanitation as a major component of the programme. It recognizes school sanitation as an entry point for wider acceptance of sanitation by the rural allocations for hardware and support services for school sanitation have been made under the Total Sanitation Campaign, which hopes to achieve 50% coverage of the rural population by the end of the 9th Plan.[23]

Objectives

Awareness Creation in School Children about the Concept and Components of Sanitation

This is carried out by taking up each of the components as the thought for the day; organizing inter-school competitions at block, district level, etc.

Inculcation of Hygiene Practices in School Children

By involving teachers in monitoring hygiene practices such as hand washing with soap and water; assigning activities related to water handling, disposal of waste waster, garbage disposal and so on to the students of higher classes, etc.

Involvement of Parents and the Community

Establishing a Parent Teacher Association in every school, motivating parents and the community to contribute voluntarily towards the water and sanitation facilities in the schools, etc.

Improving Access to Water and Sanitation Facilities within Schools

Through installation of hand pumps within schools; extending piped water supply to schools construction of storage tanks to store water for flushing, etc.

Cost Sharing for Better Ownership of the Sanitation Facilities Provided

Through contributions from the school funds, PTA funds and Panchayats.

Development of Communication Materials

Involvement of Panchayat Members

By providing incentives to most active Panchayats.

Involvement of Students and Teachers in the Operation and Maintenance of the Sanitation Facilities

Training-orientation of Functionaries Involved in the Project at All Levels

core trainers, NGOs, District and block level functionaries as well as school teachers, Anganwadi workers and other village level functionaries.

NGO's Involvement

In creating awareness at the school and village levels through community contract drives and exhibitions.[24]

5. SEX EDUCATION

A fairly new and important activity is sex education of children and adolescents. Its importance is underlined by such factors as accelerated growth and development, earlier start of puberty, modification of family structure, the breaking of centuries-old inhibitions about sexuality and the weakening of the double moral standard for men and women. Traditionally, sex education centres on sexual hygiene and prevention of sexually transmitted diseases. Its scope has now been widened to include such elements as development of the capacity to enjoy and control sexual and reproductive behaviour in accordance with social and individual ethics, promotion of happy sexual life free from fear, shame, guilt, false beliefs and other inhibiting factors. Since sexual awakening of adolescents often comes about earlier than emotional maturity, an important goals of sex education should be to help adolescents to understand sexuality and the noble ideals of humane love.

As recently shown by Dr. A. Isaev of WHO's European Regional Office, sex education in schools in various countries of Europe is in varying stages of development, being a compulsory subject in some and completely absent in others. The WHO/EURO Conference on "Child and Adolescent in Society", held in Athens last September, considered sex education an important activity to be carried out both by the family and the school. Emphasis was placed on starting sex education by the family as early as possible, and on the role of the school-teacher.[25]

6. EDUCATION ABOUT IMMUNIZATION

Leo A. Kaprio in his articles, "An element of primary care" states that Immunization and the impetus of the Expand Programme should lead to the strengthening of health services as a whole; EPI ought to be one building block in a permanent primary health care structure.

Programmes such as WHO's Expanded Programme on Immunization (EPI) are only one tool among many, all of which are necessary to improve the health of children and of the community in which they live.

Without proper nutrition, clean water, shelter, basic sanitation and protection against many other diseases (like diarrhoea and acute respiratory diseases) as well as first-aid and treatment of common ailments, even the immunized infants might easily die soon and the community concerned might remain socially as desperate as it was before an immunization programme[26].

Diphtheria

Diphtheria is a serious and highly contagious bacterial infection. The child may have mild fever, breathing difficulty, sore throat and cough. Without treatment this disease can cause pneumonia and even heart failure. Immunization is with DPT vaccine.

Pertussis (Whooping Cough)

Pertussis is a bacterial infection, which clogs the airways with mucus. This is cough with a distinctive "whoop" sound as the child tries to breathe. The dry cough sounds like a "dog barking". It may be accompanied with common cold symptoms and vomiting. The main dangers at young age are exhaustion and pneumonia. Fatality from this disease is very high. DPT vaccine proves effective in the prevention of this disease.

Tetanus

Tetanus is an infection caused by bacteria present in soil, dust, cow dung and alimentary canal of various animals. Infection is likely to occur in the newborn when the mother gives birth in unhygienic conditions or the knife used for cutting the umbilical cord is not sterilized. In older children, common causes are injury, a deep dirty wound or ear infection. The child has difficulty swallowing followed by clenching of jaws, convulsions, and this may lead to death. Tetanus is a major killer of the newborn. DPT vaccine proves effective, if taken in earlier stages.

Measles

Measles is the most dangerous of all childhood disease and can cause complications like diarrhoea, deafness, blindness, malnutrition, chronic lung infection, and even brain damage. A child if not given measles vaccine will definitely contract measles. The disease can be prevented by giving measles vaccine when the child is 9 months old along with first dose of vitamin A drops.

Others

- Hepatitis B, though not a childhood disease, can be prevented by immunizing the child with Hepatitis B vaccine.
- Vitamin A deficiency causes nutritional blindness in children. Vitamin A dose not only prevents nutritional blindness, but

also helps the child in rapid recovery from measles, diarrhoea, pneumonia and contributes immensely to lowering mortality in children.

Let us mention the:

Six Killers of Children

1. Measles

Virtually every unprotected child will contract the disease, which may be fatal for those already weekend by malnutrition or chronic diarrhoea. Complications occur in about 30 per cent of cases, and include ear infections, diarrhoea, blindness, and encephalitis.

2. Diphtheria

It causes membranes to develop in the throat, and death may follow from asphyxiation. Diphtheria bacilli in the throat also produce a toxin, which, in the blood stream, may attack the heart or nervous system with fatal results.

3. Pertussis

The disease got its common name from the "whoop" children make while desperately trying to inhale after coughing spasms. Complications include: malnutrition (due to excessive vomiting after coughing), permanent brain damage and pneumonia.

4. Tetanus

It is caused by unsterile methods of cutting the umbilical cord or by applying germladen substances to the stump. Immunization of the mother will give protection to the baby.

5. Poliomyelitis

It is the major cause of lameness in the Third World, where nearly all children get polio before they are three. Although only one out of every 200 infected children develops typical symptoms, among those with recognized polio, one in ten will die.

6. Tuberculosis

This is particularly lethal for infants. In the lungs, TB can trigger a rapidly fatal pneumonia or a slow wasting disease. In the bone, it can lead to severe deformities. When TB occurs in the brain, the results are usually fatal.[27]

Planet Earth can no longer accept that, in the age of modern technology, children should still die by the millions from diseases, which can be prevented, by available vaccines.

WHO's Expanded Programme on Immunization (EPI)—first

established in 1974 has as its goal to protect all the world's children against six killer diseases by the year 1990. Those diseases are: Measles, Poliomyelities, Diphtheria, Pertussis (whooping cough), neonatal tetanus and tuberculosis.

A sense of urgency pervades the Programme. Acceleration requires intensive efforts of social mobilization to make available the necessary health services, and to inform communities and individuals about the protection that vaccines confer. Health staff will need more training to ensure that they provide reliable services with minimal waiting time, and that they know how best to motivate mothers to return with their babies to the clinic or health centre until the immunization series is completed.

Immunization truly represents a chance for every child. But offering children the chance of a lifetime requires more than publicity alone. The real challenge is to change social norms so that it becomes unacceptable for any child to be denied the benefits of immunization[28].

A Pact of Partnership

Our children are the future of our country. The shape of tomorrow depends entirely on what we give to our children today. The best gift that we can bestow upon a child is the gift of health. A healthy child today means a stronger and more prosperous India tomorrow.

In our country, despite progress in several areas and a well-organized health structure, every year millions of children fall victim to devastating childhood diseases that either prove fatal or end with complications that last lifetime.

Some of these diseases are:

Tuberculosis, poliomyelitis, diphtheria, pertussis (whooping cough), tetanus, measles, with complications like diarrhoea, pneumonia and blindness. However, these six childhood diseases have one important fact in common.

They are all vaccine preventable diseases.

They can all be prevented by immunization.

In addition, hepatitis B, which leads to primary cancer of the liver, can also be prevented by vaccination.

Immunization: The Simple Intervention

Immunization is a way of protecting the human body against infectious diseases through vaccination. This process starts even while the child is a foetus, by giving certain vaccinations to the pregnant mother. A great number of human lives can be saved by these simple yet effective measures.

The Immunization Programme

The Government of India launched the Expanded Prorgramme on Immunization (EPI) in 1976-77 and an accelerated version of the same known as the Universal Immunization Programme (UIP) in 1985 with the aim of protecting pregnant women, infants and young children from the debilitating effects of diseases such as tuberculosis, poliomyelitis, diphtheria, pertussis (whooping cough), tetanus and measles by one year of age.

As a result of UIP, a lot of infrastructure improvements and build up, especially in establishing cold chain systems, enhancing indigenous vaccine production capacity and monitoring inputs were added. Subsequently, the introduction of the Child Survival and Safe Motherhood (CSSM) Programme in 1992-93, and then the Reproductive and Child Health (RCH) programme in 1996-97, have retained the UIP as a crucial link between child survival, reduction in infant and child mortality and population stabilization. As part of polio eradication efforts, the Government of India launched National Immunization Days known as Pulse Polio Immunization Programme in 1995-96 with the objective of immunizing children of age 0-5 years in a pulse mode. In 2002-03, the Government of India introduced hepatitis B vaccination in 15 cities and during 2003-04 it was introduced in 32 more districts as a part of routine immunization schedule with the aim of universalizing hepatitis B vaccination by end of the Tenth Five Year Plan in 2007.

Despite yielding good results in terms of decline in vaccine-preventable diseases, infant mortality rate (IMR) and under-5 mortality rate (U5MR), full immunization coverage levels remain around 50% countrywide (Coverage Evaluation Survey, 2000-01). Interstate disparities are glaring, with majority of Hindi-speaking states being able to immunize only about a quarter to newborns every year. The reasons for this low coverage are inadequate access to immunization services, lack of knowledge regarding the importance of immunization, and unfounded myths and beliefs amongst the target population.

The important factors that can contribute to the success of any programme, apart from making services available at community level, are demand creation through behaviour change communication and social mobilization. Informed public and individuals are hence a prerequisite to the realization and sustenance of the aims of the UIP.

Tools and Strategies

To make the immunization programme a success, several tools and strategies have been developed.

Cold Chain: A Vital Link

Vaccines have a specific life period and have to be utilized before their expiry date. This requires special storage and transportation arrangements to retain their efficiency.

Cold chain is a system of transporting and storing vaccines at the recommended temperature from the manufacturer to the point of use. All vaccines can be stored at temperatures between +2°C. However, for long-term storage, OPV and measles vaccine can be stored at sub-zero temperature in deep freezers.

Cold Chain

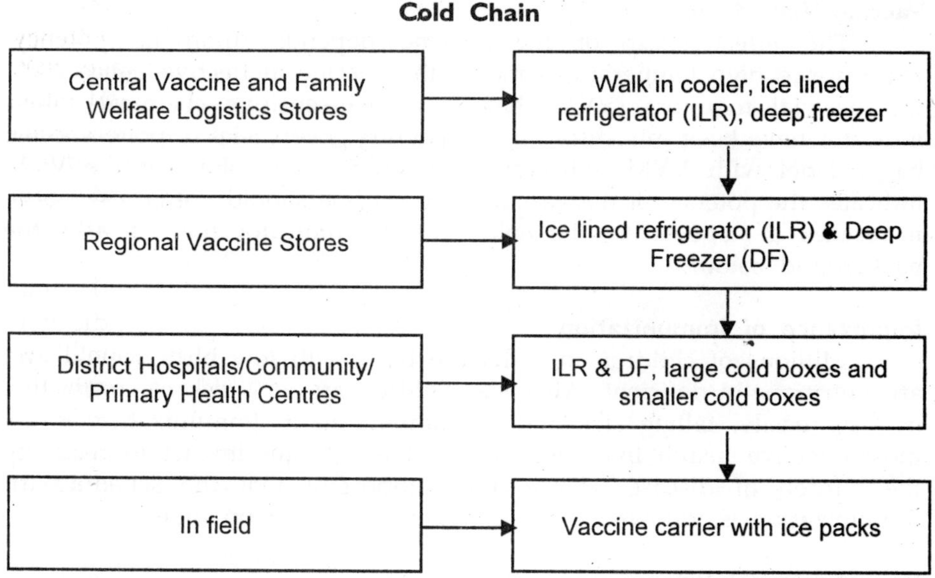

From manufacture down to the filed where the vaccines are administered, various types of equipment are used as part of the cold chain.

The cold chain is a vitally important link in the immunization process and the government has taken steps to strengthen the cold chain system.

Injection Safety

This is one of the most important aspects of the immunization programme. While immunizing the child, care should be taken that vaccination does not become a means for spread of diseases by infection through syringes and needles.

For sterilizing needles and syringes, autoclaves are available at all Primary Health Centres (PHCs), Community Health Centres (CHCs), district hospitals, etc. At the sub-health centres, pressure cookers have been provided along with appropriate drums for sterilizing needles and syringes.

Under the hepatitis B programme, auto-disable syringes (ADS) have been provided in 15 cities during 2002-03. These syringes get locked after single use, thus preventing the possibility of re-use. These will be introduced in routine immunization by the end of the Tenth Five Year Plan.

Training provided to the health staff involved in administration of vaccines and vitamin A.

Vaccine Vial Monitor

The effectiveness of the vaccine depends upon its potency. Exposure to high temperatures makes the vaccine ineffective. Since 2000, vaccine vial monitors (VVM) having a heat-sensitive chemical colour indicator have been introduced in the country. Every vial of polio vaccine has a label with VVM indicator stuck on it. The colour of the VVM indicates the potency of the vaccine. The vaccine should not be used once it reaches a stage when the colour of the indicator merges with the background colour.

Importance of Immunization

Millions of children in India are born with low birth weight and are nutritionally deficient. All these children are at a risk of contracting diseases easily, falling sick and succumbing to it. Immunization is the most effective health intervention, and has a major impact in reducing the burden of disease. Hence, it is important that the schedule for immunization is followed carefully, completely and on time.

Immunization Card

It is the most important way for the mother to know whether her baby has received all the vaccinations. It also helps the health worker to keep track of the immunization status of the pregnant women and infants in her area.

Immunization Schedule

A schedule of vaccinations has been drawn up, explaining which vaccine is most beneficial to the pregnant women and child and at specified ages.

Recommended Immunization Schedule

For the Pregnant Woman	
Early in pregnancy	TT-1 (injection) or TT booster (injection)
One month after TT-1 (injection)	TT-2 (injection)
Iron tablets	Take one tablet a day for 3 months. Take at least 100 tablets.
For the Infant and the Child	
At birth	BCG (injection) Polio (zero dose)
At 1-1/2 months (6 weeks)	BCG (injection) DPT-1 (injection) OPV-1 (dose) Hepatitis B-1 (injection)
At 2-1/2 months (10 weeks)	DPT-2 (injection) OPV-2 (dose) Hepatitis B-2 (injection)

At 3-1/2 months (14 weeks)	DPT-3 (injection) OPV-3 (dose) Hepatitis B-3 (injection)
At 9 months (after 270 days)	Measles (injection) Vitamin A-1st dose
At 16-24 months	DPT booster (injection) OPV booster (dose) Vitamin A-2nd and 3rd dose

Immunization Sessions

Immunization sessions are held on certain fixed days in every village health institution and urban wards in the country. All parents and partners should have information of where and when can they get immunization service in their locality—whether it is a village or a town.

The Pact of Partnership: Our Role as a Partner in the Immunization Process

The immunization programme consists not only of the actual process at the field level but also of a series of activities that have to be undertaken prior to it. This is where our role as a partner in the immunization process becomes important. Every time we facilitate the immunization of even one child, we are paving the way of that child to be healthy and free from diseases. There are several ways in which your help as a partner will be welcomed and appreciated—

- Ensure that all vaccines are available at all the immunization sessions, and at the health centres. As per the instructions of the Government of India, even if there is a single child to be vaccinated, a fresh vial should be opened and no child should remain immunized. All vaccines are available free at health centres.
- Help in maintaining and monitoring cold chain system, to ensure that only good quality and potent vaccines are given to the mother and child. In case of electricity failure you can help in getting ice for preserving the vaccine, and arrange for repairing the cold chain in case of breakdown.
- Assist in arranging the immunization session on fixed days, in giving wide publicity to them, and identifying and enumerating children and pregnant women in collaboration with anganwadi workers (AWWs) and auxiliary nurse midwives (ANMs).
- Ensure that each mother and child is provided with the immunization card. You can help the ANM in filling the card correctly. You can also remind the mother about the next vaccination and the date on which she should come for the next dose. Identify children who are due for booster doses

and inform the parents about the next immunization session.

- Cooperate with private practitioners and non-governmental organizations in making the immunization process smoother. You as a partner can help in arranging for transport to take mother to the site where the immunization is being organized.
- Monitor the progress of immunization in a geographical area by being present at the immunization session and follow up by motivating the dropouts to take all vaccinations.
- Monitor the quality of counselling provided by ANM to the mothers. Provide correct information about the small papule that will form at the site of BCG vaccine and pain at the site of the DPT injection. Assure them that it is normal and indicates that the vaccine is effective and protecting the child. In case of fever, advise them to give the child one-fourth of 500 mg tablet of paracetamol (i.e. 125 mg).
- Arrange for wide publicity to ensure community participation. For this purpose publicity material published by Government of India and state governments such as posters, booklets, flyers, videos, films audio cassettes, etc. are obtainable from the state government family welfare offices, chief medical officer's office at the district level and the block extension educator at the block level and non-governmental organizations.
- Educate and dispel myths and superstitions by giving correct scientific knowledge and information in an easy to understand manner to the mothers and family.
- Compile and disseminate the information about the names and addresses of ANM, AWW and local health centres, where information and services on immunization are available.

If all of us act as responsible partners in this pact of partnership, we can ensure that the immunization activities are a success. We can save great many human lives and build a better and healthier future for our country.

Organization of Health Education Activities in Schools

Principles for health education in the school to be meaningful:

(i) It must be closely related to the children's day-to-day activities, both at school as well as at home and in the community.

(ii) It should be based on their interests and physical needs as regards adequate nutrition, healthful environment, rest and sleep, physical activity and protection from illness and injury.

(iii) So also, it should be related to their mental and emotional needs for attaining scholastic merit and for feeling that they are wanted, understood, accepted and respected by their teachers, companions, and family members.

(iv) It should not be taught as a separate subject, thus adding to the already heavy burden of teaching and learning, but it should form an integral part of existing curricular subjects, e.g. environmental studies and language, as well as the co-curricular activities such as games, PT and handwork.

(v) It should be imparted in an interesting and exciting manner, using a variety of methods and devices appropriate to the age and ability of the students.

(vi) It should be carried out in cooperation with the parents, community members, health staff, and other block level workers. In this way, the student will learn to recognize the relationship of health to other aspects of family life and community development.[29]

Intensive Health Education

Teachers' Involvement

Active involvement of teachers is very important as they are the pivot of the whole programme. Their involvement will be sought in the following areas:

(i) Intensive health education of the students using child-to-child or youth-to-child approach for developing self-health care.

(ii) Inculcation of healthy habits with a view to developing healthy lifestyles.

(iii) Observation of students to identify deviation from normal health and diseases.

(iv) Screening of vision and hearing, along with taking of height and weight of students.

(v) Maintain health card for each student and discuss health problems of pupils with the Medical Officer, parents and health workers, link mothers and youth leaders.

(vi) Identify health education opportunities in the school—

1. At the morning prayer.
2. In the class room and relate with health contents given in the text books.
3. Organize enjoyable out-of-class activities like health poems, songs, skits, plays.
4. Include health activities in cultural programmes during special events such as annual days, national days, etc.
5. Supervise personal hygiene practices during lunch, after using toilet facilities and after games.
6. Organize school health days or weeks.

(vii) The above activities may be organized with the involvement of National Service Scheme volunteers, wherever available; otherwise, involve health workers, the community people or youth leaders and link mothers.

(viii) Encourage students of Classes V and IV to check the personal hygiene of students of Classes III, and I at the time of prayer, at lunch time, during recess and at home. By doing so, the older children will become conscious of their own healthy habits; it will also generate a sense of leadership.

(ix) Each child of Classes V and IV adopt two children of lower Classes, i.e. III, II and I and teach them health messages. They will also observe their practices.

(x) Coordination with Primary Health Centre for medical examination, treatment, the referral and follow-up.

(xi) Follow-up the regularity of treatment prescribed and ensure visit to Primary Health Centre.

(xii) Liaison with parents, link mothers and community for mobilizing their resources for improving environmental conditions of the schools.

(xiii) Form parent-teacher associations and seek their active involvement.

(xiv) Ensure community participation in the promotion of school health programmes by dividing the community into manageable units and allot these units to every child.

It is observed that about 10% of the population of any community consists of primary school-age children. On an average, there will be 100 primary school students in a village with 1000 population.

A population of 1000 will have on an average 200 households. So one primary school student will have to look after two households, i.e. one his own and another that of the neighbour.

Children should be used as health communicators for two households. They may disseminate health information to the members of the allotted households, observe the health habits of siblings in the home, and those of friends in the neighbourhood.

(xv) Minimal records are suggested to be maintained at the schools to avoid unnecessary burden on the teachers. A quarterly report on the activities will have to be sent to the Block Medical Officer with a copy to the Central Monitoring Cell and State Coordinator.

(xvi) Provide necessary assistance to the health team for organizing specialists' camps. These camps will be set-up in the school buildings/Primary Health Centre/Community Centre depending on the convenience, availability and easy accessibility to a large number of students or a group of villages.

(xvii) Help National Service Scheme volunteers and youth leaders of Nehru Yuva Kendra to organize village health camps by providing necessary assistance. These are:
- Physical facilities for the camps including accommodations.
- Establishing contacts with village leaders.
- Planning need-based activities like mass meetings, film shows, group-discussion, immunization campaigns, nutrition demonstration, oral rehydration solution demonstration, filling up pits, improvement of environmental conditions, etc.

(xviii) Enhancing the nutrition status of children by seeking support for programmes of better nutrition of students, providing correct and adequate nutrition knowledge and encouraging school/home nutrition gardens.

(xix) Organizing health/environmental sanitation camps and campaigns with community participation.

In order to keep the interest of the teachers sustained or to generate strong motivation, following incentives need to be provided.

1. Health check-up for teachers at the time of training and treatment in case there is need.
2. Award of certificates at the end of the training course.
3. Award of running trophies for the best school within the district. Gradation of schools on the basis of their performance may be made with the following criteria:
   - Improvement in environmental conditions.
   - Improvement in health status of children.
   - Improvement in personal hygiene of students.
   - Development of nutrition garden.
   - Involvement of parent community in school health programme.
   - Application of child-to-child and youth-to-child approaches.
   - Formation of school health committee.
   - Collaboration with NSS volunteers, youth leaders and health workers.
4. Award of merit certificate/incentive to the best health education teacher based on individual performance.
5. Training of teachers regarding their role in school health services programme will be provided by coordinating the resources like the Advisors of ICDS programme, Regional Health and F.W. Training Centres, State Council for

Educational Research and Training (SCERT), Training Orientation/Research Coordinators (TORCs), of National Service Scheme and Programme Officers of National Service Scheme, State Institutes of Education and Resources available with other special programmes.

6. A minimum of five days training for teachers along with National Service Scheme volunteers of colleges/schools, where available, and for only teachers wherever National Service Scheme is not available, has been considered necessary. Teachers must be apprised regarding portions of health cards to be filled up by them, their referral slips and the proforma for health education information to be maintained in separate note books.
7. The training programme will be coordinated by the State Project Coordinators of State Health Departments.
8. The roles and responsibilities of health and educational personnel have been drawn up exhaustively. It would be desirable to involve local functionaries during the training programmes to finalized these by raising the following questions:
   (i) How many of these activities are they already performing?
   (ii) How many more can they conveniently accept?
   (A copy of finally agreed roles and responsibilities of each functionary may be forwarded to the nodal officer).
9. A sum of Rs. 100 will be provided to the teachers as honorarium for the five-day training.
10. These teachers will be considered to be on duty for the period of training and will draw their TA from the source of their salary as per the State/UT rules. This issue may be settled at the District Coordination Committee meetings.[30]

METHODS OF EDUCATION

There are a number of ways in which health knowledge can be given and sound health attitudes and behaviour can be inculcated. Some of these are described below.

I. School Health Committee/Club

With the help of the health staff we can organize in the school a Health Committee or Club consisting of the teachers, students, parents and health staff. This committee can meet to discuss various health problems in the school, plan how to solve these problems, and carry out these plans, taking the help of the students, teachers, school authorities, parents, community members, health staff or workers of other development agencies in the area.

The committee or club can also organize health surveys, school or class health projects such as the development of kitchen gardens, filling in water collections, etc. They may also appoint a Children's Parliament, a Health Squad, a Safety Patrol, a Health Captain and Class Health Monitors. They can plan special campaigns in the school or in the community such as Health Weeks or Safety Weeks and activities connected with World Health Day (7 April), Anti-fly Week (first week of July), National Cleanliness Day (2 October), or Children's Day (14 November).

2. Demonstrations and Practical work

We can conduct health drills in which we can show the children how to carry out procedures like trimming nails, washing hands, brushing teeth, suing a handkerchief while coughing or sneezing, drawing water from the drinking water pot, etc. Get them to practice these procedures.

Each class may be given a plot in the school kitchen garden and can plan, plant and maintain it.

We can arrange for field trips in which the children will be shown how flies and mosquitoes breed and how this can be prevented, how to chlorinate wells and keep water safe, and how to use latrines and keep them clean. Or they may help in actually constructing a soakage pit or compost pit.

As a home assignment, each child may be asked to bring to school one item of food and to prepare a two-minute talk on why that food is good for health.

3. Songs, Stories, Games and Puzzles

Small children enjoy singing action songs, reciting poems, listening to stories, playing games and asking each other riddles or solving crossword puzzles. These can be effectively used for teaching them about how to keep healthy. You can prepare your own health messages and picture and fill them in on the boards or cards to make your own games. So also, you can encourage the children to make up their own poems, riddles and puzzles, or to use a popular tune for a health song.

Many children will be familiar with the local traditional folk media such as chitrakatha, folk songs or dance drama and can use these for conveying health messages.

4. Dramas, Puppet shows and Role Play

Children like dressing up and acting. You can prepare and get the students to help in preparing short plays on health themes. For instance, a play could be on 'Down with Disease' in which each child takes the part of an insect or animal which carries disease, e.g. a fly, mosquito, or rat. The village health committee discusses what they should do about these pests and decide on the measures to be taken.

Similarly, some themes can be enacted through puppets, e.g.

'Ramu and the Vegetables': Ramu's mother tries to get him to eat vegetables like carrot, pumpkin, green leafy vegetables, beans and karela, but he doesn't like them. Each character and each vegetable can be represented by a glove puppet or a card puppet.

The students can also-play situations, e.g. children teaching younger brothers and sisters how to develop healthy habits.

5. Health Parades, Competitions, Class Charts, Scrap Books and Diaries

Each morning as the children come into class, they can have health parade in which the class monitor inspects the nails, hands, teeth, hair and clothes of each child. The class can be divided into two houses, which may be given the name of a flower. Bird, or national leader. Each student will get plus or minus marks for cleanliness, which will be added to his house marks. This will encourage the children to help each other to remain clean and gain marks for their house.

You can also hold inter-class competitions in which the class, which is judged most clean and tidy throughout the year, will get a floating trophy.

The students could work together in preparing health charts; or they may keep a bar chart showing the height of each of the boys and each of the girls in the class. The children can be encouraged to create health posters, paint pictures illustrating different health themes, or write essays on health topics. Each class can make a class scrap-book or magazine, about 45 cm × 30 cm in size, containing the children's poems, pictures, puzzles, riddles, etc., relating to health, among other topics.

6. Exhibitions and Display Boards

The school can put up an exhibition, e.g. on the theme 'Our Health is Important'. Each class can be given one topic to plan for, e.g. 'Water and Health', 'The Food we Eat', 'Safety First', 'Carelessness costs lives'. They will collect or draw pictures, make models, or make health rangolis of coloured fruits, vegetables or grains.

The school wall newspaper can include items on health, and the class bulletin board can have health corner, which can be devoted to a different health topic each week or fortnight. The bulletin board can be the responsibility of groups of students by turns.

7. Talks, Debates and Discussions

From time to time the school may invite doctors to give talks or demonstrations on health topics to the children, or the students, may take part in debates, symposia, panel discussions or group discussions related to health. These assignments can be given as a part of different subjects.

8. Visual Aids in Teaching

Teaching can become more attractive and striking with the

judicious use of suitably chosen audio-visual aids. While most of our schools do not have sophisticated equipment such as slide and filmstrip projectors, overhead projectors, tape recorders or TV sets, simple visual materials on health can be obtained from the Block Extension Educator at the Primary Health Centre, or from the District Extension and Media Officer. With a little imagination and ingenuity, you can make your own visual aids such as flannelgraphs, flip charts, or flash cards. If the blackboard is properly used, it can also be an effective aid to teaching.

9. Involvement of Parents

Some schools have a Parent-Teacher Association through which the parents and teachers can meet from time to time to discuss the problems of the children, including those relating to health. They can also use these occasions to plan together for activities such as setting up a school canteen, or organizing a programme for providing a mid-day meal or nutritious snacks. The parents can be involved in these activities not merely by giving donations in cash or in kind (utensils, furniture, food), but by taking turns in planning the menus or in helping to cook and serve the meals.

The parents can also be represented on the School Health Committee or Club.

Children take home many ideas from school and want to try them out. Unless there is understanding and cooperation between the parent and the teacher, this can cause conflict and confusion in the mind of the child.

10. Child-to-Child Health Activities

In rural areas older children are often required to feed, bathe, dress and play with younger brothers and sisters and to protect them from injury. Sometimes, especially in the case of girls, they are kept away from school for this purpose. Try to persuade parents not to keep their children away from school in this account. At the same time you must remember that school-going children can play an important role in the care of young children.

If school children are taught a few simple ways of caring for small children, they will serve as an important resource in providing childcare and in promoting the well-being of their younger brothers and sisters.[31]

A CASE STUDY—SCHOOL SANITATION

According to the Multiple Indicator Cluster Survey (MICS) 2000, only 56 per cent of Assam's rural population has access to toilets. Of these, 57.2 per cent have facilities within their premises. The causal disposal of excreta, combined with the characteristically heavy monsoon in the area, results in diarrhoea and other water-borne diseases, which often assume epidemic proportions.

Points for Health Education

Encourage the children to concern themselves with the health of younger children in their homes. They can do this in the following ways:

(i) By teaching the smaller child to develop clean habits like washing its hands before meals, brushing its teeth, etc.

(ii) By preventing flies from sitting on the child's face and eyelids, and by protecting the child from ants, mosquitoes, cockroaches, rats, dogs, etc.

(iii) By teaching the small child to keep the home and its surroundings clean, e.g. by not defaecating or urinating anywhere about and by throwing rubbish in the right place. Little children can be taught to use a small pit dug near the house for defaecation and urination until they are old enough to use the latrine. When the pit is filled with earth, another pit can be dug.

(iv) By feeding the young child at the proper time, giving the child nutritious food like carrots, leafy vegetables, beans khichadi or dal-roti, and by ensuring that the food is clean and protected from fillies and other creatures.

(v) By protecting the child from accidents due to—

- swallowing small objects like beads or coins.
- putting small objects in its nose or ears.
- going near open fires, playing with matches or touching hot vessels.
- playing near ponds or other collections of water.
- handling knives, pins and other sharp objects.
- swallowing medicines and poisonous substances.
- touching electrical appliances, electric wires, switches and plug sockets.
- playing in places where there may be snakes, scorpions or poisonous plants.
- wandering on to the road.
- falling-off heights.

(vi) By knowing what to do in case of accidents.

(vii) By giving the child plenty of clean water and other fluids to drink, especially when the child has diarrhoea, fever or other illness.

The school sanitation project in Kamrup was launched to create awareness with regard to sanitary practices and provide the district population with access to water and sanitary facilities. It aimed to create awareness of sanitary practices in the community through school-going children and teachers. The project has brought about tremendous change in the attitude and motivation of the community. Supported technically and financially by UNICEF, the project aimed at improving the health status and awareness of the community. This was made possible through cost-effective interventions and the strengthening of the ongoing Rural Sanitation Project (RSP).

The field note attempts to capture the spirit and content of interventions in Kamrup district and impact they have had on the community.

Background

The interventions in water and sanitation in Kamrup district have their genesis in the Intensive Sanitation Project (ISP) 1993, with technical and financial support from UNICEF. The ISP was a comprehensive project aimed at generating household demand for cost-effective sanitary latrines, by creating awareness regarding sanitation and hygiene. The current programme was launched by the PHED in Kamrup, with a view to extending the progress made under the ISP as also filling any gaps of the earlier project.

Sanitation programmes had been running in Assam earlier. However, most of these, like the Central Rural Sanitation Programme, launched in 1986, did not directly target schools. The Tenth Finance Commission had made provisions for the installation of hand pumps and construction of latrines in 5,000 primary schools in the state. However, considering that there are 30,000 primary schools in the state, hand pumps and latrines alone cannot create a sanitary environment. A state-wide school sanitation programme was clearly needed. In this regard, a significant beginning has been made in Kamrup district, which can be replicated in other districts.

In Assam, the school sanitation programme (SSP) has been implemented in two phases, which can only be differentiated in terms of technology and cost.

Objectives

- Moulding the future generation by making school children adopt sanitary and hygienic habits at an early age.
- Provision of water supply, sanitary latrines, urinals hand-washing and other WATSAN facilities in primary schools.
- Promotion of sanitation and hygiene as one comprehensive package.

- Creation of greater capacity and establishment of a self help system, which will enable students, teachers and the community at large to maintain WATSAN facilities.

Institutional Level Partners

The PHED has been the nodal agency for project implementation. Its activities include overseeing the construction of facilities, allocation of funds and overall planning and monitoring.

The Elementary Education Department has been responsible for gathering information related to school health and hygiene, creating awareness, organizing training camps, monitoring the utilization of funds and the maintenance of facilities at the school level.

Some other departments are also involved in the programme.

The Forest Department is providing seedling of trees to improve school environs.

The Health Department is organizing regular student health check-ups and educating both teachers and children on primary health care.

The District Rural Development Agency (DRDA) is responsible for the construction of WATSAN facilities, fencing of compounds, etc.

UNICEF, as the sponsor of the programme, is providing technical expertise, funds and assistance in planning, implementation and monitoring of the programme.

Community Level Partners

Local NGOs, clubs and Mahila Samitis have associated themselves with the programme by providing physical labour and financial help and making efforts to spread awareness.

Project Implementation

Phase I

The plan was to cover the entire district in three phases. Phase I was launched in five blocks, and till date, has covered 736 schools. The major activities undertaken in this phase include:

- District-level sensitization workshops for coordinating departments, to promote sharing of responsibilities.
- Block-level orientation programmes for headmasters and a core group of teachers from each school.
- Setting up school committees and strengthening existing committees for programme implementation.
- Training programmes for officials of the NGOs involved in the programme.
- Identification of community motivators and training them to spread awareness on sanitation.

- Providing school committees with hygiene education materials and sanitary hardware, and training them in the construction of WATSAN facilities.
- Organization of campaigns, rallies and competitions to motivate the teachers and students to cooperate in the programme.
- Motivating teachers to monitor the personal hygiene of students.
- Encouraging schools to involve students in awareness campaigns and providing financial support of Rs. 1,000 to each school for the purpose.
- Setting up sanitary marts so that sanitary hardware and other related items are easily available and are affordable.

Phase II

The ongoing Phase II was launched in the year 2000 after the completion of Phase I in the district.

All the activities undertaken in Phase I the campaign for awareness creation; motivation of school teachers and students to ensure their participation; orientation, sensitization and training of the core groups of teachers and school committees—are being carried out in Phase II. Additionally, there is a qualitative enhancement in the technology employed and consequently, in the budget for construction activities.

Under Phase II, 2,995 schools are to be covered (13 blocks of five districts). Sanitary blocks have been constructed in 291 schools and another 152 are under construction.

Achievements

- Funds have been allocated to 736 schools as of year 2000. In all, 328 sanitary blocks have been constructed and 312 more are under construction.
- In order to make sanitary hardware easily available to households, 35 sanitary marts have been established in 11 districts.
- Schools committees and students have actively participated in the construction and maintenance WATSAN facilities.
- Health and sanitation are now subjects taught in schools.

There has been a remarkable rise in the level and quality of community participation, both in financial and material terms, in the construction and maintenance of the facilities under the project. There have been many instances of members of the community bearing head-loads of material over rocky terrain, for hours. Today, the project is not only self-sustaining but is also quick to respond to the demand.

Lessons Learnt

The key to the success of the project lies in the continuous enhancement of community motivation.

The project has been successful despite the challenges of remoteness and insurgency. This clearly shows that careful organization of funds and materials, as well as clear guidelines for implementation, are necessary for successful and effective coverage of all target areas.

Historic Handpump

The first Tara handpump in India was installed in Ajara village. The caretaker of this hand pump is Sahida Bibi. The pump works as well as it used to when it was installed, a few years back. Around 1,000 people in the village drink water from this pump.

Practical Lessons

Noorjahan Begum, a student of Pudchesa Mukh Prathmik Vidyalay, in Pudchesa village, is very happy with the toilet block in the school. Now she does not have to go home in the middle of the day. The School Sanitation Project has given the children practical lessons on how to use a toilet and pour water in the toilet after use; it has also trained them to wash their hands after using the toilet, cut their nails, and have a bath daily.

Not Just Construction but Motivation as Well

The sanitary mart run by the NGO Astha, stands near Kochpara Lower Primary School. It supplies material, both to the school as well as to villages of the block. Jogan Das, the head mason of this sanitary mart, has been working there for the past four years. He is not merely a mason engaged in production, but plays the role of a motivator, both in his village as well as in the neighbouring village. He learnt the science of masony and the art of motivation at the seven-day training organized at Hengrabari, Guwahati. He owes his association with the project to one of the assistant engineers of PHED, a resident of his own village. It has enabled him to earn wages as well as contribute to the implementation of this very necessary programme.

Local Initiatives and Responsibilities

- In some schools there was no source of water, earlier. Now water is provided through the Tara hand pump.
- The funds received for the project are being transferred directly into the account of the school committees. The committees purchase all the construction material themselves.
- Local masons have been trained so that one toilet block in a school can be constructed within seven days.

- Schools are made self-sufficient with regard to the maintenance of toilets and other sanitation-related activities, through the provision of material such as soap, buckets and nail cutters, etc. Schools are generating funds for these through contributions.

An All–round towards Village Sanitation

Gosain Medhipara in Rampur block is nearing its goal of becoming a full sanitation village. Different sections—students, school sanitation committee, village committee, school staff and Mahila Samiti—have all contributed to making this village a model for others.

Shoulabala Goswami, former Secretary, Medhipara Mahila Samiti says:

"When we started motivating people in the village we faced a lot of resistance. Paucity of finances and the age-old habit of defecating in the open fields were the main deterrents. However, the Mahila Samiti continued its mission and was successful. Today, there are only 15 families in the village who do not have latrines in their homes, most of them being below the poverty line. As soon as the funds are sanctioned to these families under the CRSP, the village is expected to become a full sanitation village."

Padmeshwar Goswami, President, School Committee observes:

"The sanitation drive in our village began with the School Sanitation Programme. Apart from our role in this programme, the role of the students has been commendable. Whatever the students learnt in the school about sanitation, they shared with their parents at home. As a result, some of the parents also got motivated through their children. The sanitation programme has been very successful in helping our children become aware of the importance of environmental and personal sanitation."

Ashok Goswami, member of Village Committee states:

"This programme initiated by UNICEF and the Government is commendable because this is the first time that I have seen the community so involved in any developmental programme. It's admirable that people from the community are being trained, as they are the ones who implement this project and also carry out its assessment. If the community is involved in any programme then there is no chance of its failure. We have seen this in West Bengal and now we are seeing it in our own state."

Umesh Goswami, assistant teacher feels:

"Ever since the school sanitation programme started in the primary school, it has brought about a lot of change. Moreover, behavioural change can be very effectively achieved at an early age. This is clearly visible in our village. Sometimes elderly people do not wash their hands after defecation but these children never forget to wash their hands after defecation."

Bishwadeep Goswami, an elder comments:

"When I compare my time with today's situation, I see that lots of changes have taken place, after the implementation of this sanitation programme. Not only has the environment in our village changed but the health of the people is also improving rapidly. Earlier, some person or the other used to suffer from some type of diarrhoeal diseases, but now such cases are rare in our village."[32]

CONCLUSION

The transfer of knowledge cannot be considered the final goal of health education; the child has to learn how to use this knowledge and how to make the best choice in a given situation.

While general education has contributed immensely to the health improvement of the people, the importance of special health education efforts aimed at parents, children and adolescents has always been recognized in most health service systems.

Traditionally, health education aims at fostering hygienic habits, promoting adequate nutrition, and creating environmental conditions conducive to health by physical and mental growth and development. Much importance is attached to prevention of disease, recognition of the first signs of illness and elementary treatment procedures. At school, children are introduced to the basic knowledge of anatomy, physiology and hygiene, which constitute the core of school health education programmes.

Rapid changes in lifestyles, and the evolution of views on health and disease call for new departures in health education. Quick glance at health education material of even one generation ago will show how fast it tends to get out of date. Medical facts, it has been estimated, get outdated within a decade or so. Effective health education therefore requires a continuous stream of knowledge, development of the people's ability to absorb it, and decisions taken on the basis of a constantly changing body of information.

There is another, and perhaps more important reason for new health education efforts to be made. The WHO definition of health stresses that health is not only the absence of disease or infirmity but a state of complete physical, mental and social well-being. Such a concept of well-being should include not only the individual's ability to function normally under optimal or near-optimal conditions, but also to stand up to increased loads, strains and stresses by summoning up resources that usually lie dormant.

Raising the Quality of Life

If the contents of "traditional" health education are analyzed from this standpoint, it would be clear that a substantial part of it is aimed at prevention of diseases and creation of optimal environmental conditions for the child's growth and development, while a comparatively minor role is given to health promotion that would prepare an individual to function properly under the stressful conditions of life today. This is no to say that "traditional" health education has not value—which it certainly has—but there is need to underline the importance of health education aimed at health promotion and at raising the quality of life, and not limited merely to prevention of disease or health protection.

One of the best examples of such an approach is to engage children in physical training and sports, which lead to harmonious growth and increased capacity for physical work. In the USSR, a set of indicators, differentiated by age-groups, has been developed, to serve both as a target of physical training of school children and as a measure of physical activity performance by individual children. Research is needed to formulate precise indicators for physical training of preschool children, as well as of children with various infirmities who need physical exercise as much, if not more, than healthy children.

However, the aim of physical education goes even beyond this: it should help to create in adolescents an internalized need for physical activity, an ability to maintain a balance between physical and mental work, which is the best way to combat hypodynamia—diminished power—a quickly spreading modern "disease".

It is well known that even children in equally good health do not react the same way to various stress factors. For example, some may catch cold even after a short exposure to cold weather, while the majority of children remain unaffected. "Tempering" or toughening up of the children to gradually increase their resistance to cold is one of the most important elements of healthy development, particularly in cold climates. Introduction of tempering (for example, through shower baths of decreasing temperature) in many pre-school institutions in the USSR brought down respiratory morbidity to one-half or one-third. These measures cannot, however, be effective if parents are not made to stop over-clothing the children and keeping them in a hothouse atmosphere. Hence the need for systematic educational efforts in childhood and adolescence to motivate future parents.[33]

Immunization against childhood diseases starts at birth or as soon after that as possible, and the schedule is completed by the age of 18 months. There has been a gradual increase in the number of children immunized as well as the numbers receiving the third doses of DPT (diphtheria, pertussis and tetanus) and poliomyelitis vaccines.

Nutrition and growth supervision of the children is carried out monthly. Children are weighed, immunized and given appropriate nutrition intervention where the child's growth is not proceeding satisfactorily. Health education of the mother is an important part of these visits. Attendance at these pre-school clinics is fairly regular during the first 24 months, and tends to drop after the first immunizations are completed.

As most of the services are preventive, the importance of people's participation is vital to the life of the programme. Over the last five years, the number of mothers and children who come to MCH facilities has been increasing steadily. This has been the result partly of providing rural health facilities within easier reach, but the FWES' increasing contact with the community and their role in motivating the mothers to use the faculties have also been vital factors.

Promoting better health for mothers and children, and through them better health for the whole family, is the vital nucleus of action towards better health for all. Let us hope that increasing coverage in antenatal care, delivery under supervision, family planning and immunization will lead the country to the desired goal of a drastic reduction in infant deaths and sickness.[34]

Thus, education for health in modern society should be carried out not only by health professional, but by parents, teachers and also by other social figures. A multi-disciplinary approach becomes indispensable as soon as the problem is seen in a wide perspective beyond its "medical" and "prevention and cure" aspects. The medical profession will no doubt continue to play an important role, particularly health professionals who come in close contact with people. But new tasks call for an increasing use of non-medical persons, such as parents and teachers, with medical workers serving them as resource persons, consultants and, in many respects, educators.

An important role could be played by psychologists in creating a healthy psychological climate among groups of children, assessing, together with teachers, the psycho-emotional development of children, and instituting promotional or correctional activities.

The school, along with the family, peers and society at large, is an important socializing factor that helps children in assimilating basic social values. Socialization is greatly promoted by out-of-school, extra-curricular activities, which also stimulate the children's creativity. This is amply proved by the USSR experience where a network of out-of-school institutions—young pioneer palaces, sport and music schools, children's theatres, libraries, and so on—provide tens of million of children with scope for the exercise of their creative talents and cultivation of social values.[35]

Notes and References

1. WHO: Donald Reid, Learning good health, *World Health*, Jan.-Feb., 1994, pp. 5-7.
2. WHO: Frank Falkner, The vital years, *World Health*, Feb-March, 1979, p. 8.
3. *Ibid.* op. cet., p. 11.
4. Dr. H. Mahler, World Health Organization, February-March 1979, pp. 2-3.
5. *Ibid., op. cit.*, p. 4.
6. *Ibid.*, p. 7.
7. Jagannath Mohanty, Teacher Education, 2003, pp. 273-74.
8. School Health, M/o Health and Family Welfare, GOI, 1984, p. 1.
9. WHO: V. Tatochenko, Education for Health, *World Health*, Feb.-March, 1979, p. 27.
10. School Health, M/o Health and Family Welfare, GOI, 1984, p. 28.
11. Anjali Pattanaik, 1994, Nutrition, Education and Child Development, Deep & Deep Publications, New Delhi, pp. 1-3.
12. *Ibid.*, pp. 31-32.
13. School Health, Ministry of Health and Family Welfare, GOI, 1984, pp. 29-30.
14. WHO: Moises Behar, Nutrition and Child Health, *World Health*, Feb.-March, 1979, p. 16.
15. *Ibid.* p. 19.
16. Anjali Pattanaik, 1994, Nutrition, Education and Child Development, Deep & Deep Publications, New Delhi, pp. 45-48.
17. *Ibid.*, pp. 48-51.
18. School Health, M/o Health and Family Welfare, GOI, 1984, pp. 31-36.
19. *Ibid., op. cit.*, p. 39.
20. WHO: V. Tatochenko, Education for health, *World Health*, Feb.-March, 1979, p. 26.
21. School Health, M/o Health and Family Welfare, GOI, 1984, pp. 93-94.
22. *Ibid., op. cit.*, p. 103.
23. A Better World for Children, School Sanitation in Ambala. p. 35.
24. UNICEF: A Better World for Children, School Sanitation in Ambala, p. 3.
25. WHO: V. Tatochenko, Education for health, *World Health*, Feb.-March, 1979, p. 26.
26. WHO: Leo A. Kaprio, An element of Primary care, *World Health*, Jan.-Feb. 1987, p. 18.
27. WHO: Ralph H. Henderson, *World Health*, January-February 1987, p. 7.
28. WHO: Sir John Wilson, Vaccines Versus disability, *World Health*, January-February, 1987, p. 16.
29. School Health, M/o Health and Family Welfare, GOI, 1984, p. 45.
30. Intensive Health Education, M/o Health and Family Welfare, GOI, New Delhi, 1989, pp. 8-10
31. School Health, M/o Health and Family Welfare, GOI, New Delhi, 1984, pp. 46-52.
32. UNICEF: School Sanitation, Ways to WATSAN, Field Note, Assam, pp. 1-8.
33. WHO: V. Tatochenko, Education for health, *World Health*, Feb-March, 1979, pp. 24-25.
34. *Ibid., op. cit.*, p. 31.
35. *Ibid.*, pp. 26-27.

CHAPTER 6

FAMILY HEALTH EDUCATION

> Each family has its own dynamics of formation, growth, maturation and dissolution. Now health workers should look after family units rather than individual cases
>
> —*F.J.W. Miller*

Family Health Education

Since children in schools remain in home for more time, therefore, family education is essential to educate the children in health education. Schools must maintain contact with families.

World Population Conference Plan of Action, states that:

> "The family is recognized as the basic unit of society. Governments should assist families as far as possible to enable them to fulfil their role in society. It is therefore suggested that:
>
> (a) The family be protected by appropriate legislation and policy without discrimination as to other members of society; and
> (b) Family ties be strengthened by giving recognition to the importance of love and mutual respect within the family unit."

"All couples and individuals have the basic right to decide freely and responsibly the number and spacing of their children and to have the information, education and means to do so."

". . . Ensure that family planning, medical and related social services aim not only at the prevention of unwanted pregnancies but also at elimination of involuntary sterility and sub-fecundity in order that all couples may be permitted to achieve their desired number of children, and that child adoption be facilitated." "Special attention should be given to rural family policy and to the formulation and implementation of a complex of economic and social measures calculated to meet the specific needs of the rural family." "Recognizing . . . that the promotion of the status of women is an integral factor in the development process."

> Health education based on man's active involvement in his community is the most effective and economic way of building up family health and understanding.
>
> —The Corner-Stone, by *Akbar Moarefi*

Each family has its own dynamics of formation, growth maturation and dissolution. Now health workers should look after family units rather than individual cases.

Universally the family is the primary social unit and a significant force in human development. Its influence on mental health is beyond question. For most people the family is the matrix within which the individual is moulded and developed, the area where his strongest emotional ties are formed, and the background against which much of his most intense personal life is enacted. It is the family, which serves as a link between successive generations, and most societies expect the family to prepare the children for adult life in the larger community of the clan, the village, the town or the country. This means, depending on the culture and socio-economic status of the society, enabling the child to realize its potential abilities and attain varying degrees of physical, economic and emotional emancipation.

CHART 6.1

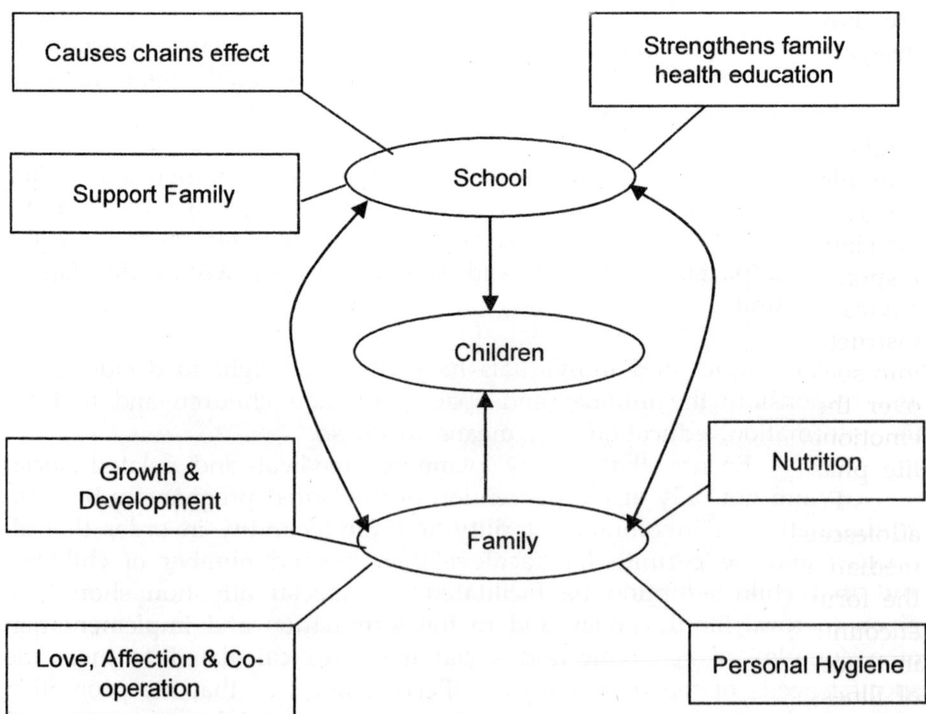

In Western industrialized countries where the nuclear type of family is the general rule, where emphasis in on self-sufficiency and self-reliance, and where there exists some form of national social security for the unemployed and the financially, socially, physically and morally handicapped, this emancipation may be complete.[1]

Numerous arguments have been put forward to explain what is happening. Some have claimed that the family has proved particularly vulnerable to the pressures of changing social conditions and has been weakened. Others have argued that the family has simply shown an evolutionary ability to adapt and mould itself to fit the requirements of modern systems of life and behaviour.

Whatever the appropriate explanation, it is clear that as society has become more urbanized, and as urban life in turn has become increasingly complex, so the patterns of family formation have changed.

From various parts of the world comes evidence that the traditional extended family, which, in its various forms, appears to have been a relatively universal phenomenon, is gradually being replaced by the nuclear family. The unit is becoming smaller, more remote physically and economically from other family groupings and, in terms of many of its functions, it is moving toward a shorter life span.

What is the significance of these changes and what are their various implications for the health of the family, its members and society in general? The answer may be found in part by examining the different functions which the family traditionally fulfilled in the past and which are now, as a result of its emerging structure, being increasingly delegated to non-familial bodies to perform or, all too often, are simply being neglected.

Throughout history the family has played a unique and fundamental role. With relatively few exceptions, it has provided, for example, the most effective and socially appropriate milieu in which procreation could take place, and in which the physical and emotional development of children could be ensured. Through the routine responsibilities and interaction of its adult members, it has constituted an environment in which offspring could be gradually exposed to, and instructed in the values and customs considered necessary for integration into society; at the same time it has provided a source of informal control over their activities. For older members it has represented a source of emotional and economic support as they themselves pass through their life phases[2].

From the time of conception and birth, through childhood, adolescence, parenthood and old-age, the family has been an inter-mediating force between the individual and his community. It has been the forum in which the major part of the significant life experiences are encountered and coped with. Within the framework of the family, for instance, the individual has been exposed for the first time to the concept of illness, has learnt how to adapt to it and, more importantly, has been assisted through it. In many respects, the family has traditionally constituted a unique unit of primary health care, a front line in the sequence of education, prevention, diagnosis, treatment and rehabilitation of its constituents. And indeed to a significant percentage of the world's population for whom alternative health strategies are not available, or to whom new approaches do not always prove acceptable, the family still remains the only viable health care resource.

Changes and pressures on the family disrupt many of the relationships that are required if these functions are to be performed adequately. Just as the family has the potential to act as a unique agent of therapeutic intervention, so changes or a temporary dis-equilibrium in its structure can actually generate problems for the physical and psychological well-being of its individual members. With this in mind a number of areas of concern have emerged in recent years.[3]

Child Care

The transition to the smaller nuclear type family has coincided with the increased involvement of women in the labour force. This has often curtailed their continued care of small children. In the absence of elder parental figures and female relations, who in many societies assumed automatic responsibility for children, childcare has been increasingly delegated to extra familial, professional or quasi-professional bodies. To a great extent these organizations have in part replaced many of the roles of the mother and of the extended family. Nurseries, kindergartens, day centres, whether provided by the State, industry or private organizations, have allowed mothers to follow active working lives or simply to liberate themselves from traditional female roles and seek further self-development.

But the widespread dependence upon day centres has raised certain questions about the effects of maternal deprivation on child development. Attention has been focused on the fact that, while these organizations have been meant to replace maternal care, they have in some instances done little more than simply provide shelter, supervision and basic educational training; they have not been able to give the type of individual care and attention that is basic to healthy physical and psychological growth.

Even if centres that are optimally planned, staffed and administered can genuinely meet the needs of the child and mother, it remains true that these standards are difficult to meet and still more to maintain. Availability and training of staff varies widely between and within different countries, and physical facilities, playrooms, sanitary arrangements and educational play materials—are all conditioned by different economic and social factors, which are difficult to control. The costs of care, when this is not provided by state or industry, often put them beyond the reach of the population at large.

Adolescence

The question has been asked, "Can the nuclear family is transitional and highly urbanized and industrial societies really attend to the many different needs of the adolescent?" Age groups that have been relatively neglected, adolescents, are now acknowledged to have quite specific health needs, particularly with respect to sexual behaviour and reproductive health. Their vulnerability to sexually transmitted diseases, unwanted pregnancy and illegitimacy has been epidemiologically established in many different countries, but particularly in those areas where society is undergoing rapid and fundamental changes. In developing regions of Africa, for instance, it has been pointed out that few mechanisms have been developed to replace the intricate relationship that previously existed between the socializing functions of the family and the social rituals which its members observed and which provided specific guidance and control. Meanwhile, in highly industrialized societies of Europe and North America, studies have indicated that many adolescents are unable to discuss important questions concerning reproduction with their parents, and therefore embark on sexual relationships relatively unaware of their potential consequences. Educational institutions, upon whom the responsibility for preparing young people for adulthood has been increasingly placed, have themselves been unable to keep abreast of the changing situation.

Introduction to the prerequisites of adulthood, marriage, procreation and child-rearing is being left to schools and other organized groups, even though doubts remain as to how effective they can be in replacing the informal preparation that the large extended family was able to provide through routine exposure and example.

Changing Role of Women

In most industrialized and industrializing societies, the participation of women in the labour force has increased significantly. The statistical fact of this may however belie the reality of the situation; for regardless of the degree of occupational involvement that has been achieved, the traditional concept of the woman has not changed significantly in many settings. All too often she is still seen first as a mother and as someone whose responsibility is the care of the domestic situation. While involved in industry she has often remained peripheral to the labour market, has been paid less than men are for doing similar tasks, and has had fewer opportunities for advancement. Her occupational status has remained ill defined and the different roles she has been called on to play have often tended to lack precision. Available evidence about the effects of such inconsistencies on mental health shows that all too little attention has hitherto been paid to the working and living conditions of women.

Similarly, although the small family is by now a well-established fact in the industrialized countries of Europe and North America, social pressures on the woman to plan her family have not been reduced. Indeed they may well have increased. Yet while there has been much progress in the development of contraceptive technology, the educational services and techniques for disseminating information about family planning have not been sufficiently developed.

In industrialized countries, where it is apparent that the planned childbearing period for most women is being completed earlier than ever before, the need for protracted contraception has increased. There has been little development of counselling services specifically geared to this issue, or indeed to the needs of couples who essentially cease parenthood while still relatively young. Limiting family size has often meant that children attain adulthood and economic independence and leave home while their parents are themselves relatively young. This pattern of family life represents a significant change in many societies and is one whose ramifications for the parents have been little explored. Psychologists, for example, have pointed out that children constitute a stabilizing force within the household; they not only symbolize the aspirations and expectations of parents, but act as agents of cohesion. And while women have been increasingly integrated into non-domestic activities, many of them continue to see children, in the traditional way, as a symbol of their accomplished maternal role. Their adaptation to a long period of childless life while yet physically active is a phenomenon for which society has not adequately prepared the family. In terms of the mental health of the mother and the couple, and in terms of conjugal life, these are further questions that need to be examined more thoroughly.

The Couple

At the level of the couple too, it is evident that the movement away from the large extended family has brought with it changes in responsibilities. Students of the family in the United States, for example, have questioned the ability of the small family to accommodate itself, alone, to many of the economic and social stresses of life. Accommodation to familial problems, coping with demanding work hours, unemployment, chronic illnesses, alcoholism and death may be more difficult when the number of kin with whom these responsibilities can be shared is small. This is particularly the case in family situations where the couples are both involved in following their own work careers and must plan ahead somewhat independently of each other. Decisions about who should be the one to donate time to family responsibilities may take on a much more stressful character in such circumstances.

Old Age

To older people, the changes that have taken place in the family have inevitably been of great consequence. Particularly in societies where the relationship between status, lifestyle and occupation is close, old age, symbolized increasingly by retirement, presents many psychological problems. Cut-off from friendships and associations that have been formed and maintained throughout the working career, many individuals are left with few opportunities for occupying their time with satisfying activities. In situations characterized by small families where it has become increasingly accepted for children to move away from the household of origin when they start their own families (or even earlier), many of the ties that in traditional family systems ensured the welfare of old people are severed; old age often means isolation. The consequences of this type of isolation are far-reaching. In the United Kingdom and the USA, failure to retain an active role in society and be an active member of a family has been identified as one of the chief causes for the admission of old people to mental hospitals. It is also one of the reasons for their delayed recuperation, and for the explicit preference expressed by many for institutionalization rather than rehabilitation and a return to their own homes, where they fear repeated isolation.

The inability of the small family to maintain the welfare of older relatives has also meant that problems that could have been dealt with effectively in the home environment are increasingly left to professional bodies. The consequent burden on health services, particularly in situations where specialized geriatric services do not exist or are not equipped to meet a large demand, has been and continues to be considerable.

The magnitude of this problem cannot be over-emphasized. Recent demographic projections for Europe alone indicate that by the year 2000 one in every 20 Europeans will be aged 75 years or over, a 100 per cent increase over the comparable situation in 1950. Similar growth in the populations of old people in other parts of the world can be anticipated as longevity increases.

The health-related needs of such groups cannot and should not be seen as solvable simply by extending the existing geriatric services. Much more important will be the close examination of older people's needs in modern society and the development of appropriate counselling, educational re-training and recreational services, all orientated towards the continued functional integration of the aged in society.

What do these issues mean for health and health planning? That the family is changing is clear. That the implications for the individual, the family and the community are significant is also apparent. Many of the changes may be inevitable, and it would be both inappropriate and purposeless to make any moral evaluation of the changes in family structure. It is, however, imperative that these changes be carefully taken into account by those who plan health and social services, so that the ramifications of the transition that is taking place be anticipated in terms of services designed to meet the various needs of the family and its members. In developing countries the rapidity with which these changes are occurring makes it imperative that attention be focused on their problems. In developed countries, meanwhile, it would be naïve to suppose that the situation has been adequately met, for indeed it is in these countries, where the change has been relatively gradual, that too much has been taken for granted and too little adaptation in terms of services has been attempted.[4]

To sum up it may be said that:

1. There should be awareness and acceptance of the inevitability of change and increased mobility of families, which make community relations more difficult.
2. There is an urgent need for planned scientific research into the extent, nature and root causes of the psychopathological states associated with ongoing change in the family structure.
3. At an early stage, the mental health team should collaborate with those working in the planning and delivery of health care; and, a step further.
4. Health service administrators should collaborate with planners in other disciplines such as economics, architecture and town planning, agronomy, agriculture, etc. as appropriate.

There are occasions when medical intervention is appropriate, although neither disease nor impairment is directly involved. Intervention of this kind may be preventive or supportive. Either way, it is an imperative step in the interests of family mental health.[5]

Education for Family Health

Although the basic conditions of organization of services for family health are necessary, the attainment of true family health depends upon the education both of members of families (nearly every member of the general public is a member of a family) and of health workers of all categories. (See Table 6.1) This education and training will be effective only when behaviour is altered and decisions are made with new knowledge and different attitudes as the family member understands more of family dynamics and relationships, and as the health worker sees beyond the individual into the family. This is manifestly easier said than done. For instance, the idea that the family itself is the greatest potential contributor to family health is not new, but the incorporation of education for family members at different ages as integral parts of health and educational services is far from being realized in practice. The education of health workers in family health, getting them to see the family as a group of inter-related persons, would also be a radical departure from almost every type of traditional training.

Thus medical and health training for primary health care would once again be shared between community and hospital, the "normal" family and its dynamics would be understood as a background to the "abnormal" just as "physiology" and "anatomy" can be integrated with "pathology". Teaching and learning would then be related to the social

TABLE 6.1

Areas of Family Functioning

Biological	*Psychological*	*Socio-cultural*	*Economic*	*Educational*
(i) Reproduction of the species	(i) Emotional Security of members	(i) The transfer of values relating to behaviour, tradition, language and mores	(i) Acquisition of resources to fulfil other functions	(i) Inculcation of skills, attitudes and knowledge relating to other functions
(ii) Rearing of children	(ii) Sense of identity for members	(ii) Socialization of children	(ii) Distribution of resources, expenditure, saving	(ii) Preparation for adult life
(iii) Nutrition of family members	(iii) Maturation of personality	(iii) The formulation of norms of behaviour for all stages in development and adult life	(iii) Economic buffering of members of family	(iii) Fulfillment of adult role
(iv) Protection of health of family members at all ges	(iv) Psychological protection			
(v) Recreation for family and its members	(v) Ability to make relationships outside the family			

Source: WHO: *World Health*, Aug.-Sept. 1975.

context of the region in which the teaching organization was situated, and the hospital would act as an institution within society rather than the centre of society as it seems to appear to so many medical teachers.

In all health care there is a large element of education yet generally speaking health workers are relatively ineffective as educators. The reasons for this are complex; one is because most of their training is still directed to the alleviation of symptoms or of episodes of illness or disability, and does not lead or compel them to think through the symptoms of illness to its prevention in the future or to consider the long-term prevention of disease by changing patterns of individual or family behaviour. No one pretends it is easy to change such set patterns of human behaviour but it is regrettable that most training schemes for health workers do not even make the student aware of the problem, let alone give them any grasp of the techniques by which changes can be accomplished.

The delivery of health care will vary from one society to another and, as it does, so too will the roles of the various categories of health workers. Yet ultimately the effectiveness of all health workers depends upon their awareness of their own role in society and their attitude towards and understanding of the society in which they work. Understanding of society in its trunk begins with understanding of family, so that an awareness of family dynamics and family health should form an integral part of the training and later of the practice of every health worker whatever their role or category.

The organization of primary care service to provide family health care with the family as a health unit would require an educational set-up very different from that, which obtains today. Our submission is that at whatever level of development it could be applied, beginning with maternal and child health and family planning and progressing to a full primary care health team, such a set-up would give a better return for expenditure, lay a better foundation for health and provide a scheme for continuous development of family care and family health. The primary problem is to change the outlook, attitude and education of the health workers themselves.

Viewed from this standpoint, the health of the family might appear to be simply the sum of the health of all the individuals making up the family. In fact, it represents much more than this, since it takes into consideration the interpersonal relationships within the family group and the biological and social environment in which the group functions and lives. In this light, the most important indices of family health are probably the composition of the family, the patterns of its growth until it is complete, and the physical and psychological development of the children. The quality of life or of happiness is difficult to quantify, and there are such negative factors as the effect of morbidity and mortality on the family structure, or crises, both transitory and lasting, which may tend to break up the group.

Family health and community health are distinct entities, even though closely linked with each other. A community cannot be healthy if the families of which it is composed are themselves in a poor shape. One of the afflictions of many modern societies is the existence of underprivileged, excluded or marginal families cut-off from the benefits of expansion and socio-economic progress. These constitute what has been very vividly described as the "Fourth World". Coping with the problems they face simultaneously promotes the health of the community. To go one stage further, it may be asserted that every family should be induced, by means of education rather than coercion, to assume responsibility not only for its own health problems but also for the well being of the community of which it is a part. Through reliance on such families, public health will be able to make its objectives and activities acceptable.

In our era of rapid change, it is fundamental to have a proper grasp of the concept of the family within the context of its everyday life in order to plan judiciously the services, which are required to meet health needs. The family represents an essential element in the functioning of society; in return, it is entitled to expect society to provide a certain number of services, notably access to education, to welfare and to progress in all fields—not least, in that of health[6].

The rapid social changes in many parts of the world especially taking the form of over-urbanization, have brought about important changes in values, family structure and community experience, which in turn interfere with some of the important psychosocial and health needs of human beings. The shrinking of the extended family and the disintegration of communities have resulted in less effective social support networks and less likelihood of giving or receiving emotional support; in less responsibility for local affairs; in fewer opportunities for cooperative small group interaction and action; and in fewer activities in general that stimulate a sense of personal involvement, belonging, comradeship and responsibility. Gripped by a sense of isolation or alienation, young people particularly, in their search for group membership and values worth identifying with, that is, in quest of a sense of belonging and responsibility, simply cannot satisfy those needs in healthy ways. They become all the more subject to health risk behaviour like addiction, or to manipulation or abuse by political and criminal organizations.[7]

If the world of tomorrow is to be an improvement on what we have today, it will be inhabited by people capable of creating new shapes and forms through grafting on to what was best in the past.

It is observe that the view of those gloomy prophets who say that, because of high divorce rates, falling birth rates, the dispersion and mobility of families and changes in moral codes and occupational patterns, the family as an institution will disappear. It has been stressed that today's medical establishments are not doing enough to provide health care for the family. Once the problems facing primary health care are better apparent to all, it will no doubt be seen that most of the relevant technology can be reduced to a series of routine patterns—most of which can be carried out by auxiliary personnel, or even entrusted to the family. Such radical changes in family health care, however, will depend upon the ability of the health professions to listen to the needs and desires of the people.

What is needed is something of a moral revolution. Health is the business of the individual, the family and the community. Health services must be restructured in a manner that consistently aims at increasing human well-being. If the ethic of providing better health care for every body can prevail, then we shall see changes in the health of the family that will augur well for the health of the entire human family.[8]

In this labyrinth of conjecture and confusion about causes, effects and the mechanisms involved, certain aspects of the new type of familv set-up are repeatedly mentioned as being potentially pathogenic. Chief amongst these are:

1. The weakening of authority and relaxation of primary control by the elders of the extended family.
2. A change in the traditional role of the womenfolk, who nowadays frequently work outside the homestead and, in effect, cope with at least two full-time jobs.
3. The present day competitive economy with growing inflation and unemployment, and the consequent emergence of a vigorous individualism; and
4. Exposure to the influence of new moral values, ideals and practices in the outside world, awareness of which gives rise to new statuses based on education and affluence and causes conflicts in individuals which are particularly difficult for the adolescent to resolve and may lead to identity crises and a variety of disturbed or delinquent behaviour.[9]

GUIDE TO FAMILY HEALTH

"Health Begins at Home" was the theme chosen for World Health Day, 1973, on the 25th Anniversary of WHO, in recognition of the important role of the family in promoting and protecting the health of its members. The mother and children are not only at the very centre of the family unit, but they are also subject to special health risks. The care of mothers and children, including nutrition and family planning as important components of family health, is briefly reviewed in the following paragraphs specially chosen to illustrate some of the problems and public health actions, which can be usefully taken in this field.

Family Diet

Eating well. A pleasant and healthy diet, not necessarily an expensive one, is one of the most satisfying and stimulating activities of family life. It contributes to the physical, mental and social well-being of all members of the family.

A Family Disease

Malnutrition is a social disease. Treating one person only will not solve the basic problem. Other members of the family will continue to be at risk. The needs and problems of the whole family have to be considered and met.

Pre-Natal Care

To ensure the normal outcome of a pregnancy—a healthy mother and a healthy child—periodic examinations during pregnancy with appropriate health and nutrition education can help to avoid most of the possible complications. This pre-natal care can be entrusted to properly trained health workers using simple and safe procedures.

Birth

At birth a baby is already nine months old. During this crucial period in his mother's womb the unborn baby develops from a single cell—the fertilized ovum—to a healthy new born. Adequate care and hygienic conditions are essential to both mother and baby to ensure a healthy birth.

Use of Common Foods

Man does not always instinctively choose the right foods for maintaining his health. He is influenced in his food habits by religion, culture, social status, tradition and beliefs.

Nature abounds in good nutritious foods—within reach of economically under-privileged families. A balanced diet does not mean an expensive diet. Good nutrition and sound health can be maintained by a suitable combination, in sufficient amounts, of cereals, legumes, vegetables and fruits of all kinds with a little fat or oil. Small amounts of animal products like milk, cheese, eggs and meat when available can help in achieving a good diet, but they are not nutritionally indispensable.

With proper education, families with limited financial resources can take better care of their nutritional needs.

Post-Natal Care

After adequate training, a rural health worker has the confidence required to show a young mother how she can take proper care of her first baby. Many other basic and simple, but fundamental, concepts and practices of health can be explained, making use of what is available at home.

Breast Feeding

Baby's few months of life are bliss! Sheltered in the warmth of mother's bosom, Mother Nature looks after all his nutritional needs through breast milk. It is the most hygienic, most nutritious and the cheapest food for human infants. It is the best insurance against malnutrition in infancy and it also increases the resistance of the body to severe infections. Nursing mothers need an adequate diet to produce a sufficient quantity and quality of milk.

Bottle Feeding

The alarming decline in breast-feeding among the low socio-economic urban communities in recent years and its replacement by bottle feeding with unsatisfactory milk substitutes, prepared and given in the most unhygienic manner, have produced serious health problems.

The incidence of malnutrition and gastro-enteritis has jumped during the early months of infancy.

The feeding bottle is indeed a dangerous instrument in low socio-economic communities and should be avoided. For supplementary feeding of breast-fed babies the cup and spoon can and should be used.

Supplementary Feeding

By the time a healthy infant is one year old he should have tripled his birth weight. When he is two years old, almost eight-tenths of his brain is formed and the other organs and tissues are growing rapidly. Mother's milk alone is not enough after 4-6 months. The vigorously active, rapidly growing baby needs good sources of energy, protein and other nutrients in gradually increasing amounts to supplement mother's milk. Cereals, legumes, vegetables and fruits, properly prepared, can provide the additional calories and nutrients required while the baby continues to have its mother's milk for as long as possible.

The Adventure of Growing up

Through his mother, a baby first learns to love and accept love, knows the feeling of security and joy in achievement and comes to recognize himself as an individual. The psychosocial stimulation of the child in a healthy environment is fundamental for his normal development.

Weaning

The weaning period is a crucial phase in human life representing a transition from liquid to solid feeding. The child moves from a period of close proximity to and dependence on the mother, to a more mobile independent existence. Filling up baby with liquid starchy gruels in place of or in addition to milk is a mistake, which many mothers make and for which the children have to play with malnutrition. The combine effect of malnutrition and infection is responsible for most deaths and ill-health at this age.

Checking on Growth

Children suffering from malnutrition and disease over a long period reach a "point of no return". Several irreversible changes are produced in his body—which may handicap him for the rest of his life. Screening children for early growth retardation is a vital necessity, so that appropriate simple measures can be taken. Advanced cases require hospitalization for long periods, and this is difficult to achieve in countries with a scarcity of hospital beds.

Screening can be done by the use of a simple growth chart. WHO has prepared such charts, which can be conveniently used by primary health workers.

Housing

Disease and socio-psychological problems are to a great extent determined by the immediate environment of the family—its home. A clean and functional house, not necessarily expensive but adapted to the environment and favouring a healthy way of life for its inhabitants, is an important factor in the prevention of many of the diseases and other problems now afflicting large population groups in rural areas, and even more so in city slums.

Health and School

Children who are ill or malnourished are in no condition to benefit fully from their teachers' lessons. Their performance is poor and the number of dropouts is high-big loss for socio-economic development. Early detection of disease, and preventive measures, such as immunization, health and nutrition education, and a healthy school environment, are essential.

Day Care Centres

Day care centres for pre-school children are becoming a necessity in many places, especially in industrialized countries where a large proportion of mothers go out to work. They should be used for educating children as well as for providing them with adequate health services.

Periodic Control

The first years of life are full of health hazards, particularly in developing countries. Periodic examination of small children by properly trained health workers can contribute to preventing or overcoming most of these health hazards. Over 90 per cent of the diseases afflicting children in developing countries are preventable or can be cured by very simple measures if treated in time.

Nutrition and Infection

Malnutrition and infection are a deadly combination. Each aggravates the other, resulting in alarming mortality and morbidity patterns among children in developing countries. Common diseases like diarrhoea, respiratory infections and measles can be fatal for malnourished children. On the other hand, these infections are frequently the main cause of severe malnutrition in children living on a bare subsistence diet, but which could be adequate for their health if they were not frequently suffering from them. Nutrition promotion and control of communicable diseases, implemented together, reinforce each other.

Immunization

Many of the dreadful diseases of childhood including diphtheria, whooping cough, tetanus, poliomyelitis, tuberculosis, smallpox, measles and others can be prevented by vaccination. All children in the world must have the right to enjoy the benefits of the great advances made by medical science.

Family Planning

Family planning is concerned with the quality of life. In the context of family health, it is a way of helping families to be healthier and happier. With family planning, pregnancies can be spaced so that a woman can regain all her strength and take good care of a new child. Many different methods of family planning are available today, which enable couples to determine when and how many children they wish to have.

Accidents

Accidents constitute a common health hazard for children. The nature of these may vary in different areas, but they are always an important cause of death or disability. In any health programme proper consideration should therefore be given to prevention of accidents and rehabilitation of the injured.

Environmental Sanitation

An insufficient supply of water, inadequate disposal of human and other waste, an abundance of insects and other disease carriers are among the environmental factors continuously menacing family health. Many of the still highly prevalent diseases responsible for death and weakness, especially of children, like diarrhoeas and parasitic diseases are the result of living in an unclean area.[10]

CONCLUSION

Viewed from this standpoint, the health of the family might appear to be simply the sum of the health of all individuals making up the family. In fact, it represents much more than this, since it takes into consideration the interpersonal relationships within the family group and the biological and social environment in which the group functions and lives. In this light, the most important indices of family health are probably the composition of the family, the patterns of its growth until it is complete, and the physical and psychological development of the children. The quality of life or of happiness is difficult to quantify, and there are such negative factors as the effect of morbidity and mortality on the family structure, or crises, both transitory and lasting, which may tend to break up the group.

Family health and community health are distinct entities, even though closely linked with each other. A community cannot be healthy if the families of which it is composed are themselves in a poor shape. One of the afflictions of many modern societies is the existence of underprivileged, excluded or marginal families out of from the benefits of expansion and socio-economic progress. These constitute what has been very vividly described as the "Fourth World". Coping with the problems they face simultaneously promotes the health of the community. To go one stage further, it may be asserted that every family should be induced, by means of education rather than coercion, to assume responsibility not only for its own health problems but also for the well being of the community of which it is a part. Through reliance on such families, public health will be able to make its objectives and activities acceptable.

In our era of rapid change, it is fundamental to have a proper grasp of the concept of the family within the context of its everyday life in order to plan judiciously the services, which are required to meet health needs. The family represents an essential element in the functioning of society; in return, it is entitled to expect society to provide a certain number of services, notably access to education, to welfare and to progress in all fields—not least, in that of health.[11]

Notes and References

1. WHO: Bertha C.A. Johnson, "Changing Patterns", *World Health,* August-September 1975, p. 16.
2. WHO: Manuel Carballo, "Need for Adaptation", *World Health,* August-September 1975, p. 34.
3. WHO: Manuel Carballo, "Need for Adaptation", *World Health,* August-September 1975, p. 34.
4. *Ibid.,* pp. 34-37.
5. WHO: Bertha, C.A. Johnson, "Changing Patterns", *World Health,* August-September 1975, p. 21.
6. WHO: Michel Mañciaux, "The Health of the Family", August-September 1975, p. 9.
7. WHO: Rene Diekstra, City lifestyles, *World Health,* June 1988, p. 19.
8. WHO: Halfdan Mahler, "A Moral Revolution", August-September 1975, p. 3.
9. WHO: Bertha, C.A. Johnson, "Changing Patterns", August-September 1975, p. 20.
10. WHO: Appendix Guidelines to Family Health, August-September, pp. 22-28.
11. WHO: Michel Manciaus, The Health of the Family, *World Health,* August-September, 1975, p. 9.

CHAPTER 7

HEALTH EDUCATION: SEXUALITY AND SEX EDUCATION

> Healthy and objective information on sex will not only help in ensuring better adjustments that are often marred by sexual frustration but will also help in securing satisfactory relationship among people when they get married. Experts have considerably emphasized the need for sex-education among juveniles so that mis-information may not lead them to commit wrong actions, which is likely to lead them to tragic goals of life. Therefore, schools have to provide certain basic information on sex behaviour in human beings the knowledge of which will enable boys and girls to understand the behaviour in proper scientific perspective.
>
> —*C.L. Kundu and D.N. Tutto*
>
> Educational Psychology

Health Education: Sexuality and Sex Education

> Through sex-education, we also aspire to achieve the reduction in sexual offences including juvenile delinquency. Sex education will build self-confidence in children and free them from the evil feelings. Self-confidence is so essential for smooth sailing in this sphere. Modern young man is haunted by a peculiar kind of neurosis—that they will not be able to carry out their duties as husbands in a satisfactory manner, all because of lack of sex-education and proper attitude towards sex. Schools can promotes sex education in an authentic way.
>
> —*S.K. Nanda*
>
> Indian Education and its Problems Today

The onset of adolescence is a critical period of biological and psychological change for the individual. For many, it involves a drastic change in social environment. These years are highly formative for health-relevant behaviour patterns such as the smoking of cigarettes, the use of alcohol or other drugs, the driving of automobiles, habits of food intake and exercise, and patterns of human relationship.

The onset of adolescence is triggered by events in the brain. Information is transmitted from the brain to the pituitary gland, and pituitary hormones then stimulate the secretion of sex hormones, which have important effects on various tissues of the body, including the brain. These hormonal changes are probably related to concomitant changes in sexual, aggressive, and emotional behaviour. It is remarkable that so little psychobiological evidence is available on such relations, but much new information may be expected in the years ahead.[1]

Major changes are taking place today in the roles of men and

CHART 7.1

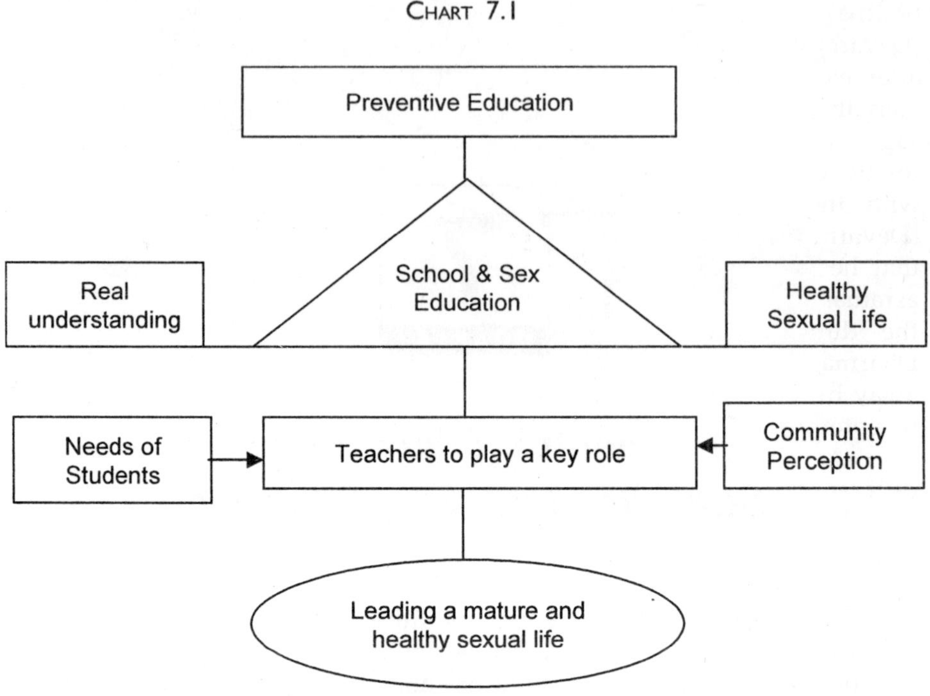

women, which are now less polarized than ever before. The dependence of women is on the decrease and male supremacy has almost disappeared. Clearly defined forms of masculinity and femininity have given way to a diversity of make-up, to increasing individualization or forms of behaviour independent of sex, and to uncertain and conflicting expectations.

Marital relations have altered. The family has become smaller while relations between family members have become closer and more intimate. Century old anti-sexual tendencies have broken down. Sexuality has entered the arts, and nudity and is no longer a taboo. The expression of one's emotions is accepted.

The double standard (for men and for women) is less apparent; overall sexual activity has increased. The widening gap between sexuality and its purely procreative role is reflected in increasing sexual contacts among people of all ages, a weakening of sexual restraint, early commencement of sexual life and relatively tardy social maturity.

According to Dharma, one has to lead his complete life in four asramas, viz Brahmacarysrama, Grhasthasrama, Vanaprasthasrama and Sannyasasrama. Dharma has ordained specific duties and goals for every asramas. The asramas system helps a man develop himself physically, psychologically, intellectually and socially. According to the Dharmasastras every man has three debts (Rnas) viz. the debt to sages

(Rsirna), the debt to the ancestors (Pitrrna) and the debt to the gods (Devarna). Manu instructs that one should set his mind on the Moksa after clearing away these debts.[2] To clear away these debts one has to pass the former three asramas. A man can clear away his debts to the sages (Rsirna) by studying Vedas in accordance with the rules laid down for their study, to the ancestors (Pitrrna) by begetting sons in accordance with the norms laid down in the Dharmasastras and to the Gods (Devarna) by offering sacrifices according to one's capacity.[3] Manu opines that he who seeks Moksa without fulfilling his duties in the first three asramas will sink low to damnation. Therefore, a man has to perform all the duties relating to the asramas as per the injunctions of the Dharmasastra. The Dharmasastra clearly mentions that one has to clear away his pitrrna by begetting a son in the rightful way. For this, one has to enter the Grhasthasrama.

Man and the woman, though they belong to human race, have different types of bodily structures. There are various erotic points in their body. The emotions and the expression of emotions vary from man to woman. Thus there are many distinctions in physical and psychological elements among men and women. Man and woman, at first, have to understand the physical and emotional condition of their partner. Then only he or she will get the real pleasure of sex. Especially the body structure and the personality of the woman is a complex element. Therefore, a man has to understand his mate before indulging in sex-sports. The texts on erotics or sex-education will help him in this regard. It will help understand the nature, the desire, the passion and the longing of the spouse. Therefore, the study of the Kamasastra or the science of Erotics is essential.

Kalyanamalla, the author of Anangaranga opines that the man who does not know the science of sex behaves like an animal. He does not experience the sex pleasure which is equal to Paramananda, i.e. Brahmananda.

This new ethical climate in many parts of the world has obliged doctors, teachers and parents to try to understand the difficulties children and adolescents face in adapting to such a mobile society, and has made them aware of the need for sex education. However, many people believe that the aims, principles and content of sex education are still unclear or open to argument.

The purpose of sexual education is to help people to lead a satisfactory and healthy sex life. Requirements for sexual health can be summed up as: the capacity to enjoy and control sexual and reproductive behaviour in accordance with a social individual ethic; freedom from sentiments of fear, shame, guilt, false beliefs and other psychological factors inhibiting sexual response and impairing sexual relationship; freedom from organic disorders, diseases and deficiencies that interfere with sexual and reproductive functions.[4]

When we look at the special health problems of the young, the mortality rates for accidents, the problem of sexually transmitted diseases, and the various nutritional, psychological, recreational and health service needs of the adolescent, it must not be forgotten that all these are intimately related to the fundamental, social and cultural context in which the adolescent lives.[5]

No less important and disturbing than this quantitative aspect, we have to bear in mind the qualitative aspect underlying the alternatives stated above; behind the bald statement quoted from the WHO document there lies a whole series of fearful choices for the adolescent girl:

- whether or not to embark on a career of heterosexual activity; if so, when and in what circumstances—in the lasting delirium of a grand passion or in the vapours of alcohol after a hectic party; or if not, how to resist the pressures of teasing (and possibly envious) comrades, the demands of boys or men, or the permissive atmosphere of contemporary urban society;
- whether or not to increase the relationships and/or the number of partners, with a consequent risk in the second case of adding to the risk of infection;
- whether to worry about the risk of pregnancy and to obtain the best possible means to prevent it, or not to worry and to do nothing about it. The most recent British figures show a certain proportion of the "sexually active" who only rarely take sensible precautions (WHO, 1975);
- in the event that pregnancy is suspected, whether to put off indefinitely any medical or biological confirmation or to face up to the reality as quickly as possible, however catastrophic that reality might be;
- once pregnancy is confirmed, whether to lock up the secret and conceal the "accident" for as long as possible or to seek early advice, help and support from wherever it is certain to be forthcoming. According to Deschamps, "the pregnant adolescent girl is psychologically and socially alone in assuming her role of mother";
- when the pregnancy is conceded as an unforeseen mishap during a stable relationship with a loving partner who is also valuable as a confidant, whether to discuss with him the best steps to take, or to leave him under one pretext or another—a simple enough solution in the absence of marital ties;
- finally, when the outcome of the pregnancy, for one reason or another, is the birth of a healthy but illegitimate baby, whether to keep it despite all the obstacles which society in most countries still puts in the road for the unmarried mother, or to resign oneself to having it adopted. Such a separation can be a rending experience for an adolescent mother uncertain of the fate and future happiness of the child she will never see again.

Young girls today, generally present an appearance of blooming health. But in the domain of sexual relationships, a whole series of fearful choices may lie before the growing girl. Whatever choice she makes demands a high degree of maturity, and the risks of making an error of judgment are all the greater if she is at a younger age, or is less knowledgeable about sexual matters.

It is time for the health professionals to show sufficient imagination and initiative to ensure that adolescents prefer contraception to abortion; and it is up to medical science to discover vaccines against syphilis and gonorrhoea and thus make a significant contribution towards the battle to control these diseases[6].

The content of any sex education programme must of course be adjusted to the particular sociological environment. Vague though this statement might appear at first sight, it calls for a great effort to provide enough knowledge to enable the students to put the sexual attitudes and rules of their own society into a historical and sociological framework. Why do we put so much effort into teaching, for instance, the history of religion, while totally neglecting the historical evolution of human sex.[7]

It is not altogether surprising then that a so-called generation gap should have emerged to further emphasize the marginality of the adolescent from the core of the social framework or that adolescence shows an inclination, albeit an unnecessary one, to become a problem period of growth. It is, after all, this fact that has contributed to adolescence attracting the attention and concern that it has today. But it is perhaps ironic that—in an age when so much is known about the needs of human beings with respect to personal and social life—more is not actually done to structure the context in which adolescents function in such a way that meaning and identity would be easier to define and, once defined, would show more consistency with the society concerned.[8]

So what are the aims and nature of sex education? Sex education comprises all that which helps to shape the total personality of an individual capable of recognizing the social, moral, psychological and physiological characteristics of his (or her) sexual make-up and establishing optimum interpersonal relationships with persons of his own and the opposite sex. Knowledge of sexual functions helps to allay feelings of shame, taboo, ignorance, mystery and fear in relation to sexuality. This knowledge should prevent the development of bad habits and help children to adapt to their nascent maturity; it should not only prepare the way for sound development of reproductive functions but also inculcate a sense of responsibility for the health and welfare of the future partner and future children, and prevent conflict in marital relationships.

While it takes a number of years for children to learn about their anatomical and physiological characteristics, many more are needed for them to acquire the psychological traits of masculinity or femininity and to understand and internalize the sexual role. The timeliness and completeness of this process provide the basis for self-confidence, fullness of emotions, clarity of intentions and adequacy of interpersonal relationships within the family and the community.

Sex education is often regarded as an intimate process, which cannot take place in a large group of people and especially not in the presence of strangers. This has prompted parents in some countries to request the removal of specific topics from school curricula. It has been found, however, that even well informed parents do not attend to sex education. Some people have concluded that such education should only be given at school; but this is contrary to the view that it should be started at a very young age. What is needed is to bring together the parents, the school and the health services as educators.

The mass media (press, radio, films, television) have a stronger influence on children and adolescents than on adults. The absence of a firm line of conduct or of definite standards of taste, and the fragility of nascent moral values, make films and reading materials dangerous since children and adolescents are not ready to understand them fully. The ambiguity of certain subjects, their incomplete treatment, or the exposure of naked human relationships lead to an incorrect moral appraisal of the behaviour of heroes and heroines and their adoption as models. Educators and parents have the responsibility not only for selecting reading materials for young people but also for ensuring that they understand them and can make a moral appraisal of what takes place. Discussing a book or a film together is more useful than prohibitions or locking up book cases.

All educational measures must be appropriate to the child's development. It is important to talk to the child about matters on which he asks questions, or which he understands. Account has to be taken of the child's intellectual level and his sexual knowledge. Nowadays parents and teachers generally try to discuss the relevant topics years after the children have learnt about them on their own. The fact is that no information, conveyed in a readily understandable way and adapted to the child's particular interests and ideas, should be regarded as premature. All information received by the child produces an emotional reaction and it is therefore important that parents teach the child as early as possible to look on pregnancy, birth and attraction to the opposite sex as positive occurrences that bring happiness.

In summary, then, the attention of parents and the entire community must be drawn to the need to prepare children for life with a partner, marriage and family life. It should be made clear that sex education is one aspect of the formation of a complete and socially active personality, with awareness of the sexual role and the capacity for concern and acceptance of responsibility for one's own behaviour and for the welfare of one's partner and future children.

Parents must learn to help children to become properly aware of their sexual role; and they should start sex education as early as possible in the family and then cooperate closely with the school in this sphere. During the educational process, children and adolescents must be free to discuss all sexual matters, and must be encouraged to make moral appraisals in an active way so as to acquire adequate knowledge and, where necessary, to seek help and advice and also contraceptive services. In the interest of parents and the community as a whole, governments should be encouraged to use legal means to make sex education compulsory at teaching institutions.

Finally, the educational process cannot be complete without the participation of medical specialists. Physicians not only provoke counseling for children and adolescents with sexual problems but they also educate teachers and parents, and they make a particularly important contribution by disseminating the rules of hygiene and knowledge of all aspects of sexuality.[9]

The alternative to concerted public health action to control AIDS is the unchecked spread of HIV infection throughout the world, ultimately reaching all segments of the population. The particular biological and epidemiological features of this infection require that the HIV pandemic be seen as a unique public health problem, and not just as another of many communicable disease problems facing the world today. Uninfected populations must be protected, as HIV infection in itself is an adverse health outcome of profound personal and public health importance. The apparently healthy infected person is not only at substantial risk of severe illness at a later date, but creates a public health risk because of the ability to infect others. Public health control of HIV cannot wait for the possible development of effective anti-viral and vaccines. The solution to pandemic health problems calls urgently for international cooperation and global coordination.[10]

Ensuring the safety of blood and blood products:

- The public should be clearly informed that blood donation itself does not incur any risk whatsoever of infecting donors with the AIDS virus.
- Donor education and selection programmes are guaranteed to eliminate potentially infectious units of blood and plasma from being collected.
- Donors should be made aware in advance of their donation that their blood will be tested for the presence of serological markers of virus infection.
- Blood for transfusion and preparation or components should be tested for antibodies to HIV when the risk of transmitting the virus is significant, and when the benefits of such testing outweigh other important factors in providing blood.
- Blood from which plasma derivatives are manufactured should be shown to be free of serological markers of HIV in areas where the virus is prevalent. Specific exceptions might

be considered appropriate by national control authorities based on therapeutic benefit and safety of the product.

- Countries which import blood products should consider, wherever feasible, reviewing manufacturing protocols so as to assess the acceptability of the products, taking into consideration these conclusions and recommendations.
- WHO should provide reference material and sera for use in evaluating and standardizing laboratory tests.
- WHO should attempt to establish uniform scientific criteria for heat inactivation, chemical treatment and serological testing of blood products regarding AIDS.
- WHO should revise its requirements to take new manufacturing and screening procedures into account.[11]

What the sexually transmitted diseases (STDs) have in common is that they are transmitted predominantly by sexual contact; but there are at least 20 causative agents, and they include bacteria, viruses, protozoa, yeast and even arthropods (parasites).

In addition to the five classic "venereal diseases" which include syphilis and gonorrhoea, an increasing number of disease conditions have been found to be spread from one person to another by sexual contact and are often referred to as the "second generation" of STDs. They include conditions such as nongonococcal arthritis (which is often caused by the virus-like bacterium, Chlamydia trachomatis), genital herpes, genital warts, hepatitis B and others.

The most recent addition to this group of diseases is the acquired immunodeficiency syndrome (AIDS), which, because of its high mortality and its rapid spread throughout the world, has become the most talked about STD in recent years. Many of these second generation diseases have been known for years but their extent, method of transmission and clinical consequences are only now appreciated because of advances in diagnostic technology or because of changes in sex practices in some groups.[12]

ACQUIRED IMMUNODEFICIENCY SYNDROME (AIDS)

This apparently new disease labeled by journalists as "Killer Sex Disease" is currently occupying the front pages of most newspapers all over the world. Many cases have been documented in both developed and developing societies. More than 14 African countries have now been epidemiologically linked with the disease and there is alarm that it may spread to other areas. The main feature of this disease is that it destroys the body's natural immunity, leaving the victim highly susceptible to simple infections, which are normally repulsed without harm. While the majority of cases in the "Western" world are linked with homosexuals and intravenous drug users, on the African continent heterosexual transmission is the usual mode of infection. AIDS has now become one of the most serious communicable diseases to threaten mankind, and is certainly the most serious STD.

Sexually transmitted diseases pose major public health problems all over the world. Unfortunately social taboos about even discussing them, let alone controlling and preventing them, act as a powerful brake on the energetic counter-action that needs to be taken. Only by facing frankly the less palatable facts of human nature, and by recognizing the vast scale of problems that are all too often "swept under the carpet", can health care providers and consumers alike give adequate priority and provision to controlling and preventing these diseases.[13]

Prevention of disease transmission and early detection of disease: these are the two activities, which will have the greatest effect in reducing the impact of sexually transmitted diseases (STDs). And in practice these two activities should not be separated.

Although early detection is often aimed at preventing complications of infection in the individual, it may have a greater impact on disease transmission because it removes a source of infection from the community. Prevention of disease transmission to newborn infants may be achieved most effectively by early disease detection in the mother.[14]

Today the society is changing rapidly. Human relations are losing their values. The system of divided family has become a fashion and an unavoidable element. The small families are coming up. Father and the mother both have to work for a moderate and dignified life. They are ready to spend any amount of money for the welfare of their children. But they have no time to discuss or to chitchat with their children. Such children, when attain youth, indulge in illegitimate activities, as they are not guided properly by any member of the family or of the society. Such youths indulge in pre-martial sexual activities. Many youths visit brothels with curiosity with the desire of sex-sport or to test their virility. If they enter once, they become the slaves of sex-sport. Prostitutes swindle their money and health and in turn they cause diseases to them.[15]

Sex education explains the various responsibilities of husband and wife. Both have to take those responsibilities sportively. Then only their life becomes happy. Sex education explains the importance of family planning, the various methods of contraception, the proper age to become a mother, the duties of a pregnant lady, the medicines and the nutritions which are necessary for a pregnant lady, the importance of the breast milk, triple antigens, immunizations, etc. which are necessary to lead a happy life. Therefore, it is necessary even for the married people.[16]

(1) Health Education about the knowledge of growth, development and activities of the Human Body with special reference to genital organs—sexual urges develop as the body changes take place in males and females. A good sex health education would prevent many problems through biological understanding of the sexual phenomenon.

(2) Sex Education need to dispel myths associated with sex . . . sex is considered as a sin and thus anything related to sex is considered bad. Sex is a biological necessity and when undertaken after proper education is not wrong. Hence health education should promote real attitudes towards sex.

(3) Sex education should promote satisfying sexual relationship—Sex is not one sided affair. Sex involves two partners—male and female. Thus, the true success would be possible only when both of them desire and are in a mood. It is not male dominated or female dominated.

(4) Sex Education to avoid sexual diseases—Sexual enjoyment is accompanied by some diseases if sex rules are not followed. Therefore, sex may not be done with different partners.

(5) Sex education should help in procreation—The ultimate purpose of sex is to give birth to healthy children who are the future of the country.

(6) Abstinence: It is obviously a foolproof method, but equally obviously it is unacceptable to many people. So a number of other preventive methods need to be recommended. In order to avoid catching an infection you can—stay away from casual relationships and reduce the number of your partners; use barrier methods such as condoms, diaphragms and vaginal spermicides which may provide protection and should be encouraged regardless of the need for contraception. To be effective, condoms must be used consistently and correctly and must remain intact. Their use protects both the wearer and his partners. Although urinating and washing the genital area after intercourse have not been proved after to be effective in preventing STD transmission, they may help you to avoid some genital infections.

(7) Health Education for Early treatment: If you think you have an infection, consult the nearest clinic or your own doctor right away. The sooner an infection is recognized and treated, the easier it will be for the doctor to cure you.

Here are some possible signs of infection:

- heavy and unusual discharge from the vagina;
- discharge from the penis with staining of underwear;
- a sore, a blister or a rash near the vagina, penis or anus;
- pain or a burning feeling when urinating and a very frequent need to urinate; and
- pain when having intercourse.

Sometimes there are no symptoms at all, especially in women; so if one has any reason to think that she might have been infected, go for a check-up. Remember: early treatment prevents serious complications.

(8) Health Education to Ensure Patient cooperation: This is a vital

part of disease control. All too often, patients stop taking their medication as soon as the symptoms disappear. Do keep to the instructions given by the doctor and do not forget any subsequent appointment, so that the doctor can make sure you have been cured. Most of all do not try to treat yourself. Medication given by a "friend" could do more harm than good, as the drug given for somebody else's problem might not be what is required for you. Taking drugs without a proper diagnosis and prescription may only reduce the symptoms without getting rid of the disease.

(9) Health Education to Ensure Treating contracts: If you have been diagnosed as having an STD, you should stop having sex until treatment is completed. But any sex partners you have had over the previous months, casual or steady, should also consult the clinic or a doctor and be given the benefit of treatment, since they may be infected without knowing it and may be infectious to others—including yourself.[17]

TALKING TO TEENAGERS ABOUT SEX

Mexico's answer to the problems of adolescent sex is known as CORA. This is a network of "orientation centres" (Centros de Oreintacion para Adolescentes), which for nearly a decade has been providing health services to young people, with special emphasis on sexual and reproductive health. A non-profit-making, private association, CORA in fact offers a whole range of educational, social, psychological and medical services to adolescents, their families and the professionals who work with them. Drug abuse is another special topic at these centres.

Since adolescents may be found either in school, at work or on the streets, CORA—the first institution of its type in Latin America—has designed different strategies to reach them, wherever they are. Youth promoters, young students aged between 17 and 24, organize sporting, recreational and cultural activities in order to encourage youngsters to attend the centre during their leisure time.

The network provides contraceptive methods and information about sexually transmitted diseases in schools, factories and communities. And youth teams, based either in the centres or in nearby youth clubs, go out to talk to young people in the streets or at work.

CORA has collaborated with Televisa, a commercial television station, in making a TV "soap opera" called "Caminemos—Let's Walk." The programme has a story line specially aimed at young people and their parents, and includes fairly frank discussions of sex education and family planning.

Another very successful strategy has been the annual contest to find the best Adolescent Theatrical Playwright. The contest has been run since 1980 in collaboration with the National Institute of Fine Arts (INBA) and the office of the Mayor of Mexico City.

Contestants must be between 12 and 22 years of age, and the objectives are:

- to offer young people a forum for self-expression where they can reveal their health problems and concerns;
- to prevent problems of vagrancy by channelising their energy in a positive direction.
- To stimulate artistic expression; and
- To sensitize community leaders to the needs of young people.

Over the past eight years a total of 308 groups, averaging 20 members each, have participated, and about 30,000 people have seen the performances. In an effort to reach still more young people, their parents and the professionals who work with them, five of the best dramatic works were chosen to be put on videotape. They are:

- *Susana*: A story of two teenagers who experience the consequences of an unplanned pregnancy.
- *Jovenes Desoreintados (Disoriented Youth)*: Lack of communication with his parents causes a youth to run away and become involved with drugs and delinquent behaviour.
- *Dos Adolescentes (Two Adolescents)*: A friendship develops between two teens with different sexual histories. This video deals with rape, sexually transmitted diseases, gender roles, and communication within the family.
- *Poesia en Voz Muda (Poetry in a Mute Voice)*: The story highlights the factors that cause the breakup of relationships among young people, such as immaturity and lack of financial resources and support.
- *Requiem para el No Nacido (Requiem for the Unborn Child)*: Abortion as an alternative to unwanted pregnancy seen from the point of view of two couples from distinct social classes.

(These videos are available for purchase, and may be obtained by contacting CORA, Apartado Postal 21-205, 04000 Mexico D.F.)

Puppet theatre is a tool we have found to be vary effective. We use it to promote our services, explain the work of the youth promoters, and motivate young people to learn about AIDS, contraceptives, unwanted pregnancy during adolescence, drug abuse and other health topics. We combine puppet shows with games of chance such as bingo when we have tables available, although theatre is often used in the streets where bingo is not permitted.

We regard comic books as very important educational tools for adolescents. So we have developed a series of three comics on sex education (including prevention of STDs and AIDS, contraceptives, and pregnancy). These are targeted at adolescents from 12 to 15 years old, but we are planning another series of five comic books for older adolescents. All the comics will be on sale in ordinary shops.

We also use more traditional books and pamphlets, and in addition have had some of the books made into slide-tape shows for use with large groups. These materials too are put on sale.

During its ten years of experience, the lesson that CORA has learned is that adolescents are very creative and discover for themselves how best to communicate with their peers. Consequently, instead of providing them with material developed by adults, the best approach is to allow them to create their own materials and to learn from the process.[18]

CONCLUSION

In many countries, boys and girls at school have the opportunity to receive sex education directly from teachers and occasionally from school nurses. As already mentioned, this is primarily offered within a biological framework, and mainly deals with conception, pregnancy, childbirth, contraception, induced abortion, venereal diseases and sexual minorities. Some biological and sociologically important subjects like spontaneous abortions and infertility seem to have escaped attention. Until recently, comparatively little time has been spent on imparting knowledge about sex life in general, and with few exceptions practically nothing is taught about the task of parenthood.

During recent years some sex educators have advocated that young people should have the opportunity to receive much more detailed information than that included in the obligatory school education programmes. However, this new trend has been limited by its over-emphasis of sexual technology, primarily based on some sex research data from USA. A few Youth Sex Guidance Centres seem to have gained a deeper insight into the need for a more integrated outlook on sex education, including tactful talks about psychological factors.

Good and informative books on sexology are generally available. Access to them, however, requires the initiative of a selective search in bookstores or libraries. On the other hand, the general interest in sex matter is reflected not only by a large direct outflow of articles on the subject in many newspapers and magazines, as well as in film, radio and television programmes, but also indirectly by the element of sex built into commercial advertising. The message of the latter—that your likelihood of becoming appreciated, respected, loved in dependent on the extent to which you can conform to a narrow standard of beauty, emphasized or changed by some superficial attribute like clothing or cosmetics—is easily swallowed by the still insecure adolescent trying to orientate himself or herself in a complex society with confusing sexual and moral attitudes. However, many young people seem to have started to get a clear insight into this, and to be reacting against it.[19]

Notes and References

1. WHO: Beatrix and David Hamburg, "Becoming mature", December 1976, p. 12.
2. Manu-VI, 35.
3. *Ibid.*, 36.
4. WHO: D.N. Isaev, "Learning about sex", October 1979, p. 20.
5. WHO: "Adolescence the crucial years", December 1976, p. 1.
6. WHO: Olivier Jeanneret, "that awkward age", December 1976, pp. 10-11.
7. WHO: Maj Hulten, "lowering the taboos", December 1976, p. 25.
8. WHO: Manuel Carballo, "Search for identity", December 1976, p. 29.
9. WHO: D.N. Isaev, "Learning about sex", October 1979, p. 23.
10. WHO: Jonathan Mann, "Acquired Immunodeficiency Syndrome (AIDS)", November 1986, p. 15.
11. From Weekly Epidemiological Record: No. 18, 2 May 1986
12. WHO: George Antal, "Healthier Sex", November 1986, p. 3.
13. WHO: A.O. Osoba and B.O. Ogunbanjo, "Syphilis and gnorrhoea have company", November 1986, p. 7.
14. WHO: Gavin Hart, "Prevention and detection", November 1986, p. 18.
15. Sex Education, Indian View, p. 79.
16. *Ibid.*, pp. 80-81.
17. WHO: "The Keys to STD Control", November 1986, pp. 16-17.
18. Anameli Monroy de Velasco, Talking to teenagers about sex, The World Health Organization, January-February 1989, p. 15.
19. WHO: Maj. Hulten, *World Health*, December 1976, p. 25.

CHAPTER 8

ENVIRONMENTAL HEALTH EDUCATION

> Environment is the most essential for survival and healthy living. Children must be taught about environment to promote healthy living.
>
> —*Author*

Environmental Health Education

Environment has been defined by Webster's New Collegiate Dictionary as "the aggregate of all the external conditions and influences affecting the life and development of an organism". Shri T.N. Chaturvedi in his Editorial to IJPA July-Sept. 1989 (Special Number on Environment and Administration) rightly sees the intimate relationship between human beings and nature since times immemorial. To quote: "Man, since his origin, has lived in harmony with Nature through the ages, holding Nature in awe and reverence. The Vedas, folklore and scriptures of different religions, faiths and beliefs also speak of the need for harmony with the universe, which is the habitat not only of man but also of all animals, bird, insects, plants and vegetation. The mutually supportive role of all living things is often mentioned as a crucial factor for a balanced social and harmonious existence. The ecological balance is inherent in the very process of creation. Everywhere, the seers, poets and thinkers, through the ages, have referred to the need for living in harmony with environment. In fact, the Taitariyopanis had looks at the relationship between man and his environment in its totality and stresses complete harmony and interdependence between them in order to attain real prosperity."

Dr. Hiroshi Nakajima, Director-General of World Health Organization, sounded a warning alarm about degradation of this planet in his Article, "A Wounded Planet."[1] He rightly visualises that it is now increasingly evident that more and more diseases stem from the degradation caused by man to his own environment. The potential harmful effects of industrial development on our global ecosystem are now better known. Ozone layer depletion, acid rain, climate change, chemical pollution are some examples of the man-made wounds to our planet.

We are at a turning point; warnings of the damage to our health and quality of life are growing louder. An increasing number of people are acting to stop the degradation of our environment. Lt. Gen. I.F.R. Jacob, PVSM (Retd.) Governor, Punjab in his message, "Fifty years of Indian Republic" in the *Daily Tribune* (26th January, 2000), remarked that with our rising population the civil services and environment, especially in the urban areas, are under great stress and strain. The degradation of our environment has to be arrested immediately otherwise it would have long-term impact on the quality of life of future generations. We should also take this opportunity to educate our children regarding the importance of the preservation of our environment. Dr. Wilfried Kreiser also elaborates the aspects of environment which affect health of mankind.

How can we make environmental health a more potent force to serve people faced with growing threats to their health? How can our improving environmental health technology be better used to foster positive health? I know of no country-developing or industrialised in which this issue is not urgent and important. I know of many countries in which it is critical. The remarkably wide range of environmental concerns include the international problems of acid rain, the greenhouse effect, and depletion of the planet's ozone layer. It includes national concerns with medical wastes disposal, radioactive and toxic wastes control, transportation accidents, health aspects of urbanisation and traffic, occupational health and safety, and air and water pollution. It also includes local concerns over inadequate water supplies and sanitation facilities, water quality, clean air, solid wastes management, and finding a balance between the economic incentives of development and a decent quality of life. In the report on Our Common Future, the World Commission on Environment and Development (sometimes called the Brundtland Commission) pointed out that the situation is getting increasingly critical. WHO, South-East Asia Regional Office Declaration on Health and Development in the South-East Asia Region in the 21st Century mentions that significant differences exist between the environmental problems of rural and urban areas. In rural areas, poverty, unsafe drinking water, inadequate excreta disposal, combined with contaminated food and illiteracy, are responsible for a majority of illnesses. Poor ventilation, coupled with the use of poorly-designed cooking stoves, causes severe indoor air pollution and health problems, particularly in children and infants. With the intensification of agricultural activities large quantities of pesticides and herbicides are being applied without taking adequate precautionary measures.

In urban areas, on the other hand, environmental problems are the result of rapid and massive population migration from rural to urban areas and of uncontrolled industrialization. Municipal services are unable to keep pace with the urban growth, like providing adequate water supplies, sewerage and sanitation. Overcrowding, inadequate housing with poor ventilation and absence of protection against rain, heat and cold add to the stresses and dangers of urban living. Industries are often located in and around urban areas with uncontrolled disposal of wastes. The Bhopal gas tragedy in India over a decade ago is an example.

Of course, there are other major environmental concerns such as deforestation, global warming, ozone depletion, cross-border movements of hazardous products and other forms of environmental degradation. Protection of the environment and of health endangered by environmental hazards comprises a very large and important international public policy agenda. In developing countries the problems are doubly difficult because of the immediacy of local environmental threats as well as the larger regional and global issues.

ENVIRONMENTAL ADMINISTRATION IN INDIA: GENESIS, GROWTH AND LEGAL FRAMEWORK

As stated in India 1999-A Reference Annual published by Ministry of Information and Broadcasting, in the beginning of the Fourth Five Year Plan problems and issues centred around environment. This resulted in the establishment of the National Council of Environmental Planning and Coordination in 1972 at the Department of Science and Technology. Another empowered Committee was set-up in 1980 for reviewing the existing legislative measures and administrative machinery for ensuring environmental protection and for recommending ways to strengthen them. On the recommendations of this empowered Committee, a separate Department of Environment was set-up in 1980 which was subsequently upgraded in a full-fledged Ministry of Environment and Forests in 1985 to serve as the focal point in the administrative structure of the Government of India for the planning, promotion and coordination of environmental and forestry programmes. The state department of environment, Central and state pollution control boards, the Botanical and Zoological Survey of India, the Forest Survey of India, the National River Conservation Authority (formerly Central Ganga Authority), the National Afforestation and Eco-development Board, the Indian Council for Forestry Research and Education. the Wildlife Institute of India, the National Museum for Natural History, etc. are the Ministry's partners in carrying out of environmental protection activities.

Prevention and Control of Pollution

The policy statement on Abatement of Pollution, adopted in 1992, provides instruments in the form of legislation and regulation, fiscal incentives, voluntary agreements, educational programmes and information campaigns to prevent and control pollution of water, air and land. Since the adoption of the policy statement, the focus of activities has been on issues such as promotion of clean and low waste technologies waste minimisation reuse/recycling, improvement of water quality environment audit, natural resource accounting, development of mass-based standards, institutional and human resource development, etc. The whole issue of pollution prevention and control is dealt with by a combination of command and control methods as well as voluntary and regulatory fiscal measures promotion of awareness and involvement of public.

Central Pollution Control Board

The Central Pollution Control Board (CPCB) is the national apex body for monitoring and control of water and air pollution. The executive responsibilities for enforcement of the Acts for Prevention and Control of Pollution of Water (1974) and Air (1981) and also of the Water (Cess) Act, 1977 are carried out through the Board. The CPCB advises the Central Government on all matters concerning the prevention and control of air, water and noise pollution and provide technical services to the Ministry for implementing the provisions of the Environment (Protection) Act, 1986. Under the Act, effluent and emission standards in respect of 61 categories of industries have been notified.

Education, Awareness and Information

Priority is accorded by the Ministry of Environment and Forests to promote environmental education, create environmental awareness among various age-groups and to disseminate information through Environmental Information System (ENVIS) network to all concerned. Special emphasis is given to non-formal environmental education through seminars/symposia/workshops, training programmes, eco-camps, audio-visual shows, etc. The Ministry has been organising a National Environment Awareness Campaign (NEAC) since July 1980. As a part of this campaign, 19 November to 18 December every year is observed as the National Environment Month. The main themes for the 1997-98 campaign were Pollution Prevention and Control, and Conservation and Plantation of Trees for Environmental Protection. A large number of organisations have been granted financial assistance by the Ministry to organise various activities for creating environmental awareness. The Ministry also provides financial support for setting up eco-clubs at schools and for production of films on environment.

A New Scheme

Paryavaran Vahini, was launched in 1992-93 to create environmental awareness and to ensure active public participation by involving the local people in activities relating to environmental protection. Paryavaran Vahinis are proposed to be constituted in 194 selected districts all over the country which have a high incidence of pollution and density of tribal and forest population. The Vahinis also play a watch-dog role by reporting instance of environmental pollution, deforestation, poaching, etc. They function under the charge of District Collectors, with the active cooperation of the State/Union Territory governments. This scheme is entirely financed by the Ministry of Environment and Forests.

International Cooperation

The Ministry of Environment and Forests functions as a nodal agency for United Nations Environment Programme (UNEP), South Asia Cooperation Environment Programme (SACEP) and International Centre for Integrated Mountain and Development (ICIMOD), International Union for Conservation of Nature and Natural Resources (IUCN) and various international agencies, regional bodies and multilateral institutions.

India is signatory to the following important international treaties/ agreements in the field of environment: (i) International Convention for the Regulation of Whaling, (ii) International Plant Protection Convention, (iii) The Antarctic Treaty, (iv) Convention on Wetlands of international importance, (v) International Convention on International trade in endangered species of wild flora and fauna; (vi) Protocol of 1978 relating to the international convention for the prevention of pollution from ships, (vii) Vienna Convention for the protection of the ozone layer; (viii) Convention on Migratory Species; (ix) Basel Convention on trans-boundary movement of hazardous substances; (x) Framework convention of climate change; (xi) Convention on conservation of biodiversity; (xii) Montreal protocol on the substances that deplete the ozone layer; and (xiii) International Convention for Combating Desertification.

Environmental Legislation

Major legislations directly dealing with the protection of environment are the Wildlife (Protection) Act, 1972, the Forest (Conservation) Act, 1980, the Water (Prevention and Control of Pollution) Act, 1974, the Water (Cess) Act, 1977, the National Environment Appellate Authority Act, 1977, the Air (Prevention and Control of Pollution) Act, 1981, the Environment (Protection) Act, 1986, the Public Liability Insurance Act, 1991 and the National Environment Tribunal Act, 1995. The Constitution (Forty-Second Amendment Act of 1976) gave Parliament the power to enact laws on virtually any entry in the State list, and through Article 253 brought environmental regulation under the Concurrent List. India has increasingly institutionalized its environment concern after the United Nations Conference on Human Environment at Stockholm in 1972, to serve as a guideline to the governments, both Central and State, Article 148A was added to the Directive Principles of State Policy in 1976, which said, "The state shall endeavour to protect and improve environment and safeguard the forests and wildlife of the country." In a new chapter entitled 'Fundamental Duties', Article (51Ag) imposed a similar responsibility on every citizen to protect and improve the natural environment including forests lakes, rivers and wildlife and to have compassion for living creatures. Supreme Court of India has held whenever a problem of ecology is brought before the Court, the Court is bound to bear in mind Art. 48A of the Constitution.

ENVIRONMENT VIS-A-VIS DEVELOPMENT

Nature and Scope of Environmental Health Programme

Meaning

Environmental health refers to the ecological balance that must exist between man and his environment in order to ensure his well-being. The deterioration of the human environment through the population explosion, pollution of air and water, and other disruptions of the ecological balance pose a major international health hazard and a serious challenge. Professor J. Logan, in a paper published in *American Journal of Tropical Medicine* in 1960, was able to show that environmentally transmitted diseases were responsible for the sufferings of 500 million people every year particularly among infants and children. The UN Secretary-General's report on problem of the human environment sounds a similar ominous note: "If current trends continue, the failure of life on earth could be engendered and thus, it is urgent to focus world attention on these problems which threaten humanity in an environment that permits the realisation of the highest human aspirations."[5]

The close relationship that exists between an unhealthy environment and the economic condition of a community was pinpointed by a panel of experts which met in 1971 to discuss the environmental problems of the developing countries. "Poverty and the very lack of development", these experts said, "constitute an essential environmental problem in the developing countries. They recommended an attack on the problems of inadequate water supply, poor housing, sanitation, nutrition and widespread disease as prime targets in an effort to improve the environment of millions of people, and to lay the groundwork for their economic betterment."[6]

Ninth Five Year Plan (Draft) also warns about the bad consequences of poor environment on Health. Environment can affect human health in many ways. Deficiency of iodine in soil, water and foodstuffs is the cause of iodine deficiency disorders. Excessive fluoride content in the water is the cause of fluorosis. Environmental degradation may affect air, land and water. Pollutants may enter the food chain. All these may enter human body through various portals and affect the health status.

Rapidly growing population, urbanisation, changing agricultural, industrial and water resource management, increasing use of pesticides and fossil fuels have all resulted in a perceptible deterioration in the quality of environment and attendant adverse health consequences. Environment pollution due to developmental activities are increasingly becoming the focus of concern. The interactive interdependence of health, environment and sustainable development was accepted as the fulcrum of action under Agenda 21 at the Earth Summit in Brazil in 1992. Environmental health in its broader perspective would have to address the detection, prevention and management of:

(i) existing deficiencies or excesses of certain elements natural environment;
(ii) macro-environmental contamination of air, land, water and food; and
(iii) disaster management.

Aspects of Environmental Health

The environment can be defined as an aggregate of all the external conditions and influences affecting the life and development of an organism. Human environment means everything that is experienced by man and it is the total nature of this experience that determines the quality of life. According to Roggers, "the environment appears to possess two main avenues by which it may, reach man and affect man's health: it may act upon his body as a material agent or it may act upon his mind and emotions as non-.material agent. although sooner or later this may very well produce a material effect.'" The effect of both is the pollution of environment. Prof. Samuel Halter. Professor of Public Health at the University of Brussels defines pollution as "the presence in the ambient environment of chemical, physical or biological factors capable of inducing disturbances in the normal physiology and functioning of human organs.[8]

We can classify the environmental factors impinging on the health of the people as follows:

(a) Physical, Chemical and Biological factors.
(b) Social, Economic and Cultural factors.
(c) Ecological, Economic and Aesthetic factors.
(d) Individual human system.

All these agents in the environment interact with one another and produce the favourable or unfavourable impact on the health of the people.

MEANING AND ROLE OF ENVIRONMENTAL HEALTH ADMINISTRATION

Environmental Sanitation Administration is an activity of diagnosing and controlling the environmental factors which exercise or may exercise a deleterious and unhealthy effect on the physical, social, and mental life of the people, The Draft Five Year Plan (1978-83) has rightly mentioned: "The essence of sound environmental growth lies in a happy blend of the realisation of the physical out limits to the exploitation of environmental resources and the inner limits to human needs and aspiration." Environmental health administration is quite complex and complicated owing to the complexity and diversity of the socio-political and institutional arrangements in which the programmes are implemented and the complexity, multiplicity of the physical, biological, social and economic factors that they must take into account. The objective of the environmental sanitation administration is to plan thoroughly to change favourably the environment itself and modify the interaction of human beings with the environment so that the people can enjoy a good quality of life. The administration of environmental programme is not within the purview of any single discipline but presents a challenge to many disciplines. The administrators responsible for such programmes must plan to attack the unfavourable factors in concern with one another. We may mention some of the important areas which need the immediate attention of the planners, policy-makers and administrators to solve these impending problems—potable safe water supply and water pollution, solid wastes management, air pollution control, occupational health, food sanitation, urban planning and housing, slum clearance, soil erosion, noise pollution, etc. The administration must define in the geographical context the magnitude of each problem, its relationship with others and the benefits expected, direct outputs, intermediate effects or impacts and the ultimate effects or benefits. Some of these have been indicated in the form of a table (see Table 8.1). The administration of environmental health programmes are very expensive and complicated. In order to translate the benefits of such programmes to the society, the administrators must ensure that the programme:

(a) receives acceptance and support;
(b) achieves the desired objectives and results;
(c) links its efforts with those of other health and socio-economic development programmes; and
(d) accomplishes its work economically, with a minimum waste of money and other scarce resources.[10]

We may now take up two important aspects of environment, i.e. water supply and sanitation which affect health development in a big way.

Water Supply and Sanitation

Safe water and improved sanitation are a necessary condition for better health, and there can be no lasting improvement of public health without them. There is no denying the fact that inadequacy of safe drinking water, improper disposal of human excreta, solid and liquid wastes leading to unfavourable environmental condition have been the causes of many killer diseases.

M. Aktar has stated that inadequacy in the availability of safe drinking water, unfavourable environmental conditions and lack of personal hygiene have been the major causes of disease and disability among people. As per WHO statistics, 80 per cent of diseases in the developing countries are related to unsafe water supply and inadequate sanitation causing high child mortality, low life expectancy and poor quality of life. In India, more than one million children below 5 years died from dehydration caused by diarrhoea annually, while another 250 thousand are victims of tetanus. Poliomyelitis has been a cause of lameness among 170 thousand children per year. There is also a very high rate of occurrence of intestinal worms, particularly in West Bengal, Bihar, Orissa, Andhra Pradesh, Tamil Nadu, Kerala and Maharashtra. The national goal to reduce child mortality from 146 per thousand to 125 by 1995 and 70 per thousand by 2000 cannot possibly be achieved without a significant change in the existing mortality/morbidity related to water and sanitation. Also important is to change the peoples' perception about the link between sanitation and health. According to a recent KAP survey in the country, 37 per cent people do not know/do not believe that exposed excreta can harm health. Outdoor defecation is not generally seen as a problem except in terms of inconvenience during rain, night or winter and to women.

Y.N. Nanjudiah has stated that majority of the rural people practice open air defecation as the coverage of sanitation facilities has reached only a negligible population. For want of awareness on health on the part of users quite a large number of latrines are out of use or misused. Further, open air defecation generally enjoys social acceptability. It is considered hygienic and wholesome and in tune with the nature and fresh air. At the same time toilet has a poor image. It is believed to be dirty and a breeding place for flies and mosquitoes. Social surveys carried out so far have highlighted that there is lack of knowledge regarding latrine, which can be summarised as under:

(a) Faecal-borne diseases can be prevented by using a latrine.
(b) Pathogenic microbes survive from days to years in the moist soil and may become wind borne.
(c) Social status and prestige can be attained by having a latrine.
(d) Constipation, particularly among rural women can be eliminated.
(e) Privacy can be achieved.
(f) Low cost sanitation options are available and these can be maintained in an eco-friendly way.

Dr. H. Mahler, former WHO Director-General, has rightly said that, I am utterly convinced that the number of water taps per 1,000 population will be an infinitely more meaningful health indicator than the number of hospital beds per 1,000 population. Mr. Kurt Waldhelm, former UN Secretary-General also stressed that, the provision of safe water and sanitation does not merely mean happier, healthier citizens; it also means increased economic productivity.

Nikolas P. Napulbow in his editorial, "Water For All, a Human Right" has rightly said that, "water is a basic human need for health—

indeed, for survival—and therefore it is not an exaggeration to call it one of the basic human rights. Without safe water and sanitation, there is no real development. A community ravaged by diarrhoeal diseases, dracunculiasis or schistosomiasis cannot look beyond its immediate problems towards social and economic welfare. Safe water is the doorway to health and health is the prerequisite for progress, social equity and human divinity."[11]

Infectious diseases resulting from water pollution can be classified into four groups, depending upon the ways in which their incidence can be lessened by improvements in water supply. (See Chart 8.1)

CHART 8.1

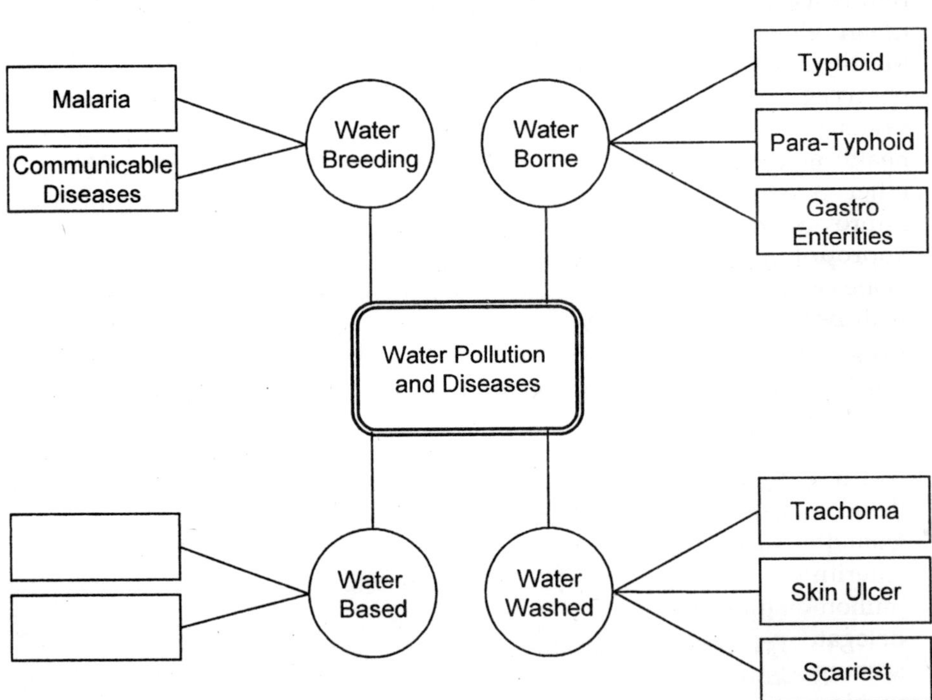

(1) "Water-borne" diseases are those in which infectious agent remains alive in drinking water e.g., typhoid, paratyphoid, gastroenterities, etc. The incidence of these diseases can be reduced by the purification of water.

(2) "Water-washed" diseases include infection of the outer body surface, e.g., trachoma, skin ulcers, scabies and typhus, bacillary and amoebic dysentery and gastroenterities be incidence can be reduced by augmenting water quantity.

(3) "Water-base" infections, i.e., schistosomosi, guinea worms. The Infection occurs when the skin is in contact with water or through drinking water.

(4) "Water breeding" or water promixity diseases are caused by mosquitoes or flies living near aquatic conditions.

There is probably no single factor that has a greater effect on the health, well-being and development of a community than the provision of ample and convenient supply of wholesome and good quality water. In towns and cities water supply is recognised as a basic necessity for industrial and commercial purposes; it is vital for the maintenance of public health and the prevention of epidemics. Dame Barbara Ward, President of the International Institute for Environment and Development, rightly observes that, "Water is everywhere, the key to human health. Clean water is a key to human comfort, health and even survival.[12] Martin Boyer, Adviser, Drinking Water Programme, UNICEF has observed that "The provision of ample supplies of safe water and the sanitary disposal of excreta have a direct and far-reaching effect upon the health and well-being of rural populations. Indeed, it is believed that no other single measure can make a comparable contribution to the improvement of their health and standard of living. The choice of an appropriate technology depends on local conditions.") To quote WHO: "One hospital bed out of four in the world is occupied by a patient who is ill because of polluted water. Provisions of a safe and convenient water supply is the single most important activity that could be undertaken to improve the health of people living in rural areas of the developing world."

WHO estimates that as much as 80 percent of all diseases in the world are associated with water. Lain Guest (Geneva), a specialist in development topics submits that an astonishing number of people suffer from these water related diseases at any time, 400 million with gastro enteritis, 160 million with malaria, 30 million with river blindness, 200 million with Schistosomiasis.[14] At the 1969 World Health Assembly, a delegate from the region (SEA) estimated that water-borne diseases accounted for 40 percent of all morality, and 60 percent of all morbidity in his country.[15]

I.V. Rajeshwar, ex-Governor of West Bengal in his article, "Endemic Problems defying solution" in the *Daily Tribune,* dated January 16, 2000 rightly says that fifty-two years after independence even basic amenities like drinking water supply and unpolluted air are not available to most citizens. At present, water supply is available to 84.33% of urban population and 76.68% to rural population. However sanitation coverage is 49.91 to urban areas and 14.02 to rural areas.

Ninth Plan finds that the existing norms for rural water supply is 40 liters of drinking water per capita per day (LPCD) and a public stand post or a hand pump for 250 persons. Further, the sources of water supply should be within 1.6 km. horizontal distance in plains or 100 metres elevation distance in hills. For cattle in Desert and Drought Prone (DDP) areas, an additional 30 LPCD is recommended. Against this, the norm for urban water supply is 125 LPCD piped water supply with sewerage system, 70 LPCD without sewerage system and 40 LPCD in towns with spot sources. At least one source for 20 families within a maximum distance of 100 metres has been laid down.

As against these norms, the studies as on 1.4.1997 reveal that there were 61,724 habitations without any safe source of drinking water (called not covered habitation). 3.78 lakh habitations which were partially covered and 1.51 lakh habitations which had quality problems like excess fluoride, salinity, iron and arsenic, etc. Apart from the provision in the state plans for water supply, there are major Centrally Sponsored Schemes called the Accelerated Rural Water Supply Programme and the Urban Water Supply Programme for small towns with population of less than 20,000. In order to cover this backlog in rural drinking water supply, it has been estimated that approximately Rs. 40,000 crore will be required including the funds required for operations and maintenance and funds to tackle quality problems. Similarly, the estimates of investment required for full coverage of urban water supply is Rs. 30,734 crore. Drinking water and sanitation improvements could reduce the overall incidence of infant and child diarrhoea by one quarter and cut total infant and child mortality by more than one-half. Country programmes are increasingly taking measures to improve water supply and sanitation within their primary health care programmes. Guinea wonn disease can be effectively prevented by providing safe drinking water and its global eradication is clearly possible within the next few years. As for schistosomiasis, some 60% reduction could be achieved by improving water supplies. Building latrines, giving health education and introducing selected drug therapy could reduce the prevalence even more.[16]

A great surge in the population of India's big cities poses huge problems for safeguarding water supply. We suggest here the methods of conserving water supply:

- Integration of water and waste water management, coupled with health education for cost-effectiveness and promotion of preventive measures for health;
- Prospecting for water resources through state of the art techniques of remote sensing and geophysical surveys;
- Protection of water sources against pollution;
- Decentralization of water supply matching the required quality and quantity through waste recycle and reuse;
- Maintenance of the water distribution system, which can prevent up to 50% of the purified waste water from being lost; and

- Application of mathematical programming techniques with exact fluid flow relationships in the design of water and waste water systems, so as to ensure functionality and to conserve material and financial resources.

Lack of sanitation causes many diseases related to human excreta, sewerage disposal.. Garbage and the use of pesticides and the industrial and radio active wastes. (See Chart 8.2). Following the suspected plague outbreak in the country during 1994 the Planning Commission constituted a High Power Committee on Urban Solid Waste Management in India under the Chairmanship of Member (Health). This committee understood a comprehensive review of current situation of urban solid waste management, specially in cities with one million or more inhabitants and made recommendations for safe methods for collection, transportation of waste and suitable cost-effective, environmentally friendly methods for disposal of these wastes. Pilot projects exploring the dimensions of the problem and aimed at seeking realistic solutions were

CHART 8.2

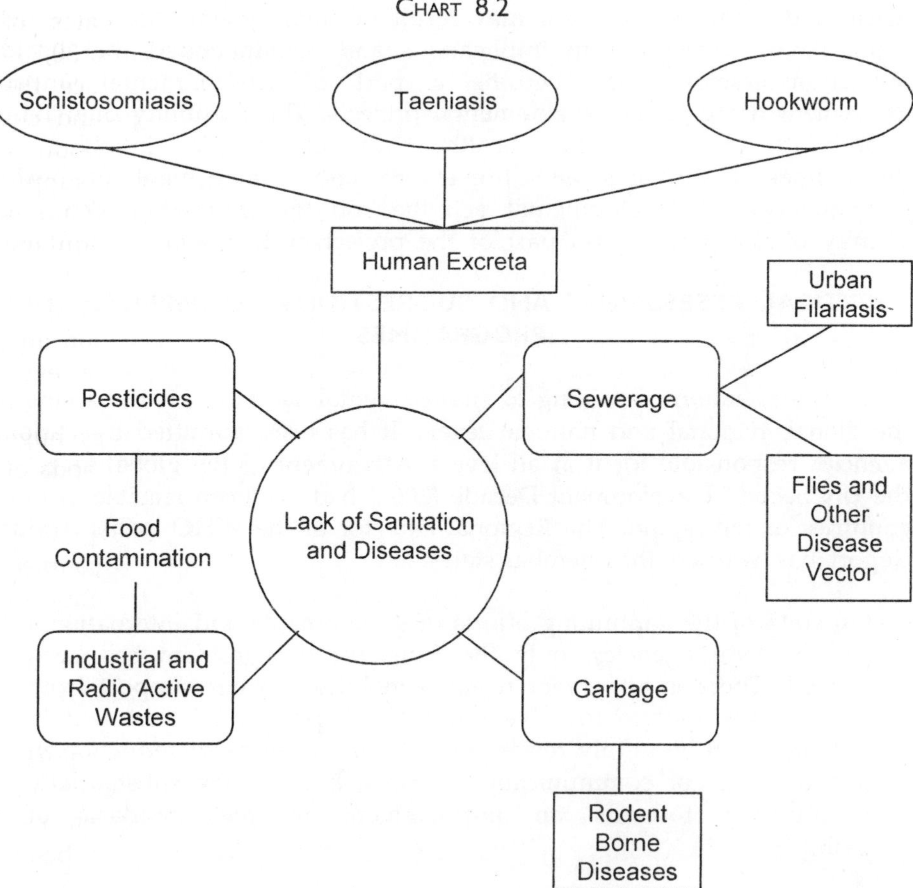

initiated during the Eighth Plan period. During the Ninth Plan period it is expected that many more cities will initiate programmes for the efficient methods of management of wastes generated and improve environmental sanitation.

So far, the major focus has been on communicable disease burden due to poor environmental sanitation in urban areas and due to improper disposal of human excerta, garbage and waste water in rural areas and methods to tackle these. These efforts will be intensified during the Ninth Plan. In addition, efforts to reduce pollution and related non-communicable disease burden will also be strengthened. Efforts will be made to document the extent of the problem of environmental pollution and its impact on health status of the population through linkages between existing environmental monitoring data and data on health status of population living in these areas. Prevention and management of health consequences of environmental deterioration will receive increasing attention.

The Expert Committee on Public Health System had noted that major developmental activities in any field such as agriculture, industries, urban and rural development may result in environment changes which could have adverse health implications and recommended that health impact assessment may become a part of environmental impact assessment of all large developmental projects. The feasibility of making appropriate provision for health care of people involved in developmental activities and prevention and management of health consequences of developmental activities on the population living in vicinity of the project as a part of the project budget will be explored.

CRITICAL ASSESSMENT AND SUGGESTIONS TO IMPROVE THE PROGRAMMES

The situation pertaining to environmental sanitation is horrifying at the global, regional and national levels. It has been admitted by various agencies responsible for it at all levels. Attainment of the global target of the UN Second Development Decade (2002) had not been feasible in most countries of the region. The Regional Director of the WHO in his Annual Report has warned the member-states:

> "In spite of the continuing efforts of governments and international and bilateral agencies, only the fringe of the problem has been tackled. There is an urgent need to mobilise further support from all available sources to solve this difficult problem. Investment in this field will be amply rewarded not only in terms of reduction in the incidence of communicable diseases, but also by substantially contributing towards an improvement in the standard of living."[18]

Dr. Abel Wolman, one of the "father-figures" of environmental health and Professor Emeritus of Sanitary Engineering at the Johns Hopkins School of Engineering, Baltimore, USA says while talking of the world health situation: "It always leads great conferences to pass resolutions to do something about providing water to impoverished people. Resolutions become opiates because they are gratifying substitutes for action."[19] He warns the policy-makers and administrators against complacence and says, "Viewed on a global basis, we have little to be sanguine about. The disease-consequences of poor and insufficient water, of living with human excreta, and of unhygienic personal habits, are disastrous—they have been familiar for so long a time that they no longer excite even the statistician or epidemiologist. People accept their devastation, as they so often abjectly bear their real and spiritual poverty. We speak of the toll of deaths, due to environmental deficiencies in a casual way, even though the figures mount to hundreds of millions. The communicable diseases, often the sequels of poor sanitation are maiming and killing men, women and children—not computer data."[20] It is beyond doubt that a lasting solution to many of the existing and future problems of public health require control on environment. The question arises as how to provide sanitary facilities to hundreds of millions of people still without even minimum sanitary facilities? How to tackle such programmes? How to find the resources required for these programmes? What should be the administrative set-up to ensure speedy implementation? What are the responsibilities of planners and policy-makers to ensure integrated approach? We shall discuss the facts and suggestions to provide good environment for the healthy growth of the people.

(I) Cooperation and Coordination among Allied Programmes

There is a close relationship between the environmental programmes and other programmes. In practice, this relationship is ignored by the planners and administrators of these programmes, e.g., a dam has to be constructed for irrigation and power purposes; its consequences on human health or soil salinity are ignored or underestimated. To remedy such unfortunate situations it is suggested that an 'integrated' approach may be adopted. It presumes an unprecedented, ungrudging cooperation between different services, as well as between various brands of natural scientists on the one hand and of social and human scientists on the other. We have to encourage such integrated approach to have full impact rather than piecemeal goals and approaches. It was mentioned in a WHO document that, "more effective administration requires that planners and managers take account of the full range of implications of their own programme goals and further, that they actively seek to participate as consultants and collaborators in the planning and execution of other community programmes that demonstratively or potentially interact with environmental health."[21]

UNESCO's MAB Programme (Man and the Biosphere Programme) coordinates various disciplines by mobilising applied research efforts all over the world on major man environment resources interactions. It relies on international cooperation among governments and the participation of all specialists. A major UNESCO research programme is closely studying the effects of human interventions in the environment and man himself in all the major socio-economic systems. We can get benefit out of such programmes.[22]

(2) Improve Administrative Capability and Competence

Environmental health programmes are administered by technically qualified people but such people lack administrative capability and capacity, i.e., the ability to achieve results. We have doctors, engineers, town planners, inspectors, nutritionists, geologists who are responsible for improving the environment. Every programme has its administrative component which is the heart and soul of that programme. It is suggested that the persons engaged on these programmes may be given suitable training in administration to enhance their competence.

(3) Deploy more Resources

The Environmental Health Improvement programmes require considerable financial investment. The World Bank and WHO reported to the Mar Del Plata Conference that $ 140,000 million would be needed to reach the target of clean water for all by 1990. Today, we need double this amount to cater to increased population. Where will it come from? External aid is limited. So, there is a need to exploit the resources available within each country. It is only a question of proper allocation of resources. Voluntary effort can be encouraged to accelerate the pace of development. With exploitation of local self-help, money can be generated. It is also a question of political will. This programme must be made an integral part of the community development programme. It should take the form of self-aided programme. The funds allocated should be used to achieve the aim of the policy and care should be taken that the funds are not diverted for other purposes. It was mentioned by Dr. B.H. Dieterich, Director, Division of Environmental Health, WHO that "Development planners confronted with meagre budgets are often forced to keep some projects in abeyance and give priority to others that may bring immediate economic benefit. It is now being increasingly realised that it is not a practicable or economically sound idea to defer environmental health projects. Planners are beginning to look at environmental health projects in the context of the ultimate socio-economic objectives of the development process."[23]

(4) Research to Meet the Requirements of Different Geographical Areas

There are many potential health hazards. We know much about some of these hazards and little about many of them. We must encourage research in the experimental laboratory and epidemiology to pin-point the areas of ignorance. Secondly, national institutes should carry out research to develop models for adapting measures to reduce costs. They may also find simple disinfection devices suited to rural needs. We may not adopt costly western models to supply safe water and sewerage disposal, e.g., the British Development Agency, Oxford has made a latrine which turns the human excreta into organic manure producing some 6,000,000 tons a year. In the Republic of Korea, human excreta is being exploited to produce methane gas. There is need to change the attitudes of experts so that they can design the machinery and equipment suitable and feasible in our country.

(5) Local Participation

Public Health administration is manned by and meant for human beings. It is therefore necessary to associate the people with the programmes of water supply and rural sanitary latrines. Sociologists, behavioural scientists and public relation experts should be associated with programmes to make the local involvement more effective.

Social mobilisation, People's participation and health and sanitation education are essential inputs into water supply and sanitation programmes. These help to make sure that the proposed activities fit into the targeted population's habits and socio-cultural environment. Where they do not suggest changes, it intends to ensure that the proposed water supply and sanitation technologies and activities are appropriate to men, women and children.

(6) Strong Political Will and Determination

It has been mentioned that the programmes of environmental health are deferred because of the lack of resources or the apathy on the part of the politicians. This assumption is totally wrong and baseless. "The major cause for delinquent action lies in the motivation of governments. Do they really mean what their resolutions say—militantly enough to go into action? Is only lip service the main response of Presidents, Prime Ministers, kings and ministers? The task for the future is difficult but possible. People should not be consigned to premature death simply because we are less than courageous and diligent. The pace must be accelerated."[24]

(7) Effective Maintenance

It is not only important to build the infrastructure for the environmental sanitation programmes but also to see that these projects function efficiently and regularly. We must ensure their competent construction, efficient and fool-proof operation and maintenance of completed supplies and effective surveillance on quality of drinking water. The maintenance is very poor in the developing countries. Even in the planned cities like Chandigarh—the headquarters of three governments—we are shocked to find germs, mosquitoes and flies coming in the tap water. Besides, the dirt is scattered in the whole of the city. Thus, there is a need to maintain the services once provided to the people through efficient and economical administration, involving the people.

(8) Guidance and Assistance from Bilateral and Multilateral Agencies

The capacity of the developing countries to solve the problem pertaining to environmental sanitation programmes are limited. International and bilateral agencies should be encouraged to increase their direct technical assistance to member-countries in the following ways:

(a) In making assessment studies;
(b) In the establishment of information systems and programme formulation, implementation and evaluation;
(c) In identifying and helping to meet specific needs for multilateral or bilateral assistance by way of expertise, equipment, materials and soft loans;
(d) In setting up research and training centers and collaborating laboratories;
(e) In assisting training programmes, including programmes for the production of manuals and training guides;
(f) In establishing health criteria and codes of practice; and
(g) In the local production of materials.

In addition to providing assistance itself, WHO should act in a coordinating capacity in respect of assistance received from these and other sources."[25]

(9) Civic Consciousness

Environmental sanitation cannot be achieved by the effort of the Government alone. It requires the active support and cooperation of the people. It was indicated to the writer by the authorities responsible for water supply that 25 per cent of the resources are being wasted because the people do not care to use the services only when in need. Most of the public and private taps remain working without any utility. Besides, the people lack civic consciousness and they do not cooperate in the maintenance of hygienic conditions. One is shocked to see the beautiful city of Chandigarh with heaps of debris all around. The difficult task of improving environmental sanitation is possible only if the people develop civic consciousness.

(10) Environmental Education

Dr. T. Sundaran in his Article from literacy to health in Kurukshetra (Oct. 1992), suggests Health education and personal hygiene are necessary components of all such plans. Such education inputs may relate to:

(a) washing hands before collecting and carrying water, and pouring out water from a storage container without touching it or using a clean long handled dipper to take the water out;
(b) making sure that the water container, the cups and mugs used for drawing water are clean and that the water is kept covered at all times; and
(c) washing hands after defecation, before preparing and eating food, cutting of nails and other such basic measures; Special care to ensure implementation of these measures in hotels and other public eating places is more difficult essential to really checking diseases like typhoid.

The Stockholm Conference held in 1972 drew the urgency of tackling environmental problems through various efforts. One recommendation of this conference called for development of 'environmental education' as one of the most important steps to attack world's environmental crisis. The conference pleaded that "new environmental education must be broad-based and strongly related to the basic principles outlined in the United Nations Declaration on the New International Economic Order". Environmental education has been defined as an educational process dealing with men's relationship with his natural and man-made surroundings, and encompass the relation of population, health, pollution, technology, urban and rural planning, housing, proper nutrition to the total human environment. The scope of environmental education is vast, touching every aspect of man and environment. The purpose of environmental education is to provide knowledge to the people so that they can adjust with the environment and enjoy decent environment. The goals of environmental education as discussed in the Inter-Governmental Conference on Environmental Education, organised by the UNESCO in cooperation with UNEP, at Tbilisi (USSR), from October 14-26, 1977, are mentioned below:

(a) To foster clear awareness of and concern about economic, social, political and ecological interdependence in urban and rural areas;
(b) To provide every person with opportunity to acquire the knowledge, value, attitudes, commitment and skills needed to protect and prove the environment; and
(c) To create new patterns of individuals, groups and society as a whole towards the environment.

The Secretary-General of the UN in his report on Population, Resources and Environment sums up the benefits of environmental improvement programmes. He mentions four social and economic benefits that would result from government action for environmental betterment in the poor countries besides the improvements in the people's health from control of infectious diseases.

(a) Employment of large number of poor people in public works projects;
(b) Reduction of food requirements and costs by lessening the mal-absorption caused by intestinal parasites. This might ultimately save $ 2,000 million per annum in India alone. This annual saving would be equal to the entire capital cost of needed water supply improvements in the whole of rural India;
(c) Increases in potential economic productivity through improved health of adults; and
(d) Greater receptivity of children at the early ages by improvements in health."[26]

(11) Appropriate Technology

A.S. Bal, A.N. Khan and P.R. Sarode in their Article, "Technological Options for Rural Sanitation" in *Kurukshetra* (October 1992), rightly suggest that high incidence of excreta related diseases in the developing countries warrants that the sanitation programmes be designed with the primary objective of bringing about improvement in public health. This objective can be achieved through alternate sanitation technologies which are simpler and cheaper as also socially acceptable. An inter-disciplinary sanitation programme could prove to be more successful not only from the sanitation point of view but also from the point of view of problems faced by the local bodies by way of poor financial returns from provision of sewerage facilities in the low income areas. Selection of appropriate sanitation technology for a given community and its proper operation and maintenance after installation is ensured only when socio-cultural aspects are considered along with economic, financial, ecological and technical features in the planning process. The task of providing water and sanitation to the unserved population is so immense that it would be almost impossible to accomplish it without the development and application of low-cost technologies. Low-cost technologies are generally applied at the peripheral level, where construction, operation, maintenance and surveillance may vary greatly from one location to another, affected by the level of community motivation and participation.

Non-sewerage onsite sanitation facilities may be all that are needed when water supplies are limited, but if improvements result in greater water usage then eventually the need will escalate for sewers and offside disposal. In this case it can create a need for concentrated population to be controlled by treatment.

(12) Holistic Approach

Nirmla Deshpande, an eminent Gandhian has stressed the need to adopt holistic approach to sanitation, it is necessary to approach the problem in a holistic manner by linking sanitation with religion, culture, health, agriculture, environment and production of energy. The basic attitude that needs to be formed is to link it with Bhakti. It has to be stressed that cleanliness is godliness and unless cleanliness becomes a part of our lives, we cannot be true devotees of God. Construction of toilets, their proper use, maintenance and clean habits should form part of the psyche. The wrong notion that night soil is not to be touched has to go. Cleaning should become a part of daily practice. The linkage of cleanliness with health is also very important. It has to be impressed upon the minds of the people that this programme is essential for keeping good health and protecting the family and village from various diseases. With charts, slides, films, songs, cultural shows, this knowledge can be imparted. Imaginative and innovative methods have to be adopted to make people aware of health.

CONCLUSION

Dr. Zbigniew Bankowski,[27] spells out the code of ethics to protect the environment. It would be unrealistic, however, to suppose that the damage that has been done, and still continues to be done, can be arrested and undone in the short-term. Rather, long-term global policies must be envisaged and, if they are to be successful, they will require changes in our perceptions of man in nature. If our global physical environment is not to be further degraded, we must change our conceptual environment, our ways of thinking and behaving. Perhaps the worst environmental pollution is pollution of the mind, and the greatest need is for well thought out principles of environmental ethics. All spheres of human conduct—private and public, are subject to ethical principles or rules. When governments or other corporate bodies despoil the environment in the name of development or political dominance or national security, when government adopt *laissez faire* policies that permit the exploitation of nature for narrow, short-term gains. they contravene the basic ethical principle of the greatest good for the greatest number of people.

Sh. M. Akhtar, Chief WESS/ICO UNICEF, New Delhi, in his Article. "Strategies for Rural Sanitation (UNICEF Experience)" suggested the following based upon UNICEF experience to ensure fruitful application of strategies for safer water supply and sanitation (*Kurukshetra*, October 1992).

1. If sanitation has to be a 'way of life' it should be treated as a package of facilities/services and not identified with latrines. All the low-cost sanitary facilities, both at domestic and community level, such as latrine, soak pit, garbage pit,

smokeless chulha, bathing cubicle, drainage improvement, ground water sources and other community-based facilities should form a part of the package. A distinction may have to be made among 7 components of sanitation. These are: (i) Handling of drinking water; (ii) Disposal of waste water, (iii) Disposal of human excreta; (iv) Garbage disposal; (v) Home sanitation and food hygiene; (vi) Personal hygiene; and (vii) Sanitation in the community. This should be supported by a strong IEC back up to create awareness with regard to various sanitary practices including personal hygiene. It is necessary to modify the guidelines both at the Government of India and State Government levels to reflect the package deal and how to achieve the same.

2. In order that sanitation becomes a "peoples' movement", it is essential that their active involvement and participation receive due importance. In this regard subsidy can play only a limited role. Alternate financing mechanisms have to be developed to facilitate greater adaptability.
3. The low-cost sanitary facilities should have different technological options to suit different geohydrological conditions and also the varying socio-economic segments of the population. Such technologies should be affordable, acceptable and replicable. Identification and use of alternate materials should be a continuous process so as to keep the cost escalation under check.
4. Demand generation for sanitary facilities should get a high priority in Rural Sanitation Programme. For this purpose, a comprehensive and systematic communication strategy has to be developed and all possible methods and channels should be used to motivate people. In this regard inter-personal communication through village level motivators seems to be quite promising. Willing village level functionaries like Anganwadi workers, DWCRA group organisers. Traditional Birth Attendants, Primary school teachers, Youth Club/Mahila Mandal office-bearers, etc. could be the core group of motivators. The panchayat members can also play an active role in this regard.
5. The demand generation strategy should be backed up by an efficient delivery system which need not be a part of the subsidy-oriented programme. At present, even if a person wants to have his/her own latrine in rural areas, it is not easy to find the required pan/trap/pit cover, etc. as adequate infrastructure has not developed as yet. Only in an area where government programme is under implementation, things are more readily available. It is, therefore, necessary to create alternate delivery channels/mechanism to have improved sanitation coverage.

6. Private initiative is a must to make the sanitation programme a success. The government-supported activity could at least be a stimulant. The results of the 44th Round on Sanitation Coverage is a pointer to this assumption. While figures from the government sources show a 3 percent coverage, the NSS survey reveals that more than one-tenth of the households were using latrines. The difference could be accounted for by the spread effect of the government programme. It is high time that a clear cut policy on how to encourage private initiative outside the subsidy-oriented approach is laid down. The policy should keep a flexible approach and suggest alternate social marketing strategies to promote sanitation through private initiative. Involvement of industrial houses/ public sector units including the manufacturers of sanitary goods could form a part of it.
7. NGOs can play a very crucial role in promoting rural sanitation. They can very effectively be used to encourage private initiative because of their rapport with the community and can serve as an efficient channel for information dissemination, awareness creation and motivation. Only those NGOs who have the required capacity to take up activities at a district level or at least for a group of blocks should be encouraged. The Government should come out with separate guidelines for involving NGO's in the Rural Sanitation Programme. The State Government should be well aware of such guidelines.

Dr. Martin Kaplan[28] has desired to look positively and is hopeful of solutions by mankind. He stated, "hazards to human health arising from environment factors are many and varied. We know much about some and little about many of them. We must therefore depend on future research both by the experimental laboratory and by epidemiology to clarify many of our areas of ignorance. The development of surveillance and monitoring mechanisms for changes in health status correlated with environmental components should provide the warnings necessary to avoid serious harm to present and future generations of the human race. In reviewing all these environmental effects and their possible dangers, we should not however reach too gloomy a conclusion. A comforting finding, which may be extended to many other aspects, is the recent discovery that fish caught in the last century and preserved in museums have been found to have similar mercury levels as those found in fish today. And afterall, the human race with its great adaptability has survived the innumerable disasters and environmental hazards it has encountered for several million years. Modern life and represent for man merely a new set of ones, and there is no reason to doubt that negligence will prevail as far as environment."

Notes and References

1. Hiroshi Nakjima, "A Wounded Planet" in *World Health*, January-February, 1990, p. 3
2. Dr. Wilfried Kriesel, "Environmental Health in the 1990s" in *World Health*, 1990, p. 5.
3. WHO : SEARO, Declaration on Health Development in the South-East Asia Region in the 21st Century, New Delhi, 1997, pp. 17-18.
4. WHO, *World Health*, May 1972, p. 28.
5. U. Thant quoted in Clellan, M.C. and S. Grant (ed.), Protecting our Environments (New York, 1970), p. 206.
6. WHO, *World Health*, May 1972, p. 29.
7. Edwards S. Roggers, Human Ecology and Health Environment, Administrator, New York, 1960.
8. WHO: Samuel Halter; "Man and his Environment" in *World Health*, July 1975, p. 11.
9. GOI, Planning Commission, Draft Five Year Plan (1971-73), p. 117.
10. WHO, *World Health Paper*, S-9, p. 12.
11. Nikolas P. Napulbow, Water For All: A human right, in *World Health*, July-Aug., 1992, p. 3.
12. Barbara Ward, "The Key to Health" in *World Health*, January 1977, p. 3.
13. UNICEF, Assignment Children, 34, April-June 1976, p. 11.
14. WHO, *World Health*, January, 1979, p. 3.
15. UN, 1970, Report on the World Social Situation, New York, 1971, pp. 167-61.
16. *World Health*, July-August 1992, p. 7
17. Purshotam Khanna and Bindo Koshy, "When City Growth Exceeds Supply" in *World Health*, July-August, 1992, p. 11.
18. WHO, SEARO: Annual Report of the Regional Director, 1976-77, pp. xii-xiii.
19. WHO, *World Health*, January 1977, p. 17.
20. *Ibid.*
21. WHO, *Public Health Papers*, S-9, p. 116.
22. Satisse Michel, "Man and Biosphere" in *World Health*, June 1971, p. 4.
23. WHO, *World Health*, May 1972, p. 29.
24. WHO, *World Health*, January 1977, p. 17.
25. WHO, SEA/RC27, p. 41.
26. UN, ST/ESA/SERA/S7, New York, 1975, p. 101.
27. Zbigniew Bankowski, "A Code of Ethics" in *World Health*, January-February 1990, p. 11.
28. Dr. Martin Kaplan, "Environmental Hazards for Human Health" in *World Health*, May 1972, p. 11.

CHAPTER 9

VALUE EDUCATION

"Devoid of Sathya, Dharma, Santhi, Prema and Ahimsa"
All Education is a zero.
Bereft of Sathya, Dharma, Santhi, Prema and Ahimsa
The value of all meritorious deeds is a zero

—*Ministry of HRD*

Value Education

"Our power of life lies in thoughts. Thought is the secret key of our mental software. Human Resource Development should take us from negative thoughts (darkness) to positive thought (light), from Untruth to Truth, from Immortality to Mortality."

—*Ministry of HRD*

Swami Visharananda in his book, "Human Values" beautifully states that to be happy is the universal urge of all beings and at all times. One has to be at peace with oneself to be happy. There can be no peace for a turbulent mind. Vasanas, desires, take away the peace of mind. It is only when we follow a value system that we can have a serene, contemplative mind. When mind is calm, we can turn it within to 'see' the treasure of pure consciousness. No treasure on earth is equal to a slice of that tattva. Mind has to be loosened from durvyapara (misdeeds) and engaged in acquiring sadgunas (virtues). In Gita, Krsna talks about the developing human values and says that a mind which has daivisampatti (divine qualities) has *santi* (Peace). These values make us introspective and correct our personality.

Education institutes today are engulfed by materialistic values. Teachers have become salesman while the students indulge in indiscipline, take drugs, alcohol, and smoking. This scene has emerged as teachers in higher education do not take interest in the development of the personality of the students. (See Chart 9.1)

R.T. Deopurkar in his article, "Values in the Modern Indian Education Thought" rightly observes: Plain living and high thinking is becoming a out-dated notion. Increase of one's needs and desires and the

---

* See Appendix 9.1—Human Values in Srimad Bhagavad Gita, Chapter 13.
See Appendix 9.2—UGC Xth Plan Guidelines about Values.

CHART 9.1

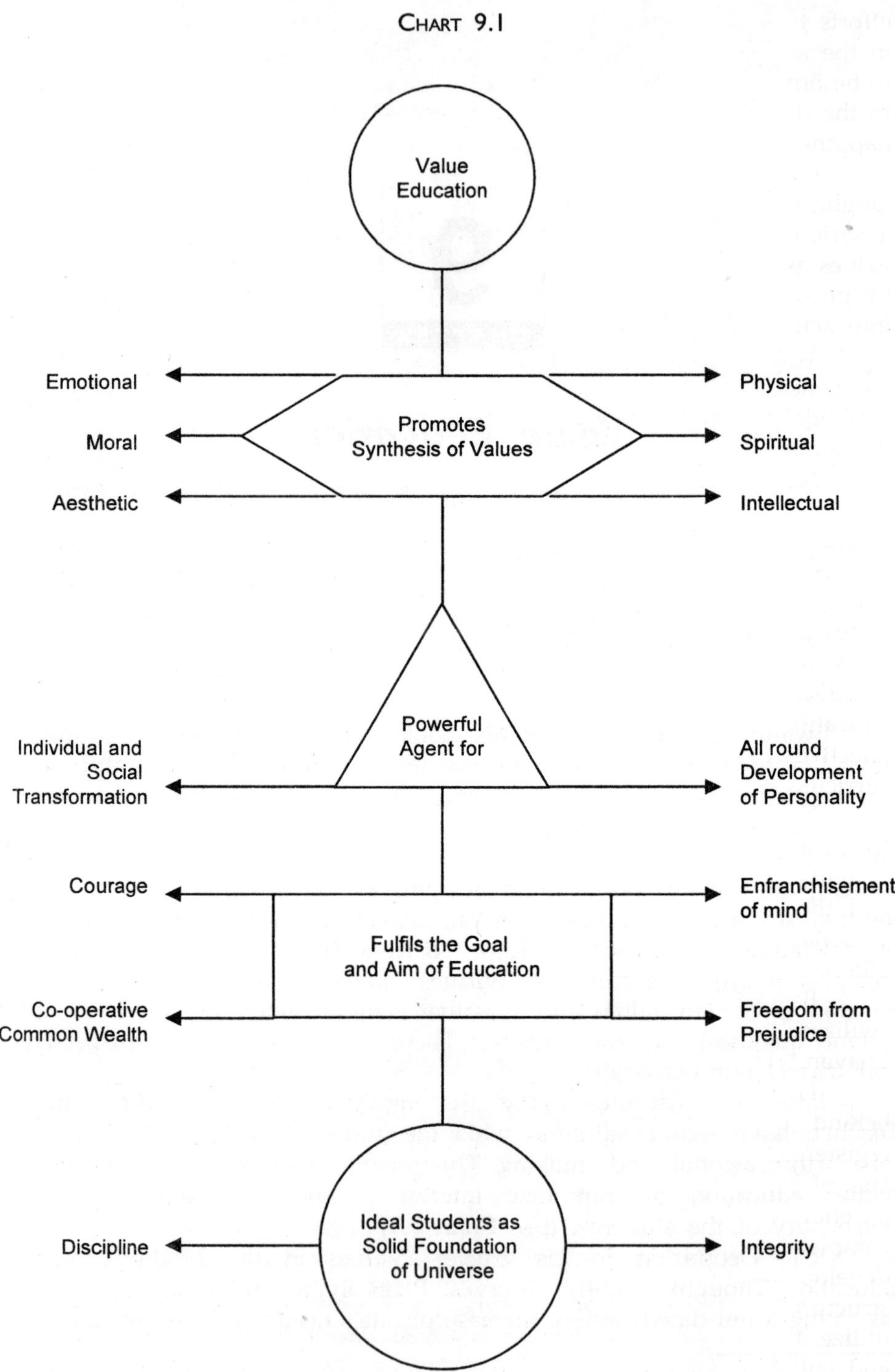
Value
Education
Emotional
Moral
Aesthetic
Promotes
Synthesis of Values
Physical
Spiritual
Intellectual
Powerful
Agent for
Individual and
Social
Transformation
All round
Development
of Personality
Courage
Co-operative
Common Wealth
Fulfils the Goal
and Aim of Education
Enfranchisement
of mind
Freedom from
Prejudice
Discipline
Ideal Students as
Solid Foundation
of Universe
Integrity

efforts to fulfil them all has become the philosophy of life and education in the modern world. Control of one's own sensual desires is considered to be out of date. The number of desires cherished increases in proportion to the desires fulfilled, and so the sum total of happiness is the same as happiness is equal to the desires fulfilled upon desires cherished.

Craving for cheap popularity on the part of the teachers and the taught, short cuts in study, a longing of easy life, guide books—all need a serious attention on the part of the modern Indian educators. Their values and places must be fixed once and for ever and the decisions taken by great educationists in the interest of the nation should be strictly put into actual practice.

To get through the annual examination in a higher class has become the general immediate goal of education in India and it tells upon the methods of learning and teaching and on the national character as such in the long-run. The whole attitude to education needs revision.

N.N. Prahallada in his Article, "Contemporary Significance of Higher Education" beautifully explains the role of Moral values in Education. To quote him, "Indian Culture is rooted deeply in her spiritual values and unless these values find their way into the life of students, education will lose its significance and will not fulfil its function of endowing the students with a vision to life and by and with ideals to work for, therefore, indifference to the cherished goals of democracy, socialism, humanism and secularism, it is very essential that our education system should evolve a new positive morality which could effectively be built into the school, under-graduate/Post-graduate curriculum.

Value education involves social education but extends beyond it in so far as it covers the way the individual deals with his own powers and potentialities as well how he behaves in his relationship with other people and the community at large. It is as much concerned with striving for personal wholeness as with generating a responsible attitude towards others and an understanding of right and wrong behaviour.

Background papers, New Delhi Conference on Dialogue among civilizations "Quest for New Perspectives" held on July 9-10, 2003, Vigyan Bhavan, New Delhi spells out the need for values. To quote:

Humankind is passing today through an acute crisis, and the reason behind this crisis is a disequilibrium between the progress that has been registered in recent times in the externalities of life and the progress or lack of progress in the inner realms of life. The human mind has achieved an enormous development in the building of a structure of hugeness and complexity. On the other hand, the contemporary human beings has not developed enough spiritual and moral capacity to manage the hugeness of structure and its complexity. Inwardly, man has remained too small to utilize and manage the complex political, social, administrative, economic and cultural machinery. The world has become global, but man has not developed yet the required global consciousness. It is this disequalibrium, which is reflected in the great challenges that the contemporary civilizations of the world are confronting.

The necessity to develop quality education is paramount. The notion of quality education does not merely encompass aspects of educational attainment, but especially the aspects of curricula and their content focusing on peace, shared values, human rights, democracy, tolerance and mutual understanding. Educational institutions and educational materials should serve as a vehicle for peace, dialogue and intercultural understanding, but not be instrumentalized for and used as vehicles to spread misunderstanding, intolerance and hate. For its part, UNESCO has deliberately placed programmes related to education for peace and human rights within the area of quality of education, emphasizing the importance of addressing these issues in any long-term education strategy.

Quality education for peace and security should focus in particular on:

- Improving knowledge of cultures, civilizations, religions and traditions;
- Developing an understanding of universally shared values; and
- Encouraging the development of key competencies for peace and the prevention and resolution of conflict.

There is a widespread feeling among a cross-section of the people in India today that, all is not well with our body politic and that education must contribute actively and positively to find a part of the solution. The growing malaise in modern education is that it is seen and practised merely or mainly as a means of acquiring techno-informative knowledge and skills, with little or no anchoring in cultural roots of the country and its perspectives. Unless education helps the students to develop not only a personal identity (which essentially means a set of value perspectives and world views, linked to ones cultural traditions) education cannot be said to have fulfilled its essential role.

Leaders, not only in the field of education but also in other fields have tried to enhance the quality of life. Various kinds of remedies have been applied or tried but, of late, it has become, the united voice of all that Moral, Social and Human Values are the ultimate and the much-needed remedy.[1]

G. Chandralekka Rao in an Article; value education for college students rightly feels that realizing this need our curriculum needs to insist on educating the young students in the art of living with values. If learning remains detached from value judgements, scholarship runs the risk of degenerating into indifference. Value judgements actually enhance the accuracy of learning, teachers, therefore, should be aware of the important role they are called upon to play as professionals and citizens, as agents of development and change. They must make an effort to light a candle instead of cursing the darkness and sow the seeds of value education with a fond hope that they would diffuse their own fragrance towards the creation of a just and new society as they sprout and blossom. Can we be good role models if we are not ethical ourselves.

University education which is worthwhile should lead to the development of integrated personality and inculcate values like patriotism, spirit of national unity and a healthy appreciation of the rich variety of cultural expressions and promote a humanistic outlook. It is only in the highest education stage that the students can be enabled to acquire intellectual, democratic and aesthetic values and a deeply felt concern for the environment.

The content of value-oriented post-graduate education should include: (a) a yearning for knowledge and capacity to utilize it for the good of the society, (b) Democratic education, (c) Aesthetic education, (d) a course in ethics, (e) spiritual education, and (f) provision for activities involving values.[2]

R. Satya Raju in his Article, "Human Values in University Management" suggests the following:

(a) Value education means a positive effort for bringing about a synthesis of physical, intellectual, emotional, aesthetic, moral and spiritual values in a human being;
(b) Due to total neglect in the last five decades after independence, the present focus is on revival of moral and spiritual values in education; and
(c) The government should have no reservation in introducing and funding universal religion of human values in the form, in the contents and in the methodology of education at all levels.

Let us understand three areas of education and our values; viz.:

(a) "truth" seeking through scientific and objective processes which are followed by the scientists;
(b) "beauty" creates appreciation through the processes of artistic and unique expression followed by artists; and
(c) "goodness" constructed through the processes of subjective and meaningful contracting followed by social scientists. There is danger in trespassing the boundaries of sciences to arts-to-social sciences without transforming our own respective perspective and amending the tools of analysis used by our own discipline areas. This has implications of prioritizing values in various disciplines and their scholars. These scholars in turn influence the value substance and methodology prescribed for institutions in a centralized model of education.[3]

All these three aspects if practiced would make students value conscious. The need for value education has been stressed by all the commissions set-up for educational development from time to time.

Radhakrishnan Commission (1948)

"If we exclude spiritual training in our institutions we would be untrue to our whole historical development."

Sri Prakasa Committee on Religious and Moral Instruction

"Every effort must, therefore, be made to teach students true moral values from the earliest stages of their educational life."

Kothari Commission (1964-66)

"A serious defect in the education system is the absence of provision for education in social, moral and spiritual values. A national system of education that is related to life, needs and aspirations of the people cannot afford to ignore this purposeful force."

National Policy on Education (1986)

"The growing concern over the erosion of essential values and an increasing cynicism in society has brought to focus the need for readjustments in the curriculum in order to make education a forceful tool for the cultivation of social and moral values."

Programme of Action NPE (1992)

"The framework emphasized value education as an integral part of school curriculum. It highlighted the values drawn from national goals, universal perception, ethical considerations and character building. It stressed the role of education in combating obscurantism, religious fanaticism, exploitation and injustice as well as the inculcation of values."[4]

In addition to the emphasis of commissions on moral education, persons of eminence have also advocated the cause of moral education for all-round development of the youth.

Education is a powerful and pervasive agent for all-round development, individual and social transformation. This alone can sustain culture and civilization. A balanced development of mind and body in harmony with the spirit is the key to the enrichment of human personality and also the key to 'true education,' which must in the ultimate analysis help humanity to rise to a higher level of consciousness. Gandhiji said: "Unless the development of mind and body goes hand in hand with a corresponding awakening of the soul, the former alone would prove to be a poor lopsided affair. By spiritual training, I mean education of the heart. A proper and all round development of the mind, therefore, can take place only when it proceeds *paripassu* with the education of the physical and spiritual faculties of the child . . . . Our children must from their infancy be taught the 'dignity of labour'. Thus, the true meaning of education is harmonious development of head, heart and hand, i.e. enlighment of mind, compassion and dignity of labour." Such qualities would automatically promote the development of youth.

Sarvepalli Radhakrishnan said: "The three things—vital dynamism, intellectual efficiency and spiritual direction together constitute the proper aim of education. Moral and spiritual training is an essential part of education. Enfranchisement of the mind, freedom from prejudice and fanaticism, and courage are essential. What we need today is the education of the whole man—physical, vital, mental, intellectual and spiritual . . . . If education is to help us to meet the moral challenge of the age and play its part in the life of the community, it should be liberating and life giving. It must give a basic meaning to personality and existence and equip us with the power to overcome spiritual inertia and foster spiritual sensitivity . . . . Seat of learning should produce men and women who will move together to develop common ideals and purposes, love each other and co-exist to create a co-operative common wealth."

Swami Vivekananda had proclaimed: "We must have life-building, man-making, character-building education." Shanker Dayal Sharma, former President of India, the scholar-educationalist had said, "The aim and objective of all education is to maintain, sustain and develop a healthy mind in a healthy body. Co-curricular and extra-curricular activities have as much place in our system as the curriculum and the syllabus. The lack of such activities is the reason for the growing evils of habitual smoking, drinking and drug-addiction fast growing amidst our student community . . . . Education is not injection or injunction. It is not indoctrination of views and ideas or just an imposition of one's views upon others. In short, education should not be an infliction. The moment education becomes such an infliction, the consequence will be student indiscipline, strikes and agitations within the campus." Pandit Nehru rightly said—"A vast responsibility . . . . rests on our universities and educational institutions and those who guide their destinies. They have to keep their lights burning and must not stray from the right path even when passion convulses the multitude and blinds many amongst those whose duty is to set an example to others."

Gurudev Rabindranath Tagore had a vision for such an education: "Education must aim at the development of moral, spiritual and ethical values and we should seek them in our own heritage as well as in other cultures and civilizations . . . . It should be such that Indians do not lose sight of their rich heritage—their thought must be rooted to the ideals set forth in the great writings and works of our sages, poets and philosophers. The noble goals and high values set forth in our precious culture must be adhered to."

Shanker Dayal Sharma had said: "Thus, a teacher must succeed in conveying the larger ideals of service to the community, virtues of tolerance and respect for all faiths, the importance of character, integrity and discipline and the value of humanism to his pupils. They should also be made aware of our heritage and culture." He was a great advocate of 'developing a mature attitude towards religion'. To quote him again . . . . "Acquaintance with prayers of different religion and hymns and songs of various faiths could also, surely, help our youth to recognize the intrinsic purity, beauty and practical usefulness of different religious thoughts."[5]

Value is a "conception explicit or implicit, distinctive of an individual or characteristic of a group of those desirable traits which influence the selection from available modes and ends of action" (Wuchohn, 1957). (Rokeach 1973) defined values as "enduring belief, a specific mode of conduct and state existence along a continuum of relative importance." Values are the criteria for determining levels of goodness, worth or beauty.

Values in our education is a hotly debated subject nowadays. This is because of the chaotic conditions observed in almost all spheres of our national life. It is conjectured, not without reason, that this chaos is mainly due to *lack of values* in the education being imparted in India. This was formulated, as is well-known, by Macaulay in 1836 more to enslave the Indian mind than to liberate it, so that Indians would remain loyal to British Raj, being alienated from their native Vedic culture, education and Sanskrit language. As planned, this gradually weaned our intellectuals away from our classical heritage and from the Sanskrit language, in which lay all our spiritual, cultural, social, and political traditions. We lost our indigenous system of education in which hearing, chanting and memorizing played a great part, assimilation of ideas took place through a well-planned life of service to teacher, contemplation and meditation, all under his guidance. Thus, the educated ones in that system were men who had not only knowledge but also character. Knowledge had become a part of their life, influencing their thoughts, emotions and actions.

The Sanskrit for values is dharma or Sadacara. Dharma is described as 'the set of values that sustains the creation without which the very existence of it would be threatened.' Sankaracharya defined Dharma as the values that sustained human beings and helped them to enjoy happiness both in this as well as in the spiritual world.

Thus, education in India meant not merely intellectual cramming of information into the brain but the application of them into one's life so that life became better at individual, social, secular, spiritual levels. Education was a life-transformer. That is real education which liberates.[6]

Eminent Journalist, Mr. V.N. Narayanan, Editor, *The Hindustan Times*, delivered the Convocation Address at the XV and XVI convocation of the Nagarjuna University. He said, "When we face problems of ethics, we tend to solve them by research, by statistics, by the use of instruments and resources rather than by moral energy. The Victorian society in Britain, the pre-Independence Congress party under Mahatma Gandhi, Abraham Lincoln's era in U.S. politics displayed this moral energy. This is not to be confused with excessive Puritanism or moralism. All it demanded of the people was the feeling that they were put on this earth in order to leave it a better place than you found it."[7]

RATIONALE AND PHILOSOPHY OF VALUES

A recent conference, "Dialogue among civilizations quest for new perspectives", July 9-10, 2000 elaborated the concept of values as:

Values may be defined as those desirable ideals and goals which are intrinsic in themselves and which, when achieved or attempted to be achieved, evoke a deep sense of fulfilment to one or many or all parts of what we consider to be the highest elements of our nature. Values are norms, which hold and sustain life and society and establish a symbiotic and interdependent relationship between humankind and ecosystem. Values denote a fundamental category; in a common understanding they correspond to what we mean when it is said that Truth, Beauty and Goodness are the Supreme value of life. They occur to us whenever we try to conceive all those states of our being or becoming in which we are likely to find some kind of ultimate fulfilment. (Chart 9.2)

There are, indeed, values of physical life, values of emotional life, values of mental life, but these values constantly point towards certain basic and ultimate values, which are moral and spiritual in character.

Moral and spiritual values are the foundations of the highest peaks of civilization, and since they emancipate humanity from narrow grooves of thought, they deserve to be understood more and more clearly and more and more meaningfully. Moral and spiritual values appear to be the common elements of various religions promoting everlasting peace and universal harmony; we look up to the ethical and spiritual values in our effort to rise above differences among religions. In recent times, a vast effort has been made to discover the pursuit of those values—moral and spiritual—which are to be found among all religions. And it has been rightly argued that what is most important in religions is the pursuit of ethical and spiritual values, which transcend the externalities of religious institutions.

Science, morality and spirituality are intimately intertwined and they should not be viewed as antagonistic to each other. Indeed, the survival of human race at the present critical juncture of human history will depend upon the pursuit of ethical and spiritual values. It has been rightly contended that peace is a most desirable objects of the present world and that peace cannot be achieved unless individuals and increasing masses of people contemplate and practice ethical and spiritual values such as those of unity, harmony, mutuality, friendship, faithfulness, sincerity and respect for diversity.

Spirituality is premised on universal consciousness, which can serve as the basis of the unity of humankind, and ethical systems derive their force and sustaining power from spiritual consciousness. In the field of education, ethical and spiritual values need to be encouraged, since they are directly related to the character development of students. In the latest reports of UNESCO, "learning to be" and "Learning: Treasure within", the highest ideals have been put forward. The concept of "To Be" is so

Chart 9.2

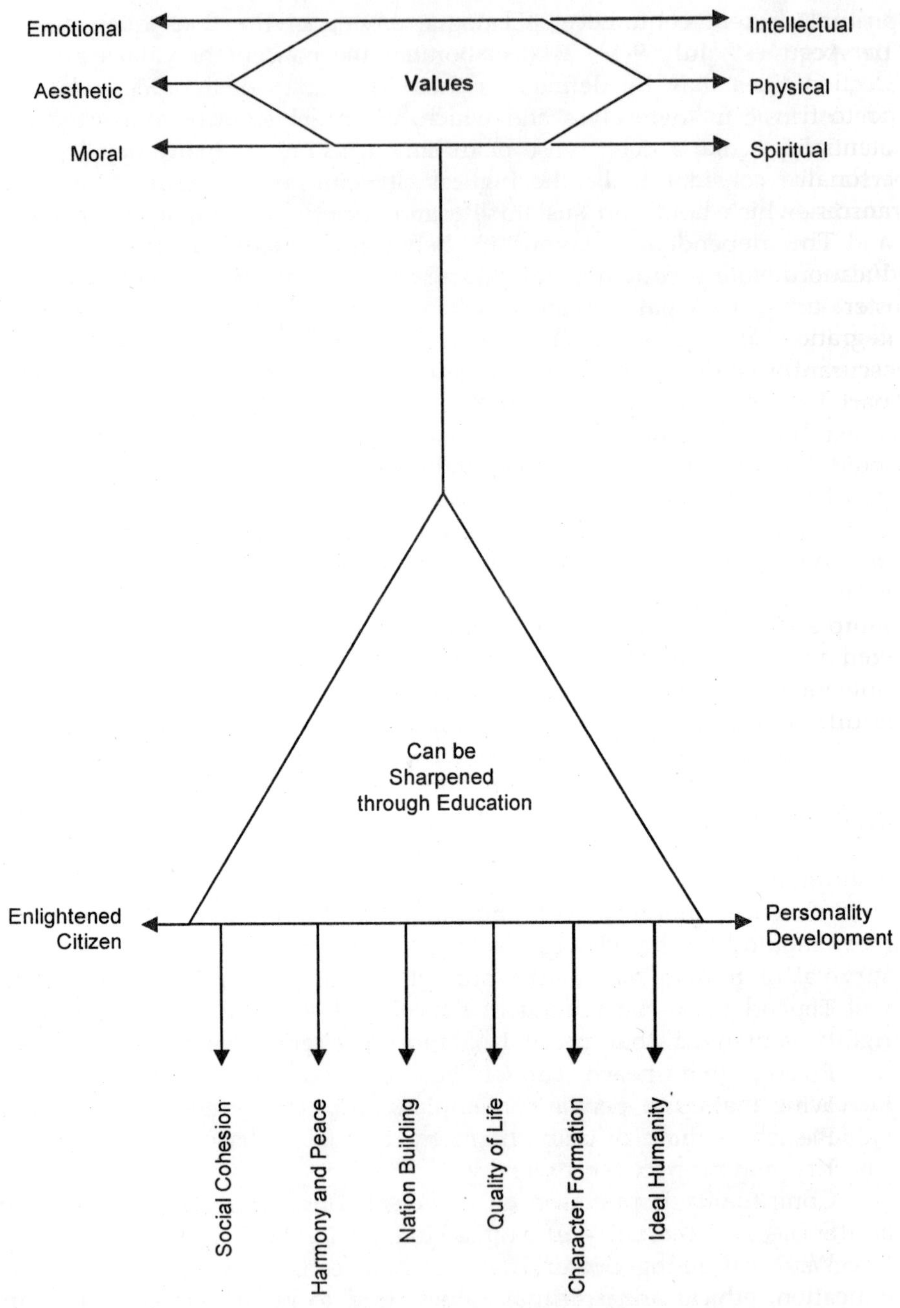
Emotional
Intellectual
Aesthetic
Values
Physical
Moral
Spiritual
Can be
Sharpened
through Education
Enlightened
Citizen
Personality
Development
Social Cohesion
Harmony and Peace
Nation Building
Quality of Life
Character Formation
Ideal Humanity

defined as to mean development of the fullness of personality in all richness. And this fullness of personality involves fullness of ethical and spiritual development. The ideal of "To Be" is distinct from the ideal of "To Acquire" and "To Possess." The ideal of "To Be" refers to that direction of effort which leads the individual to look deeply within oneself and to find in his or her inner being the source and treasure of his or her potentialities and actualities, the source of a harmony of the complexity of personality, and the source of fulfilment in some kind of perfection that transcends egoism and which rests in a vast and integrated self-hood.

The National Policy on Education has laid special stress on value-education. It has said, "In our culturally plural society education should foster universal and eternal values, oriented towards the unity and integration of our people. Such value education should help eliminate obscurantism, religious fanaticism, violence, superstition and fatalism. Apart from the combative role, value education has a profound positive context based on our heritage, national goals, universal perceptions. It should lay primary emphasis on this aspect."

R. Natarajan, Chairman AICTE has rightly said in his convocation address at Tirupati:

When we say that a person has 'values', we imply that he has certain fundamental beliefs about what is desirable or good, and that he attempts to use these in directing his life. For beliefs of this kind to be called values, two conditions are generally held to apply:

Values are formed as a result of reflection and judgment; this they are different from desires—

- A person's values are beliefs which he sees as applicable not only to himself, but also to others; essential to the idea of value is the function of commanding.
- A person's values are beliefs which he sees as applicable not only to himself, but also to others: essential to the idea of value is the function of commanding.[8]

The Seven Sins, according to Mahatma Gandhi, are:

Politics without Principle.
Wealth without Work.
Pleasure without Conscience.
Knowledge without Character.
Commerce without Morality.
Science without Humanity.
Worship without Sacrifice.

To quote Anita Shetty again:

Values are those standards or codes of conduct conditioned by one's cultural tenets, guided by conscience, according to which one is supposed to conduct himself and shape his life pattern by integrating his benefits, ideas and attitudes to realize the cherished ideals and aims of life. By values we mean the criterion or basis for choosing between alternative courses of action. High values lead to objective, fair, correct decisions and actions and ensure the welfare of all concerned. Low values do exactly the opposite. Therefore, what we need more today is moral leadership focused on courage, intellectual integrity and sense of values. There is no substitute for a sense of value.

Sir Aurobindo says: "In the right view both of life and of yoga all life is either consciously or subconsciously a yoga. For we mean by this term a methodized effort towards self-perfection by the expression of the potentialities latent in the being and a union of the human individual with the universal and transcendent existence we see partially expressed in man and in the cosmos."[9]

To quote Anita Shetty: "Value is a conception, explicit or implicit, distinctive of an individual or characteristics which influences the selection, from available modes and ends of action." Wuchohn (1957), Rokeach (1973) defines values "as an enduring belief, a specific mode of conduct or end state existence along a continuum of relative importance."

Values may be described as a system of personality traits which are in harmony with the inner nature of an individual and which are in accordance with the values approved by the society. The process of valuing is what we go through when we make judgment about things, events and people that we encounter in our day-to-day life.

Adisankaracarya has given many values which can make life beautiful. Let us mention some of them.

Yogah Karmasu Kausalam

Yoga is special skill in the performance of activities. The skill consists in maintaining the uniformity of mind in success and failure. The person who maintains this skill performs all the works as his duty. He dedicates his mind to God.

That is Knowledge

Samacittatva is unfailing equanimity—or evenness of mind in all situations—favourable or unfavourable. The person is not elated when good things happen nor gets angry when misfortune betides. This unwavering evenness of mind is true knowledge.

That is Yoga

That is knowledge, understanding of things like the self, acquired from the scriptures and the preceptors. The single-pointed and striking realization of these truths, by controlling the sense organs is Yoga.

Achieve the Goal

Here in this present human life the Self must be known. This is the injunction. How? If the Self is known in this birth the life's goal is achieved. This is the supreme truth. His life is fruitful. If the Self is not known in this life, that would become useless.

Experience True Knowledge

Tapah, the concentration of the physical body, the sense organs and the mind; **damah,** discontinuance from sense objects, Karma, Agnihotra, etc. rituals. One who attains holiness by means of purification of the heart through these things can get the knowledge of Brahman.

Don't Speak Untruth

Not that there ever was or is in them any falsehood. Contrary to that speaking untruth is the behaviour of bad people. Can any body become free from death? and decrepitude by his falsehood. For which reason (martyah), man (sasyam iva) like corn, (Pacyate), tatters and dies and after death (punah) again; sasyam iva ajavate, (reborns like conr). Thus, what one can gain in this impermanent human world by breaking his own words?

Classification of Values

Values have been classified differently by different educationists and philosophers. Mascarendhas classified them as professional values, operational values and dynamic values. National Education Policy (1986) classified all the values into three main categories—Personal values, Social values and National values. All the three supplement one another. Adherence to personal values would promote better social and national values. (Chart 9.3)

Education with Value Focus: Sri Sathya Sai Institute of Higher Learning Prasanthi Nilayam (AP)

Sri Sathya Sai Institute of Higher Learning Prasanthi Nilayam (Andhra Pradesh) founded on November 22, 1981, by Bhagavan Sri Sathya Sai Baba which grew out of the Colleges founded earlier by Bhagavan Sri Sathya Sai Baba at Anantapur, Andhra Pradesh, Whitefield (near Bangalore, Karnataka) and Prasanthi Nilayam, Andhra Pradesh.

Bhagavan, in His Divine Message to the students, announced that the main purpose of establishing the Institute of Higher Learning was to help them cultivate self-knowledge and self-confidence, so that each one of them can learn self-sacrifice and earn self-realization. He defined the goal as spiritual upliftment, self-discovery and social service through love and detachment.

The consistent endeavour of the university since its inception has been to develop core courses bringing out value-orientation in an appropriate manner, blending of science and spirituality, providing interaction between head and heart through self-reliance programmes and

CHART 9.3

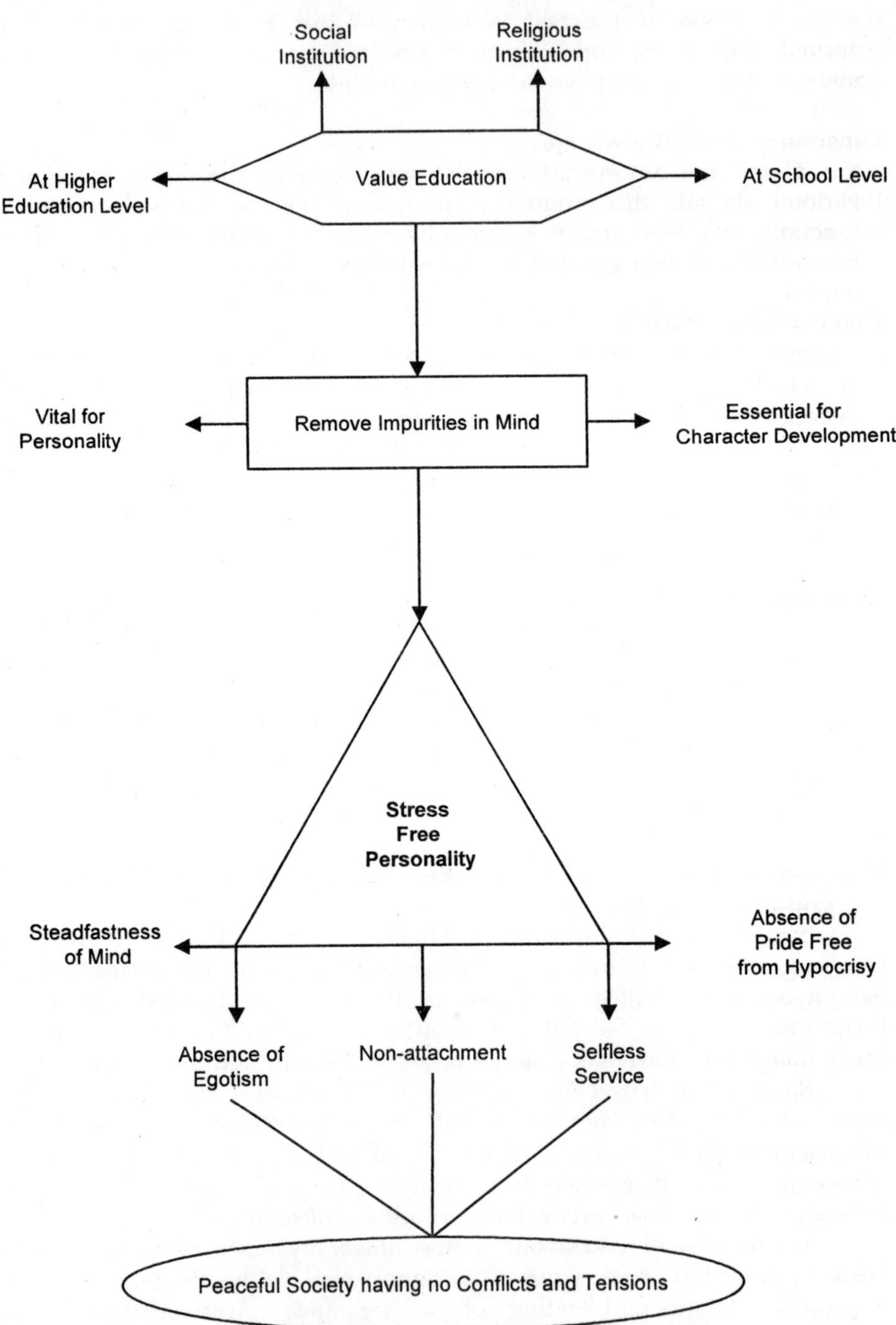
Social
Institution
Religious
Institution
At Higher
Education Level
Value Education
At School Level
Vital for
Personality
Remove Impurities in Mind
Essential for
Character Development
Stress
Free
Personality
Steadfastness
of Mind
Absence of
Pride Free
from Hypocrisy
Absence of
Egotism
Non-attachment
Selfless
Service
Peaceful Society having no Conflicts and Tensions

co-curricular activities, designing Awareness and Foundation courses and incorporating these as part of the curriculum with credits.

The philosophy of education of the Institute is based on the appreciation of the need to provide full scope for the development of body, mind and heart. Discipline, duty and adherence to basic human values are deeply appreciated as the best qualities of students in the Institute. These are being observed in various situations in the hostel, on the playground and in the Campuses and during the celebration of various festival and organization of festivals and other important functions. It is precisely because of the importance of these activities for the overall development of personality, that the Institute attaches great importance to integral items of education like Yogasanas, games and sports, attendance in morning prayers and meditation, attendance in universal prayers and participation in morning assembly talks, attendance in classes and social work/self-reliance programmes. These are incorporated in the total system of our education offered in the Institute.

A society without values will cease to be human. The more human values are cherished, the better will be the growth of society, the nation and the world. We cannot rest content with an educational system which is confined to academic achievement. It has to promote human virtues simultaneously. The main problem of our education today is how to adapt the spiritual and cultural traditions we have inherited from the past to our present day life.

The Institute believes that teaching of values cannot be confined only to specific programmes such as Awareness Programme under Under-graduate and Post-graduate Courses and foundational courses in Professional Studies. Values will have to be presented as a part and parcel of teaching of the subject. In the process of teaching of various subjects, whether it is physical sciences, biological sciences, social sciences or Commerce and Management, the values are appropriately incorporated in the subjects in order that the students would appreciate and imbibe the practical applications of values in their day-to-day living.

Even research is value-based. For years, the Chemistry department has been focusing on the Chemistry of Natural Products, and in particular on the possible use of various native plants for producing drugs. Many of the Dissertations of the students of M.Tech. [Computer Science] address the needs of the Sri Sathya Sai Institute of Higher Medical Sciences [popularly known as the Super-Specialty Hospital]; and so on.

On the sports field, the stress is less on competition and more on collective enjoyment. Indeed, the events presented on the Institute's Annual Sports and Cultural festival held every year on January 11th are carefully planned to promote such a spirit.

"We do not need today a new faith or creed, nor a new system of education. Nor need we create a new society. All we need are men and women who have pure and loving hearts. Their hearts must be filled with sacred feeling. The transformation has to be effected in the minds of the people."

"Our educational institution (University) is making an endeavour so that in a few years from now we shall have thousands of those students who will scatter themselves to all parts of the world. The uppermost thing for the students is that they should futher this moral aspect of ours." Most of the research studied carried out in the field of value education revealed the following:

1. Educational system at present is not congenial to value promotion.
2. Teachers, themselves lack knowledge and rationale of values. They do not follow values.
3. Literature on value education is limited. Whatever is available is not of good quality.
4. Students are enarmoured by modern fashion.
5. Families are also forgetting their role as the first school of citizenship.
6. Materialism has left no place.
7. Leaders have no values.
8. The aim of students is to pass the examination and not personality development.
9. Negative values like drinking, smoking, gambling are common among teachers and students.

Let us discuss the role of Values in education. (see Chart 9.4)

I. Building of Human beings with Strength and Power based upon our Ancient Values

Even during the last century Swami Vivekananda had issued the following warning: "All political and social system and organizations basically depend upon the goodness of man. Men cannot be made virtuous by an Act of Parliament. It cannot be taken for granted that if the Parliament enacts good legislation a nation becomes automatically strong. But if the people of a country become good and great, that country becomes automatically good and great. Of all forms of wealth in the world man is the most valuable.

"Acts of Parliament, Government, political administration, all these are indeed means, but they are not our final goal. Beyond them there is a goal, which is not governed by any of these factors. Christ discovered that moral fervour and purity of heart are true sources of strength. Our sages proclaimed the same truth. It is thus, that religion strikes at the root of the problem, it moulds man's character.

"So every improvement in India requires first of all an upheaval in religion. Before flooding India with socialistic or political ideas, first deluge the land with spiritual ideas. The first work that demands our attention is that the most wonderful truths confined in our Upanishads, in our scriptures, in our Puranas must be brought out from the books,

CHART 9.4

Personal

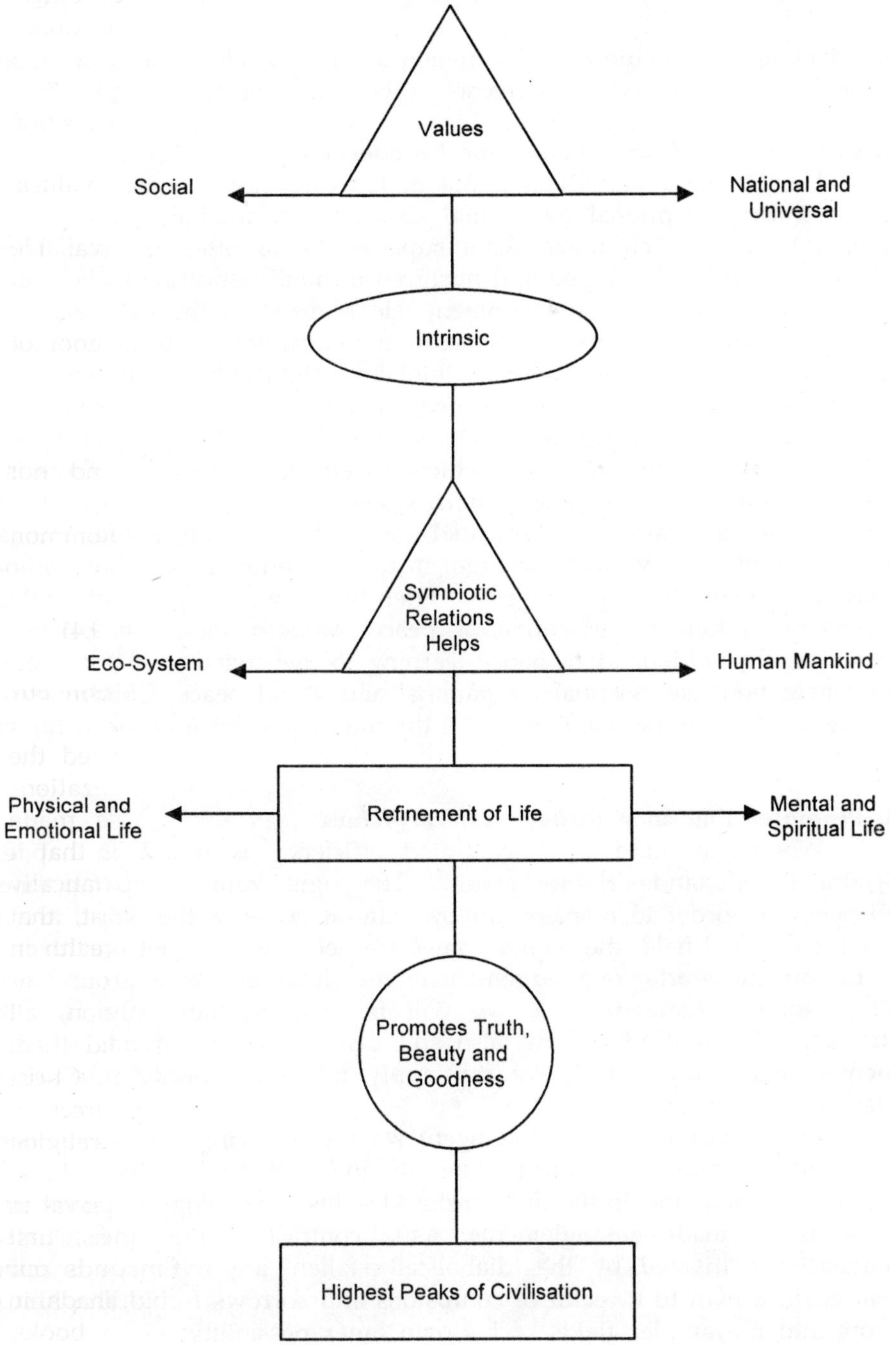

brought out from the monasteries, brought out from the forests, brought out from the possession of selected bodies of people, and scattered broadcast all over the land . . . .

"The secret of achieving national spirit in our country lies in regaining our spiritual strength, which seem to have been lost. If we have to lift ourselves up, we should stop quarrelling among ourselves. Keep the motto before you—"Elevation of the masses without injuring their religion."[10]

2. Education for Peace: Values for Co-operation

His Holiness The Dalai Lama in his extension lecture at NCERT spoke of the exceptional intellectual abilities and qualities possessed by human beings, which make them superior to all other species. These qualities could be developed and nurtured through education to help man achieve higher levels of development. He referred to the rich legacy of Indian tradition, its ancient system of education, which promoted spirituality and produced great thinkers, philosophers and spiritual leaders. The inculcation of good human qualities like compassion, respect and sense of truthfulness, caring, etc. have been a part of the Indian way of life. But now when India has achieved tremendous progress, there is a decline in human values. The modern system has no place for spirituality whereas human values are essential for leading a happy life. Human values, therefore, have to be brought in the education system but without attaching them to any religion. Friendly relationships with others according to him are essential for peace. Modern society is becoming increasingly interdependent hence learning to live together in the family, with neighbours is essential for national and world peace. Children from young age have to be made aware of the interdependence between human beings.[11]

3. Promotes Efficiency through Ethical Values

When the mind is concentrated efficiency is found to happen. Swami Purananda rightly states:[12] The right values step up one's efficiency. In order to manage our own life at home in the world and in our professional field, the higher values are necessary, so that our reaction to the outside world, our judgement of the situation that is around us—all is totally changed. And, we will be able to, not only face the challenges in front of us, but also still discover in our minds a lot of mental energy left, which we can apply for our quantity purpose of planning the future.

Ethical virtues are the intelligent ways of reviving man's exhausted energies and fatigued spirit to live. By living these healthy values of righteous living, the individual unshackles his psychological personality from its self-made entanglements. As a contrast to this, the negative tendencies cultivated by the 'diabolically fallen' are self-made shackles that chain a man to a realm of confusions and sorrows forbidding him to grow into the ampler fields· of his own inner possibility.

4. Co-ordial Relations between the Teacher and Students: Values of Respect, Love and Affection

Swami Lokeswarananda observes that according to the Indian tradition, a teacher is like a lighted lamp from which other lamps may be lighted. This underlines the fact that a teacher must himself be a highly educated man, otherwise he is not entitled to teach. Can a blind man lead another blind man?

But it will be a mistake to think that academic qualification is the only criterion of a teacher. He may have encyclopaedic knowledge, but to this must be added moral excellence of the highest order. He need not teach high moral principles, he has to live them. A teacher should be an example of what is best in man. He can inspire by what he is and not by what he knows. 'To know is to be'—runs a popular dictum in India. Knowledge is useless if it does not make a man perfect—perfect not merely in skills and abilities, but also in character.

The teacher's task is to impart knowledge but to do this, he must first enkindle in the pupil a thirst for knowledge. He must also train his pupil's body and mind, train his faculties, so that the pupil can use them to his best advantage. Mind is man's most powerful organ. A healthy mind under control is man's best friend and guide. Given such a mind and a desire to learn, a student can learn by his own efforts, with the assistance of the teacher or even without. In fact, one learns best when one learns by one's own efforts, for how much knowledge can a teacher pass on to his pupil? Also, the knowledge that the teacher imparts may turn out to be outdated, if not also wrong. The most a teacher can do is to give his pupil a sense of direction, that is, tell him what to learn and how to learn it and also how to apply that knowledge for his own good and the good of his community.

The relationship between the teacher and the taught is exactly like the relationship of the gardener and the flowers on the bush. The gardener does not create the flowers from the soil and the manure; the flowers must themselves come from the bush. The gardener can only tend its roots, water it, protect it, see that it has the correct amount of sunlight and shade—all these externals he can provide. But no mere gardener can guarantee the blossom; it can come only from the bush itself.

Similarly, the teacher's job is to nurture the student with right thoughts. The student must be given a conductive and protective environment where he or she need not overstrain to live. But the blossoming—the real fragrance and beauty of the personality—must come from within.[13]

If contemporary education is to be value-based, it can never be done without the teachers themselves understanding, appreciating and upholding the life-sustaining moral values. The teachers cannot have any excuse whatsoever. If one cannot practise these values, one should not dream of teaching as a job. In fact, teaching is not a job. It is a mission and vision for life and for posterity. Swami Vivekananda established the Ramakrishna Mission order in 1897. Now there are a number of educational institutions, administered by Ramakrishna Mission throughout the country. They are transmitting the universal values of austerity, brotherhood, compassion, dedication, empathy, faithfulness, grace, hardwork, integrity, justice, kindness, liberty, mercy, non-violence, obedience, perseverance, fortitude, rationality, selflessness, truth, unity, virtue, wisdom, yoga and zest. A unique enterprise in educational endeavour is Shri Sathya Sai Baba Institute of Higher Learning, a deemed university, for the promotion of value-based education. It is situated at Prasanti Nilayam (AP), the headquarters of Sri Sai Baba mission. There are similar institutions, run by other missions in the country. If these educational institutions can be strengthened further, of course, within the secular framework of the Indian Constitution, India will ably meet the challenges of the twenty-first century.

K. Muralidharan in his article, "Value in Education: A Changing Concept" in *University News*, January 7-13, 2002 strongly feels that:

The Indian culture is deeply rooted in spiritual values and unless these values find their way into the life of students, education will lose its significance and will not fulfil its function of endowing the students with a vision to live by and with the ideals to work for. Therefore, in deference to the cherished goals of democracy, socialism, humanism and secularism, it is very essential that our education system should evolve a new positive morality, which could effectively be built into the school curriculum.

It is essential that the teachers also should be exposed to the traditional values and ethics of education through training programs from time to time. They should not confine to their job to a mere matter of completing syllabus and following the curriculum. There should be a platform for teachers to deliberate on any sensitive issues or topics as and when the need arises. They should also explore the ideas of accepting modernisation, globalisation and liberalisation from the academic point of view. They should also learn while imparting their duties for which they are meant. By creating a conductive atmosphere for intellectual rigor and freedom of expression and thought, one can practice values in education.[14]

The National Commission on Teachers (1852), also known as Chattopadhyay Commission, observed:

"There has been a feeling of grievance on the part of the teachers that they do not receive the status and respect from society that their profession and role demand. . . . It may be recalled that the Guru never demanded reverence by the Shishya, his parents and the adult community gladly and gratefully proffered it to the teacher. So must the teacher earn status through achievements. The closer the teacher the more he is able to link himself and his vocation with the mission for the nation, the more relevant he will become and more revered by students, parents and society. We underscore that the primary task of the teacher is concerned with man-making, namely, the making of the Indian of tomorrow. The

Universal; the Guru (Teacher) is personal in relationship. The illustrious poet, Kalidasa, speaks of the Guru in the following words: "He converts darkness into light and makes the invisible God visible."

5. Value Education Promotes Personality Development and Social Cohesion

Value education helps oneself and one's relation to society. Value education makes one peaceful and by his personality, he adds peace to the society. Individual and society supplement each other.

Education is a personality building process. It has always been linked with society. It has both a personal and social dimension, and like the two sides of the same coin, these are inseparable. According to Gandhiji, real education did not consist in packing the brain with information, facts and figures, or in passing examinations by reading the prescribed number of books, but by developing the right character. At present, our education system is largely involved in preparing the younger generation for developing their cognitive domain. It is mainly based on the preponderance of public examination and excessive competitive spirit at the cost of developing the more important affective domain. Today, what is being done is to educate the heads and hands and not the hearts. Essential education must lead to internalisation of the obligation on the part of each human being to be value-conscious in word, thought and deed. Lack of value education has been an important factor in the global scenario of growing violence and terrorism, pollution and ecological imbalances. The Education Commission (1964-66) and the National Policy on Education (NPE-1986) stressed the importance of value-oriented education in our country. The Rammurthy Committee Report (1990) recommended that the imparting of value education should be an integral part of the entire educational process.[15]

6. An Integral 'Vision' for National Regeneration: National Values

Value education makes the youth powerful. They contribute a great deal to the national reconstruction and national development.

An old Jewish proverb says that 'a man without a dream and a nation without a vision shall perish'. We need a great vision to build a great nation. In the multi-religious context of India, this vision has to be an inclusive one. It must be deeply rooted in the truth, goodness and beauty of our ancient culture and tradition and at the same time, it must also be in harmony with the scientific developments of the era. We are fortunate that our Constitution has been able to capture and embody this spirit of unity and harmony of cultures and religions and the scientific temperament of the modern world.

I am inspired to present to you here a vision of a great India firmly rooted in her own rich spiritual and cultural heritage and at the same time fully open to the scientific development of humankind. I have termed this great India of our vision Bharatiya Dharma Rajya or Dharma Bharathi in short.

Bhartiya Dharma Rajya is the vision of an India of love, unity and peace built on the integral concept of Dharma and on the ensuring Bharatiya Dharma as embodied in the Preamble and Article 51(A) of the Indian Constitution. This is the vision of an awakened India of political stability, social harmony and economic prosperity built on an integral vision of life and reality. It is the vision of a disciple nation of God on earth where all religions and cultures will be respected for their unique insights into Truth and valuable contributions towards human welfare, an India where all living beings will live in harmony and peace with one another as the fulfilment of our age-old dream of a Vasudhaiva Kutumbakam. This is our vision of the great India of the third millennium that will be a land and light of Dharma in humanity's quest for a culture of life, unity and peace on earth.

'Peace and Value Education for Schools/Colleges' should present and promote this noble and inter-religious vision of Bharatiya Dharma Rajya in our intuitions of learning and among our youth if it is to lead to the much needed national regeneration of India. This is a religious task more than a political task that can only be achieved through interreligious cooperative action. It will be difficult for political parties and governments to take up this task on their own, they can only support and collaborate with religious-minded and peace-loving patriotic citizens of India in this divine mission.[16]

7. Value Education will Build Character

At present, the Government of this country is striving to bring about universal education. In this context, it will be useful to consider what the purpose of education is. Great men of this land have declared that education should foster character, help the acquisition of good qualities, or seela, and eradicate vices, knowledge should also enable us to understand the truth about things. Saivite and Vaishnavite saints have proclaimed that God alone is Truth, and the rest is maya or illusion. These sages and saints endeavored to realise Truth, that is God. In Him they found their supreme joy. They looked at everything else as the sources of evil and suffering. In the Vedas, the Paramatman is spoken of as Truth. When it is declared that everything connected with this world is mithya, or false, it to so much to condemn the world as to affirm that the Paramatman alone is true.[17]

Right education should make us know that God is the Truth. Knowledge must fill one with good qualities through which alone one can realize the Truth, that is God. Therefore, the goal of knowledge is the understanding of the Ultimate Truth. The first fruit of education must be humility and self-control. Education that does not produce these qualities is useless. We find that people in countries where modern education has spread are not as virtuous as they should be. Unsophisticated illiterates, like those slaving in the tribal areas of South African jungles, are found to be more honest than those who have received the doubtful benefits of modern education. It is sad to Note that in our own schools and colleges, indiscipline is rampant nowadays. Even girls, who are by nature docile, have caught this infection of indiscipline. All these developments give rise to the question whether this kind of education is after all necessary or useful. Such education is the cause of stress among students.

From time immemorial, the necessity to acquire knowledge is being emphasized and he who has had no education is considered an animal. Vidyaa viheenah pasuh says Bhartruhari. But what is the type of education our ancients had in mind when they said: Vidyaa vinaya sampanna? A thing can be done either in the dharmic way or in the adharmic way. Good results will flow when a thing is done in the right way.[18]

8. Study of the Life of Great Men to Learn from their Practice in Life

We must train our people from an early age to study the lives of great men who led an unattached life, free from debasing passions like lust, anger, greed and fear and, following their example, develop faith in God. This will help them to grow up into dutiful and honest citizens, disciplined to lead a moral and ethical life. If the government also takes sufficient interest in making provision for teaching moral and spiritual values to children, it stands to gain much. For one thing, expenditure on police and law courts will get reduced. They will also be free from the troubles arising from strikes and other forms of student indiscipline.

"The Inculcation of moral and spiritual values in the minds of the people from the early years is most desirable that provision should be made for the teaching of moral and spiritual values in educational institutions."[19]

9. Nation-building and Promotion of Peaceful World Order

In the words of Sri Sathya Sai Baba, education is for man-making, nation-building and promotion of peaceful world order. At the dawn of the new millennium and in the changed policy framework of the Government, there is an urgent need among teachers to inculcate values among students so that they develop into integrated personalities blossoming mentally, emotionally, intellectually, ethically and spiritually (Khandelval, 2001). Teachers in higher education have to act as a role model to bring back values among students, educational institutions and in the society as a whole. They have to act as role models in terms of their honesty, sincerity, hard work and determination towards their duties and responsibilities in order to create an example before their students. The students at this stage are at the cross-road of their career and life. At this stage, normally students seek to identify with some role models for their life. Therefore, the role of teacher at this level of education is to create and recreate the values among students, in educational institutions and the society as a whole. They have a greater responsibility in shaping the destiny of future generation and the country as well. They should also come forward catering to the educational needs at primary and secondary levels in the society. They should be conscious about their social responsibilities. No external force should be required to inculcate in them a sense of dedication and responsibility. The role of teacher at the higher level is different from their counterparts at other stages on account of these teachers' greater involvement with activities related to research, publications, training and administrative responsibilities.[20]

10. Core Value-Based Education Promotes Ideal Humanity

The Parliamentary Standing Committee on Human Resource Development in its Eighty-first Report on Value-Based Education (1999) has highlighted that Truth (Satya), Righteous Conduct (Dharma), Peace (Shanti), Love (Prema) and Non-violence (Ahimsa) as the Core universal values, which need to be identified as the foundation stone on which the value-based education programme can be built-up. All the religions of the world have also emphasized that non-violence, tolerance and peace are the fundamental components of humanity. Great philosophers and social thinkers of East as well as West have seen education as a process leading ultimately to spiritual development. UNESCO in the context of peace, refers education not only to general education acquiring cognitive capital but ability to live together.[21]

11. External and Internal Values must Act in Harmony

The wonderful development of science during the past three hundred years concerns the external nature and the world outside. The study of the nature and potentialities of the human mind is of more recent origin—it has a history of about hundred years. It is true that with the help of scientific equipment, like the microscope and telescope, the scientist has understood innumerable minute details of the exterior world. But many of the scientists are realizing, though belatedly, that the nature of the mind, its constant tendency to flow outward, prevents it from getting an insight into many other aspects of the mind which can be achieved only by the practice of meditation.

Scientists have provided us with various kinds of conveniences and comforts by discovering innumerable natural laws and thus, uncovering the secrets of nature. It has to be admitted that the human power of investigation has reached an all-time high; man has displayed the peak of his intellectual ability. But is it not within his power to create a beautiful world full of honesty, justice, brotherhood, mutual understanding, cooperation, peace and tolerance? Why has he not succeeded in creating such a world?

The following voice of a poet reflects the present predicament of mankind:

People fear people
Doubt reigns everywhere

Behind the curtain of peace
Martial moves the revolution
Meanness yet unheard of
Devilishness in patriotic garb
Tuskers among nations crush life apace
Not to speak of the bloody flame
Rising high on the West
Bullets are at play
Mad after martial joy

The scientist can make the five elements dance to his tune, he can transverse land, water and space at a marvelous speed, and he can drive away terrible epidemics, which threaten the human race. Can't he instill in the hearts of men, who live and thrive now, but who are liable to decay and die, a sense of brotherhood and friendship? Can't he quench the primordial fire of hatred by pouring forth the ambrosia of love?

The following is the answer to the question:

Progress is to take place in two fields. It relates to the two faces of nature:

The one is the physical nature, the nature of the external world. The other is the inner nature of man. The one is related to the world that we see. The other one is related to the inner-self of man with whose help he is able to see the world outside and investigate.

If man is able to increase his power to free himself from the hold of the surrounding world or environment, if he increases his freedom, if he gains control over nature, we may say that the change we call development leads to progress. In this respect, the innumerable discoveries of scientists have helped us gain control over the outside nature. Undoubtedly, we are moving on the path of outward development and progress. But is there a comparable development in the regions of the mind?[20] Upon this understanding depends the solution of educational problems.

12. Ethical and Moral Values: The Foundation of the Quality of Life

Ethical and moral values are the basis of good life as ethical culture indeed ennobles human life. Ethics, religion and spirituality have become synonymous terms in common parlance as they co-exist in the development of moral culture and of righteous and virtuous life. Moral living starts through dedication to ideal principles, maxims and human values. A righteous and virtuous life and a clear conscience provide the backbone of spiritual as well as a humane material progress of the civilized man and his society.

No ideal, ideology, institution or religion is self-operative. It is through human agency alone that ideals and institutions established for their realization are made operational. History bears witness to perversions, distortions and abuse or misuse of ideals and institutions for the reason that human being is essentially imperfect though he seeks perfection. It is true that perfection is not attainable by imperfect beings, however, it is always worthwhile attempting and this depends largely upon a meaningful education of man with a view to fertilizing the soil within so that the vessel may bear rich, juicy and truthful fruits. Sustenance of human values, ethics and morals in human society and spiritual enlightenment of man seem to be decidedly more effective and meaningful goals of educational philosophy to follow. It is principally inadequate appreciation of the essentially spiritual nature of man and prevailing disrespectful attitude towards the role of true religion or spiritualism in protecting and promoting the spiritual core of human beings which accounts for the crisis of our times.

Ever since the dawn of human civilization, conscious efforts have been made by man to cultivate values in order to humanize himself by conquering his animal instincts and ennobling his life by harmonious development of all the faculties. When one realizes that one's actions affect the entire society, the value system that we live by and the choices that we make acquire paramount importance. Living a life based on noble values enables human beings to refine their character which is called culture. The culture of a people or a nation is based upon the values that those constituting it live and uphold in their lives. When the cultural values deteriorate, civilization declines but when these are promoted civilization flourishes. Whenever higher ideals are abandoned and fundamental cultural values of the society are totally ignored, civilizations have disappeared. If perversions of man's desires and natural urges transgress the control and limits set by nature, it results in the loss of culture which is his internal aspect. When his culture declines, it eventually results in withering away of civilization which essentially manifests external aspect of man's social life.

The modern world is marked by a widespread explosion of knowledge and tremendous achievements in Science and Technology, coupled with a general decline and reversal of human values as well as an alarming deterioration of moral and mental health both of individuals and societies. The recent spate of crimes, violence, terrorism, and drug abuse makes us aware of the significance of human values, without which human life loses all meaning. It is also evident that a mere economic prosperity and material wealth cannot result in a lasting well-being of mankind. The inner strength of mankind springs from within, which seems ill-nourished now. To fill up the void regarding human values, the richest resources are available in the texts and scriptures of all the religions of the world which have guided people in their thoughts, feelings and actions for ages. Human virtues have been propounded and preached by many great sages, Prophets and teachers who had perceived subtle truths of human life, for the benefit of their adherents and for those who would derive benefits by studying their sayings and advices. Some of their sayings were understood by people in letter and spirit, enriching and elevating them, but some others were not understood well, ending up as mere outward rituals, blind faiths, intolerance with others and hatred for other faiths. More than a century ago, Swami Vivekananda had said: "We want to lead mankind to the place where there is neither the Vedas, nor the Bible, nor the Koran, yet this has to be done by harmonizing the Vedas, the Bible and the Koran. Man ought to be taught that religions are but the varied expression of the religion, which is oneness, so that each may choose the path that suits him best."[23]

13. Growth in Spiritual Values

One of our noblest duties in life is to grow. This is the screaming cry of all evolution. Growth in the biological apparatus was the command in the lower stages of evolution. After having attained manhood, the demand is to grow our moral stature, in our spiritual worth, in our cultural dignity. This is where study of the scriptures, regular and continuous, and sadhana, constant and sincere, come to serve us. The study clearly points out the goal and the way—the sadhana yields to us the energy and vitality to walk the path and explode into the goal. These we must.

14. Harmony and Peace: Values for Tolerance

In the world today, we are living through an age of confusions and tensions, both within and without us. The external challenges persecute us and render our lives unhappy and sorrow ridden. The intelligent philosophy of the Rishis advises man 'to live in harmony' with the situations in life and steadily work on to meet them with discretion and constant application. When we live thus, for a period of time, a subjective poise develops, giving us inward peace and tranquillity, which, thereafter, remains unaffected by external threats and onslaughts.

Revered Shri Vethatheri, Maharishisays' has beautifully written that 'Harmony is a precious treasure of human life'. Real success and satisfaction, happiness are the different facets of harmony. If one is to enjoy the benefits of life to the fullest, it is necessary to develop and maintain harmony; and for this understanding the philosophy of nature is required.

Harmony should be maintained in all spheres of life, and these are:

- Between body and life;
- Between wisdom and habits;
- Between self and society;
- Between the purpose of life and the method of living; and
- Between will and nature.

The more one understands life, the more one will achieve harmony; and success will be proportionate to that. No doubt, harmonizing life is a difficult task, but its worth all the striving, for it is the only way to equip oneself to enjoy life to the fullest extent and to reach the goal of life, which is the perfection of consciousness. By the development of knowledge man comes to understand the cause and effect system which is the law of nature.

15. Values of Devotion and Dedication

Of the innumerable techniques prescribed by the rishis for self-development, the most popular ones are the path of selfless dedicated service (karma yoga), the path of discriminative knowledge (jnana yoga), and the mystic path of self-development through disciplined contemplation (raja yoga).

According to Sage Narada, true devotion for the Lord is superior and nobler to all these, because devotion is the final outcome of all other methods of self-development.

This supreme devotion is indeed, as a technique, even superior to the path of action, the path of knowledge, and the path of disciplined contemplation. (Narada Bhakti Sutra II:I:25)

All the other paths are the means that take the seekers to the final goal of spiritual experience, but in devotion there is very little difference in essence between the means and the end, between the way and the goal. Love alone is love's own end and fulfilment. Devotion is both the means and the end. As long as residual vasanas (inherent tendencies) are still lingering in the devotee's personality, so long is devotion only the path. But when, as a result of his love for the Lord, his vasanas disappear totally, a stage comes when his supreme love itself becomes the Lord of love Supreme.

Than all other paths, devotion is the one most readily available and most easily attainable. (Narada Bhakti Sutra VI:1:58)

Having dedicated all activities unto Him, the devotee should turn all desire, anger, pride, and so forth toward Him alone (Narada Bhakti Sutra VI:2:65).

Having gained this supreme devotion, the devotee attains perfection and immortality and becomes extremely satisfied. (Narada Bhakti Sutra I:1:4)

Acharya Vinoba Bhave says: Knowledge, love, and constant effort are the three legs on which life stands. If one of the legs of a tripod is broken, it cannot stand, since all three legs are needed. This is also the condition of life. Even if we logically distinguish between devotion (bhakti), knowledge (jnana), and action (karma), we cannot divide them in experience. The three together make up one great entity.

CONCLUSION

The worst days of a serious threat to Indian society are over. Under foreign domination and western influence we had developed the foolish notion of degrading everything, morals, ethics and spirituality and were easily swept-off our feet by the glamour and glitter of the exotic. The wonderful phenomenon that is taking place now is that we are returning to these things which have lent stability and strength to our culture over the centuries. Because the various educational programmes launched by the NCERT, UGC and other organizations (such as Sri Sathya Sai Organization) ranging all the way from nursery to post-graduate level, are bringing into proper focus the valuable ingredients of our culture. By far the most important aspect of these programmes is that besides giving a theoretical and conceptual base in the curriculum they also seek to transform the quality of life through inculcation of human values of peace, love, truth, spirituality, right conduct, ahimsa and, above all, national character which, in effect, represent the highest and the noblest in our culture system.[24]

About ethical or approved conduct Apastamba-Dharma-Sutra (22.14) enjoins:

Absence of anger, elation, indignation, avarice, delusion, vanity and enmity; speaking truth; moderation in eating; refraining from exposing others' weak points; freedom from jealousy; sharing one's good things with others; sacrifice; straightforwardness; gentleness; quietude; self-control; friendliness with also beings; absence of cruelty; contentment—these form the approved conduct for men of all stations of life. By observing them duly one becomes universally benevolent.

Suresh Prasad Singh in his Article "Emerging Values in Modern Education" suggests an integrated vision to promote value education. To quote him:

The power of modern education can be better realized by achieving a happy integration of utility and value, integration of body and mind, emotions and ideas, individual and society, and the world. The vision of progress must not be devoid of human element, the aspect of vision which makes the progress meaningful and purposeful. The progress that is aimed at the desired, is an assertion of the powers of human imagination, and soothe fruits of this progress must be realized with the ends of humanity in mind. The tools of change are powerful but their application must be human and they must be employed for pious purposes.

In the wake of the phenomenal developments on the educational front, re-orientation of values in the post-modernist education assumes special significance. Here are certain concrete recommendations for tempering utilitarian pursuit of together education with desirable ideals and visions of human happiness;

(a) Education must promote rational outlook on life and scientific approach to issues confronting the real life situations;
(b) An imaginatively farmed course in fundamental freedom and human rights must constitute of our degree level curriculum;

(c) Power that education generates must be employed for constructive human purposes;
(d) Education must develop sensitivity to environment and must foster human ethos for the enjoyment of the fruits of progress;
(e) Humanism should be the central concern of education in all circumstances, and it must promote quality concern for corporate behaviour and corporate life; and
(f) Education must be able to develop a working mechanism to fight the evil of consumerism and acquisitive culture so that environment may be protected and development may remain sustainable.

In New Delhi Conference on "Quest for New Perspectives", held on July 9-10, 2003 feels that:

As we reflect today on the theme of dialogue of civilizations, it seems imperative that education should be so developed that a new mentality is created which spontaneously turns to dialogue rather than to conflict, which spontaneously responds to the call of interchange, and which is spontaneously eager to see problems from various points of view and which is capable of synthesizing different points of view without sacrificing uniqueness of various truths that are synthesized. We have to develop particularly a new curriculum that aims at explaining the basic theme of human progress as a mighty expression of an adventure of continuous self-exceeding. This curriculum should inspire students to work for unity even while rejecting uniformity; this curriculum should also encourage students to respect cultural diversity. Finally, this curriculum should develop a new science and art of living together which necessitates adherence to the law of mutuality rather than conflict and the law of variety of expressions rather than any uniform monotone. It may also be urged that since science and technology characterize a large part of modern civilization, we should develop a new curriculum where by a fresh impetus is given to scientific studies that are in harmony with the study of values. There is, today, an increasing awareness that unless science and value are blended together, humanity will have to face a great peril, the peril of inner human suffering even in the midst of increase of knowledge and increase of material comforts. It is in the hands of educationists today to develop a new dimension in education so that education can not only build the defences of peace in the minds and hearts of people but also build bridges between the past and the future, and serve the great ends of the dialogue among civilizations.

What is now needed is a concerted action at the development of a curriculum that can bring home to the students three important lessons, namely, (i) that the entire humanity shares one basic impulse towards progress and by sharing this impulse humanity can be seen as one vast surge of adventure which aims at continuous self-exceeding; (ii) that humanity, in its mature developments, tends to reject uniformity and adopts the law of unity that permits and respects cultural diversities; and (iii) that the future progress of humankind is bound up with the development of a new science and art of living together which necessitates adherence to the law of mutuality rather than conflict and the law of varied expressions rather than any uniform monotone. Education should aim at strengthening democratic and universal human values and respect for human rights. Education is the most powerful instrument for preparing a mind which can promote the culture of dialogue.

Notes and References

1. Anita Shetty and K. Pushpanadham, Valuing Values, *University News*, Dec. 29, 1997, pp. 7-8.
2. H. Venkataiah, Value Education, Curriculum for Graduates and Post-graduates in *University News*, June 22, 1998.
3. R. Satya Rajiv, Human Values in University Management, in AIU, *Value Education in India*, New Delhi, 2001, pp. 86-87.
4. Quoted in Anitha Shetty *et. al.*, Value Education: Need of the present generation in *University News*, Oct. 13, 1997, p. 12.
5. Quoted in N.P. Sinha, Towards inculcating values in Education, in *University News*, Oct. 22-28, 2001, pp. 1-2.
6. Swami Gautamananda, Values in our Education, in *Values: The Key to a Meaningful Life*, Ramakrishna Math, Madras, India, pp. 83-85.
7. *University News*, Dec. 9, 1996, p. 22.
8. R. Natarajan, *University News*, July 21-27, 2003, p. 16.
9. Sri Aurobindo, The Synthesis of Yoga, 1976, Sixth Edition, Sri Aurobindo Ashram, Pondicherry, p. 2.
10. Swami Jagadatmananda, Learn to Live, Vol. 2, Ramakrishna Math, Chennai, 2000, pp. 154-57.
11. H.H. The Dalai Lama, Education for Peace, in *Journal of Value Education*, Vol. 2, No. 1, January 2002, p. 1.
12. Swami Purnananda, Making Life Valuable by Imbiding Values, in *Journal of Value Education*, Vol. 2, No. 1, January 2002, pp. 30-31 (NCERT).
13. *Ibid.*, p. 15.
14. P. Dhannavel, Importance of Value-based Teachers, in *University News*, May 1, 2000, p. 2.
15. Hemanta K. Khandai, Value Oriented Approach from Primary to University Education, *University News*, March 31 to April 06, 2003, pp. 9-10.
16. Swami Sachidananda, Vision and Values for National Regeneration, *Journal of Value Education*, Vol. 2, No. 1, January 2002 (NCERT), pp. 70-71.
17. H.H. Jagadguru's Madras Discourse Acharya Call, Part III, Peetam Kanchipuram, 1998, pp. 66-67.
18. *Ibid.*, p. 192.
19. *Ibid.*
20. Nageshwar Rao and R.P. Das, Bringing Values Back: The Role of Teachers in Higher Education in *Journal of Value Education*, Vol. 2, No. 1, January 2002, p. 89.
21. J.S. Rajput, Symphony of Human Values in Education, NCERT, December 2001, New Delhi.

22. Learn to Live, Vol. I, *op. cit.*, pp. 139-41.
23. R.D. Dhokalia, External Human Values and World Religions, NCERT, New Delhi, 2001, pp. 10, 13, 24.
24. Girijesh Kunal, How to inculcate value education through teacher education, *Journal of Value Education, op. cit.*, pp. 118-19.

APPENDIX 9.1

VALUES IN SRIMAD BHAGAWAD GITA

Selected Slokas

Given below are the five verses from Bhagavad Gita (Chapter XIII, from 7th to 11th) enumerating the important values. The original Sanskrit test is followed by the transliteration and the meaning:

अमानित्वमदम्भित्वमहिंसा क्षान्तिरार्जवम् ।
आचार्योपासनं णौचं स्थैर्यमात्मविनिग्रह : ।। 13/7 (Srimad Bhagavad Gita)

Amanitvamadambhitvamahimsa ksantirarjavam
Acaryopasanam saucam sthairyamatmavinigrahah.

Absence of pride, freedom from hypocrisy, non-violence, forbearance, straightness of body, speech and mind, devout service of the preceptor, internal and external purity, steadfastness of mind and control of body, mind and the senses.

इन्द्रियार्थेणु वैराग्यमनहंकार एव च ।
जन्ममण्त्युजराव्याधिदु:खदोणानुदर्शनम् ।। 13/8 (Srimad Bhagavad Gita)

Indriyarthesu vairagyamanahankara eva ca,
Janmamrtyujaravyadhidukhadosanudarsanam

Dispassion towards the objects of enjoyment of this world and the next, and also absence of egotism, pondering again and again on the pain and evils inherent in birth, death, old age and disease.

असक्तिरनभिशवडंग: पुत्रदारगण्हादिशु ।
नित्य च समचित्ततवमिश्टानि श्टोपपत्तिशु ।। 13/9 (Srimad Bhagavad Gita)

Asaktiranabhisvangah putradaragrhadisu
Nityam ca samacittatvamistanistopapattisu

Absence of attachment and the feeling of mineness in respect of son, wife, home, etc. and constant equipoise of mind both in favourable and unfavourable circumstances.

मयि चानन्ययोगेन भक्तिरव्यभिचारिशी ।
विविक्तदेशसेवित्वमरतिर्जनसंसदि ।। 13/10 (Srimad Bhagavad Gita)

Màyi cananyayogena bhaktiravyabhicarini
Viviktadesasevitvamaratirjanasamasadi

Unflinching devotion to Me through exclusive attachment, living in secluded and holy places, and finding no enjoyment in the company of men.

अध्यात्मज्ञाननित्यत्वं तत्त्वज्ञानार्थदर्शनम् ।
एतज्ज्ञानमिति प्रोक्तमज्ञानं यदतोन्यथा ।। 13/11 (Srimad Bhagavad Gita)

Adhyatmajnananityatvam tattvajnanarthadarsanam,
Etajjnanamiti proktamajnanam yadatonatha.

Fixity in self-knowledge and seeing God as the object of true knowledge; all this is declared as knowledge; and what is other than this is called ignorance.

APPENDIX 9.2

ROLE OF UGC IN HUMAN VALUE IN HIGHER EDUCATION

I. A Scheme for Promoting Ethics and Human Values in Higher Education

The National Policy on Education has laid considerable emphasis on Value Education by highlighting the need to make education a forceful tool for cultivation of social and moral values. The policy has stated that in our culturally plural society education should factor universal and eternal values-oriented towards the unity and integration of our people.

In the present times of unprecedented changes dislocating traditional values and creating conflict between traditional and new values there is a universal concern in respect of erosion of values, promoting values and culture which fit in with the needs of the modern times. This concern is universal but is more acute for our country which has lead its distinct culture, worked view and a living value tradition. The process of developing into a modern nation with new social, political and economic institutions, and with emphasis on science and technology has thrown up many new values—challenges in all areas of our national life. It is important that we examine these challenges and prepare our youth to face and resolve them.

2. Objectives of the Scheme

(i) To create awareness, conviction and commitment to values for improving the quality of life through education, and for advancing social and human well-being.

(ii) To encouraging universities and colleges to undertake academic and other activities pertaining to teaching, research and extension programmes in respect of values and culture like extramural lectures, seminar, conferences, workshops and orientation programmes for teachers and students.

(iii) To encourage universities to undertake preparation and production of requisite material including books, handbooks, journals, teaching materials, video and films relating to values.

3. Eligibility/Target

All eligible Universities colleges which are included under section 2(f) and 12(b) of the UGC Act are covered under the scheme.

4. Nature of Assistance

The different activities for which support will be provided are as under: (i) Research, (ii) Teaching, (iii) Organisation of Conferences/ Seminars, (iv) Awareness/Sensitization/Programme, (v) Human

Enrichment/integrated personality development/Character Building Workshops.

The nature of research projects under this scheme would be different from the usual Ph.D. oriented academic research. They would be aimed at understanding and clarifying value issues of contemporary concern in the public and professional, and to suggest possible ways of resolving these value problems. The research could be a combination of conceptual and empirical investigations. Some of the likely areas of the research projects could be:

Value Issues in:

(i) Core values of human life with reference to the individual, family, community, nation and human society.
(ii) Values relating to Democratic polity and the Rule of Law.
(iii) Professional values, like of engineering, medicine, law, teaching, public service, management, business, etc.
(iv) Values of good governance, administration, and of judiciary.
(v) Values relating to environment, science and technology, and sustainable development.
(vi) Strategies of transmission of value through formal/informal/non-formal/education.
(vii) The role of the films and the multi-media in respect of value transmission and the potentials of multi-media learning to promote awareness and understanding of human values.

The theme should be developed in the light of Indian ethos, aspirations and social realities. The outcome of this research should be in the form of book, monograph, research papers, report, the support provided would be by way of seed money which could be utilized for the purpose of contingency, books and journals, travel, stationary, typing and hiring, etc. The duration of the research project would be ordinarily two years.

5. Teaching

Support under this head would be provided for encouraging and facilitating introduction of new courses on value-related themes like human values, professional ethics, environmental ethics, science, technology, parliamentary democracy, civil society and the rules of law and human values, etc. Financial assistance would be provided by way of:

(i) Grant to teachers teaching such courses for books, preparation of teaching material, travel grant to consult libraries elsewhere, to attend conference lectures themes related to the subject matter, preparation of manuscript for writing books, etc.
(ii) Grant to university/college, department for paying honorarium to retired teachers visiting Professors to teach such courses.

6. Organisation of Conference/Seminars

These could be of two types:

(i) Aimed at generating new ideas related to themes of ethics and human values.
(ii) To provide a platform to teachers engaged in teaching value-related courses to share ideas and experiences.

The conference should be properly focused and their proceedings should be published.

Financial support would be provided to meet expenses on TA/DA, boarding and lodging expenses, local transport, publication of report, secretarial assistance, etc.

7. Awareness/Sensitisation Programmes

These could be in a form of lectures, workshops for a day or two, aimed at specific groups, like teachers, research scholars and students of a particular discipline academic administrators, non-teaching staff, etc.

Support would be provided for meeting expenses of the programme including TA/DA for one or two persons from outside the institution.

8. Human Enrichment/Integrated Personality—Development/Character-building Workshops

These workshops could be very effective non-formal means of seeking a positive change in the value-temper of students and teachers. They could be organized during vacations or after the working hours. They could include presentations and discussions on different themes like spiritual, moral, aesthetic, societal, cultural, environmental values, values of democracy, scientific temper, communication skills, problems of youth, career choices, etc. Some of these workshops could also be for groups from outside the university, like school teachers, NGOs, government officials, corporate executives, etc. As far as possible these external workshops should be self-financing.

The support provided for this activity would be by way of TA/DA and honorarium for resource persons, contingency amount for preparation of reading material, field trips, postage, office assistance, payment to part time organizing assistants, etc.

One time grant will be provided to take up activities described above, Maximum ceiling of financial support will be Rs. 5.00 lakhs. Maximum ceiling does not mean that each College/University will get this grant. It will depend on type of activities that will be undertaken by them.

Chapter 10

POPULATION EDUCATION

The ultimate goal of the word's population policy must be to achieve an equilibrium based on low birth and death rates that can be sustained throughout a distant future for the world and its several parts.

—*F.W. Notestein*

Population Education

The programme of family welfare and family planning is in the interest of peace and humanity in order to improve the quality of life for families in developing countries particularly in rural areas and in urban disadvantaged poor.

—*Tokyo Declaration* of *Parliamentarians* issued in March, 1978

IMPLICATION OF POPULATION EXPLOSION (See Chart 7.1)

The growth rate in population absorbs the national income and lowers the standard of living. The world population conference indicated in the population plan of action that population growth and population policy must be viewed not in isolation, but in the context of development. It was mentioned by the Secretary-General that current and potential world-wide population trends evidently cannot continue for as long as even one century without causing serious dislocations and crises in many areas.[1]

Myrdal in his book "Asian Drama" gave a stern warning to the world in regard to population explosion when he said, "Demographers are of the view that if fertility does not decrease, a time will come when mortality will lose its relative independence of levels of living and begin to rise again."[2]

Thus, there is a great need of stabilizing population. According to Frank W. Notestein:

"The ultimate goal of the world population policy must be to achieve an equilibrium based on low birth and death rates that can be sustained throughout a distant future for the world and its several parts."[3]

As long as the birth rate is not restricted in these countries, it would not be possible to bring about improvements in the living standard of the people.

CHART 10.1

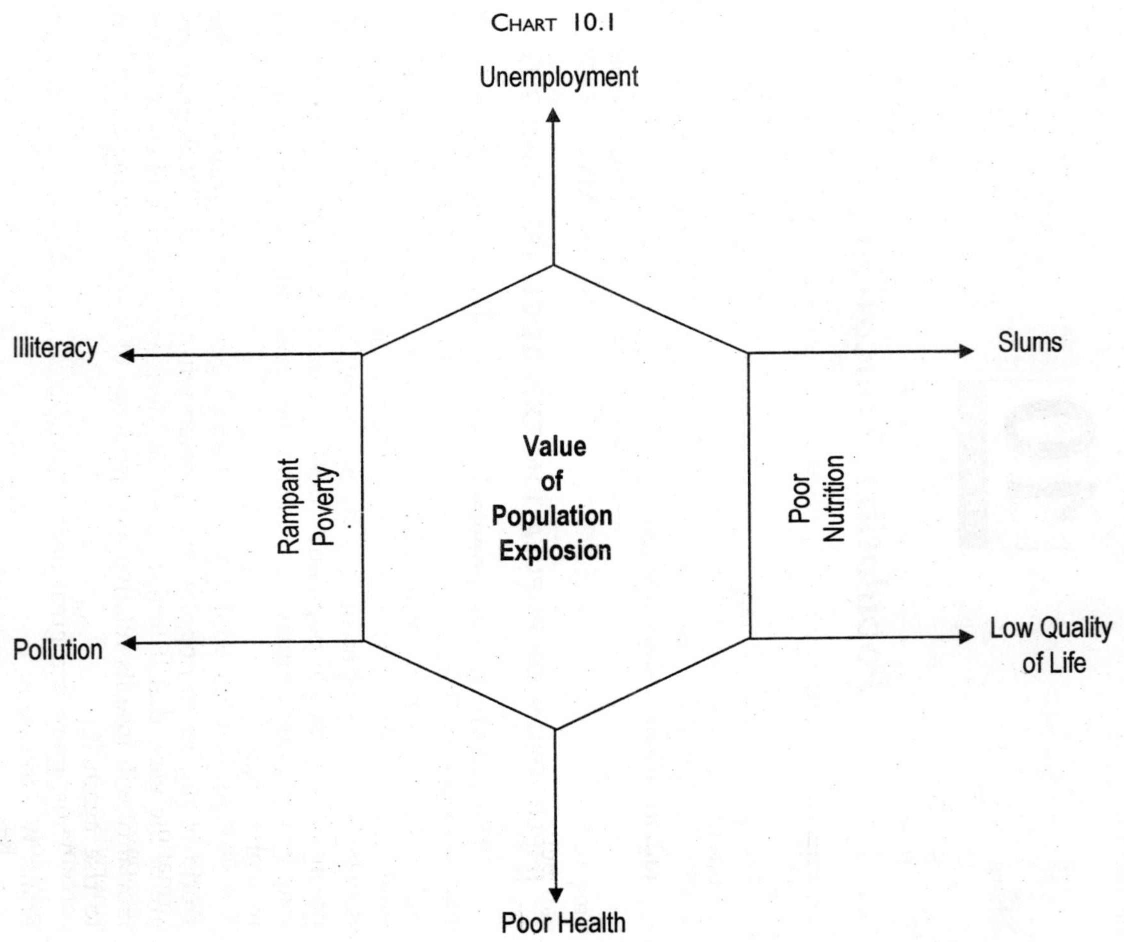
Unemployment
Illiteracy
Slums
Rampant Poverty
Value of Population Explosion
Poor Nutrition
Pollution
Low Quality of Life
Poor Health

In a 'capital poor' and technologically backward country, growth of population diminishes the rate of capital accumulation, increases the amount of disguised unemployment and lowers the standards of living of the people], resources go to the formation to population, not capital. According to Prof. A.W. Singir, population growth has a negative effect on the rate of economic development. According to him:

$$D = SP—r$$

where
D = rate of economic development,
S = rate of net savings,
P = productivity of new investment, and
r = rate of increase in population.

In the above equations, appears as a negative factor with a minus sign.

Let us examine the impact of population growth on the socio-economic development.

(1) Need of More Investments to Sustain Population Growth

The population growth requires more investment while at the same time reduces the capacity of the people to save. This creates a serious gap between investment requirements and the availability of investible funds resulting in the low rate of growth of an economy.

According to Coale and Hoover, "The significant feature of population as such is that a higher rate of population growth implies a higher level of needed investment to achieve a given per capita output, while there is nothing about faster growth that generates a great supply of investible resources.[4]

(2) Reduction in the Rate of Capital Formation

The composition of the people in underdeveloped countries (40-50% of the population in unproductive age-group) is such that it reduces the capacity of the people to save which affects the rate of capital formation. According to Prof. Meier, "This high dependency requires the economy to divert a considerable part of its resources, that might otherwise go into capital formation, to the maintenance of high percentage of dependence who may never become producers or, if so, only for relatively short working life."[5]

Recognising this, the Third Plan States:

"In an underdeveloped economy with very little capital per person, a high rate of population growth makes it even more difficult to step up the rate of saving which, in turn, largely determines the possibility of achieving higher productivity and incomes. Moreover, for a given investment, a larger proportion will need to be devoted to the production of essential consumer goods at the expense of investment goods industries thereby still further slowing down the potential rate of growth."[6]

(3) Food Problem

The demand of food is rising faster than the production of food.[7] In a study carried out by Food and Agricultural Organization, it was found that the failure of food production to keep up with population growth was especially pronounced in the case of the developing countries. Out of the total of 106 countries studied, 72 were classified as developing; but in 24 of these (or one-third) food production lagged behind the growth of population. In the more recent period, it was mentioned, the situation was even less favourable.

(4) Unemployment and Underemployment

The impact of more population would affect the employment situation as there is already a back-log of unemployment and under-employment in these countries. The growing unemployment of these countries is not only an economic but it is also a social evil.

(5) Poor Health Standards

Family planning and health are intimately related. Family planning can promote women's health through the prevention of unwanted pregnancies, limiting number of births, and proper spacing, timing of births and foetal health. Family planning also promotes the health of the child through the reduction of child mortality, and promotion of the child development. Maryellen Fullam stresses the importance of family planning as instrument for the promotion of health. He says:

> "Uncontrolled fertility directly threatens the health of mothers and infants and many undermine the health of other family members. Today, no health programme can be considered complete unless it offers ready access to the appropriate family planning measures for all potential parents."[8]

(6) Social and Psychological Tensions

Rapid population growth leads to social and psychological tensions, and breakdown of a distribution system. Civil amenities such as water and power supply, housing, transport and social utilities like schooling, educational, health and medical services fall much short of demand in spite of their constant expansion. Besides, it leads to political and social corruption and accentuates economic disparities.

Thus, we can say that the problem of growing population has reached such menacing proportions that it has become a real threat to the socio-economic stability of the country. The excessive growth in population does not affect the stability of the national economy alone, it disturbs the stability of the entire body politic. It poses a colossal threat to our social structure. In our fight against poverty, disease, hunger, malnutrition and unemployment, checking the rapid growth of population is as important as raising production in the farms and factories and provision of social services. Population control is one of the chief issues which the country has to resolve and accord top priority in its march towards social and economic development. The programme of family planning is of vital importance for our country. It is a positive and constructive approach to the betterment of the quality of life of the community. Thus, it is evident that the key to India's economic future based on social justice lies in the immediate and effective implementation of a nationwide population programme.

J.P. Singh has rightly analysed the impact of population growth. He states that according to the provisional results of the 2001 census, India's population stood at 1,027 million on March 1, 2001, comprising 531 million males and 496 million females. From 361 million at the time of Independence, the population reached one billion in 2001, registering an increase of nearly three times. All this had happened when the country is not in a position to guarantee adequate nutrition, healthcare and education to the burgeoning population. At the same time, it is also true that all this has happened because of mass poverty in the country. Indifferent governance is also partly responsible for the current demographic and health scenario. Every year about 18 million people were added to India's population during 1991-2001 as against 16 million annually during 1981-91 (see Table 10.1). In other words, each year India's population increases by the equivalents of the number of inhabitants of Ghana, Australia, Mozambique or Saudi Arabia.[9]

If the country puts for a natural course of demographic transition, then it will have to pay a heavy price in the form of unmanageable unemployment, rampant poverty, political chaos leading to ethnic violence and even dismemberment of the country in the long-run. In fact, the whole South Asia would have to encounter a similar experience and would take the shape of Africa and Europe in terms of number of independent nations fighting among themselves. Here the process have already set in, as the population bomb has already exploded. It is altogether a different matter that some of us at the helm of affairs deliverately tend to camourflage the reality or do not want to recognize it. Some of them even ignore the description of dismal demographic scenario scientists seem blissfully unaware of how rising population of India threatens its future, while the population issues have already started dominating India's future. One simply wonders whether new advancements in science and technology will really do any magic to save India from impending disaster following population explosion.

The Government of India in the year 1976-77 announced a National Population Policy. The policy covered a broad range of individual policies including such vital matters as raising the age of marriage, freezing representation of States in Parliament, linking the distribution of federal

TABLE 10.1

Decadal Variations in Population Growth in India: 1901-2001

*Census Year**	*Total population (in million)*	*Average annual exponential growth rate*	*Progressive growth rate over 1901 (in per cent)*
1901	238.4	—	—
1911	252.1	0.56	5.8
1921	251.3	-0.03	5.4
1931	279.0	1.04	17.0
1941	318.7	1.33	33.7
1951	361.1	1.25	51.5
1961	439.2	1.96	84.3
1971	548.2	2.20	129.9
1981	683.3	2.22	186.6
1991	846.3	2.14	255.0
2001	1027.0	1.93	330.8

* Including Assam and Jammu and Kashmir. The 1981 Census was not held in Assam and the 1991 Census was not held in Jammu and Kashmir due to disturbances. The 1981 and 1991 census data include estimated figures for these two states.

Sources: Census of India, 1971, General Population Tables, Series 1, India, Part II-A (i), pp. 33, 50, 536-37; Census of India, 1991, Final Population Totals: Brief Analysis of Primary Census Abstract, Series 1, India, Part 2 of 1992, p. 86; Census of India, 2001, Provisional Population totals, Series 1, India, Paper 1 of 2001, p. 34.

resources to the performance in family planning, promoting female literacy, increasing the monetary compensation for sterilization operations. The policy statement emphasized the urgent need for a direct attack on the population problem as a national commitment. It suggested a series of measures which, it was hoped, would reduce the birth rate to 25 per thousand of population by the end of the Sixth Plan.

Some of the important measures of this policy were:

1. Age of marriage to be raised to 21 for boys and 18 for girls. Offences under the new law have been made cognizable.
2. Representation in the Lok Sabha and State Legislatures to be frozen till the year 2001 A.D. at the level determined after 1971 Census.
3. Eight per cent of Central assistance to State Plans to be specifically earmarked against performance in family planning.
4. Monetary compensation for both male and female sterilization to be raised so as to provide a motivation to couples to have lesser number of children.
5. No Central legislation is proposed for the time being on the question of compulsory sterilization. States were left free to introduce compulsory sterilization if they were well equipped to meet its demands.

6. Group incentives to be introduced for panchayats, teachers and the labour.
7. Scheme for aiding voluntary organizations to be expanded to make family planning a mass movement.
8. Special measures to be undertaken to raise the level of female education.
9. High priority to be accorded to child nutrition programme to secure appreciable decline in infant mortality.
10. Population values to be introduced in the educational system to sensitize younger generations.
11. Change to be made in the Service and Conduct Rules of Central Government employees to ensure that they adopt small family norm.

The Family Planning Programme became a major political issue and the opposition coalition or Janata Party used it in the election campaigns against the ruling party. This gathered momentum and the Congress lost the election at the hands of the Janta Party. The new party changed the name of the Family Planning Programme to the Family Welfare Programme. The Janta announced the revised policy on the Family Welfare Programme on 29 June 1977.

The new approach towards family planning by the Janta Government is known as the 'Cafetaria Approach'. Under this approach, the people can choose any method suitable to them. There is no undue emphasis on sterilization. It is available only to those who desire it. The main features of this policy are:

(a) Ruling out compulsion or coercion of any sort in the field of family welfare for all times to come; while all methods of contraception will be promoted with equal emphasis, it will be left to each family to make its own choice of the method for maintaining the small family norm.
(b) Assigning a vital role to maternal and child health care by providing maternity services to all those who may need them and expanding the immunization programme further.
(c) Raising the age of marriage for girls and boys, although the statement envisaged raising the minimum age of marriage for girls to 16 years, it was decided subsequently that the minimum age for girls would be raised to 18 for the time being while that for boys would remain 21 years.
(d) Giving higher priority to the improvement of women's educational level through formal and non-formal channels.
(e) Using the population figures of 1971 as a base till the year 2001 in all cases where population is a factor as the allocation of Central assistance to State plans, devolution of taxes and duties and grants-in-aid.

(f) Linking of 80 per cent of Central assistance to the State Plans with their performance and success in the Family Welfare Programme.
(g) Giving population education the attention it deserves, specially in the courses for schools and colleges aimed at influencing that segment of population which would soon be entering reproductive age and marital life.
(h) Emphasizing a multimedia motivational approach in which all media units of the various departments in the Centre and the State would be fully associated.
(i) Involving actively all voluntary bodies and the organized sector as agents of change.
(j) Allowing full rebates in the income tax assessment for amounts given as donations for family welfare purposes.
(k) Paying special attention to the necessary research inputs in the field of reproductive biology and contraception.
(l) Soliciting active cooperation and involvement of all ministries and departments of the government of India as well as the States in the programme.
(m) Monitoring of the programme intensively and carefully. Annual review of the situation in depth is to be made by the Union Cabinet.
(n) All restrictions aimed at limiting the size of the family in the case of government employees through conduct rules and the disincentives introduced by the Ministry of Finance in respect of those who violated the small family norm have been withdrawn.

The Family Welfare Programme was included in the New 20-Point Programme of the Prime Minister announced in January 1982. It envisages promotion of family planning on a voluntary basis as people's movement.

A well-defined long-term strategy has been evolved to ensure that the adoption of the 'small family norms' is done entirely on a voluntary basis. The salient features of this strategy consist of intensified efforts to spread awareness and information through imaginative use of multimedia and interpersonal communication strategies, providing services and supplies as close to the doorsteps of the acceptors as possible, developing facilities for rapid increase in female literacy, extending population education to youth in schools and colleges as well as those out of schools, assisting and supporting the association of elected representatives of the people at all levels with the programme, developing linkages with other concerned ministries and departments, ensuring effective observance of the law relating to minimum age for marriage of girls and boys and ensuring close monitoring and follow-up of the programme at all levels.

A critical examination of the existing and past population policies indicate that the family planning programme has become more political rather than technical. Well-designed and articulated public policy can keep the structural components and their elements integrated. We should not change the population policy too often. There are no two different opinions regarding the need for control of population and reducing the growth rate to zero. The views differ regarding the methodology and strategy. We must try to evolve the strategy in cooperation with the people.

Although many dedicated and wise people have been working on the Indian population problem for several years, there are few ideas, and less agreement, about what needs to be done to recruit significantly large number of acceptors.[10]

The creation of awareness is integral to the process of social development. The possibility for the power of communication to liberate the minds and potential of people to critical awareness is real in every field linked to human development, and the generation of public will hinges on effective communication of information and ideas that relate to people's needs, aspirations and capacities for progress in thought and action. In this sense, getting the development process started is largely the task of information, education and communication.

The communication aspect of a national family planning programme is generally termed as IEC-Information, Education Communication. The Year Book (1986-87) of Family Welfare Programme in India has rightly mentioned that the success of the Family Welfare Programme depends primarily upon the voluntary and widespread acceptance of the concept of small family and delayed marriages and well spaced and properly linked births are an effective way of achieving this objective. Mass education and Media activities, accordingly, were given multi-dimensional and integrated thrust through Information-Education-Communication activities in the form of a comprehensive package of social transformation to bring behavioural and attitudinal changes in the people so as to enable them to adopt family planning as a way of life. In brief, we can simplify it, and can call it simply as communication function. Sometimes, the activities under IEC are also referred to as "Mass Communication", "Mass Education", "Mass Education and Media."

Donald J. Bogue has rightly said that IEC is a term widely used to identify the activities of family planning programme to inform the public and stimulate them to adopt contraception.[11] In every technical component of the Family Planning Programme provided by family planning workers, there exists a corresponding educational aspect, which has to be imparted more or less simultaneously, so as to enhance the continuing usefulness of the services provided at the time of need. This would have permanent value.

An added importance of communication in family planning resulted from the experience and studies which indicated that pure clinical approach did not bear fruit. A. Govindachari has mentioned some of the findings of the studies, which have brought to notice the limited impact of clinical approach. These are:

(i) The population reached by the clinics was very limited;
(ii) Education on family planning in the clinics was mostly through individual contacts. There was no organized community education;
(iii) The educational efforts were mostly directed towards women, since the clinics normally have female social workers. Husbands, who are important from the point of view of decision-making in family planning, especially in an Indian cultural context, were not given due attention;
(iv) Couples felt shy to visit clinics for fear of identification by their friends and neighbours;
(v) The working hours of the clinics were found to be inconvenient, especially for the low income groups;
(vi) There was a lack of social support for the programme due to inadequate involvement of the community;
(vii) People generally prefer to obtain contraceptives in an informal way which does not involve formal recording procedures and publicity. This was not possible in a clinic situation; and
(viii) There was very little involvement of other supporting staff, like the village level workers, extension officers, etc., in the family planning programme.[12]

Today, Family Planning Programmes around the world are applying a broad range of service delivery and communication strategies. To make family planning services and supplies more accessible, conventional clinic-based programmes have been supplemented by innovative approaches to services delivery. These include community-based outreach, social marketing through commercial outlets at subsidized prices, and employment-based programmes organized or supported by employees or Unions. Extensive communication campaigns, combining a variety of modern and traditional mass-media are spreading family planning awareness and encouraging more people to seek out family planning services.[13]

The Information, Education, Communication (IEC) component of National Family Welfare Programme is mainly to create an effective communication strategy, to inform the masses about the means and measures of Family Welfare Programme, educate them about the perils of over-population and motivate and persuade them to adopt small family norm, using all possible channels of media.[14]

In a Family Planning organisation, external communication is very important in the implementation of its programme, as information about the utility and means of planned parenthood through appropriate choice and correct use of contraceptives by the eligible married couples is important. Moreover, communication being two-way process brings to the attention of the management the needs, reactions and complaints of the people concerned for necessary initiative or remedial actions. The external communication process needs to be guided by considerations of relevance of information, the choice of communication channels and the existing understanding capacity (education, etc.) of the people concerned outside the organisation. Moreover, it should not by any means be only one sided, i.e., from the organisation to the people. The reverse flow of information from the people to the organisation would make the latter to judge the impact of the programme as well as provide the basis for any changes in the strategies of the Programme. Here again, barriers and disruptions in the two-way communication process have to be dealt with appropriately.[15]

Broadly speaking, communication is the means by which intentions of the programme are classified to ensure fruitful results. It may even be looked upon as the means by which special information inputs are fed into social systems. It is the means by which behaviour of the personnel engaged in the programme is modified; change is effected, information is made productive and goals are achieved. Barnard has aptly viewed it as the means by which people can be linked together in an organisation to achieve the objectives of the programmes. Communication is a universal phenomenon among living beings. Newman and Summer have viewed communication as an exchange of facts, ideas, opinion, or emotions by two or more persons.[16]

Family Planning Communication implies a number of actions starting with identifying the audience, assessing needs and channels for response, identifying specific messages especially in areas of resistance to change in attitude and behaviour, selecting complementary media for optimal combination, producing communication materials and refining messages and techniques after pre-testing, revision and re-testing, dissemination of communication, continuous support through stages of programmes implementation mainly to ensure community involvement and participatory monitoring and evaluation. Since, Family Planning is a challenging and arduous task, communication technology must be well planned. A successful communication effort blends the use of traditional communication media with the modern, brings together the channels of government communication with those of the community and of voluntary organisations and a variety of other groups. Family Planning ideology can be registered in the minds of the people not simply by providing the information on Family Planning, but because people can be told that they exist, shown that they work and encouraged (and empowered) to try them and make them work for themselves. This is the nature of the support which communication lends to a family planning programme.

ESSENTIALS AND ASPECTS OF MASS MOTIVATION CAMPAIGN

Essentials

Dr. John Hubley quoted by Gloria Gorden in his Article, "Let's Communicate" in *World Health* (January-Feb. 1989) has rightly described the essentials of Communication:

- Promote actions which are realistic and feasible within the constraints faced by the community.
- Build on ideas, concepts and practices that people already have.
- Repeat and reinforce information overtime, using different methods.
- Use existing channels of Communication such as songs, drama and story-telling, and be adaptable.
- Entertain and attract the attention of the Community.
- Use clear, simple language with local expressions and emphasize short-term benefits of action.
- Provide opportunities for dialogue and discussion to allow learner participation and feedback on understanding and implementation.
- Use demonstrations to show the benefits of adopting practices.[17]

E.M. Rogers mentions the following essentials:

(i) Family Planning Communication campaigns should be preceded by extensive planning of the strategies to be followed.
(ii) A Consumer Orientation in family planning communication activities will be more effective in achieving the objectives of the National Family Planning Programme.
(iii) A new family planning communication approach should be launched on a small scale pilot project basis.
(iv) Social research can perform an important function in more effective family planning communication, (a) by providing feedback for the design of communication messages through pre-testing, and (b) by yielding, evaluative data about the efforts of communication activities.[18]

Meaning and Genesis of Population Education

The National Seminar on Population Education organized by the NCERT at Bombay in 1969 observed: "The objectives of population should be to enable the students to understand that family size is controllable, that population limitation can facilitate the development of a higher equality of life in nation and that a small size family can contribute to the quality of living for the individual family. It should also enable the students to appreciate the fact that for preserving the health and welfare of members of the family, to ensure the economic stability of the family and to assure good prospects for the younger generation, that the Indian families of today and tomorrow should be small and compact."

The Seminar giving a comprehensive definition of population education emphasized knowledge about the quantity and quality of population and the need to control them for happy human existence. Population education has been regarded as a strategy for human resource development. It aims at developing desired awareness, values and attitudes both for quality and quantity of population. It must enable students to make rational decisions on population. It must enable students to make rational decisions on population matters for themselves for others by acquiring knowledge about cause and effect relationship.

The Asian Regional Seminar organized by the UNESCO at Bangkok in 1970 defined population education as "an educational programme which provided for a study of the population situation in the family, community, nation and world for the purpose of developing in the students national and responsible attitudes and behaviour towards that situation." According to Stephen Viedeeman, population education is "an educational process which assists persons (a) to learn the probable causes and consequences of population phenomena for themselves and their community (including the world), (b) to define for themselves and their communities, the nature of the problems associated with population processes and characteristics, and (c) to assess the possible effective means by which society as a whole and as an individual can respond to and influence these processes in order to enhance the quality of life now as in future.

The NCERT document (1987) has aptly enunciated, "By doing so they are expected to develop national attitude towards the desirable size and structure of our population and the quality of life in their respective family. They are also expected to appreciate and promote the development of small family norms in the society. The acceptance of observance of small family norms depends a great deal on inculcation of commitment on the part of students." (p. 68) Proper education is, therefore, felt essential to develop right attitudes amongst the vast population which is to enter the fertility age-group after a few years. Such education can enable the young people to know the actual facts and position of our country in particular and of the world in general which will motivate them with a desire to adopt small family norms.

ROLE OF HIGHER EDUCATION (See Chart 10.2)

As stated in the UGC guidelines for the Development of Population Education Resource Centres in the Indian Universities (1995), in 1983, the concept of population education was introduced in some universities by

CHART 10.2

Values of Population Education

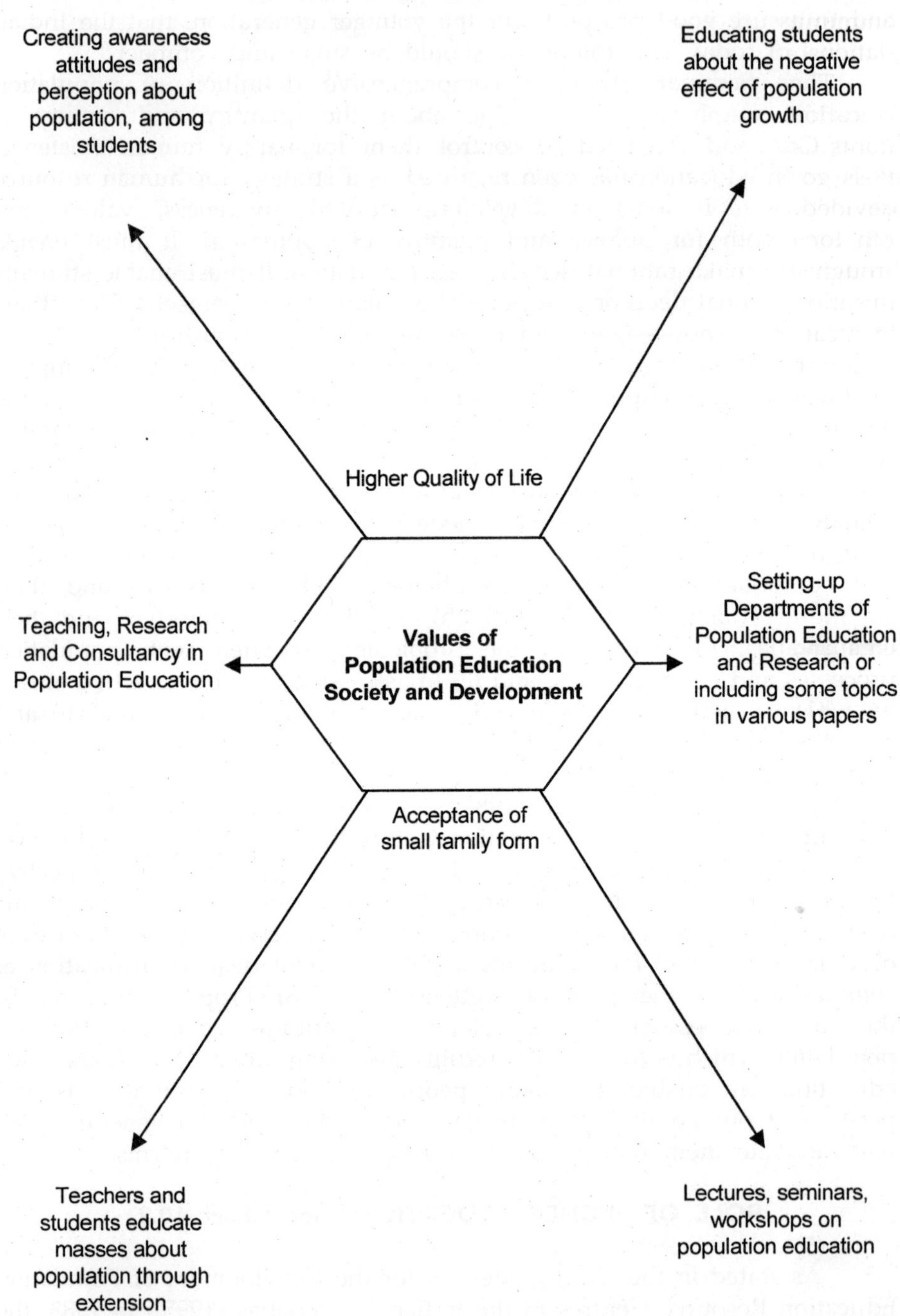

setting up population education clubs as a co-curricular activity. The main objective of the programme was to provide opportunities to the University/College youths and through them to the people in the community, on the relationship to the people in the community, on the relationship between population and quality of life.

The UGC-UNFPA projects on Population Education in Higher Education was launched in 1986. The commitment of the University Grants Commission to population education at the University and college levels go back to 1983 when about 92 universities and 1300 colleges were provided financial support to organize population education activities both for college youth on campus and through them in the communities through Population Education Clubs. The launching of the population education programmes in 1986 with the financial support of UNFPA and technical assistance of UNESCO, provided further impetus to the programme to cover the three functional areas of the universities, viz. development of population education contents for introduction into courses of study at the under-graduate and post-graduate levels, research, and extension education.

Since 1985 the programme has been implemented in 12 universities through the establishment of Population Education Resource Centres (PERCs) in the Department of Adult, continuing Education and Extension.

Aims and Objectives

(1) Change the present attitudes/values in society regarding gender's roles and rights, to one of equal participation in all social, economic and political processes and national and international development;
(2) To counter the reactionary forces emanating from certain sections of the media, economic, social and political institutions, that uncovering the demotion of superstitious from productive to more reproductive roles;
(3) To revitalize university education, bringing it closer to population-related issued to work towards their solution, and to produce sensitive persons able to play more committed and meaningful roles in development activities for the country;
(4) To fulfil a special responsibility to produce for all levels of the educational system, teachers who are aware of the need for a non-formal education, and who would actively pick up the challenge to promote, values, of social equality, including gender equality, secularisms, socialism and democracy;
(5) To update university curricula by incorporating the results of new research and the issues related to population as they challenge some of the established theories, analytical concepts and methodologies of various disciplines;

(6) To promote increased collaboration between different disciplines in teaching, curriculum designing, research and extension activities since population studies are interdisciplinary by nature;

(7) To generate new and organic knowledge through intensive field work. This would help generation of data essential for evaluation and correction of development policies and programmes and in extending the areas to academic analysis into hertherto neglected sectors. For better understanding and investigation of problems being experienced at the grass-roots, a closer contact between institution of higher education and groups directly involved in action, to assist men and women to enjoy their rights within the family, the community and at work would be very valuable. Such contact would also help universities and colleges to design their extension activities in a more meaningful manner; and

(8) To contribute to be global debate on the population problems throughout development of material, training, teaching, research and extension activities.

ACTIVITIES

Teaching

The Population Education Resource Centres would be responsible for the integration of population education in the curriculum at UG/PG/ B.Ed., M.Ed. levels. Efforts will also be made to incorporate Population Education through distance education mode.

(a) A Foundation course for all under-graduate students in all universities, professional and teaching institutions.

(b) Curriculum Development; to incorporate population dimension into courses in different disciplines.

(c) Review of existing text books and to integrate the population issues in the curriculum.

(d) Workshops to plan restructuring of courses and syllabus formation.

Development of Learning Materials (Print and Audio-Visual)

The PERCs would be responsible for the procurement, preparation of learning materials depending upon the local needs of the area. Learning materials would be in printed form as well as audio-visual cassettes. The PERC will duplicate the audio-visual cassettes to be used in their university and also in the service area.

Training (Functionaries/College Principals/Public Leaders/Medical Officers/ Students/Others)

(a) Workshop for the functionaries of the (Vice-chancellors, Principals, Medical Officers, Project Officers, etc.) Universities and colleges to generate better understanding and interest in population-related issues.
(b) Summer/Winter institutes for orientation training of teachers/ researchers, etc. to handle population-related topics.
(c) Workshops for research methodology and syllabus/curriculum restructuring at the UG/PG levels in different disciplines.
(d) Orientation of Vice-chancellors and Public leaders related to the Population Education issues.

Extension Activities

Greatest importance needs to be attached to extension work, as a learning and developmental instrument, for the benefit of the community through students and teachers. A few such extension activities are exhibitions, posters, films, songs, plays, etc. on issues pertaining to the population:

(I) To organize debates, essays competitions, elocution competitions, group discussions, symposia, drawing painting competitions/quizes.
(II) To arrange lectures by experts on population-related issues.
(III) To organize and monitor the programme of population Education Clubs in the Service area.
(IV) To enact demands/rallies on the themes on Population problems on important occasions such as World Population Day, World's Aids Day, University Day, etc.
(V) Working closely with NGOs, NSS, etc., collaboration with other departments of audit and continuing education and extension will enrich such activities.

Universities and colleges through their departments of Adult and continuing education and population research centers can help the students to understand the dynamics of population control. It can as well support the government. Universities and colleges in India are living in Ivory towers as they do not take much interest in social and economic issues found in the community. It is the duty of higher education system in the country to take interest in such issues by incorporating these into under-graduate and post-graduate syllabus or setting up individual departments to support community and government so that these issues can be solved. This is also known as extension function of the University. Faculty in the University possess immense potentially and they can take keen interest in these extension activities provided they are supported by the system of higher education with financial and material support. They can take up following activities for population education:

(a) Educating the youth about population growth so that they understand the implications of small family norms in their life.
(b) Creating understanding and a spirit in the youth about population education so that they spread the message to people.
(c) Students after getting education can work in the community to remove doubts among the people about population control.
(d) Students can convince families about quality of life, which can be possible only with small family.
(e) Prepare charts, video films, etc. for educating students and people about population education.
(f) Arrange debates and discussions on various issues of population education.
(g) Dissemination of information about population education.
(h) Prepare groups of students to visit villages on holidays to promote population education.
(i) Promote the teaching of population education as an independent subject at all educational levels or as part of the regular curricula to meet the needs of each age group.
(j) Create a better understanding of population education by organizing population education workshops for family planning administrators at various levels.
(k) Support research studies and evaluation so that the findings can be applied to further the development of population education.
(l) Encourage educational institutions and relevant agencies to carry out studies and research in order to develop appropriate techniques for implementing information, education and communication services on population activities.

Educational approach is a healthy method and will motivate people to accept family welfare voluntarily. Any other scheme without educational base will miserably fail as it will generate reaction. We must encourage population education through formal and informal education to imbibe the confidence of the people in the family welfare programme. Population education is an educational programme to develop in young mens rational and responsible attitude and behaviour towards population problem. NCERT suggested the following curriculum:

(1) The population growth.
(2) Economic development and population.
(3) Social development and population.
(4) Health, nutrition and population.
(5) Family life and population.

Wayland suggests six basic topics for study:

(1) Basic instructions in population dynamics.
(2) Development of basic understanding of the process of human reproduction.
(3) Understanding of health problem concerned with bringing up of children.
(4) Appreciation of relationship between quality of life and family size.
(5) Government policies regarding population growth and economic development.
(6) Familiarity with the family planning programme of one's own country.

J.P. Singh feels, "What has happened elsewhere can happen in India too provided there is a massive campaign to educate eligible couples, particularly in villages, about the benefits of limiting the size of the family. This point has of course been emphasized innumerable times and at different places but it has never been sincerely implemented. Rural people, steeped in ignorance and obsolete religious belief, still do not know the harm that big family size brings to them and consider every child as a gift of God. This notion must be altered if family planning is to succeed. However, the education campaign must always be backed by easy availability of modern contraceptive measures that can enable people to plan their families. One of the reasons why family planning measures have not yielded the desired results is that it has not been honestly implemented. The unmet need for family planning has been reported to be quite high. According to the National Family Health Survey the current unmet need for family planning is 16 percent and it is higher in rural areas than in urban areas.[19]

National Population Policy, 2000

Government of India has enunciated the new Population Policy in February, 2000. Commenting on the New Population Policy, *Business Standard,* Editorial, "Sense on Population" dated February 17, 2000 remarked that the new national population policy, 2000, however may have a greater chance of acceptance as it incorporates some of the lessons learnt from recent successes in curbing population growth. While the earlier attempts merely emphasized physical targets and ignored the vital aspects of health and education, especially that of the girl child, which are vitally linked to birth rates, the latest policy seeks to squarely address these issues. Besides, it also makes the right kind of noises about investment in social infrastructure as an essential prerequisite for promoting small family norms.

Success of the new policy will depend largely on the way it is implemented by the laggard states and the pace of socio-economic development (including in the field of health and education) that accompanies. It measures like freezing the number of seats in the Lok Sabha at the current level are essentially facilitators, dispelling states fears that population control will reduce their quota of MPs. There has to be an adequate political will to achieve the twin, veritably inseparable, objectives of reducing family size and improving the quality of life.

However, *The Tribune* Editorial, "Gaps in Population Policy" dated February 17, 2000, suggested the gaps in new policy and stressed the need to make up these gaps. Increasing population packs a greater destructive power than what Pakistan can cause by hurling a few nuclear bomb blasts. That is because it is concentrated at the bottom of the social and economic pyramid covering three-fourth of the population. The failure to control the exploding numbers is the most damaging of all failures. What the country needed was a radical review of the old policies, alertness to deploy all available instruments and establish enduring contacts with the target segment in rural India. Sadly these are missing in the new National Population Policy unveiled. The document still pins its hopes on a few tried incentives and shapeless promises to run in population growth. Such sops will be available only after the event—that is, after individuals or couples take themselves out of the reproduction cycle. Actually, the concentration should have been on goading people to enter the charmed circle.

CONCLUSION

Without evaluating the impact of FP education programmes on the bulk of the people, one cannot possible identify positive as well as negative aspects of the programme. An objective evaluation of the FP education programme alone can help one improve guidelines for future action. Cost benefit analysis should be an integral part of this evaluation, so that one may assess how available resources have been utilized. Through objective evaluation, one may also be able to curtail mass production of ritualistic FP education material as produced by various FP education bureaus. The amount thus, saved can be effectively utilized for a more purposeful and meaningful health education programme.

FP education is the most difficult task as habits, usages and customs are deeply entrenched. But, FP administration would fail in its purpose, if it could not produce social change, as it is easier to destroy our villages than to change our customs. Professional training helps the FP experts to deal with the health changes effectively. Their pharmacopoeia in both fields must be strong in order to translate the findings of biological investigations into social application. So over and above each technical act, there is a corresponding education function which doubles the value of the act, increases its efficiency and endows it with real human and social value.[20]

Noel David Burleson has rightly said, "The history of the twentieth century becomes more and more a race between numbers and the quality of life. If we are to utilize our intelligence in our present population dilemma, we must make our educational systems relevant. Participants and those who are about to become participants in the vital revolution will require an education that includes population education. It is felt that through education students, the future participants of population explosion will be able to understand the relationship between the increasing numbers and socio-economic development of our country. The coming generations can be made aware of the impact of population on our environment, on our resources, and on all aspects of our life and society. It is hoped that the future citizens should be involved right from their student life in understanding this major concern formation.

The NCERT document (1987) has aptly enunciated, "By doing so they are expected to develop national attitude towards the desirable size and structure of our population and the quality of life in their respective family. They are also expected to appreciate and promote the development of small family norms in the society. The acceptance of observance of small family norms depends a great deal on inculcation of commitment on the part of students." (p. 68) Proper education is, therefore, felt essential to develop right attitudes amongst the vast population, which is to enter the fertility age-group after a few years. Such education can enable the young people to know the actual acts and position of our country in particular and of the world in general which will motivate them with a desire to adopt small family norms.

Notes and References

1. UN: E.F.S. 75, XIII, 4, p. 76
2. Gunnar, Myrdal, "Asian Drama: An Inquiry into the Poverty of Nations", Vol. III, London, 1968, p. 154.
3. Frank, Notestein, W., "Population Policy and Development: A Summary View", *Population Debate,* Vol. I, Part Four, Para 5.
4. Coale and Hoover, Population Growth and Economic Development in Low Income Countries, 1958, p. 19.
5 Geral Meier, Leading Issues in Economic Development, 1975, p. 591.
6. GOI Planning Commission, Third Five Year Plan, p. 22
7. FAO: Population, Food Supply and Agricultural Development, *Population Debate,* Vol. I, Part Four, Para 8.
8. Maryellen Fullan in *People*—a Journal of the International Planned Parenthood Federation, Vol. 5, Number 4, 1978, p. 27
9. J.P. Singh, Problems of Population and Sustainable Development in India, in *IJPA,* January-March, 2003, pp. 85-86, 94.
10. World Bank, "Management Problems in National Family Planning Programme", in UN: E/F/S, 75, XIII, 5, p. 511.
11. Donald J. Bogue, "A Five Year Information—Education Communication Perspective to meet the Population, Health and Food Crisis, 1975-1980" in *Family Planning Resumed,* p. 117, 1977, No. 1.
12. A. Govindachari, "The Role of Extension Education in Family Planning", in *Aspects of Population Policy in India,* New Delhi, 1969, pp. 124-25.

13. Population Reports, Series Number 35, November 1987, p. 2.
14. Annual Report of the Ministry of Health and Family Welfare, 1998-99, p. 73
15. H. Koontz and C. O'Donnell, "Principles of Management: An Anlysis of Managerial Functions", London: McGraw Hill, Kogakusha Ltd., 1972, pp. 538-40.
16. W.H. Newman and C.E. Summer, "The Process of Management Concepts: Behaviour and Practice", Anglewood Cliffs, N.J. Prentice Hall, 1961, p. 59.
17. *World Health*, Jan.-Feb. 1989.
18. E.M. Rogers in *Joung Whang*, ed., pp. 130-31.
19. J.P. Singh, *op. cit.*, p. 93.
20. WHO, Technical Report Series, 1954, No. 89, p. 4.

CHAPTER 11

RIGHTS AND DUTIES EDUCATION

Human Rights are indeed a *sine qua non* for the development of human personality and an indispensable ingredient for the physical strength and mental fortification of humanity. As a matter of fact, human rights are an expression of dignity, freedom of conscience and a civilized means of subsistence. The genesis of the concept is to be found in the classical liberal traditions reinforced by renaissance that made a passionate defense of the principles of competitive individualism and rule of law aimed at the realization of individual dignity, liberty and freedom.

—*Prof. Mohammad Mujtaba Khan*

Rights and Duties Education

"O my Lord of Light and Love, fill my heart with light and love;
O my Lord of Bliss and Joy, fill my heart with bliss and joy;
O my Lord of Truth and Peace, fill my heart with truth and peace;
O my Lord of Transcendental Virtues, fill my heart with those virtues."

—*R.P. Dhokalia*

INTRODUCTION (See Chart 11.1)

All human beings are born free and equal in dignity and rights. The inherent dignity of all members of the human family is the foundation of freedom and justice and peace in the world as given in the Universal declaration of human rights in its preamble. Human rights are the moral claims, which are inalienable and inherent in all human individuals by virtue of their humanity alone. These are the rights of all human beings, because they are born in human family. The concept of human rights and the human rights movement is getting more and more impetus in today's social and political background because it is now universally accepted need that human rights are essential in human lives and hence they must be protected.[1]

Before we describe and analyze human rights, let us analyze the concept of human rights contained in sacred ancient Sanskrit literature which has its authenticity even today. Human rights are values recognized by national governments and are justicable.

HUMAN RIGHTS IN ANCIENT INDIA

Human rights and duties are beautifully Ingrained in the ancient Sanskrit Literature which is quite evident from the concept of Vasudhaiba

Chart 11.1

Human Rights and Duties

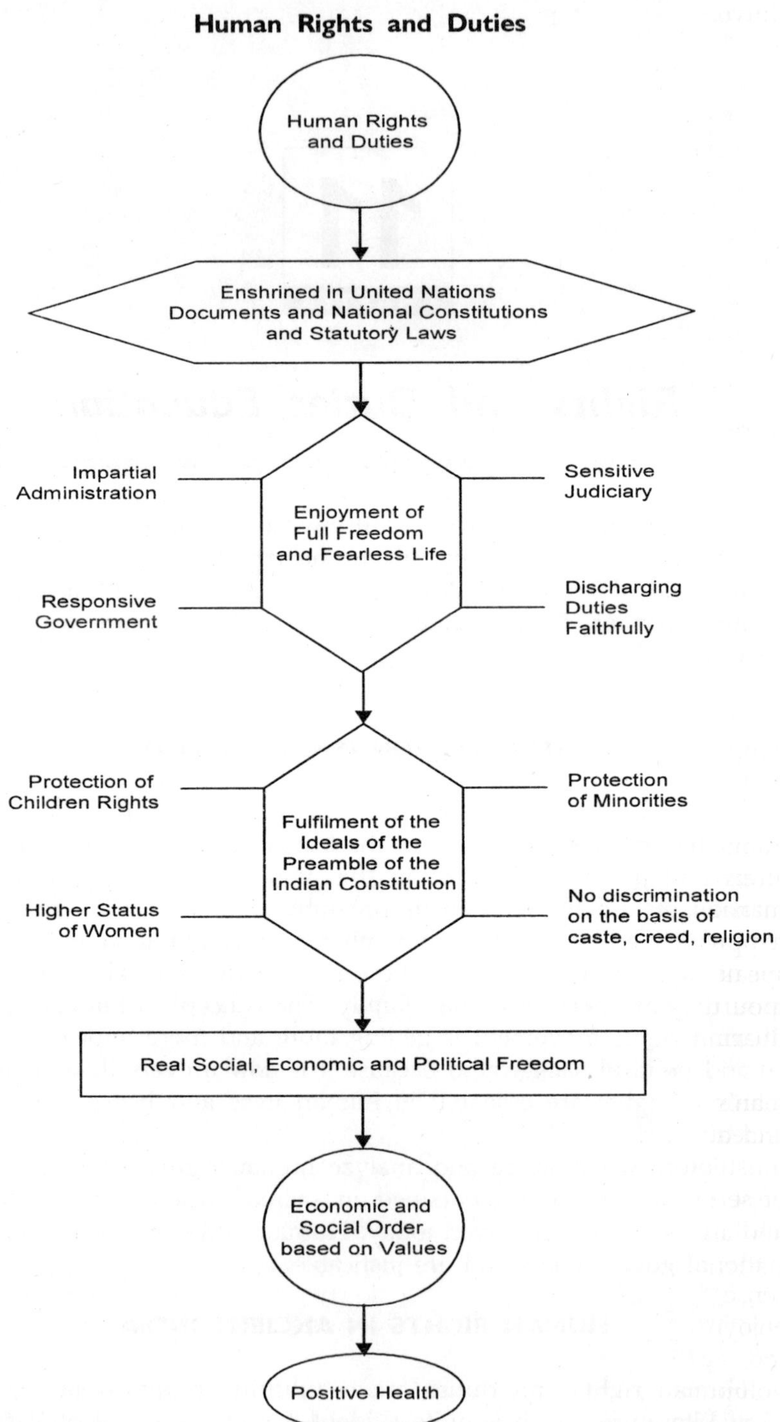

Kutumbakam (the whole universe is a family) and Nara Narayana Universal prayers in Vedic Benediction also supports the same view.

"Let all be happy
Let all be free from diseases
Let all see the auspicious things
Let no-body suffer from grief."

"Sarve Bhavantu Sukhinah,
Sarve Shantu Niramayah
Sarve Bhadrani Pashyantu
Maa kaschiddukhabhagebhavate."

Similarly a prayer in Shiksha Vali of the Taittiriya Upanishad also stress the same:

"May He (God) protect us both together
May He nourish us both together
May we work jointly with great energy
May our study be vigorous and effective
May we not hate anyone
Let there be Peace, Peace and Peace."

Ancient Sanskrit Literature allows individuals to enjoy wealth and happiness but are guided by Dharma so that they may not come a conflict with Dharma (righteous path).

Swami Nikhilananda in his book, "Self Knowledge", Madras, Sri Ramakrishna Math explains the stages to achieve moksha. We have already spoken of the division of the Vedas into Karmakanda, and Jnanakanda, dealing with man's natural desire for enjoyment of material happiness and the attainment of the Highest Good. The Vedic seers also speak of the four ideals which serve the ends of human pursuit (pourusartha). They are the springs of man's action and are known as dharma, artha, kama, and moksha.

Artha, or wealth, is a legitimate goal of pursuit at a certain stage of man's life. It is, with most people, an effective mode of self-expression and an important means of establishing fellowship with other. But wealth must be acquired according to dharma, righteousness; otherwise, instead of serving a spiritual purpose, it will aggravate greed and lust for power and ultimately be a cause of misery.

Kama is the fulfilment of sensuous and aesthetic desire. Craving for sense pleasure is present in many sensitive persons to whom the enjoyment of wealth appears gross and therefore inadequate. But kama, too, must be guided by Dharma; otherwise it degenerates into voluptuousness.

There is no desire for material possession in this state of mind.

Dharma or Karmayoga or work devoid of results has its own reward. Geeta also talks of lower and higher nature in Chapter 7, Slokas 4 and 5:

भूमिरापोऽनलो वायु: खं मनो बुद्धिरेव च ।
टंहकार इतीयं मे भित्रा प्रकणतिरघ्टधा ।। 7/4 Bhagavad Gita

अपरेयमितस्त्वन्यां प्रकणतिं विद्धि मे पराम् ।
जीवभूतां महाबाहो ययेदंधयति जगत् ।। 7/5 Bhagavad Gita

Earth, water, fire, air, ether, mind, reason and also ego; these constitute my nature eight-fold divided. This indeed is my low (material) nature; other than this, by which the whole universe is sustained, know it to be my higher (or spiritual) nature in the form of Jiva (the life principle), O Arjuna.

The satisfaction derived from the pursuit of dharma, artha and kama is neither deep nor abiding. There remains a hunger of the soul that can be fulfilled only by the attainment of moksha, or freedom. The first three ideals belong to the material world, and the happiness derived from them is therefore ephemeral and illusory. But the ideal of freedom can be realized only in the realm of spirit, and the bliss that follows is everlasting. Therefore, the realization of moksha, freedom, is the coping stone of human life; and the pursuit of righteousness, wealth, and aesthetic satisfaction only support it.

Moksha ensures bliss for all times, and at all places and in every condition.

In the Rig Veda, it has been rightly said, "No one is superior or inferior. All are brothers and all should strive for the interest of all and progress collectively." Similarly in Atharva Veda, it has been pointed out, "All have equal rights in articles of food and water." Yoke of the chariot of life is placed equally on the shoulders of all. All should live together with harmony supporting one another like the spokes of the chariot connecting the rim and the hub.

The same idealism was incorporated by Kautilya in his Arthasastra while summing up the objects and purpose of the exercise of sovereign power by the King. He stated thus:

प्रजासुखे सुखः राज्ञः प्रजानां च हिते हितम् ।
नात्सप्रियं हितं राज्ञं प्रजानां तु प्रियं हितम् ।।

In the happiness of his subjects lies his happiness; in their welfare, his welfare; whatever pleases him (personally) he shall not consider as good, but whatever makes his subjects happy, he shall consider good.

—(Arthasastra, Book I, Chapter IXXX, 39)

disciplined in sciences, devoted to good government for his subjects, keen upon working for the good of all his subjects and interested in the well-being of all beings will enjoy the earth unopposed.

विद्याविनीतो राजा हि
प्रजानां विनयें रतः ।
अन्न्यां पुथिवीं भुड्क्ते
सर्वभूतहिते रतः ।

An analysis of ancient literature would reveal that duties out weigh rights and that is why there were no exploitation. The voice about human rights in various parts of the world were voiced through full freedom functions when rights are balanced with responsibilities and choice is balanced with conscience.

There can not be the experience, individually or collectively, if attention and effort are focused only on rights and choice. When rights and choice are misunderstood or misused, debts are incurred—mentally, physically, spiritually, socially, economically, politically and so on. A responsible person fulfils the assigned duty by staying true to the aim. Duties are carried out with integrity and sense of purpose.

Rigveda has beautifully spelt out the right to equality:

Right to Equality

Right to quality is perhaps the most fundamental right without which happiness is impossible. Unjust discrimination always results in misery and unhappiness to those discriminated against. The Vedas, which constituted the primordial source of Dharma declared a charter of equality in the Vedas. It is worth-quoting.

अज्येष्ठासो अकनिष्ठास एते ।
सं भ्रातसेा वावुधशः सौभागय ।।

No one is superior (ajyestasa) or inferior (akanishtasa).
All are brothers (ete bharataraha). All should strive for
The interests of all and should progress collectively.
Let the strength to live with mutual co-operation be firm in you all.
—(Rigveda, Mandala 10, Sukta 191, Mantra 4)

Atharvanaveda—Samajnana Sukta

समानी प्रपा सह वोत्रभागः । समाने योवत्रे सह वो युनज्मि । आराः नाभिमिवाभितः ।।

All have equal rights in articles of food and water. The yoke of the chariot of life is placed equally on the shoulders of all. All should live together with harmony supporting one another like the spokes of a wheel of the chariot connecting its rim and hub.

Right to practice any religion based upon One's conviction has been

Right to practice any religion based upon One's conviction has been the hall-mark of ancient Sanskrit literature.

Special status of woman was protected and respected. The Rule of Dharma which made it the duty of male members of the family to afford protection to women reads:

पिता रक्षति कौमारे भर्ता रक्षति यौवने ।
रक्षन्ति रथविरे पुत्रा न स्त्री स्वातन्त्रयमर्हति ।।

Father protects the girl during her childhood, the husband protects her after marriage and her sons protect her in old age. At no stage a woman should be left free (Manu IX-3).

This basic human right was sought to be protected by incorporating a specific rule in rajadharma to the effect that the State was under a duty to protect every religion without discrimination. It reads:

पणण्डनैगमश्रणीपूगव्रातणादिणु ।
संरक्षेत्समयं राजा दुर्गे जनपदे तथा ।।

The king should afford protection to compacts of associations of believers of Veda [Naigamas] as also of disbelievers in Veda [Pashandis] and of others.

—(Dharmakosha, p. 870)

The Rule of Dharma which made it the duty of male members of the family to afford protection to women reads:

It was only recently that human movements got active in various countries of the world, e.g. Magna Carta in Britain in 1215 AD, Petition of Rights in 1628 AD, Habeas Corpus Act in 1628 AD, Bill of Rights in 1689 AD, American Declaration of Independence in 1676 AD and Declaration of Rights of men in France during 1789 AD and subsequently and more recently, in the Delcaration of Universal Human Rights by UN in 1948.

A mention of only a portion of the human right in ancient literature is a clear indication that in Ancient Indian human rights were far head from the thinking of presently. Human rights in ancient times were:

An analysis of existing human rights indicate that these are theoretically sound and promise a decent life to everyone born on this earth. However, majority of the people lacked the knowledge of these rights. The vested few exploited the majority making a life of hell for the majority. The main reason of this has been found to be ignorance. The need is to hammer these rights into the minds of people through education. That is why education has become the main instrument of people to know their rights and methods to safeguard them and in case of violation how to get justice. This education is the key to the achievement of these human rights, Enlightened citizenship is the need of today to enjoy decent life.

The UN World Conference of Human Rights in Vienna in 1993 drafted a Declaration ultimately inspiring the UN Decade for Human Rights Education 1995-2004. Out of the 100 clauses in the Programme of Action (POA) of Vienna Declaration, 1993 four are related directly to Education and Training which are as follows:

Art. 78: The World Conference of Human Rights considers human rights education, training and public information essential for the promotion and achievement of stable and harmonious relations among communities for mutual understanding, tolerance and peace.

Art. 79: States should strive to eradicate illiteracy and should direct education towards the full development of the human personality and to the strengthening of respect for human rights and fundamental freedoms.

Art. 80: Human Rights Education should include peace, Democracy, Development and Social Justice, as set for the international regional human rights instruments in order to achieve common understanding and awareness with a view to strengthening universal commitments to human rights.

Art. 81: Taking into account the World Plan of Action for human rights and democracy, adopted in 1993 by the International Congress on Education for human rights and democracy of the UNESCO and other human rights instruments, the World Conference on human rights recommends that states develop specific programmes and strategies for ensuring the widest human rights education and dissemination of public information taking particular account of the human rights needs of women.

The vision of UN Decade for Human Rights Education hopes that: "The vision of the Decade is that by the end of the century all humanity will become human rights literate, and participate in the decisions that determine their lives. We are all familiar with the words and concepts that assert the need for people to join in building a better tomorrow. We must work harder to make these words meaningful. With the power of knowledge and desire for social justice we will effect change and celebrate human dignity, accepting the humanity of others. The process has already begun. With the help of committed educators, individual activists, and NGO's we have succeeded in elevating human rights education to a priority on the national and international agenda. We are committed to this effort and believe that it is in our hands and within our communities that we will succeed in developing a holistic approach to human rights education. We can find our way to universality through human rights education."

The Universal Declaration of Human Rights (UDHR) and many other celebrated international human rights instruments emphasise human rights education at the core of the right to education. Thus, Article 26(2) of the UDHR ordains that:

"Education shall be directed to the full development of the human personality and to the strengthening of respect for human rights and fundamental freedoms. It shall promote understanding, tolerance and friendship among all nations, racial or religious groups, and shall further the activities of the United Nations for the maintenance of peace."

Since wars begin in the Minds of Men it is in the Minds of Men that the defences must be constructed . . . the major challenge that faces us is how to promote diversity as a positive force so that recently released energies of ethnic, religious and spiritual solidarity . . . serve as catalysts for creativity as opposed to destruction, for concord rather than division.

The UNESCO spirit is reflected in the recommendation made by UNESCO at a general conference held in Paris in November 1974 while reaffirming the responsibility that education should ensure the promotion of international understanding, cooperation, peace and respect of human rights strongly invites the . . . attention of the authorities, departments or bodies responsible for school education, higher education and out-of-school education . . . for a meaningful course of education in know-how, useful skills, work-attitudes and ethics.

UGC Ninth Five Year Plan objectives for promoting Human Rights Education (HRE) in Colleges and University observed that:

The goal of achieving human rights requires actions at various levels such as: (a) spreading awareness, amongst masses, of and about these rights and also their duty for respecting the rights of others, (b) not only creating awareness amongst masses particularly amongst weaker, poor, and vulnerable groups but also imparting capacities and confidence in them to stand for protection and preservation of their rights, (c) requiring many to shed away some of their prejudices and reform some of the attitudes which are derogatory to others' dignity, (d) creating different kind of knowledge, innovating or reforming structures, methodologies and normative regimes, and imparting new skills and competencies so that policy-making, its enforcement and realization become more sensitive to the demands of human rights culture, (e) establishing new structures of accountability and making existing modes of accountability more effective so that the State, its agencies and its personnel can be easily, effectively and meaningfully made responsible for human rights violation on one hand and can be made to internalize respect for these rights on the other.

It hardly needs stressing that the activity called 'education'—an exercise in assimilating, creating and disseminating knowledge is a powerful means of influencing and bringing attitudinal change in the citizens in general and among members of among people in general as well as professional groups in particular. Being a tool to spread awareness, information and knowledge amongst its recipients education can play a crucial role at each of the levels mentioned above for the promotion of human rights culture. But, unfortunately, the education system and more so the higher education system in India, exception in the last few years, has hardly shown any credible signs of being a partner in the efforts of evolving human rights culture in the country.

Human rights education must include also the component of obligations towards others. Mahatma Gandhi, in a letter to Julien Huxley in 1947, had said:

"I learned from my illiterate but wise mother that all rights to be deserved and preserved come from duty well done. Thus, the very right to live accrues to us when we does the duty of citizenship of the world. From this one fundamental statement, perhaps it is easy enough to define duties of man and woman and correlate every right to some corresponding duty to be first performed . . . ."

The international community has woken up to the need and importance of the right to education—emphasized in Article 13 of the Covenant on Economic, Social and Cultural Rights. General Comment No. 13 reads as follows:

"Education is both a human right in itself and an indispensable means of realizing other human rights. As an empowerment right, education is the primary vehicle by which economically and socially marginalized adults and children can lift themselves out of poverty and obtain the means to participate fully in their communities. Education has a vital role in empowering women, safeguarding children from exploitative and hazardous labour and sexual exploitation, promoting human rights and democracy, protecting the environment, and controlling population growth. Increasingly, education is recognized as one of the best financial investments State can make. But the importance of education is not just practical: a well-educated, enlightened and active mind, able to wander freely and widely, is one of the joys and rewards of human existence." (Emphasis supplied).

INTERNATIONAL EFFORTS THROUGH UN-SYSTEM

Today humanity binds us together because the global society has created oneness of mankind. Human rights and their co-relative human duties are founded on eternal and universal human values and ideals transcending all man-made boundaries—civilization, cultural or geographic. In our times of social, political and economic globalization, traditional values are being questioned and challenged and so education as a social institution is confronted with new challenges in respect to the view of man, one's perception of knowledge and the educational aims and the vision of good life and values and its substantive features. The goal of elevation of man's awareness and consciousness, and of enlightenment of his soul with a view of making a new harmonious multi-cultural world order and a more humane civilization requires a synthesis of varieties of cultural and religious diversities of materialism with spiritualism and of the values, ideals and the spirit of all major religions of the world. This further underlines harnessing of every branch of knowledge and the union of moral and secular values with constitutional and legal norms. Revival of the duty-oriented society, a spiritual basis and balancing of human rights and duties as co-relatives and spiritual regeneration of the entire human life through education in a wider sense, can pave the way for a harmonious, just and peaceful global order. Moral and spiritual source of rights and duties enjoins tenacious pursuit of worthy ideals and human values.[2]

The term 'human rights' is commonly used to denote rights which every human being is entitled to enjoy by virtue of being a human beings, and for no other reason. All cultures and societies throughout their history have been evolving conceptions of rights which they held sacrosanct. Various states in their legal systems and constitutions have incorporated rights which are inviolable. While the contemporary conceptualization of human rights which the Universal Declaration of Human Rights and its accompanying Covenants embody has drawn on the rich legacy of the past, it is distinguished by its universality, by the fundamental principle that all human rights are meant to be enjoyed by all human beings, anywhere in the world.

'Human rights' have, in practice, been redefined to encompass every aspect of dignified human existence and to make every human being an equal member of the human family. The goal is still very far, but the road to it has been marked. Mahatma Gandhi has said:

"It has always been a mystery to me how men can feel themselves honoured by the humiliation of their fellow beings."

It can not be doubted that any humiliation of a human being is an affront to his human dignity, and, thus, a violation of his human right.

NHRC took *suo-motu* cognizance also of the communal disturbances in the State of Gujarat commencing with the Godhra tragedy on 27 February 2002 and its aftermath. In this context, the commission is it so observation gave a wider scope to human rights:

"It is the primary and inescapable responsibility of the State to protect the right to life, liberty, equality and dignity of all of those who constitute it. It is also the responsibility of the State to ensure that such rights are not violated either through overt acts, or through abetment or negligence. It is a clear and emerging principle of human rights jurisprudence that the State is responsible not only for the acts of its own agents, but also for the acts of non-State players acting within its jurisdiction. The State is, in addition, responsible for any inaction that may cause or facilitate the violation of human rights."

The United Nations Charter, in its Preamble, reaffirms 'faith in fundamental human rights, in the dignity and worth of the human person, in the equal rights of men and women and of nations large and small'. Article 1 of the Charter laid down the purposes of the United Nations which included 'promoting and encouraging respect for human rights and for fundamental freedoms for all without distinctions as to race, sex, language or religion'. All the Member-states also pledged themselves 'to take . . . action for the achievement' of 'universal respect for, and observance of, human rights and fundamental freedoms'. The Charter did not define, in precise terms, the meaning of 'human rights and fundamental freedoms'. It authorized the Economic and Social Council, one of the principal organs of the United Nations, to make recommendations for the purpose of promoting respect for, and observance of human rights and fundamental freedoms for all.

The United Nations—sponsored human rights movement and their enshrinement in national constitutions have brought about a great revolution in human thoughts, relations and institutions. Abuse and misuse of human rights in the form of recurrent strikes, demonstration, rallies and animosities on the basis of status, class, castes, tribes and rural-urban divide have created social, political and economic chaos and convulsions in human affairs. On the other hand, breaches and violations of human rights in varying degrees almost everywhere and poignant gulf between law and practice have generated great disillusionment and pervasive frustration. The UN Human Rights Declaration and the two Conventions enumerate only human rights and these are spoken of as ideal standards to be achieved and as rights to be duly protected by-law and pursued in the courts of law under the constitutions of all countries. By ignoring the imperativeness of the co-relationship of rights and duties, generally law has not placed equal emphasis on duties of man. Both rights and duties essentially have moral and spiritual basis of which law provides only an external formulation for an effective implementation.

The Universal Declaration of Human Rights stirred the moral consciousness as well as the political assertiveness of the people in the countries. Another impact of the Declaration was that the various countries adopted these rights in their national constitution and laws. But the Declaration lacked the binding force of a law over the members, like Conventions and Covenants. The UN got success after 20 years of continuous negotiations, compromises and debates and ultimately in December 1966 the General Assembly promulgated International Covenants comprising three instruments:

1. International Covenants on Economic, Social and Cultural Rights;
2. International Covenants on Civil and Political Rights; and
3. Optional Protocol (on individual petition) to the Covenants on Civil and Political Rights.

The Covenants have assumed a prime place in international law as the instruments that influence and that at the same time judge the disregard of states. It is through Covenants that the conditions of individual rights in particular countries are to be assessed. India signed the Instrument of Accession to the Human Rights Covenants on 27th March 1979. By 1994, already 130 countries had become the party to the two Covenants.

Human Rights are basically the claims of the individuals throughout the world, for such conditions which are essential for the development of personality and realization of the innate characteristics without which nobody can seek to be himself at his best. There rights are inherent and inalienable to human beings and are necessary to ensure survival, dignity and personality development of the individual irrespective of race, colour, religion, sex, language, political or other opinion, national or social origin, property, birth or other status. The Human Rights represent what was agreed upon, by the international community, as the minimum of those rights and fundamental freedom which are inherent and inalienable to all human beings and which must be available to all the people.[3]

However, one must be clear in mind that all claims of individuals are not Human Rights. Only those claims are Human Rights which are recognised by the United Nations as the essential conditions for the development of one's human personality. The United Nations has also fixed *Duties* along with Human Rights and the Article 29(1) of the Universal Declaration reiterates that *"everyone has duties to the community in which alone the free and full development of his personality is possible."* On the other hand, reasonable restrictions can be imposed on the individual. Article 29(2) of UDHR says that "In the exercise of his rights and freedoms, everyone shall be subject only to such limitations as are determined by law solely for the purpose of securing due recognition and respect for the rights and freedoms of others and meeting the just requirements of morality, public order and the general welfare in a democratic society. Similarly, these rights and freedoms may in no case be exercised contrary to the purposes and principles of the United Nations [Art. 29(3) of UDHR].[4]

National Action Plan for Human Rights Education in India

Pursuant to the suggestions made at the World Conference on Human Rights at Vienna in 1993, the United Nations General Assembly through its Resolution 49/184 of 23rd December, 1994 resolved to declare the period 1995-2004 as the UN Decade for Human Rights Education. The United Nations High Commissioners for Human Rights requested the Member-States to celebrate the Decade by drawing up a National Action Plan and implement the same.

India as a Member-State of the United Nations has ratified human rights treaties which contain provisions on human rights education [e.g., Art. 26(2) of the UDHR] and thereby set-upon itself a treaty obligation to undertake human rights education, training and public information amongst its people. In order to celebrate the occasion, it was decided by the Government to set-up a Coordination Committee under the Chairmanship of the Union Home Secretary to draw a National Action Plan in consultation with other concerned. Ministries and Departments of the Government and to monitor its implementation and report to the UN High Commissioner for Human Rights on the progress made towards realization of the goals set out for this Decade. The mandate of the

Drafting Committees as follows:

(i) Assess needs and in cooperation with all concerned, formulate both a long-term and a short-term sustainable as well as achievable action plan for enhancement of awareness of human rights through training, dissemination and information effort directed to
  (a) strengthen the respect for human rights and fundamental freedom,
  (b) full development of human personality and human dignity,
  (c) promotion of understanding, tolerance, gender equality and understanding amongst all groups of people in the society, and
  (d) promote importance of democracy, rule of law, peace and sustainable development.

(ii) Build and strengthen human rights education programme in both formal and informal sectors of education.

(iii) Suggest time frame, wherever possible, for each of the action point and propose strategies for achieving the desired objective by recommending effective mechanism for measuring the achievement in a specific time frame.

(iv) Propose mechanism and identify institutions/organisations for research and development of human rights education material at all levels.

(vii) Suggest mechanism for reviewing of Action Plan approved by the Coordination Committee.[5]

Need of Human Rights Education as Envisaged by Drafting Committees

(i) The traditions of democracy in India is founded on the values of equality and equity, of tolerance and respect for freedom and human dignity and these find expression in the Constitution of India. In order to obtain the full realisation of these values, there is an imperative need to spread education and awareness amongst the citizens about these rights as protected by the State with the aim that progress comes within the framework of a respect for human rights and social justice.

(ii) Educating human rights values is one of the important steps towards promotion and protection of human rights and to bring about a change in the attitude of the people. Realizing that the change in attitude cannot be brought out overnight, the Drafting Committee urged that there is a need to have a proper high level policy on human rights education both in the formal and informal sectors.

(iii) The Committee felt that human rights education should be viewed as a strategy to prevent human rights violation and a technique to empower people to meet their needs.

(iv) It is of the view that a large mass of the people are simply not aware of their rights guaranteed under the constitution, as well as, that safeguards available in the statutes and the institutions set-up by the Government for redressal of their grievances.

(v) Realising that it is essential to educate the masses on the fundamental principles of human rights, rule of law and equality, equity and its universal application, the Committee is of the view that there is a need for creation of mass awareness.

(vi) There is need to spread awareness of the rights of women and children and weaker sections of society.

(vii) The Committee observed that currently there is a fragmented approach towards human rights education. Organizations/ Institutions, as per their need, have introduced human rights education in a piecemeal way. A uniform and consistent policy on human rights education is required to be put in place in order to achieve the desired results.

(viii) The Committee felt that there are large areas of concern which need to be looked at. There are two distinct target groups, namely, (a) the general public, and (b) the strategic groups. In order to have a pragmatic and achievable action plan, it would be advisable to focus attention on certain key groups, namely, students, teachers, curriculum developers, police, prison officials, lawyers, subordinate judiciary, government officials (including bureaucrats and administrators) and Parliamentarians.

(ix) The study of human rights should lead to an understanding of and sympathy for the concept of justice, equalities, freedom, peace, dignity and democracy.

(x) The Committee felt that illiteracy is the root cause of perpetuation of all evils in civil society. It is because of this that poor and vulnerable section of the society are unable to enjoy their rights. Realising that a large section of our children have still no access to education formal or informal, it is of the view that Ministry of Human Resource Development should take appropriate and urgent steps to make right to education as one of the fundamental rights and also endeavour to introduce free and compulsory education till the age of 14 years.[6]

HUMAN RIGHTS EDUCATION IN SCHOOLS, COLLEGES AND UNIVERSITIES (ACTION: DEPARTMENT OF EDUCATION)

(i) Generating awareness and reach through media advocacy to the deprived and special target group of children that a Right to Basic Minimum Education is their human right.

(ii) Introduction of human rights issues in the school curricula,— at primary as well as at secondary level and preparation of appropriate course material for this purpose in a way to make it part of the students all round development.

(iii) Devising a plan of action for training the teachers on human rights/values in collaboration with State Education Departments/SCERTs/NCTE.

(iv) Introducing courses on Human Rights at the under-graduate and Post-graduate level, including either a compulsory/special paper at under-graduate level.

(v) Introduction of short-term/long-term courses on human rights through the distance education programmes. IGNOU and other premier universities should be encouraged by UGC to take up these courses by liberal funding of these courses.

(vi) There is a dearth of books as well as research material on human rights. Universities should therefore, encourage research on human rights by liberally instituting scholarships and internships on issues pertaining to human rights.

(vii) To bridge the gap in the availability of research material on human rights a National Resource Centre for documentation, training, research and education in human rights is to be set-up in one of the premier Universities/research organisation under Ministry of HRD.

(viii) Gyan Darshan and Gyan Vani, the dedicated video/audio channels for education under Prasar Bharati, AIR could be put to effective use for spreading human rights education.

(ix) Colleges and Universities should be encouraged to hold seminars/workshops/debates on issues of human rights, Associations and unions in the colleges/University could be given financial assistance for such activities, Project base learning should be encouraged. Assignments and field activities like data collection, event organisation, camp activities, social service events during distress situation, etc. may be integrated into courses designing and performance evaluation.

(x) Bring out a booklet containing the basic instruments of Human Rights for public distribution.

(xi) As the subject of human rights is a matter of changing attitude, the audio-visual medium of imparting education has better impact than the class room type of learning.

Accordingly, more stress need be on preparation of course material in multimedia forms—like, videos, CDs and films. In addition for mass propagation and mass education.

(xii) Dissemination of information on human rights should also be carried out.[7]

HUMAN RIGHTS IN INDIAN CONSTITUTION

Let us now discuss about human rights as enshrined in the Constitution of India

Preamble

The Preamble to the Constitution of India which outlines the objectives of the Constitution states:

"We the people of India, having solemnly resolved to constitute India into a Sovereign, Socialist, Secular, Democratic Republic and to secure to all its citizens; Justice, social economic and political; Liberty of thoughts, expression, belief, faith and worship; Equality of status and of opportunity; and to promote among them all Fraternity assuring the dignity of the individual and the unity and integrity of the nation."

The Constitution of India has provided a detailed list of human rights and incorporated them in the form of Fundamental Rights (Part III) and the Directive Principles (Part IV).

Fundamental Rights

1. Right to Equality

Articles 14-18 of the Constitution of India deal with the right to equality—

(i) Equality before law and equal protection of law to all persons within the territory of India—(Article 14).

(ii) State cannot discriminate on grounds of religion, race, castes, sex or place of birth. It also provides public places for all without discrimination—(Article 15).

(iii) Equality of opportunity in matters of public appointment or public services—(Article 16).

(iv) Abolition of untouchability—(Article 17).

(v) Abolition of titles (other than military and academic)—(Article 18).

These provisions (Articles 14-18) clearly establish that all citizens have been guaranteed political and social equality. The constitution protects also the citizens against discriminatory treatment and provide them equal opportunity in social and public life.

2. Right to Freedom

Articles 19 to 22 cover the right to freedom.

(i) Six Fundamental Freedoms—(Article 19)

(a) Freedom of speech and expression.
(b) Freedom to assemble peacefully and without arms.
(c) Freedom to form associations and unions.
(d) Freedom to move freely throughout the territory of India.
(e) Freedom to reside and settle in any part of India.
(f) Freedom to practice any profession, or to carry on any occupation, trade or business.

(ii) Protection in Respect of Conviction for Offences (Art. 20)

This provides that no person shall be convicted of any offence except for violation of law in force at the time of the commission of the act. Nobody should be subjected to the penalty or punishment greater than that provided under law at the time of an offence. This also prohibited punishment on double jeopardy and *ex-post facto* laws.

(iii) Protection of Life and Personal Liberty (Art. 21)

The Constitution of India provides that "no person shall be deprived of his life or personal liberty except according to the procedure established by law." The right to life and personal liberty (Art. 21) is the most fundamental of all fundamental rights and it can never be suspended (along with Art. 20), not even during emergency.

(iv) Protection Against Arrest and Detention in Certain Cases (Art. 22)

(a) It lays down that no person who has been arrested shall be detained in custody without being informed, as soon as may be, on the ground for such arrest.
(b) Arrested person shall not be denied the right to consult and to be defended by a legal practitioner of his choice.
(c) Each arrested/detained person has to be produced before the nearest magistrate within twenty-four hours of such arrest and cannot be kept in custody beyond twenty-four hours without the authority of the magistrate.
(d) The Constitution, however, provides for arrest in Preventive Detention Act of a person committing anti-national activities. In such a case the initial detention may be for two months (or as fixed by the Parliament) and the further detention can only be on the recommendation of an Advisory Board under the chairmanship of a Judge of High Court also having two other High Court Judges as members.

3. Right Against Exploitation

(a) Prohibition of traffic in human beings, beggar and forced labour—(Art. 23).

(b) Prohibition of employment of children below the age of fourteen years in factories, mines or other hazardous jobs—(Art. 24).

4. *Right to Freedom of Religion*

The Constitution of India provides freedom of religion under Articles 25 to 28 to all persons—

(a) Freedom of conscience and right to profess, practice and propagate any religion (subject to public order, morality and health)—(Art. 25).
(b) Freedom to manage religious affairs, to own and acquire movable and immovable property and to administer such property—(Art. 26).
(c) No person shall be compelled to pay any taxes for the promotion or maintenance of any particular religion—(Art. 27).
(d) No religious instructions can be provided in an educational institution wholly maintained out of State funds or receiving aid from the state—(Art. 28). Similarly, there is freedom to attend religious instructions or religious worship in certain educational institutions and no body shall be forced or compelled to attend any religious instructions or functions.

5. *Cultural and Educational Rights*

(a) Protection of the interests of minorities and to enable them to conserve their language, script or culture—(Art. 29).
(b) Right of minorities to establish and administer educational institutions of their choice—(Art. 30).

6. *Right to Property*

The original Constitution provided the right to property as a fundamental right to all the citizens—(Art. 31). This included the right to acquire, hold and dispose-off property. But this right was omitted from the list of Fundamental Rights by the Forty-fourth Amendment carried out in 1978. However, right to property is still a constitutional and legal right as the 44th Amendment had added a new Article, Article 300-A in Part XII of the Constitution which provided that "No person shall be deprived of his property save by authority of law."

7. *Right to Constitutional Remedies*

Article 32 grants the right to move the Supreme Court by appropriate proceedings for the enforcement of the rights conferred by the Constitution. The Supreme Court has been vested with the authority to issue writs, orders or directions. The writs in the nature of *Habeas Corpus, Mandamus,* Prohibition, *Quo-Warranto* and *Certiorari* whichever may be appropriate for the enforcement of rights, can be issued by the Supreme Court. Under Article 226, the people can even move to High Courts for the enforcement of Fundamental Rights.

Similarly, the Directive Principles of State Policy which has been provided in Part IV of the Constitution (Arts. 36 to 51) aims at realizing the high ideals of justice, liberty, equality and fraternity as outlined in the Preamble to the Constitution. The framers of the Constitution borrowed this feature from the Constitution of Irish Republic.

Directive Principles of State Policy

Some of these Directive Principles which show resemblance with Human Rights are:

(i) To provide the right to an adequate means of livelihood for all—(Art. 39a).
(ii) The ownership and control of the material resources of the community to be so distributed as to secure the common goal—(Art. 39b).
(iii) Prevention of concentration of wealth and means of production—(Art. 39c).
(iv) Equal pay for equal work to both men and women—(Art. 39d).
(v) Protection of the health of workers—(Art. 39e).
(vi) Protection of children against exploitation—(Art. 39f).
(vii) Provision for securing right to work, to education and to public assistance in case of unemployment, old-age, sickness and disablement—(Art. 41).
(viii) Provision for securing just and humane conditions of work and maternity relief—(Art. 42).
(ix) To secure to all workers a living wage, better conditions of work and decent standard of life—(Art. 43).
(x) To secure that legal system promotes justice on the basis of equal opportunity and also provide free legal aid—(Art. 39A).
(xi) Protection of educational and economic interests of weaker sections, particularly Scheduled Castes and Scheduled Tribes—(Art. 49).
(xii) To secure a uniform civil code—(Art. 44).
(xiii) Free and compulsory education to all children upto 14 years of age—(Art. 45).
(xiv) To provide adequate standard of living and raise level of nutrition and public health—(Art. 47).

Duties of the Citizens

The Fundamental Duties are ten in number, incorporated in Art. 51A (Part IVA) which has been inserted by the 42nd Amendment Act, 1976. Under this article, it shall be the duty of every citizens of India—

I. to abide by the Constitution and respect the National Flag and the National Anthem;
II. to cherish and follow the noble ideals which inspired our national struggle for freedom;
III. to protect the sovereignty, unity and integrity of India;
IV. to defend the country;
V. to promote the spirit of common brotherhood amongst all the people of India;
VI. to preserve the rich heritage of our composite culture;
VII. to protect and improve the natural environment;
VIII. to develop the scientific temper and spirit of inquiry;
IX. to safeguard public property; and
X. to strive towards excellence in all spheres of individual and collective activity.

In respect of the situation in Gujarat, therefore, the Commission held that:

> " . . . it is the primary responsibility of the State to protect the right to life, liberty, equality and dignity of all those who constitute it. It is also the responsibility of the State to ensure that such rights are not violated either through overt acts, or through abetment or negligence."

The Commission added that:

> " . . . it is a clear and emerging principle of human rights jurisprudence that the State is responsible not only for the acts of its own agents, but also for the acts of non-State players within its jurisdiction. The State is, in addition, responsible for any inaction that may cause or facilitate the violation of human rights."

NATIONAL HUMAN RIGHTS COMMISSION: MACHINERY FOR OVERSEEING, IMPLEMENTATION OF HUMAN RIGHTS

For better protection of human rights, the Parliament of India passed the Protection of Human Rights Act, 1994. The National Human Rights Commission (NHRC), established under this Act, functions from New Delhi with jurisdiction all over India. Since its establishment the National Human Rights Commission has been engaged in protecting the human rights by investigating human rights abuses, forwarding cases to courts for trials and recommending necessary measures to the government in concerned cases.

Organization

The NHRC consists of a Chairperson, four full time members and three *ex-officio* members. The tenure of the chairperson and members is of five years or till the age of 70 years, whichever is earlier.

The Chairperson of the Commission is appointed out of those who has served as a Chief Justice of the Supreme Court. One Member is appointed who is, or has been a Judge of the Supreme Court and one Member is a person who is, or has been the Chief Justice of a High Court. The remaining two members are appointed from amongst persons having knowledge of, or practical experience in matters relating to human rights. The three *ex-officio* members are: (i) the Chairperson of National Commission of Minorities, (ii) the Chairperson of National Commission for Scheduled Castes and Tribes, and (iii) the Chairperson of the National Commission for women. There is also the provision of a Secretary General who is the Chief Executive Officer of the Commission and exercises such powers and discharges such functions as it may be delegated to him.

All the work of the Commission since its earliest days has, in a sense, aimed at creating a "culture of human rights" in the country. In the course of the past nine years, however, the commission has specifically taken a number of steps to further human rights education. These steps have, *inter alia,* included:

- Working with the Ministry of Human Resource Development, the National Council for Educational Research and Training (NCERT) and the National Council for Teacher Education (NCTE) to prepare materials for education at all levels of schooling;
- Working with the University Grants Commission (UGC) for the development of courses at the university level;
- Endowing a chair for Human Rights at the National Law School of India University in Bangalore;
- Encouraging courses on human rights in the training institutes for public servants, the police, para-military forces and army;
- Producing a handbook for judicial officers;
- Interacting with diverse groups, ranging from medical practitioners to Rotarians and the leadership of political parties, urging them to keep human rights issues on their respective agenda; and
- Encouraging and supporting the efforts of non-governmental organizations, as their role is of central importance to the better protection of human rights in the country.

The Commission shall perform all or any of the following functions, namely:

(i) Inquire, *suo motu* or on a petition presented to it by a victim or any person on his behalf, into complaint of—
  (a) violation of human rights or abetment thereof; and
  (b) negligence in the prevention of such violation, by a public servant;

(ii) Intervene in any proceeding involving any allegation of violation of human rights pending before a court with the approval of such court;

(iii) Visit, under intimation to the State Government, any jail or any other institution under the control of the State government, where persons are detained or lodged for purposes of treatment, reformation or protection, to study the living conditions of the inmates and make recommendations thereon;

(iv) Review the safeguards provided by or under the Constitution or any law for the time being in force for the protection of human rights and recommend measures for their effective implementation;

(v) Review the factors, including acts of terrorism, that inhibit the enjoyment of human rights and recommend appropriate remedial measures;

(vi) Study treaties and other international instruments on human rights and make recommendations for their effective implementation;

(vii) Undertake and promote research in the field of human rights;

(viii) Spread human rights literacy among various sections of society and promote awareness of the safeguards available for the protection of these rights through publications, the media, seminars and other available means;

(ix) Encourage the efforts of non-government organisations and institutions working in the field of human rights; and

(x) Such other functions as it may consider necessary for the promotion of human rights.

Powers Relating to Inquiries

(I) The Commission shall, while inquiring into complaints have all the powers of a civil court trying it under the Code of Civil Procedure, 1908 and in particular in respect of the following matters, namely:

(a) summoning and enforcing the attendance of witnesses and examining them on oath;

(c) receiving evidence on affidavits;

(d) requisitioning any public record or copy thereof from any court or office;

(e) issuing summing for the examination of witnesses or documents; and

(f) any other matter which may be prescribed.

(II) The Commission while inquiring into the complaints of violations of human rights may call for information or report from the Central Government or any State Government or any other authority or organization subordinate thereto within such time as any be specified by it. If the Commission is not satisfied with the report, it may initiate its own inquiry. In case the Commission does not receive the asked report on time, in such case also, it may proceed to inquire into the complaint on its own.

(III) The Commission shall have power to require any person, subject to any privilege which may be claimed by that person under any law for the time being in force, to furnish information on such points or matters as, in the opinion of the Commission, may be useful for, or relevant to, the subject matter of the inquiry and any person so required shall be deemed to be legally bound to furnish such information within the meaning of Section 176 and Section 177 of the Indian Penal Code.

(IV) The Commission or any Gazetted Officer, specially authorized in this behalf by the Commission may enter any building or place where the Commission has reason to believe that any document relating to the subject matter of the inquiry may be found, and may seize any such document or take extracts or copies there from subject to the provisions of Section 100s of the Code of Criminal Procedure, 1973, in so far as it may be applicable.

(V) The Commission shall be deemed to be a Civil Court and when any offence as is described in Section 175, Section 178, Sections 179, 180 or 228 of the Indian Penal Code is committed in view or presence of the Commission, the Commission may, after recording the facts constituting the offence and the statement of the accused as provided for in the Code of Criminal Procedure, 1973, forward the case to a Magistrate having jurisdiction to try the same. The Magistrate to whom any such case is forwarded shall proceed to hear the complaint against the accused as if the case has been forwarded to him under Section 346 of the Code of Criminal Procedure, 1973.

(VI) Every proceeding before the Commission shall be deemed to be a judicial proceeding within the meaning of Sections 193 and 228, and for the purposes of Section 196, of the Indian Penal Code, and the Commission shall be deemed to be a Civil Court for all the purposes of Section 195 and Chapter XXVI of the Code of Criminal Procedure, 1973.

Powers Relating to Investigation

(I) The Commission may, for the purpose of conducting any investigation pertaining to the inquiry, utilize the services of any officer or investigation agency of the Central Government or the State Government with the concurrence of the Central Government or the State Government, as the case may be.

(II) For the purpose of investigating into any matter pertaining to the inquiry, any officer or agency whose services are utilized, (subject to the direction and control of the Commission)—

(a) summon and enforce the attendance of any person and examine him;

(b) require the discovery and production of any document; and

(c) requisition any public record or copy thereof from any office.

(III) The Officer or agency whose services are utilized by the Commission, shall investigate into any matter pertaining to the inquiry and submit a report thereon to the Commission within such period as may be specified by the Commission in this behalf.

(IV) The Commission shall satisfy itself about the correctness of the facts stated and the conclusion, if any, arrived at in the report submitted to it and for this purpose the Commission may make inquiry (including the examination of the person or persons who conducted or assisted in the investigation).

Commenting on its work a year after it was established, the Commission observed:

"The Commission cannot begin to assert that its efforts have transformed the human rights ethos in the country or that it has as yet adequately developed a capacity to defend the least powerful of the citizens of India. But it can assert that its efforts have begun to strengthen the hands of the just and the compassionate, of whom there are legion in this country, in all States and in all walks of life.

In addition, there are State Commissions having jurisdiction in the respective states.

CRITICAL EVALUATION

C. Rajkumar has found the following limitations with the NHRC:

Lack of Functional Autonomy and Independence

The NHRCs generally do not possess any independence in their functioning, as there are several restrictions that are imposed by the statute itself or by the government in discharging their responsibilities. This casts doubts on the ability of the NHRC to conduct an impartial inquiry into charges of human rights violations against the government officials and departments.

Lack of Financial Autonomy

The NHRCs do not have finances and hence, are dependent upon the government for their funding. They are faced with severe financial crunch and hence it becomes difficult to sustain an institution of this stature.

Improper Selection of Members

The members who are selected are close to the government and hence, feel obliged to be soft with the government which has not only appointed them, but also exercises a good deal of power and authority to control their functions. This can also be done by appointing as members or other officials of the NHRC, those individuals who have held positions of power within the government.

Lack of Enforcement Powers

The NHRCs lack any enforcement powers that are needed to fulfil the direction they make to the government. In fact, the directions of the NHRCs are generally called recommendations, as their mandates do not give any more powers than making recommendation to the government.[8]

However, G. Parmanand Singh feels that the presence of NHRC has at least made human right violation more visible and has enhanced public awareness about human values. It has also been taking all possible steps to promote a culture of human rights through media publicity, human rights seminars and human rights education for police, para-military and armed personnel and in the system of general education. At times, it has drawn attention of concerned State governments to be accountable to human rights and bring human right violators to the book.[9]

In addition, there are plethora of agencies engaged in protecting women, children, scheduled castes, Scheduled tribes, backward class rights.

Let us take the case of women

Violence against women is an important force that helps to keep the structure of patriarchy intact. It makes gender discrimination a live and terrifying experience for women, and ensures their subjugation. We have used the term gender-based violence to describe acts that cause physical, sexual or psychological harm to women. Such acts are based in the unequal relations that exist between men and women in society. The most important thing to remember about gender-based violence is that, it is all pervasive—it can occur in all kinds of situations (within the family, at the workplace, in public places, in the community, and even when in the custody of the state) and at all stages of a woman's life. Domestic violence is most common.

The United Nations Declaration on the Elimination of Violence Against Women 1993 defines its scope as:

"Physical, sexual and psychological violence occurring in the family, including battering, sexual abuse of female children in the household, dowry-related violence, marital rape, female genital mutilation and other traditional practices harmful to women, non-spousal violence and violence related to exploitation."

As many incidents of gender violence are now recognized as crimes, one of the important responses is through the police and the courts of law, which is in the form of punishment after the incident has occurred. An efficient law enforcement system can also act as a deterrent to further crimes. However, women's groups in West Bengal have repeatedly been making complaints about the reluctance of the police to register complaints of gender violence. Where there is an active women's organization or any other socially aware group or individual involved, complaints by women do get registered. In remoter areas where such groups have still not been able to reach, the experience is that the police often does not register complaints of gender violence like those of battering or molestation and gives lighter sections for grave crimes.

There has also been documentation of women's experiences with courts and the police where women have complained of the expenses and delays involved and confusing court procedures. They also complain about the insensitivity of the police, lawyers and other court personnel, including judges. Courts seem to be an especially difficult experience for victims of rape or any other kind of sexual crime, where the curiosity and the questions asked prove very traumatic.[10]

The task of combating gender-based violence is therefore huge and daunting and we can only hope that all organizations and agencies, men and women who have chosen to involve themselves in this task shall do so with all sincerity and commitment.[11]

The Charter of the UN is the first international instrument to mention equal rights of men and women in specific terms. In its Preamble, the Charter reaffirms faith in the fundamental human rights, in the dignity and worth of the human person, in the equal rights of men and women and to employ international machinery for the promotion of economic and social advancement of all people. One of the purposes of the UN as set out in Article 1 is "to achieve international co-operation in solving international problems of economic, social, cultural or humanitarian character and in promoting and encouraging respect for human rights and fundamental freedoms for all without distinction as to race, sex, language or religion." Article 8 states that "the UN shall place no restrictions on the eligibility of men and women to participate in any capacity and under conditions of equality in its principal and subsidiary organs."

Articles 13, 55 and 76 of the UN charter call for the realization of human rights and fundamental freedoms "for all without distinction as to race, sex, language or religion." Under Art. 56, Member-States have pledged themselves, to take joint and separate action in co-operation with the United Nations to achieve such aims. This basic principle of equality is elaborated in the Universal Declaration of Human Rights, which declares that, all human beings are born free and equal indignity and rights, and that everyone is entitled to all the rights and freedoms set forth in the declaration without distinction of any kind, including distinction based on sex. The principle of equality of men and women and the prohibition of discrimination against women are clearly set out in both the International Governants of Human Rights.

At this stage a few lines from the poem titled Shobola, written by the great Bengali poet Rabindranath Tagore which embodied women's voice of protest may be quote:

"Why must you curtail her rights
And keep women from conquering her own fate
Oh Divine Ruler?
Why should we stand forlorn by the wayside
With bowed heads.
Waiting for our weary patient dreams.
To be fulfilled on some
Auspicious Day?
Must be always stay into vacant space?
Can we not choose for our selves
The paths to our fulfilments?

Yes, this is a right time for women to choose the path to fulfil their dreams as they approach the 21st century. At this juncture it can be said that women have just begun this journey . . . a journey for better survival or more freedom. The path is difficult to pave the way . . . but journey has certainly begun.

India has enacted the protection of Human Rights Act, 1993 for better protection of human rights. The National Human Rights Commission (NHRC) has been established under this Act with jurisdiction all over India for protection of human rights by investigating human rights abuses, forwarding cases to courts for trials and recommending necessary measures to the government in concerned cases. The Commission is even initiating *suo-moto* investigations to provide relief to the concerned person.

A recent case "Best Bakery Case" in Gujarat tells the sad tale of violating human rights while protecting the culprits—Thus, causing and concern for the promotion of human rights

The NHRC in its petition had said that the Best Bakery case's main complainant and key witness Zahira Shaikh, seven of whose relatives were killed by rioters on February 28 last year, had told it that she had resided from her statement about recognizing the culprits because there was a threat to her and her family from certain persons and no protection was provided to her by the state government.

Taking note of his arguments, the Bench told the Gujarat Government counsel, "we have no faith in your prosecuting agency. There appears to be some collusion between the government and the prosecution, which should be independent. It is a serious mater as the case relates to burning alive of 14 persons."

The blame could not be put on the courts. They would go by what the prosecution would produce before them. "The state does not show any concern. No questions were asked from the witnesses about why they had turned hostile. You will do the same in the High Court when the appeal is taken up for hearing by it," the court observed.

Describing the draft of appeal filed by the government in the Gujarat High Court against the acquittals as an "eyewash", the Chief Justice asked state government counsel Mukul Rohtagi, "What the Rajdharma is?"

Out rightly rejecting the memo of appeal, the Chief Justice said, "I have no faith in the prosecution and the state Government . . . I am not saying (about) Article 356 (imposition of President's Rule). You have to protect the citizens and prosecute the guilty. What is Rajdharma? . . . If you cannot protect them then it is better to quit."

Coming down heavily on the Narendra Modi government for the prosecution's failure in the Best Bakery case resulting in the acquittal of all 21 accused, the Supreme Court today summoned the Gujarat Chief Secretary and the Director-General of Police to explain the reasons for this lapse and about filing a "shoddily drafted" appeal in the High Court.

Stating that if the government was notable to protect its citizens, it should better quit the office, a Bench comprising Chief Justice Mr. V.N. Khare, Mr. Justice Brijesh Kumar and Mr. Justice S.B. Sinha directed top officers of the state's civil and police administration to appear before it on September 19.

Though earlier many cases of Human Rights violation have come but Gujarat Bakery case has shipped all decorum and display.

Doordarshan and AIR are nodal to the success of the raising mass awareness on human rights values. Though DD and AIR are engaged with various programmes on themes relating to social issues, a specific thrust will need to be given with the perspective of raising such awareness and education.

The greatest contribution of PIL has been to enhance accountability of governments towards human rights of the poor. The judges acting alone cannot provide effective response to State lawlessness, but they can surely seek a culture formation where political power becomes increasingly sensitive to human rights. When people's rights are invaded by dominant elements, PIL emerges as a medium of struggle for protection of their human rights. The legitimacy which PIL enjoys in the Indian legal system is unprecedented. PIL activism interrogates power and makes courts as people's court. Even if human rights have not adequately been protected through judicial endeavours, the courts shall remain the site for human rights struggle.

Since early 1980s, the Supreme Court of India has developed a procedure which enables any public-spirited citizen or a social activist to mobilize favourable judicial concern on behalf of the oppressed classes. The medium through which access to justice has been democratized is called Public Interest Litigation (PIL).

Role of UGC in Promoting Human Rights Education through Universities and Colleges

As stated in the Annual Report, 2001-02 of UGC, Role of UGC and Duties Education: In 1985, the UGC prepared a blueprint for promotion of Human Rights teaching and research at all levels of education. This blueprint contained proposals for restructuring of existing syllabi, and introduction of new courses and/or foundation courses in Human Rights. This was for students of all faculties at the under-graduate, graduate and post-graduate levels for both professionals and non-professional education.

During the year 1997-98, the Commission framed "UGC IX Plan Approach for the promotion of Human Rights Education (HRE) in Universities and Colleges" with an objective to promote Human Rights and Duties Education through the Universities and Colleges and spreading awareness about the Human Rights and Duties Education amongst the teachers and students. For this purpose, the Commission has been providing financial assistance to Universities and Colleges for introduction of PG Degree, UG Degree, Diploma and Certificate Courses at PG level in Human Rights and Duties Education. It is also providing financial assistance to Universities and Colleges for holding seminars, symposia and workshops in Human Rights and Duties Education.

The following were the objectives and strategies of UGC for promoting Human Rights Education and Duties in Universities and Colleges:

OBJECTIVES AND STRATEGIES

Mere knowledge about human rights is not sufficient. An understanding as to how human rights can easily become vulnerable to abuse of various structures and processes of power is crucial. It may be added that understanding of abuse and misuse of power alone serves no purpose unless people in general and professionals in particular are imparted skills for protection and enforcement of these rights.

Human Rights Education does not merely mean imparting knowledge in the class-room, but it also has to cover all modalities (formal, non-formal and informal) which could sensitise a person, awaken his/her conscience and develop an attitude of mind imbibing respect for human rights of others.

Human Rights Education cannot merely be an intellectual exercise alone. It requires building linkages between what happens in the society and what is transmitted in the classes to the students. It requires capturing actual experiences of violation of human rights and denial of human dignity. This kind of education needs field experience and action-oriented ways of learning and teaching.

Human Rights Education requires building strong linkages and networking between colleges/universities and various NGOs and other groups working in the field and community. Building these linkages would go a long way in giving Human Rights Education a grass-root orientation. Collecting, collating and classifying the data and experiences that NGOs and groups working in the field have already acquired can be an important aspect of human rights education and may lead to create new knowledge and research.

Human Rights Education must encompass in it a strong research component. Any teaching of or about human rights need to be backed up by strong multi-disciplinary research on various aspects of human rights and their complexities.

Training and public information are the indispensable components of human rights education. As such for carrying out awareness and other programmes, audio-visual aids and distance mode of education need to be used amongst other tools and inputs.

Extension work has long been recognized by the University Grants Commission (UGC) as an equally important component of University and Collegiate education, besides teaching and research. National Service Scheme (N.S.S.), Women Studies Research Centers, adult education and population education programmes, and continuing education are some area specific modalities. These along with field action, need to be utilized for extending the scope and access of human rights programmes to the grass-roots level.

The extension programmes in the colleges need special attention and emphasis with a view to giving them Human Rights orientation.

The legal aid programmes in the colleges could be more vigorously utilized by the law schools for the benefit of the needy to render legal advice and assistance for human rights enforcement.

National Human Rights Commission is now a statutory institution with responsibility, amongst others, "to spread human rights literacy and promote awareness of the safeguards." Co-ordination with and by the National Human Rights Commission for a more purposeful use of extension programmes of the universities and colleges is necessary. Modalities for the same need to be worked out through joint consultation between the University Grants Commission and the National Human Rights Commission.

Three alternative approaches for promoting human rights education be pursued simultaneously, viz. (a) Introducing separate courses on Human Rights, (b) Human Rights issues to be incorporated in courses already being taught, (c) Reorientation of all courses so that the human rights component is not seen as an adjunct to the existing syllabi, instead the academic packages should be so offered as to have "people" as the central theme.

The advantages of such a strategy are obvious. It is highly flexible and can accommodate the needs, pace of growth and extent of commitment to human rights education, of each institution.

It is basic to the promotion of human rights education in universities and colleges that the students after training could expect decent employment. Presently, no such avenues exist apart from extremely limited slots available in teaching and research institutions and the media.

Perhaps the setting up of the proposed human rights courts in each district all over the country could open up avenues of self-employment for a substantial number of students. Inclusion of human rights as one of the subjects in national competitive examinations also deserves consideration. Other avenues too are needed to be explored by all agencies and institutions interested in the promotion of human rights education, including the National Human Rights Commission and the University Grants Commission.

There is a need to convince all Union and State Minorities and departments especially those which provide service to the people like the railways, the post and telecommunications and electricity as well as all law courts and prisons and law enforcement agencies to appoint human rights experts as advisors and trainers.

SCOPE AND BROAD CONTENTS OF HUMAN RIGHTS COURSES

Human Rights Education should preferably be inter-disciplinary. Human Rights cannot be compartmentalized into academic disciplines; these have to be conceptualized in their entirety. These are central to all social sciences studies.

In order to inculcate a broad comprehension of human rights as "human existence with dignity", the contents of human rights courses need incorporate and reflect the concerns for democracy, development and peace. In particular in a country like India they must necessarily include issues of: social justice, distributive justice, bringing marginalised and historically deprived sections to the mainstream of national life, protecting environment and ecological balance, and ensuring steady and meaningful progress and development in individual's as well as national life (as mentioned in para 3 above).

To ensure comprehensiveness and incorporation of national, regional and international perspectives, the broad contents of courses on human rights need to cover the following:

(a) Philosophical and cultural bases and historical perspectives, theories and movements (national as well as international).

(b) Interdependence of and linkages between human rights and democracy, pluralism, development, ecological balance peace and harmony at the national as well as international level.

(c) *National Perspective*: The historical context, colonialism and post-colonialism; post-independence national development; protection regime especially for the weak and marginalised groups including minorities and for women and children; the violation of rights by the State and its agencies—the police and the criminal justice system; body of laws, bye-laws and rules, etc. inconsistent with human rights norms; violation of rights by armed political groups and terrorists; intra-societal violation of rights of the poor and weak by the dominant groups including gender inequalities exploitations and injustices; the role of the judiciary, the National Human Rights Commission and of the Statutory Commissions on Women, Minorities, SC and ST and Linguistic Minorities; the role of the NGOs and the media *vis-a-vis* protection and promotion of human rights.

(d) *Regional Perspectives*: Special features of the region in which India is located such as: pluralism, economic poverty, colonial past, rigid social structures, mass illiteracy, constant threat to political stability and democracy, growing consumerism and recently introduced economic/structural re-adjustment reforms *vis-a-vis* status of human rights.

(e) Emergence of SAARC and the debate over the need for evolving South Asia Charter of Human Rights. Other regional developments such as European Charter on Human Rights, European Court on Human Rights, European parliament, South-South Dialogue, and other such developments and arrangements.

(f) *International Perspectives*: The study of texts, treaties, arrangements and structures innovated by the international community in post-world war period for the protection of human rights; effect of cold war on the status and functioning of various institutions and structures organized for promotion and protection of human rights; the end of cold war and its influence on the regime and status of human rights promotion and other such issues. Role of developed societies *vis-a-vis* human rights. Role of institutions like United Nations Organization, ICI, United Nations High Commission for Refugees, United Nations Educational Scientific and Cultural Organization, World Health Organization, International Labour Organization *vis-a-vis* human rights. Causes of success and failure of these institutions in protecting and promoting respect for human rights.

The Commission constituted a Curriculum Development Committee under the Chairmanship of Hon. Justice Dr. V.S. Malimath to prepare the curricula for various courses under Human Rights and Duties Education Programme. It developed Curriculum for introduction of:

- Foundation Course in Human Rights and Duties,
- Certificate Course in Human Rights and Duties,
- Under-graduate Degree Course in Human Rights and Duties,
- Post-graduate Diploma Course in Human Rights and Duties, and
- Post-graduate Degree (MA/LLM) Course in Human Rights and Duties.

The UGC Model curricula on Human Rights and Duties Education have been sent to all the Universities and Autonomous Colleges as well as to the Head of the Department under which the Programme of Human Rights and Duties Education is being conducted.

During the Ninth Plan Period, the following were done:

The Commission in collaboration with the British Council organized two workshops—First on 23rd to 25th November, 1998 at Bangalore and second on 30th November to 2nd December, 1998 at Delhi.

The Scheme of Human Rights Education was renamed as Human Rights and Duties Education on the basis of Hon. Justice Verma Committee Report on "operationalization of the suggestion to teach fundamental duties to the citizen of the country." Universities and Colleges were requested to incorporate duty consciousness and essential component in the Curriculum. The report was sent to all the Universities.

Since the inception of the Programme, i.e. 1997-98, the Commission approved 31 Universities and 3 Colleges for introduction of Degree, Diploma and Certificate Courses, it also approved 48 Universities and 73 Colleges for organizing seminar/symposia/workshops during Ninth Plan Period.

Nature of Assistance

The following programmes of Human Rights and Duties Education have been identified for financial support during the Xth Plan: (for detail see appendix)

(i) A foundation course,
(ii) A certificate course,
(iii) An under-graduate degree,
(iv) A post-graduate diploma course,
(v) A post-graduate degree (MA/LLM) course, and
(vi) Seminars/Symposia/Workshops.

Facts

(1) Violation of human rights is a regular features by persons in power or persons belonging to the under-world.

(2) Police violation of human rights is a recurring phenomenon.
(3) Judiciary takes a long time in deciding the cases of Human rights violations.
(4) Women and children are abused at every place.
(5) Minorities human rights are violated on one pretext or the other.
(6) Moral and ethical values are existing in name only. No practices of values.
(7) Materialism is causing the violation of human rights.
(8) Human Rights Commissions are slow and their composition is detrimental to human rights. Instead of appointing retired people, fresh persons may be appointed to inject dynamism.
(9) Government at the union and state levels are engaged in violation of human rights purely to continue in power.
(10) Enforcement machinery is dilatory and lack the desired powers.
(11) Punishment for human rights violation is very less causing encouragement to human rights violators.
(12) Rights and duties must be pursued simultaneously.

PROBLEMS

(1) Lack of Knowledge and Implications of Human Rights

Most of the people in India lack knowledge and an awareness about Human Rights. This makes them tolerate the excesses of other people. This is more true with people living in villages, women, dalits, illiterates.

(2) Machinery designed to ensure the protection of Human Rights is not adequate to tackle large number of personnel and People are unaware of the structure and functions of such machinery

Human Rights Commissions at union and state levels are not so active as most of the persons appointed on these bodies are retired person. We must engage people on deputation so as to provide dynamism as well as provide employment to new people.

(3) There is Centralization: Need of Decentralization

It is very difficult for people to come at headquarters to file their complaints for human right violations. The machinery dealing with Human Rights need decentralization.

(4) Universities, colleges and other institutions not involved in the education of Human Rights

Universities and colleges numbering about 12000, can bring a revolution if educational system is use of for the benefit of common man. Universities are dealing only with theoretical concepts and not providing extensive services. Universities can do a lot provided the thrust is changed.

(5) Politicians of whatever political parties they belong do not adhere to Human Rights and duties

They rather create fear and exploit the people for their interest. Politicians may be made to understand that they should not indulge in Human Rights Violations rather they should maintain its dignity.

SUGGESTIONS

Human Rights Education is a difficult and challenging task. However, higher education institutes can help the help of faculty and students. Teachers have to create in students a spirit of providing extension education to the people. That is why Kothari Commission (1964-66) has forcefully stated that the destiny of a Nation is shaped in her class rooms.

(1) Rights and Duties must be Pursued Simultaneously

Human rights education must include also the component of obligations towards others. Mahatma Gandhi, in a letter to Julien Huxley in 1947, had said:

> "I learned from my illiterate but wise mother that all rights to be deserved and preserved come from duty well done. Thus, the very right to live accrues to us when we do the duty of citizenship of the world. From this one fundamental statement, perhaps it is easy enough to define duties of man and woman and correlate every right to some corresponding duty to be first performed . . ."

(2) Need of Genuine Leadership to Support Rights of Common Man

Common man in developing countries cannot enjoy the human rights as leaders both political and bureaucratic usurp all powers.

The objective knowledge, which has up till now been discovered by the man through scientific adventures is only said to be limited one. Our visionaries have given us in our religious books, that the knowledge measurable by the dimensional parameters, can be transferred and passed on from one generation to the other. Even its factual results can be verified and changed by the future scientist, but the subjective knowledge is not transferable and hence remains the prized possession of the vision and insight.

The man must remain with the essential limits for the existence of this family. The acquisition of wealth, by scams, and scandals, would ultimately take our people to mental pollution and the nation as a whole will be put to degradation, for which only the people in authorities would be responsible. It is a fact, in absolutism, that tendencies to give name and fame to money launderers, on political scenario of our country, should be discouraged in all compartments. At least we should not allow such persons to pull the strings, to unfurl the national flag, who so ever it may be. There are already under currents in our people that the battery of sycophants and jugglery of words, on such occasions, make such person enjoy the epithet of leaders or Netajee. As we see now that there is not dearth of leaders these days, while the sewadar is none. We must see reason to discard such crooks, conferred with leadership, by their relatives. Otherwise fear that the list of essentials for their existence, would not limit to the foreign bank accounts only, but they would now be aspiring for transmission channel for their entertainments in the orbital trajectories of other planets in the family of sun.

With the change of times now, the imprints of elevated consciousness and covetous preciousness of our national mind, had been camouflaged with so many question marks, on our future citadels which have now come under the control of a vertical and greedy leadership. As all the cybernetics of our prospective developments, and all the struts and columns which are supporting our system to eliminate our people from drudgery and ignorance, to boost up the spirit and esteem of the Indian mind, have now come under pressure and are exposed to rust and cracks, by the so-called leaders, whose patriotism has now mostly become a salable commodity, impregnated with diplomatic jugglery and a rank hypocracy. The common man is totally confused in the populous slogans of opportune politics which is taking the people to degeneration and denigration from the real focus.[12]

(3) Need of Sensitizing Police Personnel through Education and Training

The Commission has given high priority to the training and re-training of police personnel in human rights observance, so that they would reduce the violation of human rights by themselves and become better protector of human rights of others. On Commission's urge, with adequate governmental support the Sardar Patel National Police Academy in Hyderabad has been emphasizing on human rights education. It is a major training center for I.P.S. officers. The Commission discussed with the Director-Generals of Police of the States and Union Territories and the efforts have been successful that a three-tier model syllabus has been prepared for Constables, sub-Inspectors/Inspector, Deputy Superintendents of Police and other senior officers. This model syllabus has been circulated to all States and Union Territories with recommendation that they adopt it for training of police personnel.[13]

(4) Need of Inculcating Ethical and Moral Value

The modern world is marked by a widespread explosion of knowledge and tremendous achievements in Science and Technology, coupled with a general decline and reversal of human values as well as an alarming deterioration of moral and mental health both of individuals and societies. The recent spate of crimes, violence, terrorism and drug abuse makes us aware of the significance of human values, without which human life loses all meaning. It is also evident that a mere economic prosperity and material health cannot result in a lasting well-being of mankind. The inner strength of mankind springs from within, which seems ill-nourished now.[14]

(5) Emphasis on Human Rights Education in Universities

Education is an important human activity. It was born with the birth of the human race and shall continue to function as long as the human race exists. The importance of education can be specified by the saying "MAN" becomes "MAN" through education. It has been rightly said that without education, man is a splendid slave, a reasoning savage. Education fashions and models man for society. It signifies man's supreme position in societies. It teaches what man lives and struggles for. Aristotle says, "Educated men are as much superior to uneducated as the living are to the dead." Epithets says Education is an essential concomitant of all human societies.

Education makes man rational, reliant, selfless, self-conscious, civilized, sociable and harmonious creature. It inculcates good habits in man and makes his life systematic, develops aspirations, ambitions and desires in him, makes him powerful and paves way for his development. In other words, education opens a new world before the human beings.[15]

Colleges and Universities are supposed to provide extension services to the society as well as advice to the Government/agencies engaged in human rights. Universities are the bridges between the government and the community. What are the ways through which Colleges and Universities can play an important role in protecting the violation of Human Right? There are many methods through which colleges and universities can play this role effectively. Let us analyze them.

We may suggest the following approach to make educational programmes practical and useful for protection of Human Rights:

(a) The existing educational institutions and programmes need to be consolidated and put to optimum use to serve the goals of development in the community as a whole.

(b) Provision of suitable educational facilities in backward areas and for the deprived groups and promotion of non-formal and Distance Education programmes at all levels in a systematic way are important.

(c) Educational Planning need be linked effectively with man-power planning at all stages and aspects of skill development. Adequate attention need be paid for optimization of benefits from the existing investments and facilities.

(d) It is vital to transform the system of education qualitatively in terms of value content, standards and relevance to life. The role of education to promote humanistic outlook, sense of brotherhood and a commitment to cultural and ethical values need to be re-emphasized.

(e) The importance of educational technology has to be adequately provided for greater efficiency and effectiveness and wider reach of the educational programmes economically.

The following important areas have been identified:

(i) Informing and educating the people about their rights, duties and responsibilities in a democratic set-up through programmes like talk AIR, in English, Hindi as well as in vernacular languages. Private TV Channels should also be induced to broadcast/telecast such programmes. Such programmes should be tele/broadcasted during prime time.

(ii) Informative programmes like Quizzes/serials/soap operas should also highlight the constitutionally guaranteed rights, legal safeguards and availability of various institutional mechanisms for redressal.

(iii) Programmes on rights of women, rights of children, disabled persons, rights of HIV/AIDS affected person, drug abuse, etc. should be in drama/soap opera formats as that would have more impact than simple massaging.

(iv) Efforts should be made to include issues on human rights in the local programmes on DD and AIR.

(v) A regular slot be reserved in DD and AIR for human rights education. The education channel of DD should be effectively used for this purpose.

(vi) In order to encourage Producers/Directors to make programmes on human rights issues annual awards and incentive schemes should be instituted.

(vii) In order to encourage the Producers/Directors to make feature films/documentaries on human rights issues, special awards should be instituted for best film/documentary on human rights. Easy financing through NFDC to such Producers/Directors should also be considered.

(viii) Orientation programmes like seminars, workshops on human rights should be regularly organised by the M/O IandB, for different levels of its staff.

(ix) A meeting of media experts in the field of films, TV, publicity experts, senior Government officials, activists, and NGOs should be convened to discuss effective ways of dissemination human rights values for the people, especially weaker and the vulnerable section through mass media.

(x) Partnership be developed with the concerned State authorities in order to have wider dissemination, specially in the district/block/panchayat/village officials.

(xi) Private and corporate sector should be included as far as practicable.

(xii) The Ministry of Women and Child Development should formulate special programmes to bring about awareness of the rights of women and children, amongst different sections of society. Suitable programmes should be developed and made available to Universities, Schools and Police, Training Institutions.

In a democracy where the human rights are more important, particularly in India where the social inequalities are very sharp the human rights assume more significance. But human rights in the absence of people with proper social awareness become irrelevant and meaningless. Here comes the role of social science education. Thus, social science education is the most essential element for the promotion of human rights in the developing societies in general and in India in particular.

(6) Research and Documentation in Human Right

The higher education system in India can take up research projects in different aspect of human rights and their violation in their catchments area. Their finding can be documented by one cell set-up specially for this purpose. These documentation can be regularly sent to policy-making, planning and decision-making agencies quarterly. This would help in analysing the Human Rights Issues purely on the basis of facts and can bring forth solutions based on analyses of Data. In addition, case studies can be undertaken to throw lights on atrocities committed in depth and true perspective.

(7) Introducing Topics of Human Rights in Under-Graduate and Post-Graduate Education—To make the Youth Aware of Human Rights

The UGC must ensure that some topics of human rights suiting different areas of study should be incorporated by Universities and colleges in their syllabi on a massive scale for practical orientation and not merely understanding theory.

(8) Introducing Independent Teaching on Human Rights

Introducing independent teaching on Human Rights in Disciplines like political science, sociology, public administration, and had through one paper or set-up independent departments of Human Rights to award M.A. Degree in Human Rights.

Both the approaches are being implemented by many universities but their number is small. We have to introduce human rights programme in a big way especially in colleges and universities located in rural areas, tribal areas, urban slums and backward areas.

(9) Arranging Seminar on different areas of Human Rights through Experts from different Discipline by Engaging in Interdisciplinary Approach

UGC, ICSSR, Nation and State Commissions for women should finance such seminars liberally. These seminars must be focused and not simply a discussion house. The seminar must come out with definite suggestions which can be useful for agencies engaged in the implementation of Human Rights. We must consolidate the reports of these seminars in Human Rights Cell.

(10) Lectures to Disseminate the Current Provisions of Human Rights

Lectures to disseminate the current provisions of Human Rights to Agencies like Judiciary, Police engaged in its implementation and the procedure to deal with human rights issues. It would be of great interest if the copy of the lectures is circulated among the audience. These lectures may be later on broadcasted for the benefit of general public through radio and television.

(11) Discussion with Opinion Leaders in Cities

Discussion with opinion leaders in cities and villages like Panches, Sarpanches, Chairman Panchayat Samiti, Chairmen Zila Parishad (both men and women), Municipal Commissioners, etc. The Universities and colleges can divide the catchment area and allocate to different institutions the work of educating the masses in the scope and limitation of human rights. In addition, they can also bring to the notice of the executive agencies responsible for implementation of these human rights, the cases which have been ignored or action has not been taken. These may also be released to the press for wider use. These would create a movement wherein violation of Human Rights would be difficult.

(12) Involvement of Students

Students' team can be constituted after training in theory and practice of Human Rights which can go to different areas of cities and villages and impart education in Human Rights by discussion or lecture or informal methods. Students can be encouraged through:

(a) awarding some extra marks,
(b) giving some certificates which can help them in employment, and
(c) preference in admissions to higher education institutes.

Youth once motivated can create a momentum and people can get real education. Women faculty members and women students can mobilize public opinion and educate women about their rights/privileges. They can help the women in PRI system to prove their worth. Women studies centers wherever located can do a lot for women human rights. The need is to stress extension of education to the community.

The time has come when UGC through universities and colleges must discharge its responsibilities in the area of extension education. UGC would get a credit if it can help the universities and colleges in discharging the obligations of higher education system to the society. Higher education must play its role in solving the problems of society. Society, even after more than fifty years of independence, is being exploited in collision with vested interest. The True freedom can only be enjoyed by the people if the fundamental rights and other human rights are made a reality to them. Words written or spoken are of no use unless put to action. Higher Education System is best suited for helping the people to feel the enjoyment of fundamental freedoms granted to them.

In a democracy where the human rights are more important, particularly in India where the social inequalities are very sharp, the human rights assume more significance. But human rights in the absence of people with proper social awareness become irrelevant and meaningless. Here comes the role of social science education. Thus, social science education is the most essential element for the promotion of human rights in the developing societies in general and in India in particular.

As human rights are more important to democracy, the social science education should be properly promoted because it enhances the conscious level of the common people, without which democracy can not be protected. Hence, the protection of social sciences education is highly needed to save the democracy as well as human rights.[16]

CONCLUSION

The Human Rights Commission has been entrusted with the responsibility "to spread human rights literacy among various sections of society and promote awareness of safeguards available for the protection of these rights through publications, the media, seminars and other available means." For this, the Commission has been continuously coordinating with the Human Resource Development Ministry, the National Council for Education, Research and Training (NCERT), National Council for Teachers Education (NCTE), State Councils for Educational Research and Training (SCERT) and Universities to introduce Human Rights education programmes in their courses.

The Chairpersons of the Commission wrote to all the Vice-Chancellors of Universities and the University Grants Commission (UGC) to include human rights in the curriculum at the under-graduate and post-graduate levels and promote research, seminars and publications on human rights. Giving a positive response a large number of universities have started courses on human rights and they are also being financially assisted by the UGC in this regard. Some of these universities are, viz. Jamia Millia Islamia, Delhi University, Aligarh Muslim University, Jammu University, Andhra University, Panjab University, Banaras Hindu

University, Rajasthan University, Karnataka University, Kurukshetra University and Cochin University.[17]

Their achievements are laudable, and their further march would bring more laurels to the society and nation. But a note of caution is necessary. The concept of "progress and independent" in America destroyed the family Unit, which is the basic component of the society. It has been uprooted completely. Europe also is going the same way. African and Latin American countries are dazzled by the material progress made by U.S.A. and Europe, and they are also blindly following the same path. Some European countries like Germany and France are now seriously thinking of strengthening the basic family unit even at the cost of so-called personal liberty and independence. The disruption of family unit in U.S.A. have inevitably resulted in the mass population of destitute, orphans and illegitimate children. The problem of virgin mothers is causing additional anxiety to the social thinkers and philosophers. We have to guard against these evil consequences.[18]

No ideal, ideology, institution or religion is self-operative. It is through human agency alone that ideals and institutions established for their realization are made operational. History bears witness to perversions, distortions and abuse or misuse of ideals and institutions for the reason that human being is essentially imperfect though he seeks perfection. It is true that perfection is not attainable by imperfect beings, however, it is always worthwhile attempting and this depends largely upon a meaningful education of man with a view to fertilizing the soil within so that the vessel may bear rich, juicy and truthful fruits.[19] Sustenance of human values, ethics and morals in human society and spiritual enlightenment of man seem to be decidedly more effective and meaningful goals of educational philosophy to follow. It is principally inadequate appreciation of the essentially spiritual nature of man and prevailing disrespectful attitude towards the role of true religion or spiritualism in protecting and promoting the spiritual core of human beings which accounts for the crisis of our times.[20]

The programme for Human Rights Education is a continuous process. While certain specific areas with time targeted action programme have been identified by the concerned Ministries/Departments, further appropriate strategies for each of the action areas will be drawn up and implemented by them with specific time frames for achieving the objectives.[21]

Notes and References

1. Mrs. Snehal Fadnovas, Impact of Women's Rights Movement on the Development of Human Rights in South Asian Countries, in *Journal of the Institute of Human Rights*, Vol. II, No. 1, Jaripatka, Nagpur.
2. R.P. Dhokalia, External Human Values and World Religions, New Delhi, NCERT, 2001, p. 10.

3. Arjun Dev (ed.), "A Handbook of Human Rights", Creative Learning Series, NBI, New Delhi, 2003, p. VII.
4. Sabira Khan, "Human Rights in India (Protection and Violence), New Delhi, Devika Publication, 2004, pp. 12-13.
5. GOI, Ministry of Home Affairs, National Action Plan for Human Rights Education in India, New Delhi, 2001, pp. 3-4.
6. *Ibid.*, pp. 4-6.
7. *Ibid.*, pp. 12-13.
8. C. Roy Kumar, Role and Contribution of National Human Rights Commissions in Promoting National and International Human Rights Norms in the National Context, *IJPA*, April-June 2001, pp. 222-36.
9. Parmanand Singh, Human Rights Protection Through Public Interest Litigation, India, *IJPA*, Oct.-Dec. 1999, p. 748.
10. UNIFEM, Support Services to Counter Violence Against Women, 2002, West Bengal, New Delhi, pp. 7-11 (Sanhita).
11. *Ibid.*, pp. 13-14.
12. Gurcharan Singh, Pollution to Purity of Environment, New Delhi, Deep & Deep, 2000.
13. R.P. Dhokalia, *op. cit.*, pp. 109-10.
14. *Ibid.*, Foreward, p. viii
15. Vijay Kumar and K.V. Rama Lakshmi, Protection of Social Sciences Education to Save Human Rights, *University News*, Nov. 15, 1999, p. 3.
16. Vijay Kumar and K.V. Rama Lakshmi, *op. cit.*, p. 10.
17. Sabira Khan, Human Rights in India, New Delhi, 2004, Devika, pp. 108-09.
18. Dr. P.L. Joshi, Editorial Note, *Journal of the Institute of Human Rights*, Vol. II, No. 1, 1999, Nagpur.
19. Vijay Kumar and K.V. Rama Lakshmi, *op. cit.*, p. 3.
20. R.P. Dhokalia, *op. cit.*, p. 13.
21. National Action Plan for Human Rights Education in India, *op. cit.*, p. 9.

CHAPTER 12

SCHOOL HEALTH EDUCATION: A CASE STUDY OF HARYANA

Most emphatically, the Kothari report expressed it thus:

"The destiny of India is now being shaped in her classrooms. This, we believe, is no mere rhetoric. In a world based on science and technology, it is education that determiners the level of prosperity, welfare and security of the people. On the quality and number of persons coming out of our schools and colleges will depend our success in the great enterprise of national reconstruction whose principal objective is to raise the standard of living of our people".

—*V.R. Krishna Iyer*
"Primary Education: Some Flaws in Planning",
Studies in Educational Development,
Primary Education and Adult Literacy, 1996

School Health Education: A Case Study of Haryana

"Education does not mean teaching people what they do not know. It means teaching them to behave as they do not behave. It is not teaching the youth the shapes of letters and the tricks of numbers, and leaving them to turn their arithmetic to roguery and their literature to lust. It means, on the contrary, training them into the perfect exercise and kingly continence of their bodies and souls. It is a painful, continual, and difficult work to be done by kindness, by watching, by warning, by precept, and by praise, but above all – by example".

—*V.R. Krishna Iyer,*
"Primary Education: Some Flaws in Planning"

An Oriental proverb rightly stresses the need of Planning for children. "If you are planning one year ahead, sow rice, if your are planning five years ahead, plant trees; but if you are planning generation ahead, you must grow men."

We have divided this chapter into three parts.

A. Early Childhood Care and Education.
B. Elementary Education.
C. Secondary Education.

A. EARLY CHILDHOOD CARE AND EDUCATION (ECCE) (See Chart 12.1)

Children are our future and our most precious resources. The quality of tomorrow's world and perhaps even its survival will be

CHART 12.1

Role of Child Welfare

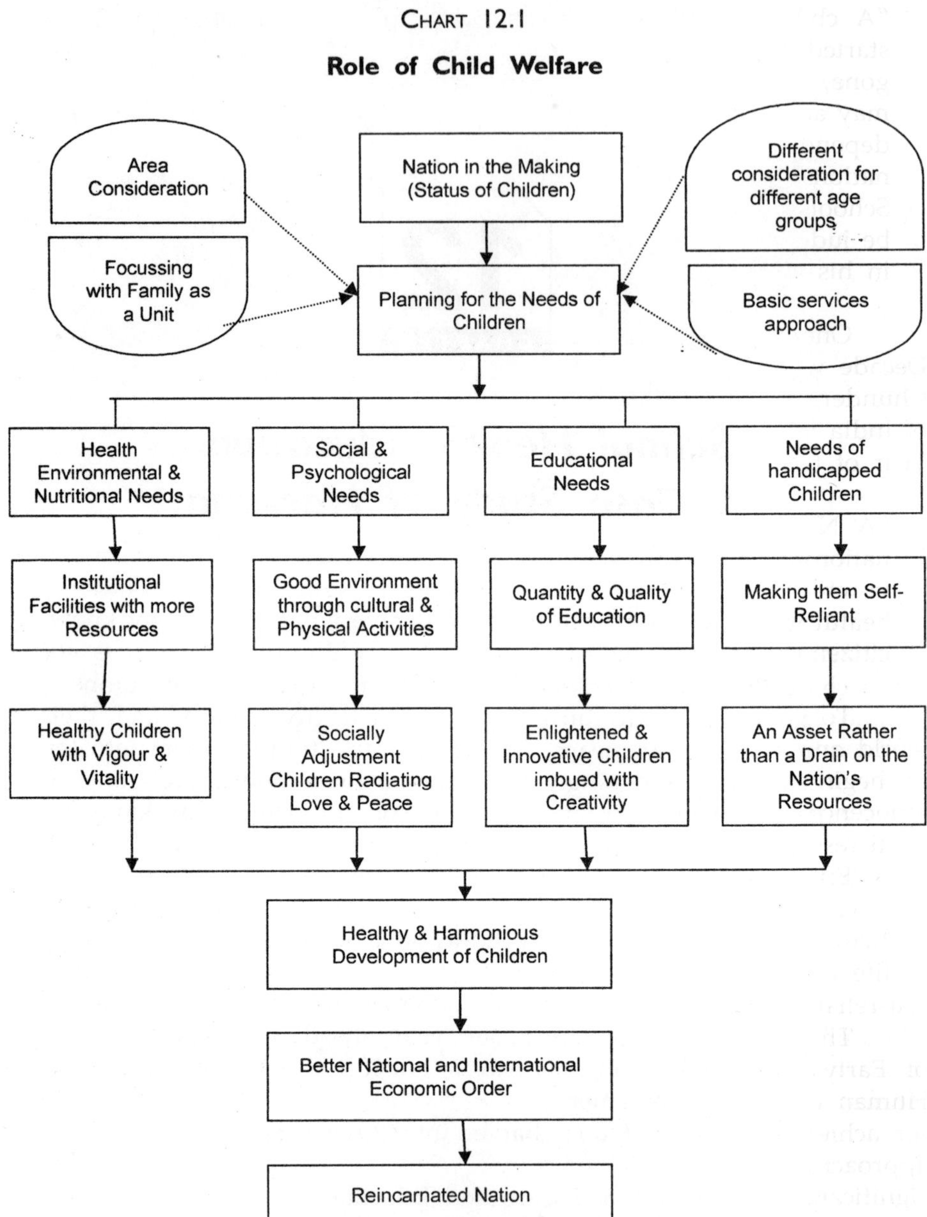

determined by the well-being, safety and the physical and intellectual development of children today. To predict the future of a nation, it has been remarked, one need not consult the stars; it can more easily and plainly be read in the faces of its children. Children are the mirrors of a nation. Abraham Lincoln nicely explained the role of the child when he said.

> "A child is a person who is going to carry on what you have started. He is going to sit where you are sitting, and when you are gone/attend to those things which you think are important. You may adopt all the policies you please, but how they are carried out depends on him. He will assume control of your cities, states, and nations. He is going to move in and take over your Churches, Schools, Universities and Corporations. All you books are going to be judged, praised or condemned by him. The fate of humanity is in his hands."

One of the specific objectives of the UN Second Development Decade was that "the well-being of children shall be fostered." Dr. P.C. Chunder, former Minister of Education and Social Welfare, Government of India in his Foreword to the National Plan of Action for International Year of the Child", 1979 has rightly said that,

> "A Nation's Children are its supremely important asset and the nation's future lies in their proper development. . . . An investment in children is indeed an investment in the Nation's future. A healthy and educated child of today is the active and intelligent citizen of tomorrow."[1]

To quote Mahatma Gandhi: "If we are to achieve real peace in this world and if we are to carry on a real war against war, we shall have to begin with children; and if they will grow up in their natural innocence we won't have to struggle, we won't have to pass fruitless ideal resolutions, but we shall go from love to love and peace to peace."

Effective national policies and plans regarding children can make a decisive contribution to all other long-term development activities and particularly to the success of the programmes aimed at raising the quality of life of lower income groups and at building national capacities and self-reliance.

The National Policy on Education (NPE) has underlined the need of Early Childhood Care and Education (ECCE) as a vital input for Human Resource Development and as a feeder and support programme for achieving universal elementary education. It also accepts integrated approach to Child Development. ECCE is also indirectly of great significance for women development and their participation in the process of Development as they would be released from Child Care activities. National Policy on Education Review Committee (NPERC) rightly suggests[2] that ECCE, therefore, is a cross-sectoral programme addressing the *intersecting needs* of women, children and girls.

Developments

Keeping in view the Constitutional Provisions, UN Declaration of the Rights of the Child, Bellagio Conference in 1965 and the UNICEF-

ECAFE Conference of Governments, and Planners held in Bangkok in March 1966, Government of India adopted a National Policy for Children in 1974. Besides National Policy Statements on Health (1983), Education (1986), Child Labour (1987), the World Declaration on the Survival, Protection and Development of Children in 1990 and Directive Principle of State Policy are other Policy statements. The policy measures ensure full physical, mental and social development of the children with a focus on areas like Child Health, Child Nutrition and Welfare of handicapped and destitute children. P.N. Luthra, the then Secretary, Department of Social Welfare, writes in an introduction to the pamphlet on National Policy for Children:

> "The Statement on National Policy is intended to serve as a pole-star to guide the official and non-official agencies alike in regard to the direction in which they should move for achieving full and integrated development of our children, who constitute our most valuable asset for posterity."

As a sequel to the National Policy For Children (1974), many programmes have been started for the development of children. Important programmes in operation are as given below:

(i) ICDS;
(ii) Balwadis and Day Care Centres run by Government and Voluntary agencies;
(iii) Pre-Primary Schools; and
(iv) Maternal and Child Health Services.

B. ELEMENTARY EDUCATION

The Directive Principles of State Policy provides for free and compulsory education till the age of 14. Since 1950, the Union and State Governments are exerting to implement the provisions of the Directive Principles of State Policy. Though, there have been achievements but still far from the goal. According to the Fifth All India Education Survey, 1986, 94.5 per cent of the rural population had schools within a walking distance of 1 km; 83.98 per cent of the rural population was served with middle schools/sections within a walking distance of 3 km.

C. SECONDARY EDUCATION

Secondary Education prepares the students for future life career as the education at this level exposes the students to differentiated roles of science, the humanities and social sciences. Secondary Education Commission set-up in September 1952 under the Chairmanship of Dr. A. Lakshmana Swami Mudaliar, suggested four aims of secondary education: (i) training of character and development qualities essential for citizenship in a democratic social order, (ii) the improvement of vocational efficiency, (iii) personality development, and (iv) Leadership Training.

Current Status

The Constitution of India has made a commitment to provide free and compulsory education for all children upto the age of fourteen. The task of providing basic education for all, with concrete plans of action, gained greater momentum with the adoption of the National Policy on Education (NPE) in 1986 and its revision in 1992. The World Declaration on Education For All (EFA), adopted in Jomtien in 1990 gave further fillip to the national commitment to provide basic education for all. India considers basic education to be the key to sustainable socio-economic development and peace and stability within and among countries, a categorical statement within the Dakar Framework for Action.

Basic Indicators of EFA

Growth of Literacy

Over the decades, literacy rates have shown substantial improvement. The total literacy rate was only 16.67 per cent in 1951, which rose to 52.21 per cent in 1991 and has further increased to 65.4 per cent in 2001. According to the Census of India, 2001, the literacy rate has gone up to 75.85 percent for males and 54.16 per cent for females. For the first time, even with an overall increase in the population, the number of illiterates has decreased in absolute terms by 31.9 million. The number of literates, on the other hand, increased by 203.6 million during the last decade.

Early Childhood Care and Education (ECCE)

Envisaged as a holistic input for promoting health, nutritional and personality development, the National Policy on Education, 1986, recommended strengthening of ECCE programmes not only as an essential intervention for human development but also as a significant support both for universalization of elementary education and women's development. The Integrated Child Development (ICDS) is the largest programme under the ECCE. It is an intersectoral programme, which seeks to directly reach out to children from vulnerable sections and of remote areas and give them a head start by providing an integrated programme of health, nutrition and early childhood education. The package of services for children below six years and pregnant and nursing mothers includes supplementary nutrition, immunization, health check-up, referral services, non-formal pre-school education and community participation. The central and state governments, to supplement the ICDS provisions and to improve its content and coverage, have also initiated several other schemes.

Schooling Facilities

Availability of schooling facilities is measured by a set of indicators concerning access. As per norms, a habitation (cluster of households) is entitled to have a primary school, if it has a total population of 300 and more, and has no school within a distance of one kilometer. For upper primary schools, the corresponding norm is the total population of 500 and more, and a distance of three kilometers. These norms are often relaxed in case of hilly and tribal areas, difficult terrains and border districts. States have their own norms according to which they provide schooling facilities.

There has been substantial expansion of primary (Grades I-V) and upper primary (Grades VI-VIII) schools in the post-independence period. The average annual growth rates of primary and upper primary schools were 2.25 percent and 5.59 percent respectively during 1950-2000. The average annual growth rates of primary and upper primary schools during the last decade (i.e. 1990-91 to 2000-01) were 1.31 percent and 3.14 percent respectively. With continuous expansion of facilities, the growth rates of educational institutions have, in fact, decreased. The ratio of upper primary schools to primary schools was 1:15 in 1950-51, which improved to 1:3 in 2000-01 (See Figure 12.1).

FIG. 12.1

Growth of Primary and Upper Primary Schools, 1950-51 to 2000-2001

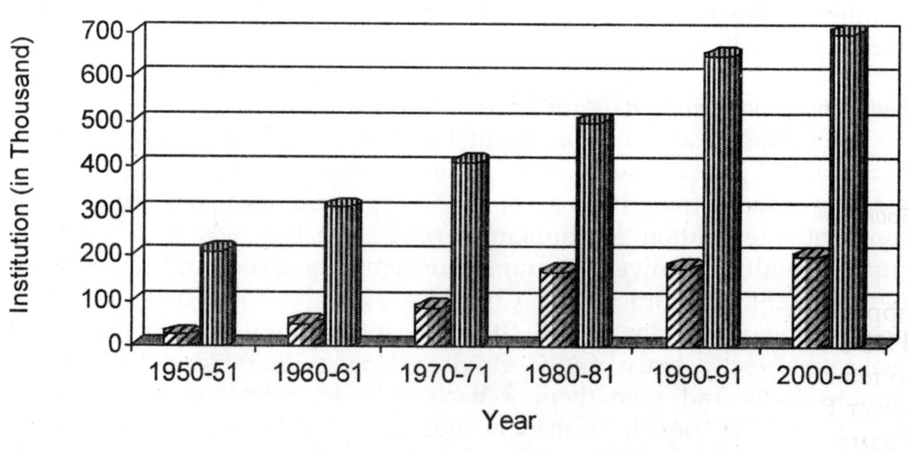

Source: Ministry of HRD, Towards Education For All, 2002

Enrolment Trends

Considerable progress has been made in enrolment at primary and upper primary levels of education. Enrolment at primary level increased from 19.16 million in 1950-51 to 113.8 million in 2000-01. Compared to primary level, the growth in enrolment at the upper primary level has been much more impressive and substantial although not adequate to reach the goal of universal enrolment of children up to the age of 14 as enjoined by the Constitution of India. From a 3.12 million in 1950-51, enrolment at upper primary level increased to 42.8 million in 2000-2001, indicating a 13.7 times increase as against six times at the primary level (See Figure 12.2).

FIG. 12.2

Growth of School Enrolment, 1950-51 to 2000-2001

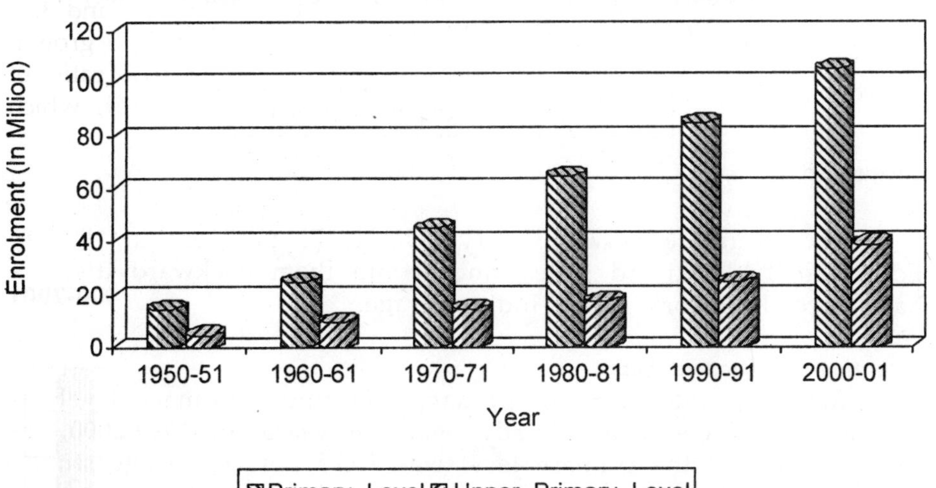

Source: *Ibid*.

The percentage share of girls to total enrolment, both at primary and upper primary levels, has increased considerably and consistently between 1950-51 (28.1 per cent) and 2000-2001 (43.7 per cent). However, girls' share to total enrolment at the upper primary level (40.9 per cent) continues to be lower than their share at the primary level (43.7 per cent) in 2000-2001 (See Figure 12.3).

The Gross Enrolment Ratio (GER) at primary and upper primary levels improved significantly between 1950-51 and 2000-2001. The boys-girls differential in GER at the primary and upper primary levels has declined significantly from 28.5 and 29.6 percentage points in 2000-2001. The Net Enrolment Ratio (NER) for boys and girls was 78 per cent and 64 per cent respectively at primary level in 1997-98 (See Figure 12.4).

FIG. 12.3

Share of Girls' Enrolment to Total Enrolment, 1950-51 to 2001

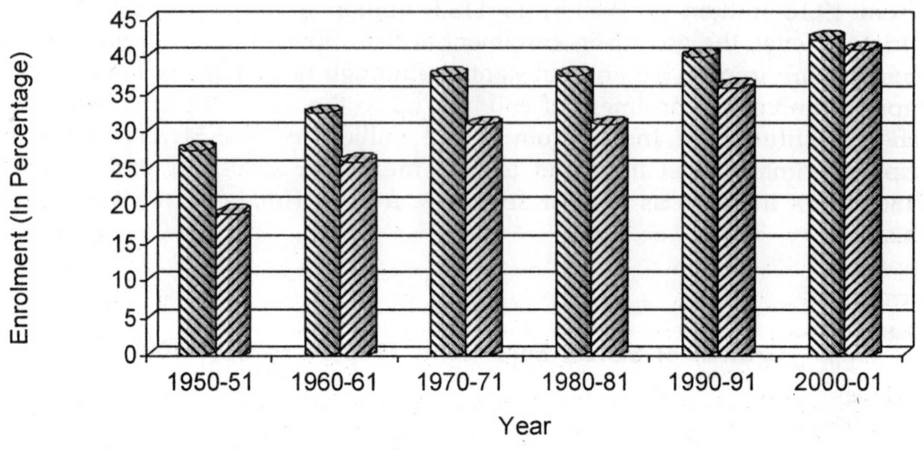

Source: Ibid.

The overall NER at primary level is 71 per cent in 1997-98. Educationally backward states, and within them backward districts, have lower NER than the all-India average.

Retention and Dropout Rates

Retention rates at both primary and upper primary levels of education improved substantially over the years. In 1999-2000, the retention rate at the primary level was 59.75 per cent, suggesting a dropout rate of 40.25 per cent. The retention rate at the elementary level (Grades I-VIII) was 45.47 per cent, suggesting a dropout rate of 54.53 per cent in 1999-2000. Dropout rates for boys and girls were 39.7 per cent and 41.9 per cent respectively at the primary level and 50.3 per cent and 57.7 per cent at the upper primary level in 2000-2001. In spite of the policy of no detention up to Grade V, a large number of children continue to repeat grades, though sex differential in their repetition rate is almost negligible.

Gender and Regional Disparities

Since education influences equity, it is important to ensure that educational provisions are equitably distributed. Primary education, being the entry level, not only covers the largest number of children but the equity in access at this level also influences access to further levels of education. Since primary education is publicly provided in India, its distribution is reflected in the policies followed by the government from time to time. Although considerable progress has been made, gender and regional disparities continue to persist. They present a major challenge for planning the provision of basic education for all.

From 1990 onwards, the policy response to address issues related to regional, social and gender disparities is through targeting. In the effort to ensure equality between women and men, India recognizes the importance of gender mainstreaming, i.e., empowerment, accountability and integration. Besides political will, the effort is to incorporate a gender perspective into the planning process, particularly those related to development planning and planning for human resource development. This gender perspective has been integrated into analysis of progress, appraisal, implementation, monitoring and evaluation policies, and formulation of programmes and projects aimed at providing basic education for all.[3]

Let us now examine about School Education in Haryana in State of India as Union:

The State of Haryana was carved out of Punjab in November 1966-67. It has a total population of 210.83 lacs in the 2001 out of which rural population is 71 per cent. It has a density 477 and literacy rate of 68.59 per cent. It has 4 Divisions, 19 Districts, 47 Sub-Divisions, 67 Tashils, 45 Sub-Tashils, 116 Blocks, 106 Towns – 6,955 villages, out of which 6781 are inhabitated villages (Census 2001).

FIG. 12.4

Gross Enrolment Ratio at Primary and Upper Primary Levels, 1950-51 to 2000-2001

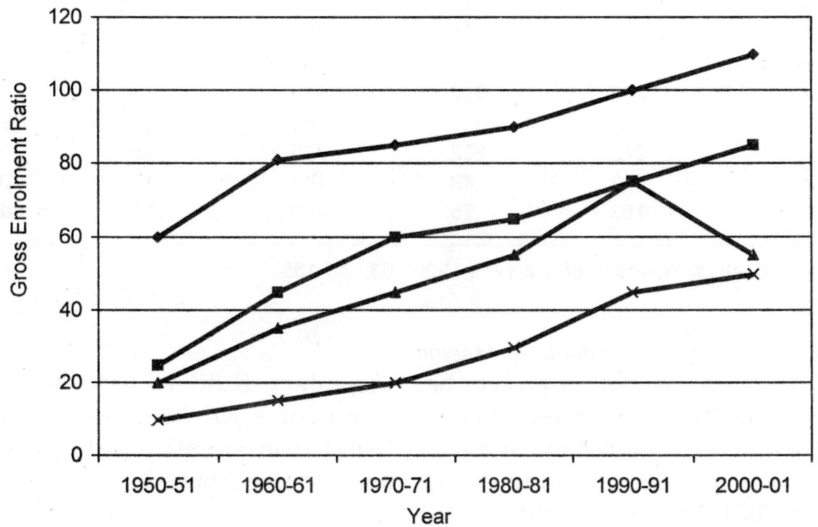

Source: *Ibid.*

TABLE 12.1

Classification of Recognized High/Senior Secondary Schools by Management in Haryana

Year/District	*Government*	*Non-Government*	*For Boys*	*For Girls*	*Total*
1966-67	440	157	488	109	597
1970-71	797	178	811	164	975
1975-76	907	222	931	198	1,129
1980-81	1,226	247	1,228	245	1,473
1985-86	1,657	289	1,643	303	1,946
1990-91	1,944	412	2,001	355	2,356
1995-96	2,345	653	2,547	451	2,998
1999-00	2,502	1,413	3,517	398	3,915
2000-01	2,620	1,518	3,631	507	4,138
2001-02	2,677	1,817	3,973	521	4,494
Ambala	125	47	154	18	172
Panchkula	50	37	81	6	87
Yamunanagar	88	93	165	16	181
Kurukshetra	82	62	135	9	144
Kaithal	118	37	135	20	155
Karnal	153	54	184	23	207
Panipat	89	44	106	27	133
Sonipat	190	128	275	43	318
Rohtak	137	169	255	51	306
Jhajjar	140	122	228	34	262
Faridabad	161	242	386	17	403
Gurgaon	156	73	200	29	229
Rewari	110	85	186	9	195
Mahendragarh	132	20	130	22	152
Bhiwani	260	230	419	71	490
Jind	181	118	257	42	299
Hisar	242	132	325	49	374
Fatehabad	110	49	142	17	159
Sirsa	153	75	210	18	228

Source: Statistical Abstract of Haryana, 2002-03, p. 135.

Status of schools and students in Haryana

The number of High/Higher Secondary Schools has increased from 597 in the year 1966-67 (440 Government + 157 Non-Government) to 4994 (2617 Government and 1817 Non-Government) in 2001-02.

The number of middle schools has increase from 735 in 1966-67 to 2170 in 2001-2002. (See Table 12.2)

The number of Primary, Pre-Primary Schools increased from 4,449 in 1966-1967 to 11,235 in 2001-02 (See Table 12.3).

TABLE 12.2

Classification of Recognized Middle Schools by Management in Haryana

Year/District	*Government*	*Non-Government*	*For Boys*	*For Girls*	*Total*
1966-67	704	31	629	106	735
1970-71	730	30	661	99	760
1975-76	742	16	673	85	758
1980-81	848	33	805	76	881
1985-86	1,062	59	990	131	1,121
1990-91	1,249	150	1,231	168	1,399
1995-96	1,194	305	1,327	172	1,499
1999-00	1,192	603	1,620	175	1,795
2000-01	1,211	676	1,706	181	1,887
2001-02	1,243	927	1,976	194	2,170
Ambala	46	11	51	6	57
Panchkula	40	8	47	1	48
Yamunanagar	54	69	120	3	123
Kurukshetra	73	21	88	6	94
Kaithal	31	41	69	3	72
Karnal	54	48	101	1	102
Panipat	41	33	66	8	74
Sonipat	74	54	112	16	128
Rohtak	33	26	49	10	59
Jhajjar	53	56	101	8	109
Faridabad	69	255	316	8	324
Gurgaon	105	75	165	15	180
Rewari	74	43	104	13	117
Mahendragarh	79	20	89	10	99
Bhiwani	95	49	126	18	144
Jind	72	40	91	21	112
Hisar	82	34	87	29	116
Fatehabad	65	10	66	9	75
Sirsa	103	34	128	9	137

Source: *Ibid.*, p. 136.

The number of students in all types of schools increased from 2,98,238 in 1966-67 to 17,11,634 in 2001-02 out of which scheduled castes have increased from 15,305 in 1966-67 to 3,79,472 in 2001-02 (See Table 12.4)

The total numbers of Teachers in all types of schools have increased from 40,417 in 1966-67 to 1,21,850 in 2001-02 (See Table 12.5).

The total expenditure incurred on Education in Schools has increased from 27,725 lacs to 38429.51 lacs in 2001-02 (See Table 12.6).

The teacher population ratio has increased from 18 in 1966-1967 to 19 in 2001-02, with a peak of 46 in 1990-91 (See Table 12.7).

TABLE 12.3

Classification of Recognized Primary (Including Pre-Primary/Balwari) Schools by Management in Haryana

Year/District	*Government*	*Non-Government*	*For Boys*	*For Girls*	*Total*
1966-67	4,344	105	4,192	257	4,449
1970-71	4,106	101	4,071	136	4,207
1975-76	5,075	81	4,892	264	5,156
1980-81	4,896	65	4,738	223	4,961
1985-86	5,018	87	4,557	548	5,105
1990-91	4,969	167	4,398	738	5,136
1995-96	5,321	180	4,451	1,050	5,501
1999-00	8,650	1,937	8,904	1,683	10,587
2000-01	8,650	2,390	9,381	1,659	11,040
2001-02	8,648	2,587	9,581	1,654	11,235
Ambala	504	78	502	80	582
Panchkula	224	61	256	29	285
Yamunanagar	492	51	500	43	543
Kurukshetra	476	84	500	60	560
Kaithal	348	114	384	78	462
Karnal	518	88	528	78	606
Panipat	242	59	252	49	301
Sonipat	460	212	565	107	672
Rohtak	240	139	291	88	379
Jhajjar	334	226	487	73	560
Faridabad	595	479	972	102	1,074
Gurgaon	802	103	750	155	905
Rewari	442	92	496	38	534
Mahendragarh	510	247	664	93	757
Bhiwani	637	304	825	116	941
Jind	465	132	448	149	597
Hisar	483	67	418	132	550
Fatehabad	348	5	307	46	353
Sirsa	528	46	436	138	574

Source: *Ibid.*, p. 137.

We have selected 50 schools in District Kaithal in Haryana to study the role of schools in Health Education. Schools are the key place to develop the mind and body of students. Based upon observation discussion with students and teachers, we mention the following problems and solutions.

TABLE 12.4

Number of Scholars in Recognized Schools in Haryana

Year/District	High/Senior Secondary/ Navodya Schools			Middle Schools			Primary/Pre-Primary Schools			Grand Total		
	Total	Boys	Girls	Total	Boys	Girls	Total	Boys	Girls	Total	Boys	Girls
1966-67	376080	286475	89605	250673	183043	67630	354764	393761	141003	1161517	863279	298238
1970-71	603396	452939	150457	245137	176703	68434	536257	386909	149348	1384790	1016551	368239
1975-76	764756	562387	202369	257983	183591	74392	659121	447692	211429	1681860	1193670	488190
1980-81	1010236	718831	291405	296027	205067	90960	598032	388175	209857	1904295	1312073	592222
1985-86	1338511	906663	431848	381174	234611	146563	694290	399432	294858	2413975	1540706	873269
1990-91	1552643	994286	558357	547105	307877	239228	784637	418887	365750	2884385	1721050	1163335
1995-96	1819148	1095605	723543	482388	263019	219369	826720	405372	421348	3128256	1763996	1364260
1999-00	1483623	867888	615735	180309	98944	81365	2083201	1099928	983273	3747133	2066760	1680737
2000-01	1576571	920408	656136	194823	105820	89003	2019795	1064811	954984	3791189	2091039	1700150
2001-02	1672264	971385	700879	178071	97048	81023	1971574	1041842	929732	3821909	2110275	1711634
Ambala	88942	45784	43158	6974	4309	2665	75845	39508	36337	171761	89601	82160
Panchkula	32152	17961	14191	3234	1729	1505	35150	19280	15870	70536	38970	31566
Yamunanagar	78232	42352	35880	6677	3702	2975	77333	40609	36724	162242	86663	75579
Kurukshetra	60762	34605	26157	8426	4222	4204	79666	43086	36580	148854	81913	66941
Kaithal	67526	40072	27454	8415	4877	3538	103527	55100	48427	179468	100049	79419
Karnal	99713	57377	42336	7669	4307	3362	106621	56171	50450	214003	117855	96148
Panipat	61403	34488	26915	6635	3357	3278	75035	38264	36771	143073	76109	66964
Sonipat	127582	77558	50024	17024	8604	8420	127633	64516	63117	272239	150678	121561
Rohtak	94564	52956	41608	5576	2651	2925	95919	48978	46941	196059	104585	91474
Jhajjar	89780	49461	40319	7512	3878	3634	88872	45548	43324	186164	98887	87277
Faridabad	163935	98781	65154	10096	5538	4558	196843	105386	91457	370874	209705	161169
Gurgaon	102939	61182	41757	13245	8791	4454	174469	103839	70630	290653	173812	116841
Rewari	66099	36093	30006	9927	4719	5208	68978	35027	33951	145004	75839	69165
Mahendragarh	69372	39037	30335	8479	4257	4222	96980	50078	46902	174831	93372	81459
Bhiwani	132434	81131	50303	20853	11574	9279	152330	77971	74359	305617	170676	134941
Jind	91563	55498	36065	11904	6335	5569	137396	72931	64465	240863	134764	106099
Hisar	123008	75034	47974	6994	3793	3201	118296	61161	57135	248298	139988	108310
Fatehabad	46542	28033	18509	6613	3671	2942	60248	31582	28666	113403	63286	50117
Sirsa	75716	43982	31734	11818	6734	5084	100433	52807	47626	187967	103523	84444

R = Revised.
P = Provisional.
Source: *Ibid.*, pp. 138-39.

TABLE 12.5

Number of Teachers in Recognized Schools in Haryana according to Type of Institutions

Year/District	High/Senior Secondary/ Navodya Schools			Middle Schools			Primary/Pre-Primary Schools			Grand Total		
	Total	Boys	Girls	Total	Boys	Girls	Total	Boys	Girls	Total	Boys	Girls
1970-71*	14298	5083	19381	5718	2240	7958	9634	3444	13078	29650	10767	40717
1975-76*	16261	7122	23383	5843	2464	8307	11707	5184	16891	33811	14770	48581
1980-81*	21889	9810	31699	5882	2851	8733	10493	4587	15080	38264	17248	55512
1985-86	25980	14963	40943	6621	4126	10747	9582	5995	15577	42183	25084	67267
1990-91	27463	17685	45148	7382	4797	12179	12118	8050	20168	46963	30532	77495
1995-96	32670	23893	56563	8057	5026	13083	95543	8398	17941	50270	37317	87587
1999-00	31818	23486	55304	5459	2744	8203	24284	23915	48199	61561	50145	111706
2000-01	33234	24245	57479	5562	2834	8396	24058	24405	48463	62854	51484	114338
2001-02	36507	26348	62855	5747	2953	8700	25372	24923	50295	67626	54224	121850
Ambala	1407	1682	3089	130	100	230	499	1515	2014	2036	3297	5333
Panchkula	376	977	1353	77	142	219	193	749	942	646	1868	2514
Yamunanagar	1290	1190	2480	230	90	320	872	1405	2277	2392	2685	5077
Kurukshetra	1250	1024	2274	260	160	420	965	1229	2194	2475	2413	4888
Kaithal	1286	630	1916	196	146	342	1262	792	2054	2744	1568	4312
Karnal	1801	1545	3346	267	167	434	1174	1188	2362	3242	2900	6142
Panipat	1162	903	2065	217	103	320	805	880	1685	2184	1886	4070
Sonipat	2978	2110	5088	407	273	680	1536	1918	3454	4921	4301	9222
Rohtak	1906	2184	4090	224	161	385	967	1694	2661	3097	4039	7136
Jhajjar	2408	1463	3871	233	174	407	1563	1815	3378	4204	3452	7656
Faridabad	3549	3703	7252	336	225	561	2617	2350	4967	6502	6278	12780
Gurgaon	1931	1671	3602	430	180	610	1589	2007	3596	3950	3858	7808
Rewari	1485	538	2023	277	108	385	1322	778	2100	3084	1424	4508
Mahendragarh	2028	419	2447	320	56	376	2105	673	2778	4453	1148	5601
Bhiwani	3868	1682	5550	875	345	1220	2356	2061	4417	7099	4088	11187
Jind	2284	115	3399	422	152	574	2040	1150	3190	4746	2417	7163
Hisar	2950	1800	4750	330	160	490	1518	1215	2733	4798	3175	7973
Fatehabad	973	569	1542	189	74	263	760	465	1225	1922	1108	3030
Sirsa	1575	1143	2718	327	137	464	1229	1039	2268	3131	2319	5450

* Teachers of pre-primary Schools not included.

Source: *Ibid.*, pp. 142-43.

TABLE 12.6

Expenditure Incurred on Educational Institutions by Type of Education in Haryana

Year	*Higher Education*	*Primary Education*	*Secondary Education*	*Total*
1966-67	22.25	86.97	168.03	277.25
1970-71	109.43	383.62	752.67	1245.72
1975-76	328.60	1441.63	1430.72	3200.95
1980-81	1022.84	2697.62	2814.95	6535.41
1985-86	1982.75	5864.43	5953.13	13800.31
1986-87	2215.13	5926.18	6395.51	14536.82
1987-88	3330.07	8460.88	9304.22	21095.17
1988-89	4007.46	8673.89	8883.06	21564.41
1989-90	5329.71	10899.80	12633.51	28863.02
1990-91	5093.00	13369.00	12321.00	30783.00
1991-92	5847.73	15243.49	13263.94	34355.16
1992-93	6476.88	11356.89	23236.90	41070.67
1993-94	7340.83	11990.27	24652.01	43983.11
1994-95	7935.89	13756.95	28370.78	50063.62
1995-96	10045.38	16571.27	34406.46	61023.11
1996-97	10650.19	20603.98	29229.66	70483.83
1997-98	12634.67	21864.38	45337.26	79836.31
1998-99	13135.86	25788.02	77144.98	116068.86
1999-00	16098.86	31537.91	67578.08	11521.85
2000-01	23177.54	37515.76	69172.87	129866.17
2000-02 (R)	22258.63	39175.28	79234.72	140668.63
2002-03	20008.29	41232.08	77189.14	138429.51

R = Revised.
Source: *Ibid*., p. 146.

Basic Education for Rural Areas

Catalyst for National Development

Education and literacy constitute the two key factors for human development of any country. Through education, learning and skill formation, people can become much more productive over a period of time, which greatly contributes to the process of economic expansion, and ultimately nation-building. Improvements in educational attainments have invariably been accompanied by improvements in health and longevity of population and also in their economic improvement. The productive benefits from education in rural areas have been particularly noticeable. According to the National Human Development Report, 2001, studies concerning 31 countries concluded that if a farmer had completed four years of elementary education, his/her productivity was 8.5 percent higher than that of a farmer who had no education at all. Likewise, it has

TABLE 12.7

Teacher-Pupil Ratio

Year/District	*Primary*	*Middle*	*High*	*Senior Secondary*
1966-67	43	30	—	18
1970-71	43	30	—	17
1975-76	39	32	—	21
1980-81	41	32	—	17
1985-86	46	33	—	17
1990-91	46	36	20	46
1995-96	47	35	18	15
1999-00	43	32	20	24
2000-01	42	32	22	21
2001-02	39	33	22	22
Ambala	38	42	19	19
Panchkula	37	29	19	15
Yamunanagar	34	33	24	30
Kurukshetra	36	33	22	24
Kaithal	50	46	23	24
Karnal	45	34	22	21
Panipat	44	34	18	34
Sonipat	37	32	25	20
Rohtak	36	24	19	22
Jhajjar	26	33	15	21
Faridabad	40	25	20	19
Gurgaon	49	32	18	26
Rewari	33	34	25	23
Mahendragarh	35	35	23	22
Bhiwani	34	37	21	17
Jind	43	33	18	21
Hisar	43	29	23	21
Fatehabad	49	33	21	20
Sirsa	44	29	20	28

Source: *Ibid*., p. 147.

been conclusively proved that adoption and spread of green revolution in the country was faster among the educated farmers. The poor countries get much higher rates of return than the rich countries from investing in education. In the case of India, returns to women's education exceeded that of man at middle, secondary and higher secondary levels. For rural areas, there were higher returns for primary and secondary levels as well as for technical diplomas.

Despite a clear acknowledgement of the contribution that education and literacy can make to the economic development and social well-being of the people, of late there has been a growing realization that India's performance in the educational sector has been rather disappointing. The

Approach Paper to the Tenth Five Year Plan says: Our performance in the field of education is one of the most disappointing development strategy. Out of approximately 2000 million children in the age group 6-14 years, only 120 million are in schools and net attendance in the primary level is only 66% of enrolment. This is completely unacceptable and the Tenth Plan should aim at a radical transformation in this situation. Education for all must be one of the primary objectives of the Tenth Plan.

Even after 50 years of planned in the education sector, nearly one-third of the population or close to 300 million persons in the age group 7 years and above are illiterate. There are critical gaps in the availability of infrastructural facilities and qualitative aspects of education including teachers' training, educational curriculum, equipments and training materials, particularly in the publicity funded schooling system of the country[4].

Since, environmental protection and conservation is very important for the promotion of sustainable development; the role of environment education, research and training assume considerable significance to create public awareness and their participation in this context today. Now, the people throughout the world asking their rights to have a clean environment through various environment movements and the political affiliations like Green Party etc., which are emerging in Europe; whereas in India, there is still a lot to do. It has become a challenge for us to get familiar with our environment issues and contribute collectively for improving our quality of life. This can only be possible through imparting both the formal and informal environment education to each of us such as not only the children, young, adult, or old, but also the women and tribals.

On 22nd April, 2004; Hon'ble Supreme Court approved the model syllabus for environment education, prepared by NCERT; which the Court had directed to make environment studies a compulsory subject up to senior secondary level; in schools. A two-judge bench of Justice N. Santosh Hegde and Justice B.P. Singh has also appointed NCERT as a nodal agency to monitor the implementation of the environment; education up to Class XII. This model syllabus took shape after the NCERT consulted more than 500 institutions, state governments, Central Pollution Control Board, individual experts and NGOs. For the students of Classes I to VIII, the subject will be part of their Social Science subject and students of Classes IX to XII would study environment as an additional subject for which separate marks will be awarded to them. The bench noted that no state government had raised any objections on the issues so far. However, state governments can put forward their suggestions regarding implementation of this programme before July 13, 2004. This brings to fruition, more than a decade old public interest crusade by environment lawyer, M.C. Mehta.

Environment has been an area of great concern. The challenge of developing a syllabus cannot be met without the active participation of and consultation with experts, educationists, environmentalists and other stakeholders for laying down a strong foundation on the following issues:

- Scope and dimensions of environment education at elementary, secondary and higher secondary levels of school education.
- Modalities of introducing environment education without increasing curriculum load.
- Environment education as an instrument for inculcating healthy personal and social attitudes towards environment and development.
- Role of community in imparting effective environment education in schools.
- Significant elements of content and process including projects and activities for environment education.
- Strategies of evaluating environment education and its place in public examinations.
- Implications of environment education in teacher education.

The foundation of this understanding needs to be laid as early as possible. One of the critical audiences, where these seeds can be sown are children, those who represent our forthcoming generation and would take over this planet from us. The school system and curriculum are one of the fundamental structures and frameworks within which the segment of school going children can be reached and addressed.[5]

Problems and Solutions

Environmental Degradation – 80 per cent of schools in Haryana are not located in good environment, i.e. either these are located in the houses, market places or such places which are not fit for study and learning. Other 15 per cent though having good environment are not properly maintained showing least concern for environment. Some of the features of school environment are:

(i) The schools look like slums, as there is neither proper cleaning nor white washing. Most of the walls remain wet giving rise to fungus responsible for many diseases. In this way, the health of the children is always at risk. No effort is made either by Government or by teachers or community to improve the school environment causing many health hazards.

(ii) Schools are used by Government to Store Grains when the Government does not find any other place causing many insects, which thrive on grass. These insects remain there even after the grains are removed resulting into many diseases affecting the school children.

(iii) There are small stalls outside the school from where the students buy eatables of very low standards causing many health problems. On personal discussion, it was found that teachers and the community do not try to persuade the students not to eat unhealthy foods and disallow these small stalls.

(iv) Inspite of teaching the importance of plants, we find very few plants and grass in the schools. Plants and flowers are both essential for health as well as aesthetic sense. Teachers do not pay attention for the beautification of schools.

In this way, we find that schools instead of promoting environmental education rather create no interest among children towards environment. We suggest the following to improve the school environment:

(i) The school and its surroundings must be kept clean. Students should be encouraged to participate in cleansing process.

(ii) Students must be encouraged to decorate the schools through good plantations bearing flowers. They must take interest in greening the fields.

(iii) The Government must ensure that school buildings must be maintained properly and these may not be used for any other purpose as these institutions are the creators of future generation with sound body and mind.

(iv) Community in the area must be encouraged to take interest in school activities and see that the school environment remains soothing for run children.

In Ancient India Schools were in deep forests under the guidance of RISHIS or rein as GURUKULS. The purpose was to provide a fragrant environment for the development of the personality of children.

Infrastructure

The school must have the following facilities to allow the students grow healthy:

(a) Playgrounds;
(b) Good Furniture;
(c) Potable Drinking Water;
(d) Urine and Excreta Disposal System; and
(e) Good Canteen.

(a) Playgrounds

75 percent of the schools do not have playgrounds resulting into seditary life causing many health hazards. Where playgrounds exist, they

are not maintained properly. Schools do not pay attention to sports. Children must be engaged in some physical exercises. Sports must be compulsory. It is strange that India does not stand anywhere in the Olympic games. The reason is that there is no place for sports in schools.

(b) Good Furniture

80 percent of schools have outdated furniture not fit for use. How can the students learn when they do not have a place to sit? In addition, the furniture is short causing many students to sit on the unclean floors. It is a matter of great shame that we are not able to provide even good furniture in the 21st century. The Government must look into it and write off the furniture, which is non-usable. Health is affected by bad postures.

(c) Potable Drinking Water

Water is life. Water is responsible for large number of diseases. 80 per cent of schools have no arrangements for potable drinking water. Students use stored water or hand pump water, which is not safe. The Government must ensure safe potable drinking water.

(d) Urinals

Most of the schools have no urinals and latrines forcing the students to ease nearly places causing pollution of environment and spread of diseases. Even the girls have to ease in the open.

Human Excreta Disposal

Human excreta consist of urine and faeces. These two substances have quite different properties.

- **Urine** is basically water and dissolved nutrients. From a health point of view it is reasonably safe, as long as it is not directly deposited in ponds, streams or lakes. In fact, it is of potential value as a fertilizer. Urine is fairly easy to dispose of within a school compound. It can be infiltrated into the ground, evaporated, or collected in a container for use (diluted with water) as a fertilizer.
- **Faeces** consist of water, cellulose fibres, nutrients, bacteria, viruses and parasite eggs. From a health point of view faecal matter is extremely dangerous and many cultures have strong taboos about handling it or cleaning up faecally contaminated environment. It is difficult to dispose of and there are no easy, low-cost methods.[6]

Schools basically have three options for human excreta disposal: drop-and-store, flush-and-discharge, or sanitize-and-refuse.

Canteens

Canteens are non-existent and wherever existent the quality is poor.

School Lack Facilities

A school need be equipped with all the facilities like Playgrounds, Lavatories, Drinking Water, etc. Fifth All-India Survey conducted by NCERT revealed that by 1986, drinking water was available in 46.6 per cent schools, urinals in 15 per cent schools, separate urinals for girls in 4.9 per cent schools, lavatory in 6.4 per cent schools and separate lavatory for girls in 2.9 per cent schools, usable conditions of playground in 34.54 per cent schools. The situation was poor in upper schools also but better than primary schools. How can a child learn without adequate facilities? It is suggested that the Government should not merely aim at expansion but should ensure full facilities to have good impact on the minds of children.

World Health Organization document (WHO School 97.2) gives the following recommendations:

Recommendations to Planners

Existing recommendations concerning minimum standards for space, lighting and sanitation should be followed and a reliable water supply ensured. But given the financial constraints in many countries, some of the recommendations suggested in the past may be unrealistic. In such circumstances the emphasis must be on achievable action. The following recommendations may provide a useful starting point:

- When a new school or additional facilities are being constructed, involve the local community from the earliest stage of site selection and design. If the community does not feel some kind of ownership it is likely that the school will fall into disrepair and be vandalized. An imperfectly designed but well-cared-for school is preferable to an ergonomically designed but neglected school.
- Where relevant and feasible, combine new schools with housing for teachers.
- Dedicate a larger proportion of available resources to maintenance.
- Dedicate more of the construction budget to building (or planting) an adequate perimeter fence.
- Dedicate more of the construction budget to water and sanitation provision.
- Provide incentives for cleanliness (for example, a prize for the cleanest school).
- Facilitate exchange of information between teachers (for example, through newsletters) on a broad range of issues but

including practical experiences of school hygiene. Encourage teachers to visit schools that use innovative techniques.

- Demand and annual audit of the school environment, carried out by the parent-teacher association, followed by an action plan. Share the most innovative action plans with other schools.
- Place more emphasis on following up health education initiatives, to find out why staff and children do not act on what they already know.
- Develop procedures to increase the use of facilities, such as shifts and alternate-day teaching, so that more resources are available for maintenance and teaching materials.
- Encourage high-profile public figures (senior politicians and sports personalities, for example) to support school health campaigns.

Recommendations to Head Teachers

Existing national recommendations concerning health education, nutrition and hygiene should be followed as far as possible. It must be recognized, however, that circumstances may impose many constraints on schools, and that such recommendations will accordingly not always be feasible. Solutions, even partial or temporary solutions, must be developed locally. The following suggestions, used in conjunction with the ideas discussed in Appendices B and C, may offer a way forward.

- Recognize that the priorities are: fencing in the school compound and keeping it free from faecal material and waste; the provision of toilets and urinals and keeping them scrupulously clean; the provision and use of hand washing facilities, and the provision of safe drinking water.
- If an active parent-teacher association does not already exist, create one. Seek out key people in the community who can help with specific activities such as fundraising, plumbing, repairs, carpentry, etc.
- Involve non-teaching staff and parents, as well as teachers, in developing ideas for improving safety and hygiene.
- If the water supply is shared with the general community, look for ways of setting up an independent supply.
- Think creatively about teaching spaces. Do not use a classroom that is dark, airless, too hot or too cold if a lesson could be better conducted outside in the open, in the shade of a tree or in some semi-enclosed space. Think of low-cost ways of creating more external covered spaces.
- Use plants creatively, not just to beautiful and build pride, but also to ensure a secure perimeter fence, to provide privacy for toilets, to supplement nutrition, to modify the microclimate, and to reduce glare in teaching areas.

- Develop daily routines which involve children and parents in health-related activities-for example, bringing water to school, subscribing to a soap fund, clearing waste from the school compound, etc.
- Organize events to raise money for the construction and maintenance of water and sanitation facilities, and to raise awareness of hygiene issues.
- In larger schools, devise incentives schemes such as prizes that encourage teachers to strive for cleanliness.
- Do not be content with just keeping the school clean. Organize events that help children to spread good hygiene behaviour to their homes and the streets.
- If a school is subject to external dangers, such as pollution and dangerous roads, encourage the parent-teacher association to take a lead in campaigning for change.
- Lead from the front. Use the school sanitation facilities yourself and be seen to be washing your hands and cleaning the compound.[7]

CONCLUSION

Developing countries are committed to achieve education for all, and quality education through a decent Educational system from Pre-Primary to Higher Education, virtually within a short span of time. The base of the Pyramid of Educational system is the School education from Pre-Primary to Secondary Education. The School Education lack good administration entailing less output and low quality. Mr. Sher Singh, Former Union Minister of State for Education in his article "Education Sans Quality, Commitment," in the *Daily Tribune*, dated 18.1.1994 rightly senses that School Education in the villages depicts a very disappointing and frustrating picture...there has been quantitative expansion, no doubt, but quantity without quality defeats the very purpose of education, the two have to be handled together. The need is to provide an efficient administration to manage School Education, which can help in mobilization of human and financial resources and generation of necessary changes. Educational administration reforms and improvements need be carried out from time to time to keep the educational system efficient and effective.

The New Policy of Education and POA suggested the following strategy to improve education at Secondary Stage:[8]

- Extending access to secondary education by setting up new schools in the un-served areas and by extending and consolidating the existing facilities, with particular emphasis on ensuring substantially increased enrolment of girls, the SCs and the STs.

- Progressively bringing in the higher secondary stage (and all its equivalents) as a part of the school system in all states.
- Formulating a National Curriculum Framework for the higher secondary stage as well as development of new curricular and instructional packages based on the semester pattern.
- Reviewing and revising the curricula of secondary education (Classes IX and X.)
- Implementing a comprehensive scheme of examination reform.
- Improving considerably the physical and infrastructural facilities in secondary and higher secondary schools.
- Providing for diversity of courses in higher secondary schools.
- Reviewing afresh the existing system of pre-service teacher education of the secondary stage and formulating and implementing an improved teacher education system.
- Institutionalizing in-service teacher training.
- Transforming the role of the Boards of Secondary Education.
- Strengthening the academic institutions and bodies concerned with research and development in the areas of curriculum, instructional materials and equipment for secondary schools.

Schools through their formal and informal teaching can equip the students with health education so that they develop into healthy citizens who can take the country to the heights of glory. Schools are the nurseries for total development of students—Physical, Mental, Social and Spiritual. World Health Organization has also deformed the health in the same way, "Health is a State of Physical, Mental, Social and Spiritual well-being and not merely the absence of disease or physical infirmity."

"Happiness, happiness, happiness
It may be different origin on this earth
But the happiness of being healthy
Is the real happiness"

—*Dashdorjin Natragdorj*

"When health is absent
Wisdom cannot reveal itself
Art cannot manifest
Strength cannot fight
Wealth becomes useless
And Intelligence cannot be applied."

—*Herophilas, C.*, 300 BC.

Notes and References

1. Government of India, Ministry of Education and Social Welfare, Department of Social Welfare, National Plan of Action for International Year of the Child (1979), New Delhi, September, 1978.
2. NPERC, p. 113.
3. Ministry of Human Resource Development, Department of Elementary Education and Literacy, Government of India, Towards Education for all India Moving Ahead, High Level Group Meeting on EFA Abuja, Nigeria, 19th–20th November, 2002, "Current Status", New Delhi, pp. 1-8.
4. V.S. Gupta, Kurukshetra, Issues Confronting Rural Development Process, Significance of Resource Education, Agriculture Transformation Through Natural Resource Management, January 2003, "Basic Education For Rural Areas," pp. 14-15.
5. Srikanta K. Panigrahi, "Environment Education: Need of the Hour", *Yojana,* Vol. 48, No. 6, June 2004, pp. 22, 13.
6. WHO: Primary School Physical Environment and Health, "Technology options for environmental sanitation", pp. 54-55.
7. *Ibid.,* pp. 32-34
8. Programme of Action, 1992, pp. 44-45.

ANNEXURE 12.1

SARVA SHIKSHA ABHIYAN

The Conference of the Education Ministers of the States resolved in 1998 to pursue a holistic and convergent approach for achieving the goal of universal elementary education in a mission mode, within a defined timeframe. As an outcome of the Conference, a Committee of Education Ministers of States under the Chairmanship of the Minister for Human Resource Development was set-up to work out the modalities of pursuing the goal of UEE in the mission mode. The SSA, the first national programme for universal elementary education, has been formulated on the basis of the recommendations of this Committee. Through the SSA, India for the first time, is attempting to translate its commitments into a programme of UEE, which provides for greater democratic participation and community involvement; decentralized planning and management with specific focus on local specific requirements; and needs of the disadvantaged regions, social groups, girls and children in difficult circumstances. The SSA, launched in the year 2000, now covers all the districts of the country.

Major Objectives

The SSA is a major intervention towards achieving the long cherished goal of universalization of elementary education (UEE) through a time bound integrated approach, in partnership with states. The SSA aims to provide useful and quality elementary education to all children of the 6-14 age group by 2010. The specific objectives of the SSA include:

- All children in school, EGS Centre/alternate school/back-to-school camp by 2003;
- All children complete five years of primary schooling by 2007;
- All children complete eight years of schooling by 2010;
- Providing elementary education of satisfactory quality with emphasis on education for life;
- Bridging all gender and social gaps at primary stage by 2007, and at elementary education level by 2010; and
- Universal retention by 2010.

Strategies Central to SSA Convergence

The SSA is conceived as an "umbrella programme" which subsumes all on-going projects, programmes and schemes aimed at developing basic education. A convergent approach will, it is expected, help overcome the problems of coordination between intra-sectoral and inter-sectoral programme initiatives and at the same time will also facilitate effective planning, implementation, monitoring and evaluation of EFA programmes. Convergence between education and development programmes, aimed at poverty alleviation, employment generation, food for work, promotion of household industries and enhancing the quality of life (health, family welfare, availability of drinking water, rural housing, etc.), is being effected. These programmes increase the capacity of households to seek and support education of children.

Institutional Reform

As part of the SSA, institutional reforms are being carried out in states. The states have to make an objective assessment of their existing education system including educational administration, achievement levels in schools, financial issues, decentralization and community ownership, review State Education Acts, rationalization of teacher deployment and recruitment of teachers, monitoring and disadvantaged groups, policy regarding private schools and ECCE. Many states have already effected institutional reforms to improve the delivery system for elementary education.

Community Empowerment

The programme calls for community ownership of schools and interventions through effective decentralization. This is facilitated by involvement of women's groups, Village Education Committee (VEC) members and members of Panchayati Raj Institutions. Local level institutions are expected to undertake training of community leaders and community representatives to enable them to undertake planning, programming and monitoring tasks.

Institutional Capacity Building

National and state level institutions like the National Institute of Educational Planning and Administration (NIEPA), National Council of Educational Research and Training (NCERT), National Council for Teacher Education (NCTE), State Councils of Educational Research and Training (SCERTs), and State Institutes of Educational Management and Training (SIEMATs) have been given capacity building responsibilities since it is realized that improvement in quality requires a sustainable support system for educational planning and management at national, state, district and sub-district levels. Of particular importance is the capacity building of local level institutions for decentralized preparation of curriculum and teaching-learning materials relevant to local contexts.

Improving Mainstream Educational Administration

It calls for improvement of mainstream educational administration by institutional development, infusion of new approaches, and by adoption of cost-effective and efficient methods.

Community-based Monitoring

It is envisaged in the SSA that the educational management

information system (EMIS) will correlate school level data with community-based information from micro-planning and field surveys. For example, every school will have a notice board showing all the grants received by the school and other details. The SSA envisages cooperation between teachers, parents and PRIs, as well as accountability and transparency.

Habitation as a Unit of Planning

The SSA works on a community-based approach to planning with habitation as the lowest unit for planning. Habitation plans developed on the basis of a realistic assessment of community needs will be the basis for formulating district plans. There is emphasis on local relevance in planning and management.

Focus on Education of Girls and Special Groups

Education of girls, especially those belonging to the scheduled castes and scheduled tribes, is one of the principal concerns in SSA. The SSA has a mainstreamed gender approach. Efforts provide for mobilization at the habitation/village/urban slum level; recruitment of female teachers; nutritional support; provision of free textbooks and uniforms; back-to-school camps for adolescent girls; organization and constitution of Mahila Samoohs, etc. There is focus on enhancing participation of children from SC/ST, religious and linguistic minorities, disadvantaged groups and the disabled children in education.

Focus on Quality and Relevance

The SSA lays special thrust on making education at elementary level useful and relevant for children through curriculum revision; introduction of child-centered teaching-learning methods; improvements in educational provisions; teachers' empowerment; value education, etc. Efforts will be made to promote individual and institutional accountability for children's attachments.

Sustainable Financing

The SSA is based on the premise that financing of elementary education has to be sustainable. Long-term perspective on financial partnership between the Central and State governments has, therefore, been proposed.

Focus on Empowerment

The SSA recognizes the critical role of teachers and advocates and emphasizes the need for addressing their professional development needs. Setting up of Block Resource Centres (BRCs) and Cluster Resource Centres (CRCs), recruitment of qualified teachers, opportunities for teacher development through participation in curriculum-related material development, focus on classroom processes, and exposure visits for teachers are some of the strategies for teachers' empowerment.

Support to Non-governmental Organizations

In view of their credibility in the community, non-governmental organizations will be increasingly involved in promoting the goals of education for all. Support will be provided to them for undertaking innovative educational programmes relevant to specific socio-economic and educational situations.

Advocacy, Campaign Approach and Mission Mode

It is recognized in the SSA that mobilizing civil society to participate for the programmes of basic education is essential for achieving the goals of universal elementary education. It is with this perspective that major efforts are being made to use all means, including mass media for advocacy and promotion of SSA activities. Further, in order to reach and involve the common stakeholders, mass campaigns have been launched for creating awareness about educational needs of children, youth and adults, and help them to develop proper appreciation of the role of education in improving the quality of life. It is also evident that programmes in elementary education have to be implemented in a mission mode involving the community in an effective manner through such mechanisms as District Literacy Committees (DLCs), Village Education Committees (VECs) and Parent-Teacher Associations (PTAs). Literacy campaigns have made big strides in this direction.

Management Structure

The central and state governments will together implement the SSA in partnership with local governments and the community. To signify the national priority for elementary education, a National *'Sarva Shiksha Abhiyan Mission'* has been established with the Prime Minister as the Chairperson and the Union Minister of Human Resource Development as the Vice-Chairperson.

States have established State level Implementation Societies for UEE under the Chairmanship of Chief Minister/Education Minister. The SSA does not attempt to disturb existing structures in states and districts, but only tries to bring convergence of efforts. The emphasis is on functional decentralization down to the school level in order to improve community participation. Besides recognizing Panchayati Raj Institutions (PRIs)/Tribal Councils in Scheduled Areas, including the Gram Sabha, the states are being encouraged to enlarge the accountability framework by involving NGOs/teachers, activists/women organizations, etc.

Source: GOI, Ministry of Human Resource Development, India Moving Ahead, Towards Education for All, 2002.

"Basic education links the children, whether of the cities or the villages to all that is best and lasting in India".

—*Mahatma Gandhi*

Annexure 12.2

FUTURE STRATEGIES

Development of basic education has always been a priority area in the five-year plans of India, particularly in the Seventh, Eighth and Ninth Plans. Now, the Planning Commission of India has formulated the Tenth Five-Year Plan (2002-07). The plan indicates the major tasks to be accomplished in the next five years, strategies that will be adopted and financial investments to be made for implementing developmental programmes including those in the education sector. An outlay of Rs. 438.25 billion has been provided for education. Out of this plan outlay, Rs. 300 billion has been allocated for elementary and adult education. The main tasks to be covered in basic education sector during the Tenth Plan period are briefly discussed in this section.

Literacy and Continuing Education

Literacy and continuing education will continue to receive increased attention so as to achieve the goal of complete eradication of illiteracy in the age group 15-35 years and to enable neo-literates to retain, improve and apply the newly acquired literacy skills for improvement of the quality of life. The emphasis will be on consolidation and sustaining of adult education processes through increased participation of NGOs, Panchayati Raj Institutions, youth organizations, teachers and student volunteers.

The focus of adult education programmes will be two-fold. While the post-literacy and continuing education needs of the neo-literates will be taken care of through provision of opportunities for self-directed learning, equivalency programmes, based on open schooling, job-oriented vocational education and skill development programmes, a fresh momentum will be given to basic literacy programmes. This is essential in order to take care of the backlog of illiterates, viz., the drop-outs and left-outs of the literacy campaigns and out-of-school children who constitute new accretions to the adult illiterate population.

Special focus will be on problems of disadvantaged groups like Scheduled Castes and Scheduled Tribes, minority groups and backward regions. During the Tenth Plan period, priority will be given to states having literacy rates below the national average and low female literacy districts. It is proposed that during the first year of Tenth Plan, i.e. 2002-03, fourteen new districts will be covered under Total Literacy Campaign. During the plan period, 166 districts are expected to be covered under Post-Literacy Programme. Under the Continuing Education Programme, it is proposed to cover 400 districts during the Tenth Five Year Plan.

Early Childhood Care and Education (ECCE)

All the community development blocks of the country will be

covered under ICDS/ECCE programmes during the Tenth Five-Year Plan. Some of the important strategies for expansion and quality improvement of ECCE proposed are: creation of a Bureau/Cell for ECCE in the Department of Education, MHRD, to initiate and monitor implementation of programmes, and ensure coordination between related sectors; strengthening of the national resource group for ECCE to carry out research, training, development and extension activities; and creating ECCE expertise in all the States/UTs, particularly in such institutions as the SCERTs, DIETs, BRCs and schools. The operational linkage between ECCE and primary education will be further strengthened through: ensuring coordination of timings and location, based on community appraisal and local micro-planning exercise; inclusion of a school readiness package at the beginning of Class I curriculum, based on local needs, to facilitate entry and adjustment of children who make a direct entry into primary school without any ECCE experience; joint training of primary school teachers and ECCE/ICDS workers/personnel to facilitate better appreciation of the nuances of ECCE—primary education the linkage and need for continuity; and experimentation, on a pilot basis, with innovative and alternative models like an integrated ECCE centre or Bal Kendra comprising ECCE and upgraded unit of early primary level education corresponding to Grades I and II.

Elementary Education

The goal of EFA is to bring all the relevant age group children into the fold of primary education. The revised medium-term targets with respect to elementary education (set forth under the Sarva Shiksha Abhiyan) are that: (i) all 6-year old children will be enrolled in Grade I by the year 2003; (ii) all children in 6-10 age group will be in primary schools or their alternatives (i.e. universal enrolment and retention) by the year 2007; and (iii) all children in 11-13 age group will be enrolled and retained in upper primary schools or their alternatives by the year 2010. It is estimated that, to achieve UPE by 2007, an additional enrolment of 4.69 million boys and 14.71 million girls (over and above the base year enrolment of 1999-2000) will need to be achieved. Thus, during this period enrolment of boys and girls at primary level of education would need to grow at an average annual rate of 1.12 per cent and 4.16 per cent respectively. The required average annual growth rate of total enrolment at primary level is 2.51 per cent during the period 2000-07.

If the goal is to achieve universal elementary education by the year 2010, the target for the Tenth Plan is to enrol an additional 8.4 million boys and 10.96 million girls over and above the enrolment in the base year (i.e. 1999-2000). The required average annual growth rate of enrolment of boys and girls at upper primary level of education will be 4.92 per cent for boys and 8.03 per cent for girls during the Tenth Plan period. Bulk of the children to be enrolled are in a few educationally backward states and within them in some districts. 'Convergence' and 'targeting' are the two major strategies to be adopted during the medium-term plan to address the issues of regional, social and gender disparities in basic education.

The access to basic education of eight years and meaningful participation in education of girls and the disadvantaged segments of the population will receive the highest priority in the development plans. Segmental plans, addressing the problems faced by the un-reached, will be developed and implemented. While establishment of full-time schools in un-served areas will continue to be adopted as a major strategy, alternative modes of delivery non-formal education centres, distance education, open schooling—will be used to provide education in sparsely populated habitations where full-time schooling will neither be economically feasible nor academically viable and for those groups who, because of their situation in life, cannot enrol in regular schools. Whether through full-time schooling or by using alternative delivery modes, children will be enabled to reach the prescribed attainment levels so that their lateral entry to full-time schooling, whenever they so desire, is facilitated. The experience of such innovative programmes like the Education Guarantee Scheme, where community initiatives to establish a school/non-formal education centre are matched by State support will be utilized to design group and community specific educational arrangements. The experiences of non-governmental organizations will help in designing suitable strategies to enhance the participation of communities/localities, yet not covered with educational facilities.

The approach, during the years to come, will be to specifically deal with the question of equity with focus on educational needs of women and girls; scheduled caste and scheduled tribe groups; working children; children with disabilities; children from minority groups; urban disadvantaged children; and educationally backward pockets in different States.

Community Participation and Capacity Building

Community involvement in planning, management and monitoring of educational activities of local benefit is expected to promote 'Education for All'. An important strategy will be to develop micro-planning, school mapping and management capacities of local communities. The capacities of such institutions as the District Institutes of Education and Training, Block and Cluster Resource Centres and State Councils of Educational Research and Training/State Institutes of Education to undertake appropriate and relevant training tasks will be enhanced. Planning and management structures at state, district and sub-district levels will be further strengthened. In the coming years, this will be a major function of NCERT and NIEPA.

Increased Role of NGOs

As a broad policy, the country proposes to promote the role of NGOs at all levels in the social sector with a view to achieving participatory development and unburdening the administration, which is unduly loaded with implementation of development programmes. Enhancing the effectiveness of the roles of NGOs in educational development programmes will follow this approach.

Decentralized Planning and Management

India is a vast country with multiple cultures, languages and religions. There are wide diversities in economic, social and educational situations. Indicators of quality of life in some states like Kerala are closing the gap with the developed countries; some other states, however, carry the burden of wanton illiteracy, poverty, social and economic backwardness, etc. These diversities and regional disparities pose serious challenges to educational planning and management. India is steadily shifting from centralized planning and management to decentralized educational planning and management. The 73rd and 74th amendments to the Indian Constitution have provided an institutional framework for participative planning and management of education at the community level. It is the vision of India that education will increasingly be planned and managed at local levels within the broad parameters of a national vision and goals. To complement the decentralized planning and management, site-based management is being promoted so that each institution can optimize its potential, creating a culture that reverberates the India's Upanishadic wisdom where all both teacher and the student—learn and grow together. The National Institute of Educational Planning and Administration (NIEPA), the apex organization at the national level, is spearheading this new vision of educational management.

It is recognized that planning at the district level has several advantages: (a) it helps in making plan strategies and approach more locally relevant; (b) it promotes participation of local people in the planning process and, therefore, develops better commitment, stake and accountability for its effective implementation; and (c) it helps in addressing the issues of inter-district disparities within the state more effectively. Keeping these factors in view, the country proposes to adopt an integrated approach for planning at the district level for development of elementary education. This approach, it is envisaged will help to identify districts needing more attention and varied types of inputs, thereby tackling the question of equity in an appropriate manner. Movement towards planning at block and cluster and village levels, in partnership with NGOs, will be encouraged and supported.

Promotion of Alternative Delivery Systems

The school education programme has to look beyond the rigid formal framework in a flexible and adaptive fashion. Part-time formal or non-formal education, seasonal learning centres for children of migrant labour, voluntary schools by NGOs, post-primary 'open' learning, the camp approach for adolescent girls, etc., will have to be systematically promoted. The government has revised the non-formal education programme recently. The new programme called 'Education Guarantee Scheme (EGS)/Alternative and Innovative Education (A and IE) will be implemented in the coming years. It provides much needed flexibility in designing educational programmes that are local specific and meet more adequately the educational needs of the community and district groups.

Public and Private Sector Partnership

Even though private initiative has always been a part of the school education endeavour, it is often felt that the country has not been able to fully exploit the potential of the private sector. Possibilities, in this regard, will have to be actively explored. It should be noted that private sector could contribute not only in monetary terms but also in the form of expertise for quality improvement through effective management of the system and development of locally relevant teaching-learning material. More collaborative efforts at institutional levels as well as programme implementation level will be designed in order to expand the profile of private initiative in elementary education.

Quality Improvement

It is recognized that quality improvement has a significant impact not only on enrolment and retention of children in the school but also on the possibilities of further education for increased productivity and exercise of citizenship rights and responsibilities. The tasks of quality improvement will be pursued through improvement in content and process of education; reorientation and strengthening of teacher education, both pre-service and in-service; provision of appropriate infrastructure facilities; focusing on strengthening institutional management processes; promoting institutional accountability for students' attainments and establishing a reliable system of learner assessment. Efforts will be made to strengthen internal management of schools; and to improve the quality of teaching-learning process.

Source: GOI, Ministry of Human Resource Development, India Moving Ahead, Towards Education for All, 2002.

"What is really needed to make democracy function is not knowledge of facts, but right education.

—*Mahatma Gandhi*

ANNEXURE 12.3

HEALTH ASPECTS OF SCHOOL ENVIRONMENT

The physical and mental health of children can be influenced by a range of physical aspects of the school environment. These can be listed as: sanitation (or the lack of it); dirty hands; water quality; the microclimate; indoor air quality; noise; light (both too little and glare as a result of too much light); dangerous structures; inadequate furniture, and a hazardous location.

Added to these is the fact that, for many children, going to school is the first opportunity to mix with people other than close relatives and near neighbours. Consequently, it may represent their first exposure to a range of infectious diseases.

Sanitation

Without sufficient clean and functioning toilets children will defecate in and around the school compound. In such situations the school and its surroundings are likely to become infested with parasitic helminths.

Dirty Hands

The availability of convenient hand washing facilities is as important as safe disposal of urine and faeces. Hepatitis A, diarrhoea caused by *Escherichia coli,* amoebic and bacillary dysentery, cholera and typhoid are among the infectious diseases, which can be spread via the faecal-oral route. Staff and pupils must be able to wash their hands after defecation as well as before eating food.

Contaminated Water

Many of the faecal-oral infections listed above can also spread via contaminated drinking-water. Children dipping their unwashed hands into a shared drinking-water supply is a typical route of contamination. But problems can also arise from water, which is not used for drinking. If rain-water or floodwater is allowed to stand in puddles, the breeding of mosquitoes and other insects may be encouraged, leading to transmission of diseases such as malaria, dengue fever and schistosomiasis. (Similar problems can arise from accumulated waste, which, additionally, may attract flies, rodents and dogs.)

The Microclimate

Microclimate is determined by temperature, humidity, heat radiation and air movement. Details of the relationship between the indoor microclimate and health remain poorly understood. However, it is evidently not good for a child to spend a large part of the day in a cold, damp and poorly ventilated classroom. Poorly nourished and inadequately clothed pupils are particularly vulnerable to acute respiratory infections. Conversely, excessively warm conditions may lead to thermal stress, fatigue, reduced learning capacity and, in extreme cases, heat stroke.

Indoor Air Quality

There is a wide range of potential indoor air pollutants, which may influence the health of schoolchildren. Pollution from heating stoves can lead to chronic respiratory diseases and carcinomas. In a crowded environment, airborne bacteria and viruses can cause cross-infection. Other threats include: rotten matter produced by moulds and fungal growths; fine dust; gaseous and particulate compounds from building materials, and radon gas. Many health problems are associated with these pollutants, including acute respiratory infections and asthma.

Noise

High levels of noise can cause irritation, encourage aggressiveness, reduce physical and mental performance, and cause discomfort and headaches. Exceedingly loud and continual noise can lead to more serious problems. Children with hearing problems, visually impaired children, and children with learning difficulties are particularly dependent on a good acoustic environment.

Light

Bad lighting can affect the well-being of both pupils and staff. Eye-strain is a frequent complaint in classrooms and other teaching spaces where light levels are low, or where glare is excessive. Eye-strain probably largely accounts for the higher prevalence of headaches in the afternoons that has been reported by children and teachers. Poor light conditions can cause children to adopt poor posture, which itself can eventually lead to physical strain.

Dangerous Structures

As well as protecting children and staff from the elements, the structure of a school building is intended to enhance health and well-being. But badly designed or poorly maintained structures may in fact threaten health. Class-rooms often require larger roof spans than traditional domestic buildings for example, and if domestic construction techniques are used for schools, they may prove to be inadequate, particularly in areas prone to earthquakes and typhoons.

On a smaller scale, cracks and inaccessible comers may provide homes for hookworms, mites and jigger fleas, while dampness and poor ventilation may lead to the growth of moulds and fungi. Broken windows, dilapidated steps, exposed nails, the lack of stair rails, missing inspection covers and other such hazards may cause injury.

Inadequate Furniture

With a widespread shortage of furniture in primary schools, many children spend much of their school days seated on possibly damp or contaminated mud floors or cold concrete floors. This can lead to infections from hookworm, urinary tract infections and problems with joints. Moreover, what furniture there may be used excessively. This can lead to overcrowding, with the attendant risk of cross-infection, for example from scabies. And with overuse, furniture may become damaged, causing injury. Classroom furniture may not always be used appropriately. Examples exist of desks designed for very young children (6-8 years) being used by older children (13-15 years) and *vice versa*. This is likely given that children attending primary schools are often above what would be considered normal primary school age. Posture problems and backache can result.

A Hazardous Location

In many cases the most dangerous aspect of a school is its location. When informal urban settlements grow up, the best land is generally taken at the outset for houses. Schools are often built on the least desirable land—for example, on the site of an old waste dump or in areas prone to flooding or subsidence. They are also often located on busy roads, increasing the risk of accidents, or at some distance from the community they are intended to serve. Size constraints at urban sites may result in over-crowding and inadequate space for exercise.

Standard school designs frequently make assumptions about the kind of site available. They require an area of flat land with specific minimum dimensions. Often, such a site can only be found a long way from where people actually live. This results in young children having to walk long distances, sometimes in the rain, sometimes along busy roads, all of which can increase the hazards they face.

While little can be done about the location of an existing school, this issue should be considered by planners and community groups at an early stage in the development of a new school. The availability of water, for example, must be borne in mind. Moreover, even in the case of existing schools, improvements are possible. For example: footpaths and bridges can be built for getting to the school; hazardous waste can be removed from the site; efforts can be made to seal-off the school from adjacent hazards such as rivers and gullies.

Prioritizing the Problems

The numerous correlations between elements of the physical environment and child health can be listed. But there are four principles, which must be considered as priority issues. These are:

- Keeping the compound clean of faecal material and waste;
- Providing or restoring toilets and keeping them clean;

- Providing convenient hand washing facilities and encouraging their use; and
- Providing safe drinking water.

If these four objectives can be achieved and sustained, schools will have a good foundation from which to start tackling other health problems.

Source: WHO: Primary School Physical Environment and Health: WHO Global School Health Initiative, Geneva 1997, pp. 15-18.

ANNEXURE 12.4

OBJECTIVE FOR A HEALTHY SCHOOL ENVIRONMENT

The previous chapter outlines the potential health hazards of the school environment. This chapter describes some key objectives for tackling them. First of all, though, it must be stressed that there is no simple technical fix for achieving a healthy school environment. A global manual on healthy school construction would not be useful. Even locally developed manuals are of limited value if they try to impose standard solutions. It is far more useful for local decision-makers—primarily community leaders and teachers - to understand a set of common broad objectives and principles.

Commitment and Motivation

There is no doubt that the single most important factor in achieving a healthy school environment is the presence of committed and informed people. The emphasis should be on the commitment: there is plenty of evidence that information is not enough. People are often well aware of the health risks and the theories of contamination but do not act on that knowledge. People who are not committed will always find reasons for not acting, while a committed person will seek ways around apparently insuperable problems. If necessary, committed people will also seek out information.

There is no simple formula for making people committed. However, recognizing and valuing people's efforts, and ensuring that there is sufficient scope for their own decision-making and creativity can go a long way towards encouraging sustained commitment. This point is particularly important since, again, it argues against standard designs. There are many manuals for school design, which prescribe every detail, down to the layout of pin boards and the arrangement of storerooms. Such advice may be technically valid but if teachers on the ground feel deprived of any opportunity for shaping their own environment, the end result is likely to be disappointing. The essence of commitment is a person's belief that his or her efforts can make a difference. If not, they will feel there is little reason to fight for change.

In at least one South American and one South-east Asian country it is well known among the locals that unless teachers can pay a sufficiently high bribe they are likely to be posted by officials in the Ministry of Education to a school distant from their own community. The immediate result is high absenteeism among staff, which damages their pupil's education. More profound, however, is the lack of commitment and involvement, which many of the teachers feel regarding their schools. Their main concern is to find ways of being posted to another school nearer to home. Unless these kinds of underlying issues are tackled, proposals for physical changes to this or that detail of the school environment will count for little.

As well as encouraging the commitment of local people, seven other basic objectives can be proposed which can be achieved by taking simple practical measures and which, once achieved, will go a long way towards creating a healthier school environment. These objectives are: a faecal-free environment; safe drinking-water; convenient hand washing arrangements; well-lit learning spaces; protection from the elements; structural safety; and adequate cleaning and maintenance.

A Faecal-free Environment

Evidently, faeces on the ground will be a threat to health. The point to be made, though, is that staff, pupils, parents and governing bodies of schools should consider the whole school environment, not just classrooms. Ideally, concern should extend to the streets and fields between home and school, and to the pupils' homes. But at the very least, it must include the school compound.

Success in eliminating faecal material from a school compound is dependent on:

- Informed and responsible pupils;
- Supervision of young children;
- A compound fence, and vigilance, to stop animals and outsiders from defecating in the compound;
- Toilets, which are conveniently located, reliable, clean, reasonably odour-free and reasonably private; and
- Some technical options for improving toilet facilities are described.

Safe Drinking Water

The conditions required for clean water are well known, but often they are unachievable. Recommendations to boil all water are of little value in a society where fuel is expensive and scarce. Advice about deep boreholes is of no use to a resource-starved school. Rather than concen-trating on the source of the water, achievable measures are often those concerned with the handling of available water.

Frequently, water from a tap or pump is reasonably clean, but has become contaminated by the time it reaches someone's mouth. For example, if people are dipping their hands into a water container to scoop up water in a cup, it is likely that they are contaminating it with germs from their hands. Simply providing a ladle can be an extremely low-cost solution. Similarly, in some circumstances, covering the water container with a lid may be an important step. In some schools in Viet Nam, each class has its own large kettle and is responsible for the cleanliness of its own water.

If the tap or water source is distant from the toilet, people are unlikely to use it. If water is stored in a relatively high-sided tank it may be awkward for younger children to use. Similarly, wells with high sides may discourage people from drawing water. Taps or water tanks, which are constantly surrounded by mud, may also be discouraging. Hand pumps may be too stiff for a small child to use, or it may be difficult to pump and wash one's hands at the same time.

A number of studies have shown that the use of soap, earth or ash for hand washing can make a significant difference to hygiene levels. Moreover, as well as its purely functional value, the provision of soap can become a means of focusing attention on the issue of hand washing. For example, teachers may need to start a small fund to raise money from parents to pay for a regular supply of soap. This in itself can help to raise awareness among both pupils and parents.

Well-lit Learning Spaces

In many places, electric lighting is either prohibitively expensive or simply unavailable. Many teaching spaces, therefore, depend on natural light. Good lighting is especially important if resources for school books are limited and learning depends on the children seeing the black-board clearly.

Frequently, climate conditions lead to poor lighting: either too little light or excessive glare. For example, in hot and humid climates people try to increase ventilation, which may result in a teacher standing against the glare from an open window. Where there is a lot of wind-blown dust, or the climate is cold, the tendency is to build small windows, resulting in dark classrooms.

However, the apparently obvious solution of having large windows running the length of the room is often inappropriate. In many places, glass is expensive, so it is most unlikely to be replaced when broken. It may even be stolen. On the other hand, if the windows are unglazed, problems of security and of exposure to the elements will arise. Even in areas commonly thought of as hot, there are often times of the year when cold is a problem. A class-room with open sides can be a miserable environment if there is a cold wind.

An alternative to large windows is the perforated screen wall. This is a solid masonry wall punctured by numerous closely spaced holes through which light can filter. If the wall is built of bricks the perforation effect can be achieved by simply leaving spaces between the bricks at regular intervals. If it is made of concrete (or earth-cement) blocks, special moulds can be used to produce blocks with decorative holes. If the inside surfaces of the holes are made light in colour, either by painting them or by using plain white cement for the blocks, the amount of light reflected through the holes is considerably increased. Where masonry is not used for construction, or where there are existing large window openings, other kinds of screens can be created, for example, using horizontal bamboos.

The advantages of a perforated screen wall are that it provides security and a relatively even distribution of light. The disadvantages are that it does not protect against wind, cold and dust, and classrooms (particularly if large) can remain rather dark unless the internal walls are also light-coloured. Care must also be taken to orient the building so that direct sunlight does not penetrate the screen wall, since this will almost certainly lead to glare.

In cold climates, where small windows are necessary to reduce heat loss, it makes sense to maximize the light, which can enter through a small opening. A roof light lets in considerably more light than a window of equal size in a wall. It can also help to bring more light into the centre of the room, which is often poorly served by wall windows. However, care has to be taken to avoid direct sunlight falling onto desks. With any window, the light entering can be increased to a surprising extent simply by painting white the surfaces of the reveal (the hole in the wall) and the window frame.

A school in the Gambia with thick mud walls and small windows had a corrugated iron roof. To overcome the inevitably poor lighting the teachers removed the sheet of corrugated iron immediately over the blackboard and relaid it, weighed down with stones, slightly to one side of its original position. This left a narrow slit, about 10 cm wide, running down the slope of the roof. The result was a strip of daylight around the teacher and over the black-board. When direct sun came through the slit there was some glare, but on the whole the arrangement gave satisfactory results. During the short rainy season the roofing sheet was returned to its original position.

Clearly, such a solution is not ideal. However, this example illustrates that it is possible to take low- or no-cost actions, which can significantly improve conditions for both pupils and teachers.

It is also important to make the best use of any light once it has entered the room. Untreated mud-and-dung plaster of the walls, for instance, will make a room relatively dark. The underside of a thatched roof will absorb a lot of light. The level of light can be dramatically increased with a light-coloured ceiling and light paint or lime-wash on the walls. These can also reduce glare by ensuring that light is reflected from all directions. In addition, making sure that the blackboard is of reasonable quality and regularly repainted can be a relatively cheap way of mitigating the impact of poor lighting.

Protection from the Elements

It goes without saying that a school building should protect its occupants from rain, wind, sun and snow. But it need only offer as much protection as necessary. A classroom of a standard required in a northern country with a cold and wet climate may be quite unnecessary and in fact inappropriate in a tropical country. The protection of a tree or a veranda may be all that is needed and often preferable to an enclosed space, which reduces light and ventilation.

In many cases the real requirement is simply for a store-room in which teaching materials can be protected from the weather and secured against thieves. In other cases, the best way of affording protection from the elements may be to organize school holidays so that they coincide with the rainiest, coldest or hottest season, as the case may be.

Schools should be designed to prevent extremes of temperature inside classrooms. However, is not uncommon for schools to be designed with large exposed windows. which can result in overheating. Classrooms either become unusable or else expensive air conditioners have to be employed. Air conditioners, apart from being a luxury that few countries can really afford, can themselves be a threat to health: they can be a home to mosquitoes and harmful bacteria, they can increase noise, and they can expose children to extremes of hot and cold as they pass from outside to indoors. One simple way to reduce overheating is to plant shade trees and climbers outside large windows.

Structural Safety

It is obvious that the health of children will not be enhanced if the school building falls down. This is more the concern of engineers and builders, but leaching staff should check their school rooms on an occasional basis for cracks in the main structure. Of more immediate importance are small-scale structural issues: doors falling off their hinges, rotten floor-boards, broken glass, exposed nails and broken paving stones. While large-scale structural problems are likely to require significant amounts of money to solve, a simple but systematic safety audit can reveal hazards which have simple remedies.

At the very least, every school should possess a hammer. This basic tool can be used to knock back exposed nails and clear away fragments of glass from a frame when a window has been broken. Such a detail may seem trivial, but in many schools, nails and shards of glass are a constant threat and a cause of injury to children. Before becoming involved in the details of, say, earthquake- and typhoon-resistant construction, basic ways to make existing schools safer should be sought.

In many societies, communal work sessions are traditional. If parents can be persuaded to work together, even just for one day once a year, then such a labour force, which will inevitably include people with specialist skills, can tackle much of the heavier structural repair work. Working together, parents can accomplish tasks such as clearing away broken concrete, rebuilding eroded steps, replacing rotten fence posts, relaying roofing sheets and repairing furniture and play equipment.

Structural safety plays an important part in good sanitation. Children are often scared that a toilet may collapse, sometimes with good reason. A toilet's squat platform or slab should be well made and protected from the elements. It must also be clearly seen to be safe. The interior of a pit toilet should generally be lined to prevent its sides from collapsing. Surface water from rain should be directed in channels away from toilets, to avoid any erosion of the pit.

Adequate Cleaning and Maintenance

Problems of structural safety can often be avoided through careful routine maintenance. Dealing with broken roof tiles or undermined foundations straightaway, as soon as they occur, minimizes the need for expensive structural repairs later. Often, where a capital budget is available for construction but resources for routine upkeep inadequate, the result is dilapidated buildings, which need to be replaced far earlier than should be necessary.

The key to good maintenance is not letting the situation deteriorate too far before taking action. Broken, clogged or soiled toilets in particular, will deteriorate rapidly if action is not taken immediately. Rectifying the situation then becomes a major task.

Often a serious problem occurs because everybody thinks it is the responsibility of somebody else. Adequate maintenance, therefore, requires that areas of responsibility are clearly defined and understood by all.

Source: *Ibid.*, pp. 14-29.

Bibliography

Anita, N.B. and Bhatia, Kavita, Peoples Health in People's Hand- A model for Panchayati Raj, FRCH, Mumbai. 1993.

Basch, P.E., Vaccines and World Health, New York, Oxford University Press, 1994.

Bhatnagar, S. and Goel, S.L., Development Planning and Administration. New Delhi. Deep & Deep Publications (P) Ltd., 1992.

Bhattacharjee P.J. and G.N. Shashtri, Population in India, A Study of Interstate Variation, New Delhi, Vikas, 1976.

Bosh, Ashish, From Population to People, Delhi, B.R. Publication, 1988.

Brown, Esther, Newer Dimensions of Patient Care, Russell Sage Foundation, New York, 1961.

Cartwright, A., Patients and their Doctors, A Study of General Practice, Routledge Kegan Paul, London, 1961.

Chanawongse Krasal, Rural Development Management, Research and Development Institute, Khon Kaen University, Thailand.

Chandra, R.C., A Geography of Population, Concepts, Determinants and Patterns, New Delhi, Kalyani, 1987.

Chauhan, Devraj, Anaita, N.H. and Ramdan, Sangita, Health Care in India: A Profile, FRCH, Mumhai, 1996.

Das, K., Civil Service Reforms and Structural Adjustment, Oxford, Delhi 1998.

Duggal, R., Nandaraj, S. and Shetty, Sahana, State Sector Health Expenditure-A Database All India, FRCH, Mumbai, 1992.

P. Jurfelds, G. and Lindbergs, Pills against Poverty—A Study of Introduction of Western Medicine in a Tamil Village, Curzon Press, London, 1975.

FRCH, Panchayati Raj Information Resource Book, Mumbai, 1996.

Ghai, Sandhaya, Bursing Services Administration: A Case Study of Nehru Hospital, PGI, Chandigarh (Doctoral Thesis, Panjab University, 1998).

Ghosh, Brindra Nath, A Treatise on Hygiene and Public Health, Scientific Publishing Company, 1970, Calcutta.

Gill, Sonya, Health Status of the Indian People, FRCH, Mumbai, 1987.

Goel, S.L., Health Care Administration Policy-making and Planning, Sterling, Delhi, 1981.

———, Health Care Administration Levels and Aspects, Sterling, Delhi, 1981.

Goel, S.L., Health Care Administration Ecology, Principles and Modern Trends, Sterling, Delhi, 1981.

———, Family Planning Programme and Beyond, New Delhi, Deep & Deep Publications Pvt. Ltd., New Delhi, 1990.

———, International Administration: WHO, South-East Asia Regional Office, Sterling, New Delhi, 1977.

———, Modern Management Techniques, Deep & Deep Publications Pvt. Ltd., New Delhi, 1987.

———, Public Health Administration, Sterline, New Delhi, 1984.

———, Public Personnel Administration, Sterling, New Delhi, 1984.

———, Hospital Administration and Management, Deep & Deep Publications Pvt. Ltd., New Delhi, 1903.

———, Distance Education in 21st Century, Deep & Deep Publications Pvt. Ltd., New Delhi, 2000.

Hanlon, John, Principles of Public Health Administration, C.V. Mobsy, Sthouis, 1969.

ICSSR & ICMR, Health for All-an Alternative Strategy—Report of a Study Group set-up Jointly by ICSSR & ICMR, Pune, Indian Institute of Education, 1981.

Govt. of India, Annual Reports of the Ministry of Health and Family Welfare, Delhi.

———, Committee on Multi-purpose Workers under Health and Family Welfare Programme (Kartar Singh Report), Delhi, Ministry of Health and Family Welfare, Delhi, 1973.

———, Govt. of India, Health in Independent India (G. Borkar Report), Delhi, 1961.

———, Health Survey and Development Committee (Bhore Committee), Delhi, 1946.

———, Lok Sabha Secretariat, Estimates Committees and Public Accounts Committees Reports.

———, Planning Commission, Five Year Plans, New Delhi.

———, Report of Health Survey and Planning Committee, (Mudaliar Committee) Ministry of Health, August-October, 1961.

———, Ministry of Information and Broadcasting, India, 1999, A Refresher Manual, New Delhi, 1999.

———, Initiatives and Best Practices of Government of India for Effective and Responsive Administration, New Delhi, Ministry of Personnel, Public Grievances, and Pensions, 1997.

———, Deptt. of Family Welfare, Reproductive and Child Health (World Bank Component), Vols. I and II, New Delhi, 1997.

———, Report of the Working Group on Health for All by 2000 A.D., New Delhi Ministry of Health and Welfare, 1981.

Gunaratne Herat, V.T., Challenges and Response Health in South-East Asia Region, New Delhi, McGraw Hill, 1977.

Hardon, A., et. al., Monitoring Family Planning and Reproductive Rights, A Manual for Empowerment, London, Zed Books, 1997.

Indian Society of Health Administrators, Bangalore.

Annual Conference Reports

Health for all by 2000 (AD 1980).
The Role of Hospitals in Health Care (1981).
Health Manpower Requirements for 2000 (1982).
Role of the Health Administrator in India (1983).
On Growing Needs of Urban Health Management (1985).
Cost Reduction in Hospitals and Health Care (1986).
Health of the High Risk Groups Mothers, Children and Elderly (1985).
Health of Women and Children for Development (1988).
Health Care for the Villages and Urban Slums (1989-90).
Health of the Youth and the Female Child.
Role of Voluntary Organizations in Health Care in India (1992).

Books

Stress and Health of Executives and Professionals.
Hospital and Health Administration.
Modern Technology for Hospitals and Health Care.
Management for Nursing Administrators.
Community Participation in Health and Family Welfare-Indian Experiences.
Health of the Metropolis-Bangalore-A Guide to Health Planning and Development of Urban Cities in India.
Leadership and Human Resources Development for Health Care.
Managerial Effectiveness for Organizational Excellence.
Computer Applications to Hospitals, Health Care and Medical Education.
Health and Development of the Tribal People in India-A Guide for Professionals and Administrators.
Retirement Planning, Adjustment and Health.
Janovsky, K., Health Policy and Systems Development on Agenda for Research, WHO/SHS/NHP/96.1, Geneva, 1996.
Jesani, Amar & Ganguly, Shilpi, Some Issues in Community Participation in Health Services, FRCH, Mumbai, 1993.
Khandewale, Shreekant V., Health Administration and the Weaker Sections in an Indian Metropolis, Devika Publications, Delhi, 1996.
Klinoboul Krienkrai, Health and Family Welfare Administration in Thailand—A Case Study of Lampang Province (Doctoral Thesis).
Kumar, R., Child Development in India, Ashish, New Delhi, 1988.
———, Environment Pollution and Health Hazards in India, Ashish, New Delhi (Year not mentioned).
———, Youth Health, Problem, Planning and Development, Deep and Deep Publications Pvt. Ltd., New Delhi, 1986.
Lane, S.D., From Population Control to Reproductive Health: An Emerging Policy Agenda, Social Science and Medicine, 1994.
Lush, L., Integrating Services, from Rhetroic to Action, Development Research Insights, 1997.

Mattoo, P.K., Project Formulation in Developing Countries, Macmillan, Delhi, 1978.

Meher, C. Nanavaty and P.D. Kulkarni, NGO's in the Changing Scenario, New Delhi, Uppal, 1998.

Miller, George E. and Tamas Fulop, Educational Strategies for the Health Professionals, Geneva, WHO, 1974.

Mishra, R.P., Medical Geography of India, NBT, Delhi, 1970.

Murray, C.J.L., Lopez, A.D., The Global Burden of Diseases, WHO, Geneva, Switzerland, 1996.

Myrdal Gunnar, Asian Drama, An Enquiry into the Poverty of Nations, Vol. III, Penguis, London, 1968.

Naik, J.P., An Alternative System of Health Care Service in India Some Proposals, Allied, Bombay, 1988.

National Institute of Health and Family Welfare, New Delhi

Management Training Modules for District Health Offices.

Management Training Modules for Health Offices.

Management Training Modules for Health Assistants (Male and Female).

Management Training Modules for Health Workers (Male and Female).

Management Training Modules for TBA.

Management Training Modules for Health Guide.

Park, J.E. and K. Park (1990), Textbook on Preventive and Social Medicine, Banarasidas Bhanot Publishers, Jabalpur.

Pai Panadiker, V.A., et. al., Organizational Policy for Family Planning, New Delhi, Uppal, 1983.

Pathak, Shankar, Social Welfare, Health and Family Planning in India, Marwah Publications, Delhi, 1979.

Rao, C. Hayavandana, Mysore Gazetteer, Vol. IV, B.R. Publishing Corporation, Delhi, 1984.

Ramanathan, S. (ed.), Landmarks in Karnataka Administration, New Delhi, Uppal, 1998 (Published for Indian Institute of Public Administration, Karnataka, Regional Branch, Bangalore).

Rafei, Dr. Uton M., Primary Health Care in Changing World South-East Asia Regional Perspectives, WHO Regional Office for South-East Asia, Delhi, India, 1993.

Ranga, R.K., Admn. of Family Planning Programmes in India—A Case Study of Haryana (Doctoral Thesis, Panjab University, 1998).

Rao, V.K.R.V., Food, Nutrition and Poverty in India, Vikas, New Delhi, 1982.

Rifikin, S.B., Health Planning and Community Participation, Crown Helm, London, 1985.

Sahni, Ashok, The Third Force in Health Care—Voluntary Sector, Bangalore Indian Society of Health Administrators (1992).

Scott-Samuel A., Total Participation, Total Health, Scottish Academic Press, 1990.

Sarjivi, K.S., Planning India's Health, Orient Longman, Delhi, 1971. Shenoi, P.V. (ed.), Contours of Social and Economic Development Political Issues, Concept, New Delhi, 1997.

Sharma, R.D., Advanced Public Administration, New Delhi, H.K. Publishers, 1994.

Singh, Sarabjit, Management Information System in a Hospital—A Case Study of General Hospital, Chandigarh (Doctoral Thesis, Panjab University, 1991).

Taori, Kamal, People's Participation in Sustainable Human Development (A Unified Approach), New Delhi, Concept, 1998.

Vaeth, R.M., A Theory of Medical Ethics, New York, Basic Books, 1981.

Vettivel, S.K., People's Participation in Social Development, Role of NGO, New Delhi, Vetri Publishers, 1992.

World, Health Organisation Alma Ata Revisited, WHO/SHS/CC/ 94.2, WHO, Geneva, 1994.

Werner, D., Where there is no Doctor?, The Voluntary Health Association of India, Delhi, 1984.

World Bank Financing of Health Services in Developing Countries, Washington, 1987.

World Bank, Development Report, 1993, New York, Oxford University Press.

World Bank, World Development Report, 1997, New York, Oxford University Press, 1997.

World Health Organisation, Annual Report of South-East Asia Regional Office, Delhi, 1997.

———, Bulletin of Regional Health Information, Regional Office for South-East Asia, Delhi, 1980, 1981, 1982, 1983, 1984-85, 1986-87, 1988-90, and 1991-93.

World Health Organization, Collaboration in Health Development in South-East Asia, 1948-88, Fortieth Anniversary Volume (Revised), Delhi, 1992.

———, Community Action for Health, SEA/HSD/185, Regional Office for South-East Asia, Delhi, 1993.

———, Development of Indicator for Monitoring Progress Towards Health for all by the Year 2000, Geneva, 1981.

———, Eighth General Programme of Work—Covering the Period 1990-95, Geneva, 1987.

———, Evaluation of the Strategy for Health for All by the year 2000, Regional Office for South-East Asia, Delhi, 1986.

———, Formulating Strategies for Health for all by the year 2000, Geneva, 1979.

———, Global Strategy for Health for all by the year 2000, Geneva, 1981.

———, Health in Development—Prospects for 21st Century, WHO! DGH/ 94.5, Geneva, 1994.

World Health Organization, Health Situation in the South-East Asia Region, 1991-93, Regional Office for South-East Asia, Delhi, 1995.

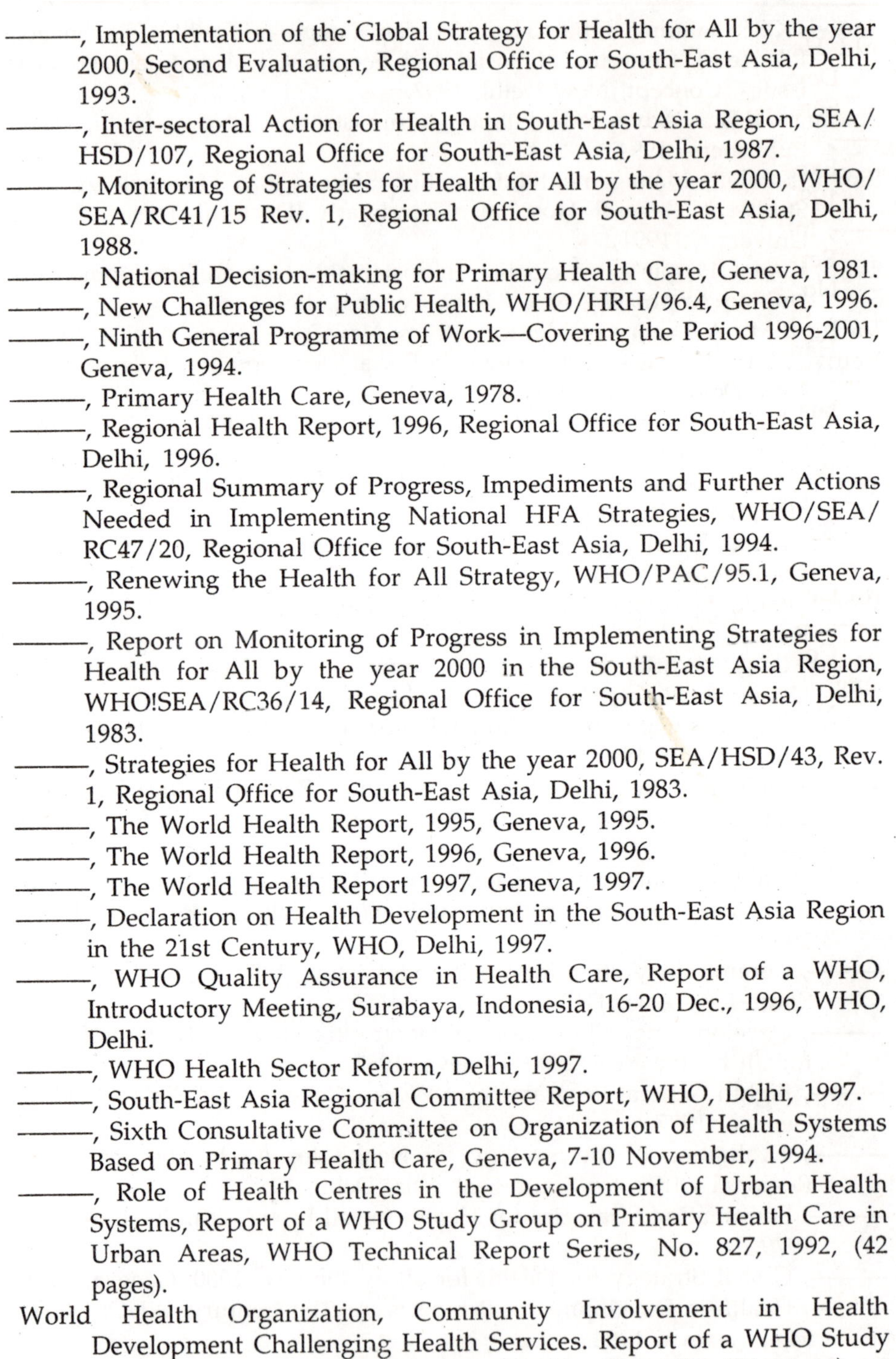

———, Implementation of the Global Strategy for Health for All by the year 2000, Second Evaluation, Regional Office for South-East Asia, Delhi, 1993.

———, Inter-sectoral Action for Health in South-East Asia Region, SEA/HSD/107, Regional Office for South-East Asia, Delhi, 1987.

———, Monitoring of Strategies for Health for All by the year 2000, WHO/SEA/RC41/15 Rev. 1, Regional Office for South-East Asia, Delhi, 1988.

———, National Decision-making for Primary Health Care, Geneva, 1981.

———, New Challenges for Public Health, WHO/HRH/96.4, Geneva, 1996.

———, Ninth General Programme of Work—Covering the Period 1996-2001, Geneva, 1994.

———, Primary Health Care, Geneva, 1978.

———, Regional Health Report, 1996, Regional Office for South-East Asia, Delhi, 1996.

———, Regional Summary of Progress, Impediments and Further Actions Needed in Implementing National HFA Strategies, WHO/SEA/RC47/20, Regional Office for South-East Asia, Delhi, 1994.

———, Renewing the Health for All Strategy, WHO/PAC/95.1, Geneva, 1995.

———, Report on Monitoring of Progress in Implementing Strategies for Health for All by the year 2000 in the South-East Asia Region, WHO!SEA/RC36/14, Regional Office for South-East Asia, Delhi, 1983.

———, Strategies for Health for All by the year 2000, SEA/HSD/43, Rev. 1, Regional Office for South-East Asia, Delhi, 1983.

———, The World Health Report, 1995, Geneva, 1995.

———, The World Health Report, 1996, Geneva, 1996.

———, The World Health Report 1997, Geneva, 1997.

———, Declaration on Health Development in the South-East Asia Region in the 21st Century, WHO, Delhi, 1997.

———, WHO Quality Assurance in Health Care, Report of a WHO, Introductory Meeting, Surabaya, Indonesia, 16-20 Dec., 1996, WHO, Delhi.

———, WHO Health Sector Reform, Delhi, 1997.

———, South-East Asia Regional Committee Report, WHO, Delhi, 1997.

———, Sixth Consultative Committee on Organization of Health Systems Based on Primary Health Care, Geneva, 7-10 November, 1994.

———, Role of Health Centres in the Development of Urban Health Systems, Report of a WHO Study Group on Primary Health Care in Urban Areas, WHO Technical Report Series, No. 827, 1992, (42 pages).

World Health Organization, Community Involvement in Health Development Challenging Health Services. Report of a WHO Study Group, WHO Technical Report Series, No. 809, 1991 (56 pages).

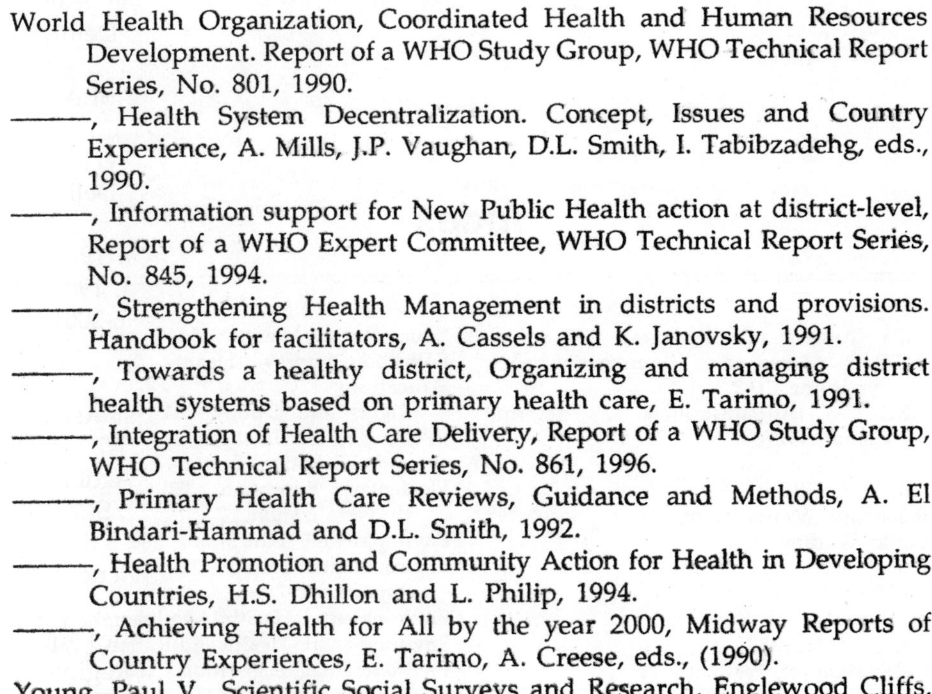

World Health Organization, Coordinated Health and Human Resources Development. Report of a WHO Study Group, WHO Technical Report Series, No. 801, 1990.

———, Health System Decentralization. Concept, Issues and Country Experience, A. Mills, J.P. Vaughan, D.L. Smith, I. Tabibzadehg, eds., 1990.

———, Information support for New Public Health action at district-level, Report of a WHO Expert Committee, WHO Technical Report Series, No. 845, 1994.

———, Strengthening Health Management in districts and provisions. Handbook for facilitators, A. Cassels and K. Janovsky, 1991.

———, Towards a healthy district, Organizing and managing district health systems based on primary health care, E. Tarimo, 1991.

———, Integration of Health Care Delivery, Report of a WHO Study Group, WHO Technical Report Series, No. 861, 1996.

———, Primary Health Care Reviews, Guidance and Methods, A. El Bindari-Hammad and D.L. Smith, 1992.

———, Health Promotion and Community Action for Health in Developing Countries, H.S. Dhillon and L. Philip, 1994.

———, Achieving Health for All by the year 2000, Midway Reports of Country Experiences, E. Tarimo, A. Creese, eds., (1990).

Young, Paul V., Scientific Social Surveys and Research, Englewood Cliffs, New Jersey, 1966.

Index